HOW TO DEFEND AND WIN LABOR AND EMPLOYMENT LAW CASES

Dedication

This book is dedicated to the respective parents of the authors:

Cora Jackson Randolph and in loving memory
of my father, Carl Jackson
Oliver Shields and in loving memory
of my mother, Oma Shields

Acknowledgments

The publication of this book would not have been possible were it not for the cooperative effort and industry of all members of the staff at Jackson, Shields, Yeiser and Cantrell. Special thanks, therefore, must go to Christine Stevens, Maria Dower, Angie Mason, Brandy Council and Jon Minkoff.

A special thanks is also extended to the legal staff at Jackson, Shields, Yeiser and Cantrell who not only supported the effort, time, and energy that went into this publication, but who also so ably assisted in numerous research and ideas that are incorporated in the book. They include James L. Holt, Jr., Ted Yeiser, Jr., Frank Cantrell and Sarah Norton.

Gordon E. Jackson wishes to express a special acknowledgment and thanks to his wife and family who, once again, survived yet another adventure with the fountain pen and "midnight oil." Thus, much love and appreciation to Sandy, Angela, Celeste, Eric, Amanda, and Alex.

Stephen L. Shields wishes to thank his wife for her understanding, cooperation, and encouragement in completing this book.

About the Authors

Gordon E. Jackson **Stephen L. Shields**

Gordon E. Jackson is a nationally renowned author and speaker on labor relations and employment law. He is the author of *When Labor Trouble Strikes: An Action Handbook, Unlawful Terminations and Employment-at-will, The Law of Employer and Employee Rights Case Manual* and *The Labor and Employment Law Desk Book.* He is also the author of *How to Stay Union-free, the Supervisor's Election Campaign Manual* and *How to Win Your NLRB Election by a Landslide.*

Gordon Jackson is a member of the National Speakers Association and a frequent speaker at labor relations seminars and conferences, averaging more than 100 speaking engagements annually. He handles labor and employment law matters for a variety of industries, businesses, and health care facilities from his headquarters in Memphis, Tennessee, where he is a partner in the law firm of Jackson, Shields, Yeiser and Cantrell. He is also a member of the lawyer-to-lawyer consultation panel, the Labor and Employment Law Section of the American Bar Association, and a member of the American Academy of Hospital Attorneys of the American Hospital Association.

Stephen L. Shields is a frequent speaker at national and regional seminars on labor relations and employment law. His speaking topics have included innovative techniques for motivating employees. He is the author of numerous articles and books including: *Employment Issues in Representing Family and Other Closely Held Businesses in Tennessee*, *Distinguishing Employees from Independent Contractors*, and *Motivating the Construction Work Force*.

Steve Shields is also an adjunct professor of law at Memphis State University, where he has taught courses on arbitration, alternate dispute resolution, fair employment practices, and labor relations. He is a partner in the Memphis-based law firm of Jackson, Shields, Yeiser and Cantrell and his practice is devoted to representing management nationwide in all areas of labor relations and employment law matters.

What This Book Will Do for You

How to Defend and Win Labor and Employment Law Cases was conceived, designed, developed, and written with one major purpose and objective: to provide both procedural and strategic guidance for defending labor and employment claims, charges, complaints, and lawsuits. This guidance is intended to help win cases, and it is meant for legal practitioners, human resource professionals, corporate attorneys, and management representatives who assist in the defense.

How to Defend and Win Labor and Employment Law Cases is uniquely designed. It is the only one-volume strategic reference guide in the nation that covers and addresses the entire spectrum of labor and employment law. It provides a step-by-step strategic approach on how to defend against a labor or employment claim from the time of the initial charge or complaint all the way through the entire appellate process.

No lawyer, personnel director, or professional manager should take on the defense of a litigation claim in the labor and employment law field without having the benefit of the hundreds of ideas and strategic safeguards contained in this book.

How to Defend and Win Labor and Employment Law Cases provides an inexpensive and indispensable quick access reference source that is unparalleled. It provides substantial understanding of the law on the subject matter in question, as well as the procedural aspects of the law in question. The book is comprehensively succinct; that is, it covers each area of the labor and employment law field in a most profound way, yet it does not exhaust you with information that is irrelevant to the strategic steps necessary to win.

How to Defend and Win Labor and Employment Law Cases is divided into seven major headings or parts.

Part I covers the various practical strategies that legal and management representatives should consider in defending labor charges and complaints before the National Labor Relations Board from the inception of the unfair labor practice charge or a representation petition to its ultimate disposition. In Part I, you will learn strategies and practical tips in formulating a proper response to an unfair labor practice charge so as to avoid costly and time consuming litigation later on. You will also learn from the information contained in Part I how to successfully seek deferral of unfair labor practice cases to a labor arbitrator. Chapter 3 discusses the deferral safeguards. Chapters within Part I contain helpful hints and practical tips on such subjects as pre-trial preparation of witnesses and evidence in NLRB proceedings and how to defend labor cases through the Federal Appellate process.

Part I of the book also discusses some useful strategies in handling representation hearings and answers such questions as who is and who is not eligible to vote in NLRB conducted elections, how to defend against unlawful strikes and how to seek injunctive relief in strike situations, work stoppages and boycotts.

Part II is devoted to a discussion of the strategies and practical tips in defending a labor arbitration case. Among the most beneficial aspects of Part II are those chapters that discuss the criteria by which an arbitrator should be chosen, as well as numerous pre-hearing checklists.

Part III is devoted to a better understanding of the defenses that can be utilized in defending labor and other forms of employment contracts. Part III addresses strategic approaches to defend against such contract theories as promissory estoppel, breach of covenant of good faith and fair dealing, retaliatory discharges for "whistleblowing," and so on.

Part IV of *How to Defend and Win Labor and Employment Law Cases* discusses new and innovative strategies that should be advanced in defending tort cases in the workplace such as:

- negligent hiring or retention
- invasion of privacy
- breach of confidential information
- libel and slander
- fraud
- mental anguish
- and other "hot" topics and theories that plaintiff lawyers are using against employers.

Part V of *How to Defend and Win Labor and Employment Law Cases* is devoted to the substantive and procedural coverage of defending employment discrimination cases, such as discrimination claims based on race, sex, religion, national origin, disability, veteran status, and so forth. For example, Part V discusses such tactics as responding properly to an EEOC charge. Part V addresses two relatively new laws in the workplace context. One is a discussion of the strategies necessary to defend an Americans with Disabilities claim; the second discusses the necessary strategies in defeating a claim under The Civil Rights Act of 1991.

Part VI addresses the strategic defenses necessary to win a wage and hour lawsuit, as well as discussing the elements of proof necessary to sustain an equal pay claim. Part VI covers techniques and tactics to use in defeating a child labor law claim.

Part VII of *How to Defend and Win Labor and Employment Law Cases* relates primarily to techniques and tactics to use in defending litigation based upon the plant closure laws. Part VII also discusses proper defenses to utilize during OSHA investigations and claims.

How to Defend and Win Labor and Employment Law Cases provides a storehouse of knowledge relative to each and every aspect of labor and employment law. It goes far beyond the hundreds of labor and employment law books on the market in two distinct ways. First, it moves you into the particular topic of interest given the user-friendly index. Second, once into the topic of interest, you are then provided essential information about the substance of the particular law in question, but far more importantly, you are given step-by-step strategies to defeat litigation relative to the legal issues involved. Thus, *How to Defend and Win Labor and Employment Law Cases* should become the one resource tool that you cannot afford to be without if you are charged with the responsibility of assisting in the preparation of defending labor and employment claims, charges, complaints and lawsuits. It is the one source book that all lawyers, human resources professionals, and management members should have on their desks or nearby bookshelves on a 24-hour basis, day in and day out.

Contents

PART VI
HOW TO DEFEND WAGE AND HOUR CASES 387

PART VII
HOW TO DEFEND EMPLOYMENT SAFETY AND WELFARE CASES 427

1

How to Defend a Case Before the National Labor Relations Board

1 What Management Attorneys and Representatives Should Know about the Federal Labor Policy

In defending labor cases, employers and their representatives, whether in the capacity of human resource professionals or labor relations attorneys, must have a fundamental understanding of the federal labor relations laws to be successful.

Unlike Canada and other countries whose labor policy is governed primarily through local and provincial laws, labor relations laws in terms of providing collective bargaining rights to employees are governed primarily by federal labor policies in the United States.

The basic labor relations law of the United States is contained in the National Labor Relations Act. The National Labor Relations Act has been amended numerous times since its origin of 1935, but still retains its original purpose of providing employees with a process of choosing a collective bargaining representative and mutual aid or protection and the protection of employees in exercising such rights. The National Labor Relations Act is the statute that established the National Labor Relations Board who has the responsibility of administering its provisions.

The National Labor Relations Act, as amended, is sometimes referred to as the Labor Management Relations Act.

FUNCTION OF THE NATIONAL LABOR RELATIONS BOARD

The use of the term National Labor Relations Board is somewhat of a misnomer. Generally speaking, both lawyers and laymen refer to the National Labor Relations Board as the overall agency, encompassing the various regional offices throughout the nation, the office of the General Counsel, the Division of Administrative Law Judges, and the official five-member Board in Washington, D.C. On the other hand, the term National Labor Relations Board is officially used to describe the five members who head the agency. The five-member Board and the agency's headquarters are located in Washington, D.C.

The NLRB, as an agency, has two primary functions: one is to process unfair labor practice charges; the second is to conduct representation elections.

Thus, in defending NLRB cases successfully, employers should appreciate, from a practicable perspective, that most of their efforts will relate to either defending an unfair labor practice charge or complaint or defending and countering a union's effort to represent a certain unit of their employees.

In unfair labor practice cases—typically referred to as Section 8 cases—the General Counsel of the NLRB has the responsibility of investigating the charge and deciding whether the charge has merit. Should the General Counsel determine that an unfair labor practice charge has merit, the General Counsel will issue a formal complaint charging that the Labor Management Relations Act has been violated and thereafter prosecute the case before an Administrative Law Judge. The case is then tried and the Administrative Law Judge makes certain recommended findings of fact, conclusions of law, and remedies to the five-member Board.

In representation cases—typically referred to as Section 9 cases—the General Counsel is not involved. Such matters that relate to election procedures are handled exclusively by the NLRB.

Some secondary functions of the NLRB include resolving jurisdictional disputes, handling deauthorization elections to determine whether employees desire to rescind a union security clause and polling employees with respect to their employer's last offer in a "national emergency" situation.

JURISDICTION OF THE NLRB

The National Labor Relations Board has limited jurisdiction in carrying out its various functions. It does not have the authority or discretion to regulate all relationships among unions, employers, and employees.

For example, the Labor Management Relations Act specifically excludes certain employers from its coverage and from NLRB jurisdiction, including:

- Federal and State governments, their agencies and political subdivisions
- wholly owned government corporations

- Federal Reserve banks
- employers that fall within the coverage of the Railway Labor Act (such as railroads and airlines)
- unions, except when such labor organizations are operating as an employer

In addition, the Labor Management Relations Act specifically excludes certain employees from its coverage, including:

- agricultural employees
- independent contractors
- domestic servants
- supervisors
- individuals employed by a parent or spouse
- individuals employed by employers exempt from the Labor Management Relations Act such as Federal or State employees, railway, or airline employees

Also, the NLRB's jurisdiction only extends to employers whose operations affect commerce in keeping with the federal constitutional authority to regulate any activity that affects commerce among the states. The courts have held that the Labor Management Relations Act has the broadest possible constitutional reach, covering virtually every small business that purchases supplies from out-of-state vendors or whose business would affect the operations of other employers who engage in interstate commerce.

However, the NLRB has taken the position that it might be too burdensome to extend its jurisdiction to all small businesses and enterprises and has, pursuant to its rule-making powers, established certain monetary jurisdictional standards that an employer must meet in order for the NLRB to assert jurisdiction.

For example, the NLRB will not extend its jurisdiction to a non-retail business that does not have at least $50,000 in direct or indirect sales outside the state in which it operates or does not make direct or indirect purchases of supplies from businesses in other states in such an amount. A retail establishment must generate at least $500,000 in an annual volume of business to meet the NLRB's monetary standards. Hotels and taxicab companies must also meet the $500,000 jurisdictional standard to fall within the coverage of the Act.

Employers and their counsel should keep in mind that even though the NLRB may not have jurisdiction, or declines to assert jurisdiction, in a given unfair labor practice charge or a representation matter, other Federal and State laws may provide for coverage.

For example, should the NLRB decline to assert jurisdiction because the employer did not meet its monetary standards, a state law—sometimes called a "Little Taft-Hartley" law—may take up the slack and provide the employee or union a right to process the unfair labor practice charge or petition for a representation election through its administrative agency. Forty-one states have some form of collective bargaining statutes for some or all public employees, including:

Alabama	Alaska
California	Connecticut
Delaware	The District of Columbia
Florida	Georgia
Hawaii	Idaho
Illinois	Indiana
Iowa	Kansas
Kentucky	Maine
Maryland	Massachusetts
Michigan	Minnesota
Missouri	Montana
Nebraska	Nevada
New Hampshire	New Jersey
New Mexico	New York
North Dakota	Ohio
Oklahoma	Oregon
Pennsylvania	Rhode Island
South Dakota	Tennessee
Texas	Vermont
Washington	Wisconsin
Wyoming	

Other states are likely to follow the trend of providing basic rights to protect self-organization, collective bargaining, and concerted activity of police officers, firefighters, teachers, and so on. Some state laws provide specific collective bargaining rights for agricultural employees, such as California and Arizona.

In addition to Little Taft-Hartley laws, Federal government workers are permitted collective bargaining rights through the Federal Labor Relations Authority. As noted earlier, the Railway Labor Act provides for collective bargaining between railway and airline employers and their employees.

A SUMMARY OF THE NATIONAL LABOR RELATIONS ACT, AS AMENDED

The first six sections of the National Labor Relations Act, as amended, sets forth the basic structure and definitions of the Act.

Section 1 of the Act details basic findings and policies and provides the congressional background as to the passage of the Act.

Section 2 of the Act contains some very important definitions that are used throughout the statute, such as Section 2(11) which subsection defines the term "supervisor."

Sections 3 through 6 of the Act establish the structure of the National Labor Relations Board.

Section 7 of the National Labor Relations Board, as amended, contains the basic rights of employees, and declares:

> "Employees shall have the right to self-organization, to form, join or assist labor organizations, to bargain collectively through representatives of their own choosing, and to engage in other concerted activities for the purpose of collective bargaining or other mutual aid or protection and shall have the right to refrain from any or all such activities."

In a nutshell, Section 7 provides that employees shall be protected in their right to collectively bargain, to engage in mutual aid or protection (protected concerted activity), or to refrain from such.

Section 8 of the National Labor Relations Act, as amended, sets forth, among other things, conduct on the part of employers that may constitute an unfair labor practice. Section 8(a) conduct is that behavior forbidden by employers and their supervisors. Section 8(b) conduct is that behavior forbidden by unions and their agents and representatives.

Since this book is primarily dedicated to employers' efforts in defending their labor cases successfully, union misconduct (Section 8(b) conduct) will not be discussed at this point. Section 8(a) conduct will be addressed inasmuch as several of the remaining chapters discuss the techniques, tactics, and strategies that should be used in defending oneself against an unfair labor charge. Employer unfair labor practices may consist of one or more of the following behaviors when managers and supervisors:

- Interfere with, restrain, or coerce employees in the exercise of their rights to organize, bargain collectively, and engage in other concerted activities for their mutual aid or protection. *Section 8(a)(1)*
- Dominate or interfere with the formation or administration of any labor organization or contribute financial or other support of it. *Section 8(a)(2)*
- Encourage or discourage membership in any labor organization by discrimination with regard to hiring or tenure or conditions of employment, subject to an exception for a valid union-security agreement. *Section 8(a)(3)*
- Discharge or otherwise discriminate against an employee because he or she has filed charges or given testimony under the Act. *Section 8(a)(4)*
- Refuse to bargain collectively with the majority representative of its employees. *Section 8(a)(5)*

- Enter into a "hot cargo" agreement with a union in which the employer promises not to do business with, or not to handle or otherwise deal in any of the products of any other person. *Section 8(e)*

Section 9 of the Act governs election procedures in representation cases and provides that the certified representative bargaining agent of an appropriate unit of employees is their exclusive representative. In addition, Section 9 of the Act:

- gives the NLRB broad discretion in determining appropriate bargaining units
- provides that security guards be certified within a bargaining unit only of security guards
- prohibits a valid election from being held more than once in any one-year period
- establishes the procedure to be followed in run-off elections
- provides a process through which employees whose collective bargaining contract contains a union security clause to hold a deauthorization election to determine if such employees want such clause rescinded

Section 10 of the Act grants the NLRB the authority to enforce the unfair labor practice provisions found in Section 8. One of the most significant features of Section 10 is its subsection (b) which states that an unfair labor practice charge must be filed within six months of its occurrence to be timely. Section 10 also establishes trial procedures in unfair labor practice cases as well as provides for certain injunctive relief through the courts.

Section 11 of the Act contains the investigatory powers of the NLRB, the manner in which NLRB documents are to be served, and other related procedural matters.

Section 12 of the Act makes it unlawful to interfere with the NLRB processes.

Section 13 of the Act preserves the right of employees to strike.

Section 14 is most famous for its 14(b) provision which permits individual states to legislate "Right-to-Work" laws.

Section 15 addresses what action is to be taken in the event of a conflict of laws question.

Section 16 is likewise procedural in form and provides that should any provision in the Act be held to be invalid, the remainder portions of the Act should not be adversely affected.

Section 17 provides that the title of the Act should be referred to as the "National Labor Relations Act."

Section 18 specifies that the failure of the AFL-CIO to have complied with certain Section 9 provisions in the 1940s would not invalidate the applicability of representation cases as provided by the Act.

Section 19 exempts individuals whose religion opposes compulsory unionism from being required to join a union or pay union dues under a union security clause, except that such an individual may be required in a collective bargaining agreement to pay sums equal to such union dues and initiation fees to a non-religious, non-labor organization charitable fund.

SUMMARY OF RELATED FEDERAL LABOR RELATIONS LAWS

The Taft-Hartley Act

The original National Labor Relations Act—the Wagner Act—was amended in 1947 by the Taft-Hartley Act, more officially referred to as the Labor Management Relations Act.

The Taft-Hartley Act sought to balance the Wagner Act by specifying certain conduct on the part of labor organizations to constitute an unfair labor practice, and added subsection (b) to Section 8 of the Act to set forth such conduct in detail.

The Taft-Hartley Amendments to the original Wagner Act limited the NLRB's discretion in determining appropriate bargaining units, provided that employers would have the right of free speech in representation election campaigns as long as such speech did not contain threats of reprisals or promises of benefits to dissuade union activities. In addition, the Wagner Act barred the NLRB from conducting more than one election in a one-year period and a number of similar changes to protect and restore a more balanced federal labor policy.

The Landrum-Griffin Act

The 1959 amendments to the National Labor Relations Act were triggered by the famous McClellan Committee hearings in the U.S. Congress that revealed an imposing history of labor racketeering, corruption, and a coercion of employees and small businesses by labor consultants serving as "middlemen."

The Landrum-Griffin amendments, officially referred to as the Labor-Management Reporting and Disclosure Act of 1959, sought to prevent such future impediments of employee rights by establishing a code of conduct for unions, union officers, employers and consultants. The code of conduct, among other things, provides union members with a bill of rights. It establishes standards for union trusteeships. It imposes a fiduciary obligation on union officers and consultants to file certain reports with the U.S. Department of Labor.

The Landrum-Griffin Act also modified certain provisions of the NLRA and added some additional provisions, as well.

Health Care Amendments

The Federal Congress added an amendment to the NLRA in 1974 that extended NLRB jurisdiction to private non-profit hospitals and nursing homes. The earlier Act had previously covered proprietary hospitals and nursing homes.

The Health Care Amendment does not provide employees the same protected right to strike as it does non-health care employees, in that unions must provide a ten-day notice to non-profit, non-governmental health care employers prior to calling a strike against such an institution.

Norris-LaGuardia Act

The Norris-LaGuardia Act of 1932 forbids the federal courts to issue injunctions in labor disputes unless certain specified guidelines are followed, such as showing that there were prior efforts to settle the labor dispute peaceably, that law enforcement officials were either unable or unwilling to safeguard the employer's property, and that the failure to deny injunctive relief would cause the employer to suffer greater loss than that of the union were it not granted.

The Hobbs Antiracketeering Act

The Hobbs Act, as adopted in 1934, prohibits criminal conspiracy to impede interstate commerce by extortion or robbery.

The Railway Labor Act

The Railway Labor Act of 1926 preceded the Wagner Act and provided a process of selecting bargaining representatives of employees of railway and airline carriers and the protection of employees in exercising their rights to self-representation and collective bargaining.

Federal Service Labor-Management Relations Statute

This particular statute, adopted in 1979, provides protection of federal service employees to exercise their right to collectively bargain.

The Postal Reorganization Act

This statute, adopted in 1970, establishes collective bargaining rights for postal employees. The Act essentially places the United State Postal Service in the same position as private sector employers with respect to collective bargaining rights and extends the jurisdiction of the National Labor Relations Board to determine employee representation issues. The Act, however, provides that postal employees do not have the right to strike and prohibits required union membership as a condition of employment in the postal service.

2 Initial Strategies in Defending an Unfair Labor Practice Charge

As noted in Chapter 1, an employer may be charged with an assortment of unfair labor practices. Employers and their human resources directors and management attorneys should know some essential strategies in countering such charges.

From a practical perspective, those employers whose employees are represented by a union are likely to be charged with refusal to bargain charges, or what the NLRB agents refer to as Section 8(a)(5) charges. Employers that do not have unions already representing their employees are mostly likely to be charged with one or a combination of Sections 8(a)(1), 8(a)(2), 8(a)(3), or 8(a)(4) charges.

In layman's terms, a Section 8(a)(1) charge is one in which the employer is charged with interfering with employee rights protected in Section 7 of the NLRA, such as by way of coercion, threats, intimidation, and so on. Almost all other charges are a derivative of a Section 8(a)(1) charge. Therefore, most unfair labor practice charges that allege specific misconduct that relate to a given subsection under Section 8(a) of the Act will typically include Section 8(a)(1) as an additional charge.

The following provides a checklist to use in defending one or more unfair labor practice charges.

TECHNIQUES TO DETERMINE TIMELINESS OF AN UNFAIR LABOR PRACTICE CHARGE

Most seasoned management lawyers, by nature, will first review an unfair labor practice charge to discern whether it was filed in a timely manner. Section 10(b) of the National Labor Relations Act specifies that no complaint may be issued on matters which occurred more than six months prior to the filing of an unfair labor practice charge, unless the charging party is in the armed services. The Act provides not only that the unfair labor practice charge be filed with an NLRB office within six months from the occurrence of the allegations, but that a copy of the charge be served on the charged party—called a respondent—within the six-month period to be considered timely filed. The consequence of an untimely filed unfair labor practice charge is dismissal.

The respondent's attorney or representative should understand that the six-month time limitation begins to run when the unfair labor practice is committed, rather than the date of the consequences of such alleged unfair act. The NLRB will recognize a continuing violation and permit an unfair labor practice charge to be filed as long as one of the continuous unlawful acts is alleged to have been committed within the preceding six month period.

However, the NLRB has been much more conservative in permitting a charge to be filed under the "continuing violation" exception than has been permitted by other Federal agencies such as the Equal Employment Opportunity Commission, assuming the primary allegations fall outside the six-month time limit. Therefore, the employer and its representatives should argue forcefully that a charge is not timely filed if not filed within the required six-month period.

Management attorneys and employer representatives must appreciate that just because some behavior or conduct occurred prior to the six-month prescriptive period does not mean that an Administrative Law Judge in an unfair labor practice trial will not permit such information to be used as background information to establish that the employer is hostile toward unionism. Hostility or animus is one of the elements of proof that an Administrative Law Judge must consider in deciding whether an employer is guilty of the alleged conduct.

TACTICS TO DISCERN JURISDICTIONAL DEFENSES TO AN UNFAIR LABOR PRACTICE CHARGE

Assuming an unfair labor practice charge is filed timely, most seasoned management attorneys and human resources professionals next seek to determine if there is a jurisdictional defense to the charge, especially in cases where there is a small business involved or there are governmental, agricultural, railway, or airline implications.

A brief summary of what is within and what is without the NLRB jurisdictional bounds was given in Chapter 1.

The vast majority of unfair labor practice charges and representation petitions for elections that are filed with the NLRB involve either retail or non-retail enterprises. Assuming that none of the statutory jurisdictional defenses discussed in Chapter 1 apply as to the NLRB's general coverage, the employer's representative should look to the NLRB's discretionary jurisdictional standards to determine whether the NLRB should or should not assert jurisdiction.

Thus, where a retail establishment has been charged with an unfair labor practice, the NLRB would not assert jurisdiction unless the retail employer had at least grossed $500,000 in its annual volume of business, including sales and excise taxes.

In a non-retail enterprise, such as in a manufacturing or processing plant, the employer must have had sales of goods to consumers in other states, whether such goods or services were shipped or furnished in or out of the state, or purchases of goods from suppliers in other states, directly or indirectly, of at least $50,000.

Aside from jurisdictional standards for retail and non-retail enterprises, the NLRB has established jurisdictional standards for certain specific employers, as follows:

- **Health care facilities**—Gross revenues of at least $250,000 per year in proprietary and non-profit hospitals; and, where gross revenues exceed $150,000 in nursing homes, visiting nurse associations and related facilities.
- **Hotels, motels, apartments, and condominiums**—Gross revenues of at least $500,000 per year in the total volume of business.
- **Colleges, universities, and secondary schools (non-governmental)**—Gross revenues of at least $1,000,000 from all sources except monies designated by the grantor of a trust as not available for operating costs.
- **Newspapers, printers, and publishers**—Gross revenues of at least $200,000 per year (assuming the interstate commerce standard is met).
- **Public utilities**—Gross revenue of at least $250,000 per year (or $50,000 annual volume of interstate business, outflow or inflow, direct or indirect).
- **Federal credit unions**—Gross annual revenues of at least $500,000 from loans, deposits, investments, and so on.
- **Gambling casinos**—Gross annual revenues of at least $500,000.
- **Law firms and legal aid programs**—Gross annual revenues of at least $250,000.
- **Radio, television, telegraph, and telephone enterprises**—Gross annual revenues of at least $250,000.
- **Transit companies**—Gross annual revenues of at least $250,000.

- **Taxicab companies**—Gross annual revenues of at least $500,000.
- **Symphony orchestras**—Gross annual revenues of at least $1,000,000.

TECHNIQUES TO DETECT TECHNICAL AND LEGAL DEFICIENCIES IN AN UNFAIR LABOR PRACTICE CHARGE

The next area to probe in attempting to defend an unfair labor practice charge is to examine the face of the charge to determine if the charging party has met all the technical requirements in filing the charge, as well as to determine whether the charge supports a sufficiency of legal details to sustain the charge.

Asserting technical deficiencies could prove to be an exercise in futility even where such shortcomings are found, simply because the NLRB will permit the charging party to amend and refile the charge to "cure" any such technical deficiencies. Strategically speaking, it may be worth the effort to attempt to assert any technical deficiencies. The fallacy may show a lack of sophistication and expertise on the part of the charging party and may provide for some additional time for the respondent to prepare its case and counter defenses. Employer representatives should also be aware that the NLRB has a very liberal policy in not only permitting a charging party to refile an unfair labor practice charge to cure any technical defects, the Board has also taken a very permissive position in permitting a charging party to amend the unfair labor practice charge to include other related allegations.

Examples of technical deficiencies may include:

- incorrect or improper spelling of home addresses of either the charging party or respondent
- a failure to sign a sworn oath that the contents are true and correct to the best of the charging party's belief
- the failure to describe allegations in the charge sufficiently to inform the charged party of the nature of the case
- the charging party may have listed incorrect dates, times, places, and so forth, in the charge sufficient to constitute a technical shortcoming
- the type or category of charge also may have been stated incorrectly

The respondent's representative should search more for legal, rather than technical deficiencies, because such deficiencies are not so readily curable. For example, should the charging party allege that he or she was discharged because of a workers' compensation claim, the charge would be dismissed by the NLRB on the grounds that an alleged retaliatory discharge falls outside the coverage of the National Labor Relations Act, as amended, unless it pertained to more than one employee and was alleged as a violation of the mutual aid or protection proviso in Section 7 of the Act. The same would hold true, generally, with other discrimination in employment cases such as those that pertain to age, race, sex, national origin, handicap, religion, marital status, and so on. A legal deficiency could arise in terms of the charging party not having standing to file such a charge. A legal deficiency can best be described where a given charge contains allegations which, even if substantiated, would make no difference inasmuch as the subject matter of the charge is not covered by the National Labor Relations Act, as amended.

STRATEGIES TO DETERMINE THE ABSENCE OF A PRIMA FACIE CASE

Once an NLRB Regional Office receives an unfair labor practice charge from a charging party, the Regional Director of that office will send the charged party a copy of the charge, along with a letter explaining the charge and procedures relative to the charge.

Soon thereafter, the respondent will most likely receive a telephone call or some other form of communications from the NLRB agent assigned to the case. Many such NLRB agents seemingly want to get the respondent's position and evidence as to why it contends it did not commit the acts alleged in the charge prior to investigating the case and gathering the necessary information and documents to determine if the charging party has been able to substantiate a Prima facie case that the allegations in the charge are true. The NLRB Rules and Regulations provide that the NLRB agent assigned to the case should first investigate the charging party's case to determine whether the charging party has supplied sufficient information to establish Prima facie evidence to support the allegations in the charge prior to burdening the respondent with a request to provide its evidence and position in defense of the charge.

Thus, the prudent response to a premature request by an NLRB agent, who seemingly wants to reverse the roles in the order of investigation, is to inquire whether the NLRB agent has a Prima facie case as a result of investigating the charging party's proof.

In the event the NLRB agent responds that he or she has not taken evidence from the charging party at that time, then the employer's representative may want to inform the NLRB agent to please make contact once Prima facie is established. If this is the case and if the charging party cannot furnish sufficient evidence to establish a *Prima facie* case, the charge should be dismissed by the NLRB without requiring the respondent to respond at all. However, the employer's representative should always defer to the Regional Office's protocol. Sometimes an agent will insist that the employer submit some type of position statement at the early stages of the investigation, prior to Prima facie being established by the agent. If so, the employer's representative should comply if he or she does not want an adverse position to be taken by the region.

In a similar vein, an NLRB agent may contact the respondent's representative and advise him or her that the investigation into the charging party's allegations has been completed and there is enough evidence from such investigation to sustain a *Prima facie* case of the alleged unfair labor practice charge. The charging party's evidence revealed information that could form the basis of one or more additional unfair labor practices and that, since the agent is requesting that the employer's representative present evidence in defense of the original charge, the agent would also like to get the employer's position and any supporting evidence relating to the evidence of possible additional unfair labor practice charges gathered through the earlier information provided by the charging party.

In this particular situation, the NLRB agent is asking the employer's representative to supply evidence to support its position to a charge that does not formally exist.

Again, the NLRB agent is attempting to get the horse before the cart, so to speak. Technically, the NLRB is to receive either an amended charge to the original, incorporating the new allegations, or to receive a new and separate charge setting forth such new allegations, prior to officially requesting the respondent to respond or present evidence in its defense that the allegations are untrue or without merit.

Thus, unless there is a substantial savings in time and costs by presenting the employer's evidence and position as to the new and additional allegations, the employer's representative may want to communicate to the NLRB agent that he or she will only be responding to the original charge if and when its evidence is presented. In addition, the representative will reserve the option to respond to any new or additional allegations only after such are presented through an amended or separate unfair labor practice charge.

One should be reminded, however, that the NLRB agent, and his or her Regional Director, may take a position that all of such new allegations are covered, inferentially, in the 8(a)(1) portion of the original charge and there is no provision in the Rules and Regulations to require the filing of a new or amended charge prior to attempting to get the respondent's evidence.

As will be discussed in detail in Chapter 4, an employer-respondent has the option to present evidence to support its position in defense of the charge or not to present such. Assuming the NLRB has a *Prima facie* case from the charging party's evidence, if the respondent fails or refuses to present evidence in support of its defense to the charge, the NLRB's option is to proceed to file a formal complaint against the employer-respondent.

3 Strategies in Deferring an Unfair Labor Practice Charge to Arbitration

When an unfair labor practice charge is filed against an employer by a party to a collective bargaining agreement that provides for a binding grievance-arbitration procedure, the employer may want to ask the General Counsel of the NLRB to defer the charge for resolution through the grievance-arbitration provisions of such labor agreement.

Likewise, where an unfair labor practice charge is filed against an employer by a party to a labor agreement providing for a grievance-arbitration procedure after a labor arbitrator has already issued an award in the same matter, the employer may want to attempt to convince the NLRB that the Board should defer to the arbitrator's decision in disposition of a pending unfair labor practice charge covering the same factual issue or issues.

Therefore, the employer's counsel and human resources directors should well appreciate that certain deferral options are additional factors to consider in evaluating overall defenses in unfair labor practice charges and a natural extension to the various defenses discussed in Chapter 2.

The NLRB will not automatically invoke the doctrine of collateral estoppel—that the decision by the arbitrator preempts further action by the NLRB—in a case where a labor arbitrator has decided the case in a certain matter and the same facts contained in the arbitration proceedings become the source and substance of the unfair labor practice charge. This means that the NLRB guards its turf very closely and subscribes to the proposition that the fact that certain conduct constitutes a breach of a collective bargaining agreement does not deprive the NLRB of the jurisdiction to hold that the same conduct also constitutes an unfair labor practice.

Strategically speaking, an employer may seek deferral of unfair labor practice charges to labor arbitration in three different situations:

- Deferral of unfair labor practice charges to the grievance-arbitration procedure enumerated in the labor agreement before the actual arbitration proceedings commence
- Deferral of unfair labor practice charges to the contractual procedure after arbitration proceedings have begun but prior to completion
- Deferral of unfair labor practice charges to the contractual procedure subsequent to the arbitrator's disposition of the case

DEFENSIVE STRATEGIES IN POST-ARBITRAL DEFERRAL

Suppose that a union, after having received an unfavorable decision by a labor arbitrator, decides to file an unfair labor practice charge with the NLRB, contending that the Board should process the case, de novo, through its own machinery, irrespective that the facts alleged and the remedy sought in the unfair labor practice charge are very similar, or even identical, to those contained in the arbitration proceedings.

Should the employer's counsel attempt to get the NLRB to defer to the arbitrator's reward and refuse to process the unfair labor practice charge? Or should the employer's counsel acquiesce in the unfair labor practice proceedings and hope that the NLRB will grant it similar relief in such proceedings?

Since the employer has already won its case in such instance, the obvious choice is to attempt to convince the NLRB that the labor arbitration proceedings were handled in a just and fair manner and that it would be unnecessarily costly and time consuming to have the same set of facts retried in an additional forum. In other words, the NLRB should be convinced that the charging party has already had its day in court and it would be redundant to hear the matter over again before the NLRB.

Were the NLRB of the disposition to agree with the employer's position, it would decide to bar the charging party from processing its case through the NLRB machinery and defer, in its disposition of the matter, to the earlier arbitrator's findings, conclusions and remedies with respect to the issues therein.

This type of post-arbitral deferral by the NLRB is known among labor relations professionals as the *Spielberg* doctrine, taking its name from the 1955 NLRB case of *Spielberg Manufacturing Co.*

WHAT THE EMPLOYER MUST PROVE TO MEET THE *SPIELBERG* CRITERIA

The employer's counsel or representative who has won its arbitration case before the labor arbitrator and who desires to convince the NLRB's local Regional Director to defer to a previous labor arbitration decision with respect to a pending unfair labor practice charge involving the same facts and issues must be in a position to demonstrate to the NLRB that the following criteria has been met:

- All parties to the pending unfair labor practice charge had previously agreed to be bound by the arbitrator's decision through the language of the applicable collective bargaining contract, or otherwise.
- The arbitration proceedings appear to have been fair and regular, affording such safeguards as due process.
- The arbitrator's decision and award were not clearly repugnant to the purpose and policies of the Act.
- The contractual dispute in the arbitration proceedings in question was factually parallel to the unfair labor practice dispute, and the arbitrator was presented with the general facts relative to the unfair labor practice dispute.

Technically speaking, the employer's counsel only has the responsibility of establishing the fact that the allegations in the pending unfair labor practice charge have already been litigated and decided through the arbitration process to shift the burden of proof to the NLRB's General Counsel to show that the *Spielberg* criteria *have not* been met in order for the NLRB to deny post-arbitral deferral in such case. However, the employer's counsel should be prepared to prove to the General Counsel that the criteria have been met. The NLRB and its General Counsel do not always subscribe to technical procedural or evidentiary requirements imposed on them through court decisions.

The employer's counsel or representative should be aware, likewise, that the NLRB will not defer to arbitration in all cases, even assuming the *Spielberg* standards are met. Unfair labor practice charges involving allegations of employer domination under Section 8(a)(2) as well as allegations of employer retaliation under Section 8(a)(4) are not deferred in such cases. Neither are issues involved in representation cases.

POINTS TO CONSIDER IN DEFERRING UNFAIR LABOR PRACTICE CHARGES TO ARBITRATION

An employer's counsel may desire to defer a pending unfair labor practice charge against it to a labor arbitrator pursuant to the arbitration provision in the employer's collective bargaining contract for a host of reasons including:

- The employer's counsel believes the employer's position and defenses in the case are more likely to be sustained by a labor arbitrator than by an NLRB administrative law judge.
- The employer's counsel believes that the arbitration process will be more expeditious and less time consuming, and perhaps, less costly if the contract provisions provide that the charging party must pay a pro-rated part of the costs (or all the costs if it loses the case).
- The employer's counsel believes that the labor arbitrator is more familiar with certain facts and issues in the case than what an NLRB administrative law judge might be, in that such arbitrator has heard other cases involving similar factual situations or employer policies and practices.
- The employer's counsel believes that matters covered in the grievance-arbitration provisions of its collective bargaining agreement with the charging party should be determined through the arbitration machinery so provided, rather than taken before the NLRB to be decided, as a matter of business philosophy.

LIMITATIONS AND RESTRICTIONS IN PRE-ARBITRAL DEFERRAL MATTERS

The employer's counsel or representative should appreciate the NLRB's general policy in deferring pending unfair labor practice charges to arbitration. The NLRB does not readily endorse the notion. Thus, the NLRB has various restrictions and limitations in pre-arbitral matters.

Moreover, even where the NLRB is of the disposition to defer an unfair labor practice charge to a labor arbitration proceeding, it will nonetheless retain jurisdiction over the case and review the final decision of the labor arbiter in question to determine if the arbiter's decision and award meet the *Spielberg* standards, as discussed above. This process of temporarily deferring the disposition of an unfair labor practice matter to the grievance and arbitration machinery provided through the applicable collective bargaining agreement is typically referred to as the *Collyer* doctrine, taking its name from a 1971 NLRB decision entitled *Collyer Insulated Wire*.

The employer's counsel or representative should be aware that the NLRB has taken the position that it will not defer such pending unfair labor practice cases to arbitration where the grievance-arbitration provisions of the contract do not culminate in binding and final arbitration or where it is shown that both parties involved, typically the union and the employer, are "hostile" to the interest of the employees covered by the contract.

In addition, the NLRB has taken a general position that it will not invoke *Collyer* and defer the following types of labor cases to an arbitrator:

- Section 8(a)(4) charges (Retaliation)
- Alleged violations of Section 8(d) of the National Labor Relations Act, as amended
- Issues involving accretion to bargaining unit cases
- Allegations of refusal to comply with previous NLRB orders
- Issues involving the validity or enforceability of certain provisions of a labor agreement
- Questions involving the statutory duty to negotiate where the underlying dispute is not determinable on the interpretation of an existing labor agreement
- Cases in which a stable collective bargaining relationship does not exist
- Cases in which the respondent to the unfair labor practice charge is unwilling to agree to arbitration of the issues involved in the matter
- Cases in which the meaning of contractual provisions are not the center of the dispute

The employer's counsel also should understand that the NLRB has had a long standing policy of deferring its determination of unfair labor practice charges to arbitration in cases where: (1) either the charging party or the respondent to the unfair labor practice charge has filed suit to, or has already secured, a court order to compel the parties to arbitrate the matter; or (2) such parties had agreed previously to do so.

4 Techniques and Tactics in Responding to an Unfair Labor Practice Charge

There are some management attorneys who are not eager to respond to an unfair labor practice charge on behalf of an employer during the NLRB's initial investigation of a charge. They apparently theorize that since the NLRB Rules and Regulations do not permit the respondent to discover the charging party's evidence, why should the employer permit the NLRB, on behalf of the charging party, to discover what proof and evidence the employer has in support of its defense against the charge? The employer's position then becomes one in which the employer's counsel or representative implicitly states to the NLRB that, "If you won't show me yours, I'll not show you mine and I'll see you in the courtroom."

Thus, one can deduce early that, assuming the NLRB has established a prima facie case of an unfair labor practice case through its investigation of the charging party's presentation of evidence, the failure of the employer to likewise "cooperate" with the NLRB and present its evidence in support of its position that it did not commit the alleged acts in the charge will cause the NLRB to exercise its right to file a formal complaint against the respondent and do just what the employer's representative implicitly suggested—see the respondent in the courtroom.

There may be some limited circumstances in which this approach may be dictated, such as where a local NLRB agent becomes overly zealous and abusive during the investigatory process, but such circumstance is truly the exception.

In a nutshell, the employer has two options once the NLRB establishes a prima facie case of an unfair labor practice:

- The employer may present its own evidence and position to the respective NLRB agent in hopes that such evidence will convince the respective NLRB Regional Director that the employer's evidence overrides the prima facie evidence and that the unfair labor practice should be dismissed.
- Or, as noted above, the employer has the option to refuse to present evidence in support of its position and take its chance in the courtroom.

The first approach—presenting the employer's evidence to the respective NLRB agent assigned to the case—provides more favorable results. True, if the employer is not successful in getting the unfair labor practice charge dismissed after presenting its evidence, the NLRB will, in turn, try to use (perhaps, misuse) any adverse evidence gathered in its investigation of the employer's evidence against the employer at the unfair labor practice hearing, but the odds are that any such evidence will be available to the NLRB's General Counsel to present at the unfair labor practice hearing through such procedural processes as the adverse witness rule, irrespective of the employer's refusal to present its evidence to the NLRB agent during the initial investigation.

More important, the vast majority of unfair labor practice charges are dismissed once the employer has presented its evidence during the investigatory stage. On the other hand, once an unfair labor practice charge proceeds to a hearing, the vast majority of such cases are lost by the employer. Thus, there is much more to gain and much less to lose by presenting one's position and evidence to the NLRB investigating agent.

THE PROS AND CONS OF SUBMITTING A POSITION STATEMENT TO THE NLRB

Once an unfair labor practice charge is filed with the appropriate NLRB Regional Office, the NLRB agent assigned to investigate the charge may well ask the employer's representative to submit a position statement and set forth the employer's response to the charge along with any supporting documents or other such evidence.

At first glance, such a suggestion may appear to provide an expeditious means by which to attempt to get the unfair labor practice charge dismissed. It may not, however, be the best method through which the employer's representative should present the employer's evidence and supporting documents simply because the process is somewhat one-sided. When an employer presents its evidence through a position statement, it does not have the advantage of interacting with the NLRB agent to really determine what the NLRB agent has already gathered through his or her investigation of the charging party's witnesses and evidence. In addition, once such a position statement is submitted to the NLRB agent, the agent—through the NLRB's General Counsel at any subsequent unfair labor practice trial or hearing—is likely to attempt to take each and every thing related in the employer's position statement out of context and try to use it against the same employer. This means, once it is submitted, it is virtually impossible to change any of its contents.

There are some limited circumstances in which the respondent may want to present its evidence through a position statement, such as where the nature of the charge relates to contract language and the labor agreement speaks for itself and needs no amplification, or where an NLRB agent insists on some type of position statement by the employer's representative to comply with the region's protocol. Another circumstance that might dictate the respondent to submit a position statement to the NLRB investigatory agent would be where the respondent has a strong legal case but a weak factual case in terms of weak witnesses who may not have the intellect or insight to present pertinent facts in the most influential and creditable manner.

However, where factual issues are involved in an unfair labor practice charge, the NLRB agent will probably request affidavits of those who have first-hand knowledge of the facts. If a witness is substantially weak due to lack of sophistication or reticence, or easily intimidated or coerced, the respondent's counsel may elect to control the presentation of his or her statements by submitting his or her own affidavits of such individuals, either with a position statement, or independent of a position statement.

So, what is a preferable method through which to present one's evidence and discover much of the charging party's evidence, while at the same time, controlling the manner in which the employer's evidence is presented?

Usually, the alternative and better approach is to inform the investigatory agent that rather than submit a position statement, the employer prefers to present its evidence through live witnesses, preferably at the employer's place of business and in the form of affidavits.

Because many management attorneys prefer to make live witnesses available to present their evidence during the investigatory stage of an unfair labor practice charge, as opposed to submitting a position statement, NLRB agents probably gather most of their evidence through such a process. It should be remembered that inasmuch as an NLRB agent, when serving in the capacity of general counsel, has the right to try to use adverse evidence gathered through employer witnesses and their affidavits in a later unfair labor practice hearing, the employer's representative should exercise some control over what goes in the affidavit and how it is fashioned as noted below.

Irrespective of whether an employer presents its evidence through live witnesses and affidavits or through submitting a position statement, the employer's representative should attempt to elicit as much information as possible from the investigating NLRB agent so that he or she cannot only respond appropriately, but also attempt to discover what the NLRB has discovered from the charging party and his or her witnesses.

TECHNIQUES AND TACTICS IN PRESENTING EMPLOYER WITNESSES DURING AN UNFAIR LABOR PRACTICE INVESTIGATION

Although the presentation of employer witnesses to an NLRB agent during the investigatory stage may be the preferred method, there are several precautions that should be taken in presenting evidence in this manner.

Review the Evidence Gathered by the NLRB

First, the employer's representative should attempt to gain as much insight as possible into the evidence already gathered by the NLRB agent in support of the charging party's position.

The NLRB agent will not directly or intentionally disclose the names of those individuals who have given affidavits on behalf of the charging party nor what any such witnesses disclosed or stated in such affidavit. However, it will be necessary for the NLRB agent to reveal to the employer's representative the names of those employer witnesses with whom the NLRB agent wishes to confer and any pertinent information or documents that the employer's representative should have available to expedite the investigation of the employer witnesses. Creative management lawyers and other employer representatives should be able to deduce from such verbal interactions with the NLRB investigatory agent, who are the charging party's witnesses and what they may have said in their affidavits now in the agent's possession.

Most NLRB agents are pleasant, personable, and cooperative—at least in appearance. That doesn't mean they are not trying to build a case against the employer in an unfair labor practice charge. It may be fair to suggest that the majority of veteran NLRB agents are, philosophically, opposed to management, and in favor of organized labor.

Therefore, an overly effusive NLRB agent may, subconsciously, be using some of his or her interactional skills and social graces to indirectly attempt to entrap an employer's witness to agree to a certain statement which, on first impression, may appear innocent enough, but when reduced to the written word by the agent on an affidavit, may have substantially adverse implications.

It is helpful then to appreciate the presence of counsel at and during the time an NLRB agent takes a statement in affidavit form from the employer's witnesses. Management attorneys are permitted to be present during such times when an employer's management member or supervisor gives an affidavit to an NLRB agent, inasmuch as such person is considered to be the employer's agent and what he or she says can be imputed to the employer. In addition, it is common practice that both the management witness and the employer's counsel have an opportunity to read the affidavit given by the respective manager or supervisor prior to the management witness signing the affidavit. Both the manager or supervisor giving the affidavit to the NLRB agent and the employer's counsel should very carefully peruse such an affidavit to ensure that what the witness said verbally was stated clearly and that no other information was written into the affidavit, either expressly or implied, that was not said or stated by such manager or supervisor.

Prepare Witnesses

Seasoned management attorneys take the necessary time to adequately prepare their managerial and supervisory witnesses prior to presenting them to the NLRB agent. (See Chapter 5 for witness preparation safeguards.)

All such witnesses should be prepared as a group so that each and every one who will be giving statements to the NLRB will understand the impact of their statements in relation to what other employer witnesses will be stating to the NLRB agent. Some NLRB agents an attempt to pit management witnesses against each other during this portion of their investigation in an attempt to obtain inconsistent statements. Witnesses should always be advised to take their time and not be intimidated or coerced by an NLRB agent to agree to some statement or position that may appear to be correct in a certain context, but when examined more closely does not relate accurate facts, as such.

The employer's counsel or representative should also be mindful of the order or sequence in which the employer's witnesses should be presented during the NLRB agent's taking of their affidavits. As much information and documentary evidence in support of the employer's position, as possible, should be presented through the employer's best management witnesses, and weaker witnesses should be used to relate less important and significant information. Stronger witnesses are those who are articulate, insightful and knowledgeable of the pertinent facts, but who are also prudent and judicious in evaluating the NLRB agent's questions so as to avoid mis-speaking themselves. Also, they typically are those individuals who have previously had to interact in adversarial environments and are not intimidated or coerced by such circumstances.

Caveats to Consider When Presenting Employee Witnesses

Although an employer and its counsel may present employee witnesses, as well as managerial witnesses in support of its position during an unfair labor practice investigation, the approach and manner in which such respective witnesses are presented is somewhat different.

The distinction lies in the fact that managerial and supervisory witnesses are part of management under Section 2(11) of the National Labor Relations Act, as amended, and exempted from coverage or protection under the Act. On the other hand, employees are covered by the Act and are protected in the exercise of their Section 7 rights, as discussed in Chapter 2. Also, the NLRB regards supervisors and managers to be agents of their employer and imputes their unlawful conduct to the employer; on the other hand, the NLRB does not regard employees as agents of their employer unless some unusual circumstances would suggest such an agency relationship.

The use of rank-and-file employees as witnesses on behalf of management can be very effective, but extreme caution should be used in preparing and presenting them.

Strategically, it is not the most prudent approach to attempt to use hostile employee witnesses, particularly if such an employee is aligned with the opposition as in the case of a strong union advocate. Although the employee may be helpful with respect to having firsthand knowledge that could serve to establish or corroborate certain pieces of evidence essential to the employer's case, the lack of trust as to whether the employee would relate the information truthfully or attempt to twist and embellish the information against the employer may outweigh the risk of taking the chance on the former. Thus, if the employer's case can be established and presented through witnesses other than an adverse employee witness, then the employer's representative should be very reluctant in attempting to use such an employee when presenting its evidence during an NLRB investigation of a pending unfair labor practice charge.

Should a more friendly and supportive rank-and-file employee have firsthand knowledge of essential information that could be helpful in proving the employer's case during the investigatory stage of a pending unfair labor practice charge, then he or she should be presented, unless there are some other pertinent circumstances that would dictate otherwise.

In either case—whether the rank-and-file employee being considered as an employer's witness to give certain information to the NLRB agent is friendly or unfriendly to management—employers and their representatives must observe certain NLRB guidelines in discussing the matter with the employee witness and must relate certain rights he or she has under NLRB guidelines prior to making inquiries regarding facts surrounding the particular case at hand.

Should an employer's representative interrogate an employee with respect to activities involving unionization or self-representation, the NLRB could find such interrogation coercive and a violation of Section 8(a)(1) of the National Labor Relations Act in that such interrogation interferes with the employee's protected rights under Section 7 of the Act.

The National Labor Relations Board has taken the position that it will not find an employer in violation of Section 8(a)(1) where an employee is being questioned about certain facts or events surrounding generally prohibited subject matters if the questioning of the employee or employees is in preparation of an NLRB hearing or investigation, provided certain specified conditions—referred to as the *Johnnie's Poultry* standards—are met, as follows:

- The employee first should be advised as to the nature and purpose of the inquiry.
- The employee should be advised that his or her participation in the discussion of such case is strictly voluntary.
- The employee should be advised that if he or she chooses not to participate in the inquiry, that there will be no reprisals taken against the employee.
- The employee should also be advised that if he or she chooses to participate in the inquiry, that there will be no benefits or reward given to the employee.
- Assuming the employee voluntarily agrees to participate in such inquiry, the questions posed to the employee must be relevant to the preparation of the employer's case.
- The questioning of the employee must take place in an environment free of animus or hostility toward unionism.
- The questioning should not otherwise interfere with the Section 7 rights of the employee being questioned.

An additional safeguard to ensure compliance with the *Johnnie's Poultry* requirements would be to read the employee his or her rights as noted above, and to have each such employee sign and date a document to that effect.

Once the *Johnnie's Poultry* criteria are met and information is revealed in the inquiry by an employee that would be helpful to the employer's case, then such an employee should be asked whether he or she would be willing to share the same information with the NLRB agent investigating the pending unfair labor practice charge, assuming that the employee is not hostile toward management and can be trusted to disclose the same information to the investigating NLRB agent.

When presenting such rank-and-file employees to an NLRB agent as part of its evidence, the employer's counsel or representative will not be permitted to be present during the time in which the NLRB agent takes the employee's statement, again in affidavit form, unless the employee informs the NLRB agent that he or she wishes the employer's counsel or representative to remain during the agent's conference with the employee. This is in contrast to the employer's counsel or representative having a right to remain during the NLRB agent's conference with a manager or supervisor of the employer.

The employer's counsel or representative should advise the employee of his or her right and option to have the employer's counsel or representative present, if desired. This should be related to the employee as a point of information only and certainly presented in a non coercive manner. Hopefully, such an employee would want the employer's counsel or representative present at such time, but it is strictly up to the employee. If pressure or intimidation is used by management to entice an employee to request the presence of the employer's counsel in such a case, the NLRB could well find that the *Johnnie's Poultry* safeguards were compromised and that the employer has violated the employee's Section 7 rights.

METHODS TO DISCOVER UNDISCOVERABLE EVIDENCE DURING THE INVESTIGATORY STAGE

The National Labor Relations Board's Rules and Regulations do not permit respondents in an unfair labor practice to discover the evidence disclosed to the NLRB investigatory agent by the charging party and his or her witnesses. The NLRB's justification in refusing to disclose such evidence to a respondent in a pending unfair labor practice charge is that the respondent may, in turn, take reprisals against the charging party and/or his or her witnesses, particularly if such persons are employees of the respondent.

The respondent and its counsel or representative are greatly handicapped in not being able to discover what the charging party and his or her witnesses have said or presented to the NLRB agent.

Most modern rules of evidence and procedure provide for very liberal discovery rights of both parties to a legal dispute as a means to fine-tune the issues in question and prevent the parties from allowing the dispute to digress into irrelevant and immaterial territories. Modern evidentiary and procedural rules that permit liberal discovery rights in other forums are justified on the grounds that any subsequent hearing or trial on the issues in question can run more smoothly and expeditiously in contrast to earlier days where each party tried to ambush the other with "surprise" evidence in the courtroom.

Since the respondent is not going to be permitted to discover the evidence the NLRB agent has gathered from the charging party and his or her witnesses through traditional channels of discovery, such as through depositions, interrogatories, or requests for admissions, the question then becomes: are there non-traditional or indirect methods available by which to discover the NLRB's evidence? The answer is yes, at least in certain cases, such as in discharge cases relating to 8(a)(3) charges.

The answer lies in using other forums in which to confront the charging party and his or her witnesses relative to the same evidence as gathered by the NLRB agent investigating the pending unfair labor practice charge.

One example would be where the charging party was discharged from his employment and thereafter files an unemployment compensation claim for benefits while also filing an 8(a)(3) unfair labor practice charge and contending his discharge was for union activity instead of for a just cause reason.

If such a circumstance should arise, the employer's counsel or representative should take every legal means available to win the unemployment compensation case and, while doing so, use the unemployment compensation hearing as a way of extracting key information from the charging party and his or her witnesses.

Similar forums through which to discover, indirectly, the charging party's proof would include the Equal Employment Opportunity Commission, the Occupational Safety and Health Commission, and various state agencies that have related functions, should the employee-charging party file claims or charges with such agencies.

TECHNIQUES TO USE IN DEALING WITH AN ABUSIVE NLRB AGENT

The respondent's counsel or representative should always be aware that the evidence presented to the NLRB agent through the respondent's witnesses, whether management and supervisory members or rank-and-file employees, is being presented on a voluntary basis. There are no legal requirements that mandate cooperation or participation on the respondent's part. What the respondent decides to present to the NLRB agent, how it is presented, and through whom it is presented is all at the discretion of the respondent's counsel.

Should the respondent's counsel elect to present the employer's evidence to an NLRB agent in the hopes that such evidence will convince the NLRB's Regional Office to dismiss the charge, such counsel should be aware that the presentation of evidence to the NLRB agent may cease at any time the respondent's counsel so desires. Thus, in the very rare instance where an NLRB agent becomes too emotionally involved in the charging party's case and, as such, becomes too aggressive or abusive in gathering information from the respondent's witnesses, the respondent's counsel has the right and privilege of ceasing to present any further evidence to the NLRB agent on behalf of the respondent and terminate its participation in such process.

One of the authors was presented with such a situation several years ago in which the investigatory NLRB agent continued to attempt to twist the statements made by the employer's witnesses out of context and reduce the incorrect information into the affidavit. Repeated efforts were made to demonstrate that the information the NLRB wrote into the affidavit was not the same as that related by the respondent's witness and that the affidavit should be rewritten to ensure that the statements made by the respondent's witnesses conformed with the information presented. In addition, after a continual refusal by the agent to grant such requests, the agent was advised that the witness would not sign the affidavit, due to its inaccuracies and that the respondent would not be presenting any further evidence of its position on a voluntary basis. After taking such a rigid stance on the affidavits, the NLRB agent reluctantly agreed to conform the affidavits, as requested, and the respondent continued to present evidence to the NLRB agent. Had the NLRB agent not agreed to "re-take" the affidavit, the conference would have been terminated immediately.

Other employer counsel should do no less, should the circumstance arise in a given case.

5 Pre-Trial Techniques in Defending an Unfair Labor Practice Case

Just because the charging party establishes a prima facie case of an unfair labor practice, and the respondent does not provide sufficient evidence to convince the investigating NLRB agent that its evidence overrides that of the charging party, does not necessarily entail that the NLRB's General Counsel will file a formal complaint against the respondent. The NLRB's General Counsel might assume that there is not enough substance of evidence to go forward; that the charging party's witnesses are not credible enough to withstand rigid cross-examination by a competent management attorney or that the issues in the case are not that significant with respect to the overall labor relations environment.

However, where the General Counsel concludes that the charging party has established a strong prima facie case and the respondent's evidence is weak or pre-textual, or the respondent's evidence presents credibility conflicts with that of the charging party, the resolution which is best provided through an unfair labor practice trial, the NLRB's General Counsel, through its local NLRB representatives, will file a formal complaint against the respondent.

FACTORS TO CONSIDER IN EXPLORING SETTLEMENT OF AN UNFAIR LABOR PRACTICE CHARGE OR COMPLAINT

Prior to filing such a complaint, or as part and parcel of the filing, the General Counsel's representative will either directly, or indirectly, inquire of the respondent about the possibility of settling the pending unfair labor practice case.

The NLRB has an inherent policy of attempting to effect settlement agreements of pending unfair labor practice cases and will intermittently attempt to settle and resolve the case up to and through the unfair labor practice trial.

The strategical challenge then becomes to what extent, if at all, should the respondent's counsel entertain or explore settlement of the outstanding issues in the unfair labor practice complaint.

The employer's counsel or representative should not summarily reject settlement proposals, outright, irrespective of his or her perception that the employer does not totally endorse settlement. Circumstances may favor settlement discussions simply because the General Counsel's representative has a weak case or there are some parts of his or her proof that could fall apart. (However, there are many management attorneys who feel strongly that these are the types of cases that the employer should not settle, but teach the General Counsel's representative that the complaint should have never been issued in the first place; that is, try the strong ones on the part of the employer, attempt to settle the weaker cases on the part of the employer.)

There are many factors to consider when exploring the settlement of an unfair labor practice case, especially once a complaint has been issued against the respondent.

Consider Monetary Costs

An employer-respondent's counsel or representative would first want to consider a proposed settlement from the General Counsel's representative in terms of any monetary costs to the employer. In many instances, the proposed settlement would not entail any monetary impact upon the employer at all, but merely require the employer to post a notice to employees that the employer would not commit certain conduct in the future.

On the other hand, especially in 8(a)(3) cases where the alleged unfair labor practices involves multiple discharges or layoffs, the monetary costs could be substantial were the employer to lose the case.

Consider Whether Terms Require Employee Reinstatement

Another factor to consider in determining settlement opportunities with the General Counsel's representative is whether the terms of the settlement proposal will require the employer to reinstate an employee, or perhaps, several employees, to their former jobs. Some employers would rather comply with any settlement conditions other than being required to reinstate employees to their former positions. Not only is such an employer typically frustrated about the returning employees being recognized as "martyrs" and "untouchables" in terms that other employees may perceive that, "They got by with it, so can we," but such an employer may also be perplexed in that an opposing union might try to use and propagandize the information to the effect that employees must have a union around to protect their job security.

Consider Time and Cost of the Trial

However, even if the monetary costs may be considerable and the settlement package may require reinstatement, employers that have a relatively weak case on the merits may want to seriously consider settlement and "cut their losses" rather than to pay the cost in money and time of going to an unfair labor practice trial only to lose the case months (or years) later.

Given the predisposition of many administrative law judges that the employer is "guilty" even prior to an unfair labor practice trial and the inherent prejudice and bias of many judges against management witnesses in unfair labor proceedings, should the General Counsel's representative offer a plausible settlement to the employer-respondent, its counsel should think long and hard before rejecting the offer.

Consider Other Company Objectives

An employer may want to strongly explore settlement, even though it genuinely believes it would prevail in an unfair labor practice trial in order to accomplish other objectives. For example, suppose that employees of a given employer have timely filed a petition asking the NLRB to conduct a decertification election, only to have the election process blocked by an unfair labor practice charge filed by the union in question against the employer. Assuming the case proceeded to an unfair labor practice complaint against the employer, rather than being dismissed, the employer's counsel may well want to consider a non-admission settlement agreement that provides for notice posting for a 60-day period, simply to get the decertification election process "back on track" in a timely manner.

The employer's counsel should be aware that a charging party, such as a union in the hypothetical case posed above, does not have to be a party to an informal settlement agreement between the NLRB and the respondent; that is, a settlement prior to the issuance of a formal complaint. The respective Regional Director on behalf of the General Counsel has the discretion to enter into such bilateral settlement agreements, but must permit the charging party to appeal its opposition to the settlement terms to the office of the General Counsel. Although there are some exceptions, rarely does the General Counsel's office overrule a Regional Director's settlement agreement with the respondent, or the Regional Director's dismissal of an unfair labor practice charge.

In contrast, certain factors may dictate that the employer's counsel not settle an unfair labor practice charge or complaint even though, under normal circumstances, settlement would be the preferred choice.

Effecting Settlement

A settlement of an unfair labor practice charge may be effected in one of three ways:

(1) an informal agreement requires the respondent to remedy the alleged unfair labor practices in exchange for withdrawal or dismissal of the charge and only requires, as noted earlier, the approval of the respective Regional Director

(2) a formal settlement agreement entails the execution of a stipulation providing for the issuance of a cease and desist order by the NLRB, specifying remedies for the alleged unfair labor practices and, sometimes, getting an appropriate court to enter a court decree to enforce the Board's order

(3) a non-Board settlement agreement occurs when the charging party and the party charged, the respondent, reach a mutually acceptable resolution of their dispute without the involvement of the Board, and, in which the charging party withdraws its unfair labor practice charge, subject to the Board's approval of the withdrawal which usually is granted unless the non-Board settlement between the parties would be repugnant to the purposes of the Act

TECHNICAL SAFEGUARDS IN ANSWERING AN UNFAIR LABOR PRACTICE COMPLAINT

Assuming that an unfair labor practice charge is not dismissed by the NLRB, withdrawn by the charging party, or disposed of through a settlement agreement, the General Counsel's representative may file a formal complaint against the respondent. The complaint sets forth the Board's jurisdiction over the matter and then enumerates the allegations of facts upon which the General Counsel's case is predicated. A notice of hearing typically accompanies a formal complaint, specifying the time and place of the hearing.

As with amendments to unfair labor practice charges, the NLRB is very liberal in permitting General Counsel's representative to amend a complaint prior to a hearing on the complaint. Should General Counsel's representative desire to amend the complaint after such a hearing commences, the administrative law judge assigned to the case must approve the amendment.

The respondent has 14 days from the service of the complaint to file the original and four copies of its answer with the Regional Director who issued the complaint on behalf of the General Counsel. Some safeguards to consider in answering a complaint include:

- The respondent's counsel or representative must ensure that the respondent's answer is filed within the 14-day time limit, or if unable to do, file a timely request for an extension of time in which to file the answer.

- Since the NLRB will treat any unanswered allegations within a complaint as admissions of truth, the respondent's counsel should respond to each and every allegation in the complaint by either denial, admission, or explanation, unless the respondent is without knowledge to admit or deny the truth of the allegation, in which case, for pleading purposes, the respondent should deny such allegations and demand proof of same.
- Should an allegation in the complaint state a legal conclusion or opinion, or assert some proposition other than an allegation of fact, the employer's representative should, in turn, relate such in his or her answer and state that the assertion, as such, does not require an admission or denial, but if required to answer such assertion, the respondent denies same.
- The respondent's counsel should not only deny allegations of facts that are not true, but with respect to any defenses arguably to be considered affirmative defenses such as prescriptive periods, he or she should plead those as affirmative defenses in the answer.
- The respondent's representative should peruse the formal complaint in a most thorough manner to determine whether the General Counsel has alleged facts simply too remote in terms of time and distance to be considered within the scope of the original charge. If not, the respondent's counsel should address such by preparing a motion to dismiss such allegations on the grounds that the allegations are not within the scope of the original charge by implication, or otherwise, and that the complaint should be dismissed.
- The respondent's counsel should be aware that he or she can readily amend its answer at a later date, should the situation arise.

TECHNIQUES IN FILING PRE-TRIAL MOTIONS

In addition to filing an answer to the complaint prior to an unfair labor practice hearing, the employer's counsel would want to determine whether he or she should file any pre-hearing motions. There are several, including:

Motion for Summary Judgment

Where the General Counsel files a complaint which contains no allegations that would constitute a violation of the Act in terms of an unfair labor practice, even if proven true, the employer's counsel or representative would want to file a motion for summary judgment, which, if granted, would have the effect of the complaint being dismissed and the hearing cancelled.

Motion for Bill of Particulars

For the most part, NLRB agents who draft unfair labor practice complaints are well trained in the art of pleading to describe the acts which are alleged to have violated the National Labor Relations Act. There may be occasions, however, where such alleged facts are so peculiar or complex or the agent doesn't have the necessary pleading skills to describe such acts in a concise and clear manner. If so, the employer's counsel may want to entertain the filing of a motion for a bill of particulars to require such NLRB attorneys to furnish more specifics relative to the allegations so that he or she will have sufficient information by which to answer the complaint.

Motion to Sever or Consolidate

Another motion that the employer's counsel may wish to consider is a motion to sever cases in which the NLRB has consolidated, especially where the issues are completely unrelated and the consolidation of the cases creates confusion and frustration. In like form, the employer's counsel may move to consolidate two or more separate cases where the allegations are related, if such consolidation could save the employer costs in terms of time and expense, especially if no strategic considerations would dictate otherwise.

Motion to Postpone Hearing

Where conflicts exist in schedules of counsel, witnesses, and so on, the employer's counsel may desire to file a motion to postpone the unfair labor practice to a later date. Assuming good reason shown, and when timely filed without opposition of the charging party, the NLRB typically will permit such postponement.

Applications for Depositions

As a matter of policy, the NLRB does not permit the taking of depositions for the purposes of discovery. Pre-hearing depositions may be permitted, however, when used for the purposes of preserving the testimony of witnesses who will be unable to attend the hearing because of illness, accident or some other type of physical disability. If so, the employer's counsel would want to, either by motion or application, request the NLRB for permission to use such limited discovery.

Motion to Oppose Section 10(j) Injunctive Relief

Section 10(j) of the National Labor Relations Act, as amended, permits the National Labor Relations Board to petition an appropriate Federal District Court for temporary injunctive relief or a restraining order in unfair labor practice cases that could be tied up for a considerable period of time through the NLRB processes, where such delays may cause irreparable harm to the charging party without such relief. It is discretionary on the part of the NLRB as to whether such action will be taken. Should the charging party request such injunctive relief, the respondent's counsel may well want to file a motion in opposition to it.

STRATEGIES IN APPLYING FOR AND REVOKING NLRB SUBPOENAS IN AN UNFAIR LABOR PRACTICE CASE

There are two types of subpoenas that may be issued in an unfair labor practice case:

- a *subpoena ad testificandum* in which the party subpoenaed will be required to attend and testify at the unfair labor practice trial
- a *subpoena duces tecum* in which the party subpoenaed will be required to both attend and testify and present certain documents so specified in the subpoena

The respondent's counsel may secure such subpoenas prior to trial from the appropriate Regional Director and during the trial from the appropriate administrative law judge hearing the case.

Some witnesses for the employer may feel more comfortable in testifying in an unfair labor practice case if they are officially subpoenaed by the employer's counsel, especially in cases in which employees may be testifying for an employer. To the extent that they be harassed by fellow employees in so testifying, they can relate that they were required to do so because of being subpoenaed by the employer's counsel.

Strategically important, also, is to subpoena those witnesses who may be somewhat frightened or intimidated by the judicial process in case they get cold feet and make up some type of excuse at the last minute for not being available for the hearing.

Probably the General Counsel will subpoena more witnesses than the employer in a typical unfair labor practice trial because most management witnesses for the employer are not usually subpoenaed. As a result, some employees so subpoenaed by General Counsel may feel that they should not have been subpoenaed because, for example, they contend that they know nothing about the facts surrounding the case. They may ask the employer's counsel what they should do. Such a question could place the employer's counsel in a sensitive position. Were the employer's counsel to become overly responsive to the situation in terms of his or her advice to the subpoenaed employee, the NLRB may subject (and possibly charge) that the employer's counsel was in some way interfering with the NLRB processes or attempting to procure the witness to commit perjury. The prudent counsel does not want to be placed in such a position. A conservative response would be to advise the employee to seek his or her own attorney's advice or relate the administrative process to the employees about how such a subpoena may be revoked.

The NLRB rules provide that a petition to revoke a subpoena must be filed within five days after the subpoena has been served. Grounds for petitioning the appropriate NLRB Regional Director prior to trial, or the appropriate administrative law judge, after commencement of trial, may be one of the following:

- the information and evidence sought to be produced through the subpoenaed party do not relate to the issues in the unfair labor practice case
- the information and evidence sought to be produced through the subpoenaed party is not sufficiently described
- for any other reason under the law, the subpoena is otherwise invalid

TECHNIQUES AND TACTICS WHEN ENTERING INTO PRE-TRIAL STIPULATIONS

Typically, prior to or immediately before the unfair labor practice trial, the General Counsel's representative will inquire whether or not the employer's counsel wants to enter into certain stipulated facts in order to save time during the hearing.

Tactically, it is beneficial to agree to any stipulations of fact that does not hurt the employer's case. The employer's counsel or representative also should be interested in saving time during trial with relatively unimportant items in which the General Counsel's representative wants a stipulation.

It may also be desirable to stipulate to matters that may harm the employer's case. If such facts are going to come out in trial, no matter what the employer's counsel does to prevent their disclosure, a stipulation will prevent the General Counsel's representative from drawing excessive attention to such facts during the trial in his or her attempt to prejudice the employer's case even more.

TIME-TESTED TIPS IN PREPARING WITNESSES FOR TRIAL

The management attorney or representative who does not take adequate time to prepare the employer's witnesses, and who does not prepare superb questions for cross-examination, is greatly jeopardizing the employer's case and serving an injustice on his or her witnesses.

It takes enormous time and effort to prepare just a minimal number of witnesses, not even considering the time that can be expended in preparing many witnesses, especially in a complex trial. The old legal warrior who used to brag that he could get the job done with just a few minutes with his witnesses at the courthouse immediately prior to the trial is either overly embellishing the glory days of the past or has lost many cases.

There actually should be at least two preparation sessions with employer witnesses when preparing employee witnesses for the employer's case.

The first session should be a preliminary dress rehearsal with respect to covering testimony that should be addressed in direct examination and questions that each witness can expect on cross-examination from the General Counsel's representative.

The Federal Rules of Evidence—rules that are applied in NLRB ULP hearings—provide that an adverse or hostile witness may be called by the opposing counsel. The NLRB's Office of General Counsel has a well-established reputation of calling key management witnesses under section 611(c) of the Federal Rules of Evidence in putting on their case-in-chief.

Thus, the preliminary dress rehearsal should include a discussion of what key management witnesses for the employer may expect from the General Counsel's representative if called as a hostile or adverse witness early in the General Counsel's case.

The first session with the employer's witnesses also should be used to determine if there are other potential witnesses, or documentary and demonstrative evidence, that could be beneficial to help support the employer's case. This reason alone, not counting many others, should be sufficient to impress upon the employer's counsel that the preliminary session with the employer's witnesses (or potential witnesses) should not be scheduled so close to the trial date that it would be too late to use information gained from it.

The second session with the employer's witnesses should be scheduled very close to the trial date so as to cover all last-minute details and provide a dress rehearsal with respect to questions that will be asked during direct examination and questions to expect on cross-examination.

Obviously, other sessions may be required in addition to those mentioned above. Irrespective of the number of discussions the employer's counsel has with his or her witnesses, it is somewhat customary that all meet at the place of hearing prior to the commencement of the trial to ensure that everyone is present and ready.

Either at a period of time just prior to the commencement of the trial or at one of the earlier sessions, the employer's counsel should discuss what witnesses should and should not do while a witness in the trial. This is probably as important, or even more important, at an unfair labor practice trial than in Federal or State court simply because administrative law judges who hear unfair labor practice cases place so much emphasis on the demeanor of witnesses in determining credibility factors to decide who is telling the truth and who is not. With the "deck" already stacked against the employer in unfair labor practice cases, particularly before career NLRB agents who ascend to an administrative law judge position, the prudent management attorney should do everything possible to educate himself or herself as to what such judges look to in determining credibility and ensure that all of the employer's witnesses understand as well, even to the extent of reviewing "body language" publications and presentations.

Checklist for Employer Witnesses

In addition, employer witnesses should be informed of some of the following do's and don'ts:

1. ***Tell the truth.*** That doesn't mean that the witness does not have to think. It merely means that truthful witnesses don't have to have long memories. Therefore, witnesses who believe they are helping their case by overly

embellishing facts only aid in the destruction of the employer's case in the long run. They will get caught up, and crossed up, in their testimony by a seasoned cross-examiner who is just waiting for that one opportunity "to go for the jugular vein."

2. ***Don't memorize what is going to be said.*** Rehearse the testimony many times and know well the sequence of facts and information that should be presented. Witnesses who have memorized their testimony easily can be "crossed up" by the General Counsel's representative during cross-examination and, in turn, not be credited as a knowledgeable and truthful witness by the administrative law judge hearing the evidence. A judge is likely to think a witness is lying if his or her testimony appears to be overly rehearsed and orchestrated.
3. ***Be respectful and courteous at all times to all parties***, including General Counsel's representative. Witnesses who appear to be a smart aleck or cocky lose respect in the eyes of the judge. Above all, do not lose your temper. Some attorneys on cross-examination purposely will try to wear witnesses down to the point they overreact and get mixed-up. Don't be a victim to such tactics.
4. ***Do not answer a question unless you know the answer to the question.*** Don't guess. Merely admit that you don't know, or don't recall, or that it will be necessary for you to review certain documents or information before you can be sufficiently refreshed to recall the facts in question (and then request such documents).
5. ***Take your time and listen carefully to the questions***, particularly of the opposing counsel. If the question is not clear, ask the person to repeat it or to explain it. Don't overact or offer a snap answer.
6. ***Temper and explain your testimony where necessary***. Do not be evasive or equivocal, but some questions cannot be answered with a simple "yes" or "no" answer. Therefore, it is sometimes best to use words of approximation as distinguished from words of exactness.
7. ***Do not volunteer information*** that may hurt your case or place you in a position of having to testify about matters with which you are not familiar. Therefore, unless some clarification or explanation is necessary, it is best to answer the question with as few words as possible, and then stop.
8. ***Testify about facts of your own knowledge***. Don't testify as to matters of hearsay or your opinion or conclusions about a matter. Only expert witnesses have the privilege of giving opinions; only judges have the privilege of making conclusions, at least, generally speaking.
9. ***Be businesslike***. Wear clean and conservative clothing. Be serious and to the point. Unless some unusual circumstance would permit such departure from the typical courtroom culture, it probably is not going to help your credibility to inject humor or laughter into your testimony. For example,

chewing gum or blowing bubbles will not endear a witness to an NLRB administrative law judge.

10. ***Testify directly to the judge***, whether the judge gives you any eye contact or not. Be natural in doing so. Speak to him or her in a frank, open, and neighborly manner, like telling a story to a friend. Don't stare at the judge.
11. ***If you answer incorrectly or mis-speak yourself***, correct your testimony immediately. Even the most seasoned television announcers mis-speak, but they correct themselves, instantly. So should a witness.
12. ***Stop immediately when the judge speaks***. The judge is in charge of the proceedings. Give him or her the deference and attention deserved if the judge interrupts the proceedings.
13. ***Speak confidently and clearly***. Speak loud enough that the judge and court reporter can hear what is said; hopefully, the employer's counsel, as well. Vocalize your answers. A nodding of the head in the affirmative or negative does not transcribe well to the written word in the transcript.
14. ***Don't look at the employer's counsel for help, or approval or disapproval, with respect to an answer***. If the question is objectionable, the lawyers will argue it out, and the judge will rule as to its propriety. If the judge directs you to answer, then answer. Don't ask the judge for advice with respect to your testimony. You are on your own.
15. ***Be aware of trick questions***. For example, the opposing counsel on cross-examination may inquire about, "What your lawyer told you to say"; or "Did your lawyer talk to you before this trial about your testimony?" Be honest. All good lawyers talk to their witnesses before trial. Such is not only permissible and proper, to do otherwise would be contemptible and probably grounds for malpractice. As to, "What did your lawyer tell you to say?" the answer should be: "He told me to tell the truth, which is what I am doing." Another trick question, in a similar form, from the opposing counsel may be, "Are you getting paid to testify in this case?" Again, if under subpoena, the answer should be something to the effect that you are not getting paid to testify, but that you are under subpoena and that you understand that the subpoena reimbursement is to pay for your lost time from work and your expense in coming to the trial.
16. ***Don't act frightened or nervous, if at all possible***. Avoid mannerisms that depict timidity, such as covering up one's mouth or failure to give good eye contact. All are negative body language signals, suggesting dishonesty. Leave the witness stand with a confident look.
17. ***Visit another trial or court prior to your testimony*** to understand the procedure and how lawyers and judges go about their business.

6 Defensive Techniques and Tactics to Use in Unfair Labor Practice Trials

The National Labor Relations Board has a Division of Judges from which an administrative law judge will be assigned to hear a specific unfair labor practice case. An administrative law judge has many responsibilities and duties, the most significant being to conduct the proceedings, hear the evidence, and make recommended conclusions of law and findings of fact.

Administrative law judges have much discretion in hearing unfair labor practice cases and are permitted to ask witnesses questions of their own, should they desire, to make sure the record of the proceedings is complete for later submission to the five member NLRB.

However, some administrative law judges, being so closely connected to the NLRB and philosophically opposed to management, seemingly take on the role of General Counsel and commence to ask questions of witnesses, especially questions of employer witnesses that should be elicited more from the General Counsel's representative as an advocate, rather than from that of a judge whose role is to be neutral and, supposedly, unbiased.

Should such a situation arise in an unfair labor practice trial, the employer's counsel may want to object to the judge's departure from his or her judicial role and argue that such conduct deprives the hearing of the necessary degree of fundamental fairness required by due process. There is a risk in so objecting because the judge's prejudice toward the employer and employer's counsel may heighten. Yet, the failure to so object will give the judge even more latitude to abuse the process and get into evidence on the part of the General Counsel, testimony that General

Counsel's representative may not have had the ability to have gotten into evidence, prompting the judge's involvement in the first place.

As noted earlier, many administrative law judges who hear evidence in unfair labor practice cases are highly prejudiced against employers, many of whom almost universally rule against each and every employer objection and who discredit each and every employer witness who appears before them, regardless of who they are or what they say.

The employer's counsel or representative may request the administrative law judge to withdraw from the case or recuse himself or herself on the basis of personal bias, prejudice or disqualification. Such a request to withdraw, or motion to recuse, should not be submitted without considering all the consequences associated with such a move. In the first place, most judges are very reluctant to disqualify themselves. Second, the standards applied by the NLRB and the courts in disqualifying judges are rather strict and stringent.

However, if a judge is so apparently hostile and prejudiced against an employer that the employer's counsel knows from previous decisions of a particular judge that it is impossible to obtain a fair and impartial hearing, the employer's counsel may want to file a motion for the judge to recuse himself or herself as a practical maneuver and to preserve such position for the sake of the record.

HELPFUL HINTS IN PRE-TRIAL CONFERENCES

As with federal and state judges, administrative law judges who are assigned to hear unfair labor practice cases desire to get counsel for General Counsel and the respondent's counsel together in a pre-trial conference shortly before the hearing commences, with several objectives in mind:

- to encourage the parties to exhaust all efforts to negotiate a settlement of the case
- short of settlement, to simplify the issues and narrow the evidence to be introduced so as to expedite the hearing as much as possible
- to avoid surprise and confusion during the hearing by clarifying the issues and theories contained in the General Counsel's complaint and the respondent's answer
- to informally dispose of any other collateral matters, not otherwise required to be disposed of on the record of the proceedings

The employer's counsel and the General Counsel's representative will be questioned by the administrative law judge as to what is the possibility of settlement. The employer's counsel probably should not take a recalcitrant position at this juncture, but merely relate that the employer is always amenable to entertain and explore settlement further, if the General Counsel desires. This does not mean that the employer's counsel should take a different posture in the settlement conference with the General Counsel's representative than that taken previously but merely to show that the employer is open minded. In actual settlement discussions during pre-trial, the employer's offer may be no more than to reaffirm its confidence in its case and state that its previous offers stand. But, at least in the mind of the judge, the parties gave settlement another chance. Refer to Chapter 5 for more detailed strategies when considering settlement opportunities of unfair labor practice cases. The employer's counsel should be aware that settlement opportunities may still be pursued even after trial commences, should the parties desire.

SIGNIFICANT STEPS TO FOLLOW WHEN SEQUESTERING WITNESSES

Prior to the commencement of an unfair labor practice trial, the administrative law judge, immediately before calling witnesses to testify, will ask the General Counsel's and the employer's representatives whether they wish to invoke the "Rule"; that is, whether they want all prospective witnesses to be excluded from the courtroom when other witnesses are testifying about events and circumstances surrounding the case about which they have already testified, or about which they will be testifying later in the trial.

The employer's counsel has two basic factors to consider in deciding whether he or she wishes to invoke this rule of sequestration. Should neither the employer's counsel nor the General Counsel's representative elect to invoke the "Rule," all the witnesses for both parties will be permitted to remain in the courtroom and hear all the other witnesses' testimony. This provides an opportunity for less honest witnesses to change and reshape their testimony during the trial to cover up and overcome unfavorable testimony of their fellow witnesses. It also permits General Counsel's witnesses to sit in the courtroom during the trial and attempt to give the appearance of a rallying group around the charging party's cause.

Should either party invoke the "Rule," all potential witnesses except the charging party (or alleged discriminatees) on behalf of General Counsel and a management representative on the part of the respondent, are excluded from the hearing except during their own testimony, even to the extent of not being permitted to talk to other witnesses after they have testified or while on recess during their testimony.

The employer's counsel should give strong consideration to invoke the "Rule" so as to avoid a potential carnival-like atmosphere in the courtroom by the witnesses for General Counsel and also to avoid having General Counsel's witnesses customize their testimony to conform to the testimony of fellow witnesses. The employer's counsel should ensure his or her witnesses are sufficiently prepared to give testimony so that they have no need or desire to customize or reshape their testimony.

There are exceptions to any recommendation, but generally speaking, "Asking for the Rule" is probably the better of the two options presented by the judge. And just in case the judge fails to inquire of counsel about the "Rule," the employer's counsel should bring it immediately to the attention of the court prior to the commencement of the hearing, if he or she wants to take advantage of it. Otherwise, the judge may infer that the right to invoke sequestration was waived.

TRIAL TECHNIQUES IN DIRECTING AND CROSS-EXAMINING WITNESSES IN AN UNFAIR LABOR PRACTICE CASE

As already discussed in Chapter 5, it is essential that the respondent's witnesses be sufficiently prepared to testify. However, there are additional techniques that may be beneficial when examining one's own witnesses and cross-examining those of the opposition in the actual trial of the case:

1. *Write out detailed questions to ask witnesses* in advance of the hearing, not only to review with one's own witnesses, but also to ensure that the questions are properly sequenced. The discipline of writing out detailed questions to ask of one's own witnesses also provides a checklist to ensure that all pertinent matters are covered through such witnesses. Also, the employer's counsel should write out detailed questions that he or she intends to use in cross-examination of General Counsel's witnesses, to be used as a checklist to ensure that all significant questions are covered during cross-examination of the opposition witnesses. An added value of writing detailed questions, in advance, is to provide a higher level of confidence in the employer's counsel who should feel more relaxed and comfortable going into trial, knowing that he or she is adequately prepared.

2. *Prepare witnesses to know each and every matter covered* in any affidavit or statement that they may have given to the NLRB during the earlier investigation of the case. Many times, there will be pertinent facts left out of such an affidavit and General Counsel's representative will try to make it appear that because the witness testified about facts at the trial that were not covered in his or her affidavit that the witness is making up the additional information and, therefore, should be discredited by the administrative law judge when, in truth, the NLRB agent who investigated the case never even inquired about such matters during the investigation. The employer's witnesses should be schooled as to such eventualities and how to respond to them. The primary purpose in encouraging employer witnesses to peruse their affidavit is that they not only read the contents thoroughly and anything in it that may be taken out of context, but also to prepare them against some form of entrapment by a seasoned cross-examiner in terms of attempting to show the judge some statement in their testimony at trial that is inconsistent with what is contained in their affidavit. To do so could very well discredit the witness in the eyes of the

judge. The employer's counsel should even go to the extent of playing devil's advocate and assume the role of the General Counsel's representative and practice cross-examination of each employer witness with respect to the information contained in the witness's affidavit.

3. *Prepare a trial notebook* with each pleading, a copy of each witness's affidavit, a list of detailed questions to ask each witness on direct and cross-examination and an original and several copies of each document or other such evidence that he or she wishes to introduce into evidence either through direct or cross-examination. To save time and confusion, it may be important to have the documents marked for identification prior to the commencement of the trial. In addition, the employer's counsel, especially when not accompanied by co-counsel, should train the management representative chosen to sit at the counsel table how to handle exhibits and keep up with them during trial as the employer's counsel will be too involved in the trial to attend to such details.

4. *Encourage the employer's witnesses who are called as adverse witnesses by the General Counsel's representative to get in as many "licks" as early as possible* to help destroy General Counsel's case. Since General Counsel's representatives have a penchant for calling an employer's witnesses early in the trial as adverse witnesses in order to seek admissions and help establish General Counsel's case, given the law of primacy in which people are likely to be influenced by the information they hear first, the employer's witnesses should try to take advantage of appearing most knowledgeable and creditable early in the trial and enjoy the opportunity to counter the General Counsel's strategy.

5. *Do not permit the General Counsel's representative* to abuse the employer's witnesses during cross-examination. Judges permit a certain amount of aggressive cross-examination to test the strength and conviction of a witness's testimony, but when aggressiveness converts to abuse, the employer's counsel should be sufficiently vocal in his or her objections to attract the judge's attention to the opposing counsel's behavior.

6. *Know the Federal Rules of Evidence and make timely objections when appropriate,* yet be aware that some administrative law judges permit almost everything into evidence. If that should be the case, the employer's counsel should pose a continuing objection to a certain line of questioning so as not to appear obtrusive or offensive to the proceedings. Moreover, if the testimony is not damaging the employer's case and an objection would not accomplish any advantage, the employer's counsel may be better served just to permit the testimony to continue, if the judge does not cut it short on his or her own.

7. *Always ask the court permission to review each General Counsel witness's affidavit or statement,* previously taken by the NLRB agent as part of the investigation, prior to his or her cross-examination of that witness. The

NLRB's rules permit such review under the *Jenck's* doctrine and the employer's counsel should ask the court for a short recess, or sufficient time to review the document, in which to peruse the document most carefully to attempt to discern whether any testimony given by such witness at the trial is inconsistent with the information contained in the affidavit, and if so, attempt to impeach the witness through cross-examination as to such inconsistencies.

8. Do not overly cross-examine General Counsel's witnesses. If the witness has given testimony that does not harm the employer's position, there is no need to cross-examine to any extent. On the other hand, if the witness for General Counsel has given testimony that is damaging to the employer's case, but which evidence can be sufficiently refuted through other witnesses and the witness has been so "coached" and rehearsed that there is no way that the witness is going to deviate from his or her testimony, to cross-examine and get a repetition of the earlier testimony has a tendency to enhance the General Counsel's case even more. On the other hand, where a General Counsel's witness has gone overboard in his or her testimony and has obviously taken liberties with "the truth," the employer's counsel should cross-examine the witness, aggressively, and attempt to impeach the witness as much as possible. Some witnesses have a tendency to overly explain matters and embellish events and circumstances. Superb cross-examination of such witnesses will usually cause such witnesses to self destruct, figuratively.

9. Be prepared to make an offer of proof in situations where the administrative law judge refuses to permit a witness to testify about a certain issue. The procedure for making such an offer of proof is for the employer's counsel to make a statement to the court as to what the witness in question would say if permitted to testify. Such an offer of proof typically is stated verbally to the court and made part of the record, and thus preserved for appellate purposes, if desired, in the event the judge does not reverse himself or herself after hearing the offer of proof.

10. Double-check the exhibit list to ensure that all exhibits introduced at the hearing are properly marked, identified and admitted into the record, to the extent desired, before the close of the trial.

HOW TO EVALUATE STANDARDS OF PROOF IN AN UNFAIR LABOR PRACTICE TRIAL

The employer's counsel should become intimately familiar with what the General Counsel must present through testimony and evidence to carry the burden of proof in order to establish a prima facie case sufficient enough to shift the burden of proof to the respondent. The mere issuance of a complaint by the NLRB is not supposed to create any presumption that the respondent violated the National Labor Relations Act, as amended.

For example, under the *Wright Line* standard, taken from a 1980 NLRB case of the same name, the General Counsel is required to establish that the employer's action or conduct in a given case was motivated by protected or union activities of one or more of its employees. Once the General Counsel's representative establishes this information, the burden then shifts to the employer to demonstrate through its own witnesses and evidence that it would have taken the same action under the same circumstances, irrespective of the employee's protected or union activities. Once the employer demonstrates such, the General Counsel must then introduce evidence to demonstrate that the employer's reason for such action was merely pre-textual and "but for" the union or other protected activity of the employee, the employer would not have taken the same action against the employee.

CLOSING SAFEGUARDS IN AN UNFAIR LABOR PRACTICE TRIAL

There are several details that the employer's counsel should address at the close of the unfair labor practice hearing.

The administrative law judge will inquire whether the parties want to present oral argument at the end of the trial. The employer's counsel should probably take advantage of such opportunity, even though the General Counsel's representative may not appear that enthused about the idea, or suggest that his or her oral argument will be contained in a post-trial brief. Two reasons suggest that the employer's counsel present oral argument to the administrative law judge at the end of the proceedings.

First, the administrative law judge will have heard much testimony by the end of the trial and will probably be perplexed as to how it all relates. Oral argument provides the employer's counsel to summarize the case, and reconfirm the employer's position into a very organized format to make somewhat of a lasting impression on the judge. A second reason that may favor the employer's representative presenting closing oral argument to the judge is to "read" the judge's body language and facial expressions during such argument to discern what to address more substantially in the employer's post-trial brief.

Next, the administrative law judge likely is to inquire whether the counsel for General Counsel and the employer's counsel desire to file post-trial briefs and possibly proposed findings of fact and conclusions of law. The employer's counsel should take advantage of this opportunity, as well, in most situations. This will give the employer's counsel an opportunity to review the transcript of the proceedings and bring to the judge's attention, in the brief, all the inconsistencies, glitches, and flaws in the General Counsel's evidence, and hopefully, give the employer's counsel an additional opportunity to reinforce the employer's position and theories, and the creditable evidence presented through the testimony of the employer's witnesses.

7 How to Appeal an Unfair Labor Practice Case to the NLRB and the Federal Courts

Within a few weeks—sometimes months—after the conclusion of an unfair labor practice trial, and after reviewing any briefs filed by the General Counsel's representative and the respondent's counsel, the administrative law judge will issue his or her decision in the form of a *recommended* findings of fact, conclusions of law, remedies, and a proposed order, if the decision is against the employer.

The employer's counsel should be aware that the administrative law judge's decision is not a decision, *per se*. It is merely a *recommended* decision to the NLRB as to what the NLRB should conclude as the proper decision.

However, the administrative law judge's *recommended* decision with respect to recommended findings of fact, conclusions of law, remedies, and a proposed order does have clout. The recommended decision will become a final decision unless the losing party files timely exceptions to the NLRB, contesting the recommendations of the administrative law judge to the NLRB.

TECHNIQUES AND TACTICS IN FILING EXCEPTIONS TO AN ADMINISTRATIVE LAW JUDGE'S DECISION

Prior to filing exceptions to an administrative law judge's adverse decision against an employer, the employer's counsel should consider the consequences and implications of accepting the decision and complying with the recommended remedies, especially if the remedies are not costly and do not provide a basis of propaganda for the charging party or union in question.

Although the NLRB gives substantial deference to the administrative law judge's findings and recommendations, the Board has full discretion to adopt, reject, or modify an administrative law judge's decision. In practical terms, however, the NLRB typically "rubber stamps" the administrative law judge's recommended decision. Therefore, once the employer has lost the initial trial, it is very difficult to get relief through the NLRB appellate process as well as relief through the appellate courts. For example, since the administrative law judge has the responsibilities of observing the demeanor of witnesses, the NLRB is most reluctant to overturn his or her determinations of credibility with respect to which witnesses were truthful in their testimony and which ones were not.

Should the employer's counsel decide to file exceptions to the administrative law judge's decision, or exceptions to portions of the decision, such exceptions must be filed with the NLRB in Washington, D.C., within 28 days from the date of service of the order transferring the case from the administrative law judge to the NLRB, or within any such further periods as the NLRB will permit or allow. Should the employer's counsel desire to request an extension of time in which to file exceptions, the request must be filed, in writing, and received by the NLRB at least three days before such exceptions are due.

Not only should an employer's counsel be sensitive to the time requirements noted above if he or she should determine to file such exceptions, counsel should also conform its exceptions to other procedural guidelines as required by the NLRB Rules and Regulations, such as:

- Set forth the specific question of procedure, fact, law, or policy to which exception is taken.
- Specifically identify that part of the administrative law judge's decision to which exception is made.
- Designate precisely each page citation of the decision and specific portions of the record relied upon as a basis of, or in support of, the exceptions taken.
- Enumerate the grounds for the exception and include the citation of authorities relied upon in the exceptions unless such supporting citations are set forth in an accompanying brief.

In addition to the right to file exceptions to an administrative law judge's adverse decision, employer's counsel also has a right to file an accompanying brief in support of its exceptions. The employer's counsel should exercise this right because exceptions, without a brief to argue forcefully the theories, issues and what the administrative law judge's recommended findings of fact and conclusions of law should have been, do not provide the impact one would want to make in such an appeal.

HOW THE NLRB REVIEWS EXCEPTIONS TO AN ADMINISTRATIVE LAW JUDGE'S DECISION

As mentioned previously, in the absence of timely exceptions by either party to an administrative law judge's recommended decision, the judge's decision automatically becomes the decision of the NLRB, including his or her recommended remedies and proposed order.

Where timely exceptions are filed, the case will be delegated to a three-member panel to decide whether the administrative law judge's recommended decision will be adopted, modified or rejected, in part or in whole, although such a case may be assigned to the full five-member Board where a decision in such a case will establish or change NLRB policy.

The Board panel is precluded from consulting or discussing the case with the administrative law judge who heard the evidence and also precluded from discussing the case with representatives of the General Counsel.

The panel reviewing the case will have the entire record before it, including all pleadings, briefs, transcript of the proceedings, exhibits, and so on.

The panel, or full Board where appropriate, may issue either a "short form" decision in which the Board, or panel on behalf of the Board, merely affirms the administrative law judge's decision and summarily incorporates such into its own decision without any substantial discussion or elaboration, or a "long form" decision in which the Board, or panel on behalf of the Board, disagrees with the administrative law judge's decision in some manner and issues its own findings of fact, conclusions of law, remedies and order, including its analysis and rationale for doing so.

The decision of the Board, or its panel, has the effect of either upholding parts, or all, of the formal complaint in the matter, or dismissing parts, or all, of the formal complaint, or a combination of both.

Where the allegations in the formal complaint are upheld by the Board, constituting a finding of an unfair labor practice or practices, the Board, or its panel on behalf of the Board, may enter an order for the respondent to cease and desist from such practices and/or direct the respondent to take certain affirmative action to remedy the violations so committed. Cease and desist orders are mandatory whenever an unfair labor practice is found and upheld by the Board, or its assigned panel on behalf of the Board. The Board's authority to order affirmative action as part of the remedy in its order is discretionary.

Cease and desist orders require the respondent found in violation of the Act to post a notice to its employees in conspicuous places at the employer premises for a period of 60 consecutive days. Such notices typically set forth what the respondent must do to remedy the violation.

Affirmative remedial action typically is ordered in Section 8(a)(3), Section 8(a)(4), and Section 8(a)(5) with respect to employer violations.

For example, the typical remedial action in a Section 8(a)(3) case in which an employer has been found guilty of discharging an employee because of his or her union or protected concerted activities would require the employer to reinstate the employee to his or her former job, or an equivalent job, plus "backpay" the employee his or her lost wages and benefits as a result of the discharge. The same affirmative remedy would hold true in a Section 8(a)(4) case where an employee was discharged because of his or her testifying or participating in some form as a General Counsel witness or, perhaps, because he or she filed an unfair labor practice against the employer.

Board orders in cases involving a Section 8(a)(5) violation in which an employer has refused to bargain with a union in good faith will require that the guilty respondent bargain with the union in good faith, or perhaps, retroactively pay the wages and benefits to the employees, in question, with respect to what they would have received had the employer bargained in good faith.

Where the employer has committed unfair labor practices in a flagrant manner, affirmative remedies could include that the employer pay for litigation costs, attorneys' fees, and other expenses of the prevailing party.

There is little an employer's counsel or representative can do during the period of time in which his or her exceptions and/or briefs are before the Board for review. Just as the NLRB panel members are precluded from a discussion of the case with the respective administrative law judge or General Counsel's representative who presented the charging party's case, the panel is also precluded from such discussion with the respondent's counsel or representative.

Once the NLRB issues its decision and order, the party adversely affected has the right to file a motion for reconsideration, rehearing or reopening of the record because of extraordinary circumstances such as a discovery of new or additional evidence that could impact upon the case. Such motions must be filed within 28 days of service of the Board's decision and order, or within any additional period of time in which the Board will permit.

The employer's counsel should be aware that the NLRB does not look favorably upon motions to rehear or reopen an unfair labor practice case once its decision and order has been issued. Motions for reopening an unfair labor practice case and rehearing evidence will be permitted only where the respondent's counsel can demonstrate to the Board the specific error requiring a new hearing, how the error prejudiced the respondent's case and where newly discovered evidence is at issue in the motion, that such evidence must have become available to the moving party only since the close of the hearing or that the evidence was submitted but rejected by the judge.

The NLRB has a history of treating motions for reconsideration with equal disdain unless the moving party can demonstrate to the Board that its decision and order is not supported by the record in the case. The NLRB will not consider favorably such a motion that merely raises the same theories and arguments that were raised in the earlier exceptions and briefs.

OPTIONS TO CONSIDER IN COURT REVIEWS OF NLRB DECISIONS

Once a final decision and order is issued by the NLRB against an employer respondent, the employer has two options: either to comply with the Board's order and remedies or not to comply with same.

Should the employer take the position that it is not going to comply with the decision and order, two courses of action are available to it. One, the employer can take a passive approach and wait until the NLRB files a petition with the appropriate federal circuit court to seek a judicial enforcement of its decision and order against the employer and respond accordingly, or, two, the employer may elect to take a more aggressive approach and file its own petition with the appropriate federal circuit court, seeking to have the NLRB decision and order overturned, dismissed, modified or remedied, either in part or in whole.

Strategically, some management attorneys attempt to "forum shop" for the federal circuit court most favorable to the employer's case, if they are contemplating filing a petition with such a court, seeking a review of the NLRB's decision.

Should an employer's counsel attempt to "beat" the NLRB to the federal circuit courts, seeking a review of the Board's decision and order, he or she should attempt to evaluate which courts are most favorable to the employer's position, and which federal circuit courts have jurisdiction over his or her potential petition and which ones do not.

Either petitions for enforcement by the NLRB or petitions for review by the employer's counsel may be filed in any federal court of appeals having jurisdiction over the geographical area in which the alleged unfair labor practice occurred or in which areas such person resides or transacts business. In addition, the aggrieved party has a right to file its petition for review of the NLRB's decision and order in the Court of Appeals for the District of Columbia. Should an employer's counsel seek to "forum shop" for the most favorable federal circuit court in which he or she may be permitted to file a petition for review, considerable time should be taken to evaluate each circuit court's previous rulings with respect to the legal theories and position encompassed in the employer's potential argument to the court.

"Forum shopping" may be a passing art, given the diverse philosophy of individual judges at the various federal circuit courts and the varying range of decisions flowing from such judges with respect to NLRB appellate cases; that is to say, that not unlike the procedure before the NLRB in which exceptions to administrative law judges' recommended decisions are referred to a three-member panel of the NLRB to review such exceptions, petitions filed by either the NLRB for enforcement or petitions filed by aggrieved parties for review of

NLRB decisions and orders to an appropriate federal circuit court are also deferred to a three-judge panel from the many judges at such circuit court, many of whom have a wide range of differences with respect to labor relations issues. Thus, there is no assurance that a given panel of judges at a particular federal circuit court will necessarily abide by previous judicial precedent with respect to a given issue or theory. The panel may attempt to distinguish the facts in the case in such a manner as to cause the decision to depart from established judicial precedent of the court that may have been more favorable to the employer's position.

The employer's counsel should be aware that there are no time limits, as such, by either the NLRB or the aggrieved party to file its respective appeal for enforcement or review. However, a federal circuit court could take a position that the petition was not timely filed if an inordinate amount of time expires between the period of time in which the decision was rendered and the time of the filing of the petition under the doctrine of laches. Practically speaking, such a position is rarely taken simply because the NLRB typically will not take very long in filing its petition for enforcement once its decision and order issues.

Once a petition is filed with an applicable circuit court, the other party must file an answer within the time limits established by the applicable court—usually within 20 days or less. Otherwise, the petitioning party may be entitled to a default judgment against the appellee.

The employer's counsel should be aware that the vast majority of federal circuit courts have a tendency to uphold NLRB decisions and orders. The reason for such a high percentage of court-enforced orders of the NLRB is that the circuit courts are very limited in their review of NLRB cases. For example, the NLRB's—in actuality, the administrative law judge's—findings of facts cannot be overturned by the appellate court unless such findings of fact are unsupported by substantial evidence on the record, considered as a whole. Too, it is the policy of the various federal circuit courts to defer to the NLRB's conclusions of law, as well, under the principle and philosophy that the Federal Congress conferred upon the NLRB the authority to develop and apply fundamental labor policy.

Whether the employer would be in a more favorable position to argue its case as a petitioner in seeking review of an NLRB decision, assuming the role of the appellant, or merely responding to a petition by the NLRB, seeking enforcement of its decision and order, is debatable. Much will depend:

- upon the philosophy of the individual judges on the panel chosen
- on the particular issues and theories in the case
- on the respective and relative abilities of each party's counsel in submitting briefs and arguments to the court on behalf of their respective clients

Should the employer's counsel prevail in the appeal, the applicable court most likely will deny enforcement of the NLRB decision or, in the alternative, remand the case to the NLRB for further action.

TECHNIQUES AND TACTICS IN PRESENTING ORAL ARGUMENTS TO FEDERAL CIRCUIT COURTS

An employer's counsel should welcome and exercise the opportunity to present oral argument to the applicable panel of judges when a matter is before a federal court of appeals, if available. It is the only means through which to detect or discern what part or portions of the employer's argument in its previously submitted brief bothers or concerns the panel of judges in question. Thus, an oral argument provides the employer's counsel an opportunity not only to detect vulnerable aspects of its case in the mind of one or more judges, but also the opportunity to convince and persuade such judge why he or she should subscribe to the employer's argument.

In order to be the most influential and persuasive counsel as possible in presenting oral argument to an applicable federal circuit court panel of judges, the employer's counsel should use the following checklist of do's and don'ts:

- *Know the record thoroughly*. The panel of judges will have the entire record of the proceedings before the administrative law judge along with the exceptions to the administrative law judge's decision that were submitted to the NLRB. The employer's counsel should index the transcript of the proceedings specifically for purposes of oral argument in addition to having previously indexed the transcript for purposes of writing the brief to the panel. The employer's counsel should become familiar with each and every exhibit that might raise questions from the panel.
- *Organize and practice the oral argument*, not in the sense of memorization, but in terms of sequencing the major points of the argument so that the argument flows smoothly.
- *Convince the panel of judges why the employer's position should be sustained* with respect to public policy considerations as well as with respect to factual and legal distinctions. Federal circuit judges typically are most sensitive to overruling an NLRB decision simply because their judicial posture has been to defer to the NLRB because of its supposed expertise in labor relations matters.
- *Understand the scope of judicial review*; meaning that if counsel's objective is to attack the NLRB's findings of fact, he or she must be able to show the panel of judges what parts of the record demonstrate that such findings of fact were not supported by substantial evidence. Employer's attorneys usually have a better chance of attacking the legal conclusions of the

NLRB as compared with an attack upon its findings of fact, particularly in those cases where the NLRB relied upon legal theories and conclusions that were contrary to its prior precedents or which legal conclusions were in opposition to the respective circuit court's position on such legal theory.

- ***Stop immediately whenever a judge on the panel interrupts*** and makes an inquiry about the case. The employer's counsel should address his or her question and then move on, particularly if the question doesn't go to the heart of the counsel's argument or, if irrespective of the answer, it is not a question of a compelling nature that would really impact one way or other on the panel's decision.
- ***Make good eye contact with all the judges.*** Try to address all the members of the panel instead of attempting to influence the one or two who make the most inquiries. The silent ones may have far more influence on the outcome of their collective decision than the one that raises the most questions.
- ***Share with the panel of judges the negative impact that the decision would have upon the public*** in general and the unconstitutionality of the decision if it is not overturned. It is important that counsel's argument addresses more than just a rudimentary legal consideration, but what impact the decision will have in terms of public policy.
- ***Be sufficiently enthusiastic and emotional to add conviction to the argument.*** Even though some of the theatrics and histrionics that typically are used to influence jurors are out of place before a federal appellate court, there must be some evangelistic quality to the counsel's argument to make it sufficiently convincing.
- ***Address the points the opposing counsel argues to the court***, but distinguish early whatever facts or legal theories the opposing counsel presents to the court and then move on and use the time allotted more productively to argue the strengths of the employer's case. Stay on the offensive as much as reasonably feasible, but be able to address any questions that the panel members might inquire about the opposition's argument.
- ***Sequence the oral argument into a timetable to ensure that there is sufficient time*** to answer any inquiries the panel of judges wish to make, but also sufficient time to cover all of counsel's argument.
- ***Stay within the court's allotment of time*** in which to present oral argument. It is important to be sensitive of the time used and the time remaining periodically throughout the argument. Ample practice of the oral argument will permit almost a subconscious sensitivity to such time factors.
- ***Be extremely polite and courteous to the panel of judges.*** Do not argue, be disrespectful or give the appearance of such. When through with the argument, merely thank the panel of judges for their time, attention and thoughtfulness with respect to the case at hand.

HOW TO SEEK A SUPREME COURT REVIEW OF THE APPELLATE COURT DECISION

Realistically, the employer's counsel will be unable to obtain a review by the U.S. Supreme Court of the applicable circuit court's enforcement of an NLRB decision and order, unless the case involves important questions of law or policy affecting the administration of the National Labor Relations Act, or unless such a review would resolve conflicting positions on the issue or issues in the case among two or more Federal Circuit Courts.

Final review of NLRB cases does, however, rest with the U.S. Supreme Court and the nation's highest court has heard numerous appeals of NLRB cases through the years.

Should an employer's counsel be disposed to seek the U.S. Supreme Court to review a federal circuit court's enforcement of an NLRB decision and order, he or she will be required to file a *writ of certiorari* with the U.S. Supreme Court, asking the Court to hear the matter. Again, unless such a labor case has national implications or resolves conflicting rulings between or among the circuits, the writ probably will be denied. The U.S. Supreme Court is not required to grant such writs or hear such matters of appeal. Typically, it does not.

8 How to Limit Liability in Unfair Labor Practices Compliance Proceedings

Should the employer-respondent not prevail before the federal appellate court or not be granted certiorari to argue an appeal to the U.S. Supreme Court with respect to an appellate court's enforcement of an NLRB decision and order, or should an employer agree to comply with the NLRB's decision and order in lieu of a petition before the applicable federal circuit court, the question becomes, "What is the employer's obligation to comply with the NLRB decision, and should the employer voluntarily comply at such point through an informal process or refuse to voluntarily comply and force formal compliance proceedings?"

Most management attorneys attempt, at this juncture, to voluntarily agree to comply with whatever the NLRB remedies entail, due partly because all appeals have been exhausted or waived and, to do otherwise, would entail additional costs with respect to a formal hearing. In addition, the failure to voluntarily comply with a federal circuit court's enforcement of an NLRB decision and order could cause the employer to be in contempt of court.

In the event the employer's counsel advises the compliance officer of the applicable NLRB region that the employer wishes to comply, the compliance officer will offer assistance to the employer in its efforts to comply, such as attempting to locate discriminatees, providing NLRB formulas to calculate backpay computation, and to explain or clarify any obligations under the Board's orders and remedies in question.

In the event the employer's counsel states that the employer-respondent does not intend to comply with the NLRB's orders and remedies, or implies that it does not intend to do so, the regional director will direct the compliance officer to coordinate formal compliance proceedings through the NLRB's Division of Enforcement Litigation.

HELPFUL HINTS IN COMPLYING WITH REINSTATEMENT ORDERS

An NLRB's decision and order obligating an employer to reinstate an employee to his or her former position, as a result of the employer having unlawfully discharged the employee for union or protected concerted activity, does not imply necessarily that such an employee be reinstated to the actual job which the employee had at the time of his or her discharge. It does mean that the employer has the obligation of reinstating such employee to a similar position to that which the employee would have had at the time of discharge but for the unlawful dismissal.

The employer's counsel or representative should attempt to evaluate what position the discharged employee would be returned to, if any, in light of what has happened with respect to the discharged employee's former job.

In the event that reinstatement to a former position is not possible because the position no longer exists or because the discharged employee would not have been in such position due to layoffs, or a reducton-in-force, the employer must offer reinstatement to the employee in a substantially equivalent position. In the event the dischargee would have lost his or her job, or would have been permanently laid off during the interim, reinstatement would not be possible, nor required. However, where an individual has replaced an employee who was discharged because of union and/or protected activities, the employer would be required to discharge the replacement employee, if such be necessary to accommodate the reinstatement of the unlawfully discharged employee.

Special concerns and considerations surface when an employer is ordered to reinstate striking employees. Employees who participate in unfair labor practice strikes—strikes occurring where employees are protesting unfair labor practices by the employer—are entitled to full reinstatement to their former positions upon their unconditional offer to return to work, even if the reinstatement requires the dismissal of the replacement employee.

On the other hand, the employer's counsel should be aware that a different reinstatement standard applies in the case of an economic striker; that is, an employee on strike against an employer for economic or other related reasons rather than those associated with an alleged unfair labor practice. An employer is not required to discharge a permanent replacement employee in order to accommodate the reinstatement of an economic striker. The employer is required to reinstate an economic striker to his or her former job if the position has not been filled by a permanent replacement employee, upon the unconditional offer of the economic striker to return to work. If the position is being filled by a permanent replacement employee, the employer is required to place the economic striker on a preferential hiring list and reinstate the economic striker to his or her former position upon the departure of the permanent replacement unless in the interim period the economic striker has acquired regular and substantial work elsewhere or unless the employer can demonstrate that the economic striker has in some way abandoned his or her right to return to work, or that the employer had some other legitimate reason for not offering reinstatement.

The employer's counsel should understand seniority implications when reinstating striking employees or unfair labor practice dischargees. The law requires employers not only to reinstate dischargees and striking employees under the conditions discussed above, but to reinstate such employees in a manner and in such shifts or departments that would not jeopardize the respective employee's seniority and other job rights. The NLRB compliance officer is unlikely to endorse an employer's reinstatement offer in which the employee is required to waive or relinquish certain seniority privileges.

ESSENTIALS TO CONSIDER IN COMPUTING BACKPAY IN A COMPLIANCE MATTER

The employer's counsel or representative should not take at face value what an NLRB compliance officer or dischargee claims as the proper backpay in a compliance case. The dischargee is likely to exaggerate the amount involved and the compliance officer, in deference to the employee, is likely to believe anything the employee suggests. Most NLRB backpay orders require the discharged employee be made whole relative to what the employee would have earned from the employer absent the discrimination, plus expenses incurred in seeking and holding employment during the backpay period, less what the employee actually earned from other employment, or less the amount of income the employee should have earned through the exercise of due diligence, during the discharge period. An NLRB backpay order does not entitle the discharged employee to a windfall or to be rewarded for not attempting to find a job in the interim period. Thus, the backpay computations must reflect more than guesswork or speculation on the part of the discharged employee.

The NLRB requires several items to be considered when figuring the gross backpay, including all wages the discharged employee would have earned from the employer, including bonuses, commissions, profit-sharing payments, vacation pay, tips, and the amount of money the employer would have contributed to a retirement fund on behalf of the employee, as well as such benefits as health and welfare payments typically spent on such an employee for the backpay period, sickness and accident premiums, life insurance premiums, and so forth. However, just as interim wages may be deducted from gross backpay wages, so may the amounts received in the form of fringe benefits earned from interim employers be reduced from gross backpay fringe benefits.

Gross backpay does not accrue during those periods of time that the discharged employee is unavailable for work, such as during periods of illness, injury, full-time school attendance, prison or other institutional confinement, retirement, and/or military service.

The discharged discriminatee has an obligation to mitigate backpay liability. Whether the employee fulfilled his or her obligation to mitigate backpay liability in terms of using due diligence in seeking other employment is a frequent issue in compliance proceedings.

The NLRB requires several factors to be considered in computing the dischargee's interim earnings, including all monies received in payment for work or services performed inclusive of tips, fringe benefits, the value of furnished room and board, automobiles and other such perks, and self-employment income, if applicable.

The employer's counsel or representative should understand, on the other hand, that the NLRB does not permit certain items of income to be deducted from the gross backpay liability such as unemployment compensation payments, union benefits, judgments or settlements from court cases, earnings from investments, or gifts. In addition, income from a second job or "after hours" job by the employee in question will be included as an amount deductible from the gross backpay computations only to the extent that such work would have been performed by the employee during his or her regular hours of work had he or she still been employed by the employer.

The NLRB permits dischargees and other discriminatees who have lost wages and benefits due to unlawful conduct by the employer to deduct from their interim earnings all expenses incurred in seeking substitute employment, including transportation costs, employment agency fees, outplacement services fees, travel expenses, moving costs, and so forth.

NLRB compliance officers are reluctant to compromise the backpay figures that they have computed. Yet, many arguments may abound from the employer's perspective to seek such. For example, the employer may contend that the dischargee failed to mitigate the gross backpay liability. In consideration of such arguments on behalf of the employer, compliance officers are amenable to "give and take" negotiations with respect to their computations in lieu of processing the matter into a formal compliance hearing.

An employer's counsel should be aware that compliance officers, subject to the approval of their regional director, may accept settlements from employers containing at least 85% of the net backpay figures computed by the compliance officer. A settlement entailing more than a 20% reduction from the net backpay computation by the compliance officer must receive approval from the NLRB Compliance Office in Washington, D.C. Whatever the amount of the final net backpay computation, appropriate taxes and other such required withholdings are to be deducted.

STRATEGIES TO COUNTER BACKPAY SPECIFICATIONS AT A COMPLIANCE HEARING

Whenever the NLRB compliance officer and the employer's counsel are unable to resolve a backpay issue in terms of settlement, or otherwise, the NLRB will transfer the matter into a formal compliance proceeding, which is commenced by the applicable regional director issuing a backpay specification—basically, the compliance officer's computation—and a notice of hearing.

In contrast to regular unfair labor practice cases in which pre-hearing discovery typically is not permitted, the NLRB actually encourages employers to review all the documents, affidavits, supporting data, and computations that it plans on introducing at the formal hearing relative to the backpay issue.

The employer's counsel should exercise his or her opportunity to review and copy all such information the regional director plans on introducing during the formal hearing to discover any weaknesses found in, or associated with, the backpay specifications computed by the compliance officer and prepared to present into evidence at the hearing, but also for the purpose of using any of the information discovered to draft an effective answer to the backpay specifications, an answer in form not unlike that required to be filed in response to a formal unfair labor practice complaint. Such answer must be filed within 21 days from the service of the backpay specification.

Inasmuch as formal backpay hearings can be very time consuming and costly in terms of the complexity of most backpay proceedings, the employer's counsel should explore settlement of the backpay liability to the fullest extent before and after a formal backpay specification and notice of hearing is issued. However, where the compliance officer has refused to acknowledge the employer's defenses such as the employee's failure to mitigate the backpay liability, such as the inability of the employee to have worked for the employer had he or she not been discharged due to the employee's illness, injury or other incapacity, such as the backpay specifications and supporting document's failure to include clearly deductible items from the gross backpay liability, and so forth, the employer's counsel may better serve his or her client by having its "day in court" relative to the backpay issue.

The hearing on the backpay liability is very similar to a formal unfair labor practice hearing. An administrative law judge is assigned to hear the case, after which he or she will draft a Supplemental Decision and Order, requiring the backpay found appropriate be distributed to the dischargee or other discriminatee(s).

The employer's counsel has the right to appeal the administrative law judge's Supplemental Decision and Order to the NLRB in a similar manner as an unfair labor practice decision is appealed to the NLRB.

9 Master Strategies in Handling Representation Cases Before the NLRB

As discussed in Chapter 1, the NLRB has two major functions. First, the NLRB has an obligation to process unfair labor practice cases under the provisions of Section 8 of the National Labor Relations Act, as amended. Unfair labor practice matters were discussed in Chapters 2 through 8. The second function of the NLRB is to conduct representation elections under the provisions of Section 9 of the NLRA, as amended.

This and the next two chapters will discuss the second function, perhaps the more important function in the mind of the NLRB and labor organizations—that of processing petitions for representation elections and conducting such elections, whether such elections are characterized as certification elections, decertification elections, or one of the other types of elections recognized and sanctioned by the NLRB.

The NLRB rules and regulations provide, as a guideline, that a union (labor organization) must have obtained at least a 30% "showing of interest" in an appropriate bargaining unit at the employer's workplace before it will process a petition for a certification election. The "showing of interest" requirement is generally satisfied by the union representatives filing along with their petition for an election, at least 30% of the employees' signatures on union authorization cards, or informal petitions in the applicable appropriate bargaining unit.

The employer's counsel and representatives should be knowledgeable of the fact that a certification election is not the sole means by and through which a union can become the exclusive collective bargaining agent of employees in an appropriate bargaining unit. A secondary means of gaining such representational rights is through the process of sending to the employer what is termed a "demand for recognition letter" in which the union in question claims it has a majority of the employees' signatures on authorization cards, or on an authorization petition, and insists that the employer recognize the union on the basis that it has what is termed "majority status." The union representatives may ask the employer to inspect or check the signatures on the union authorization cards or informal petition.

The employer's counsel should be sufficiently aware that, in the absence of the employer committing flagrant unfair labor practices, having independent knowledge that the union has majority status, or otherwise inferring that it is recognizing the union as the collective bargaining representative of its employees, the employer may refuse to recognize such union on the basis of the signatures.

However, many less sophisticated employers do not appreciate their right to refuse to recognize the union as their employees' collective bargaining representative whenever a union "demands" that the employer recognize its union as the employees' exclusive bargaining agent on the claim that it (the union) possesses majority status via signatures on a union petition or union cards. They sometimes succumb to the union's request that the employer inspect the union cards in the possession of the union representatives to determine whether the union has majority status. The employer's counsel should advise the employer and its management and supervisory staff never to fall into the "trap" of inspecting such union cards unless it wants the union as the collective bargaining representatives of its employees in the unit in question.

Anytime management members and supervisors agree to inspect or review union cards—called a "card check"—and the union has in its possession a majority of the signatures of the employees, encompassing at least 50% plus one of the employees signatures, the NLRB will infer that the employer voluntarily agreed to such a card check and if the union clearly has majority status, the NLRB will insist that the employer recognize the union as the employees' collective bargaining representative and commence bargaining with the union in good faith relative to wages, benefits, and other terms and conditions of employment, unless there is an existing contract or bargaining duty with another certified union or some similar reason that would otherwise foreclose the union's right to represent the employees.

Again, as long as the employer has a good faith doubt as to the manner in which the signatures were signed and unless the employer commits some flagrant unfair labor practice, or has independent knowledge that majority has been obtained by the union with respect to such employees, the employer has a legally protected right to refuse to recognize the union as its employees' bargaining agent based on a demand for recognition purely on the basis of union cards or an informal petition being signed by employees within a certain bargaining unit.

HOW TO REJECT A UNION'S CLAIM FOR RECOGNITION BASED ON EMPLOYEES' SIGNATURES

Most demands by union organizers that an employer recognize their union as the employees' collective bargaining representative based on a claim of majority status by virtue of employees' signatures on union cards or an informal petition are communicated in the form of a letter, telegram, or some similar written communication.

A more confrontational situation arises, however, when a union representative or official arrives at an employer's workplace and personally demands recognition based on employees' signatures to the employer's manager, and even suggests that the manager inspect the signatures (or have some neutral party inspect such cards), if the employer does not believe that the union has majority status via such signatures. As noted earlier, should the manager inspect the signatures (or have a neutral party inspect the signatures) and assuming the union has a majority of the signatures, the NLRB most likely will infer that the employer agreed to the card check and require that the employer bargain with the union.

As opposed to a union's written claim or demand for recognition based on employees' signatures in which the employer's manager or representative would have adequate time to form and draft a proper response letter, a personal visit requires some instantaneous responses. The employer's managers and representatives who may be most susceptible to such potential confrontations should have a contingency program on hand as to what to do in such eventuality. Should the employer's position be that it will not recognize a union on the basis of employees' signatures alone, whether on union cards, an informal union petition, or whatever, the employer's manager or representative should be prepared to take the following steps with respect to such a personal visit by a union representative or official:

- Inform the union representative that the employer refuses to inspect the signatures of the employees or permit a neutral party to do so on its behalf because matters of this nature involve legal considerations and have legal implications and, as a result, he or she would prefer that whatever information the union representative wishes to impart should be reduced to writing and sent to the employer by formal correspondence so that the employer's counsel may properly evaluate the information or requests, and respond appropriately.
- Inform the union representative or official that if he or she will communicate the request in written correspondence, the employer's counsel will respond.
- Should the union representative become hostile or verbally abusive, the employer's representative should be equally forceful in asking him or her to leave the employer's premises, but reaffirm the commitment that if he or she will send the requests in writing, the employer will respond to it

in writing so everyone will have a written account of exactly what occurred and who said what.

- Should the union representative leave the union cards with employees' signatures on them—which is not likely to occur given the difficulty of most union organizers to obtain the cards in the first place—the employer's manager or representative should arrange for some administrative person not a member of management or supervision to place the cards in an envelope and return them to the union, preferably by registered mail, return receipt requested, so as to preserve proof that the employer's manager or representative did not examine the signatures on the union authorization cards or informal petition.
- Once the union representative or official departs the employer's premises, the employer's manager should report what happened to the employer's counsel for further direction and advice.

Where the union's demand for recognition is in writing, the employer's counsel or representative should respond in writing inasmuch as a failure to respond to a demand for recognition possibly could be grounds for a technical refusal-to-bargain charge under the provisions of Section 8(a)(5) of the National Labor Relations Act, as amended.

The response letter may address, if applicable, at least in substance and content, the following reasons why the employer is refusing to recognize the union's demand for recognition on the singular basis that the union claims a "majority status" by virtue of more than 50% of the employer's employees having signed union authorization cards, if the employer wants to assume such position, as most employers want to do:

- Confirm that the employer has no independent knowledge of the union's allegation that it truly represents a majority of the employer's employees in any appropriate bargaining unit.
- Inform the union representatives or officials that questions of representation and proper persons to be included within an appropriate bargaining unit cannot be adequately resolved through a mere examination or inspection of signatures on union cards or an informal petition.
- Apprise the applicable union representative or official that a mere inspection of signatures on union cards (or similar documents) does not sufficiently divulge either the authority or conditions under which signatures were obtained.
- Inform the union representative or official that such matters as whether employees desire union representation or not is best left in the hands of the National Labor Relations Board through the sanctioned secret ballot election process conducted by the NLRB.

- Confirm that the employer is agreeable to abide by the results of an NLRB representation election, assuming the union has an adequate "showing of interest," and meets all the NLRB requirements for a representation election.

An additional, and perhaps a more important, reason why an employer should not recognize a union as its employees' collective bargaining representative on the basis that a union claims majority statue by virtue of employees' signatures on union cards, is that to recognize a union that does not truly represent a majority of employees as their collective bargaining representative could cause the employer to violate the National Labor Relations Act under the provisions of Section 8(a)(2) of the Act.

STRATEGIES TO GET A UNION PETITION FOR REPRESENTATION ELECTION DISMISSED OR WITHDRAWN

Some unions may file a "Petition for a Representation Election" and simultaneously send the employer a "demand for recognition" by way of separate correspondence.

Most unions know that the more enlightened employer is not going to recognize a union as the collective bargaining representative of its employees merely based on a "demand for recognition." Such unions do not send a "demand for recognition" as their preliminary step, but as a concomitant step, so that they will be able to mark affirmatively that part of the formal petition for a certification election which raises the question whether recognition has been requested of the employer.

Section 9 of the National Labor Relations Act, as amended, states that when a union's petition for a representation election has been investigated and a hearing has been held at which a "question of representation exists," the NLRB "shall direct an election by secret ballot and shall certify the results thereof." Therefore, it is the union's petition for a representation election that commences the election process by the NLRB.

The period of time during the NLRB's investigation of the petition for recognition provides the employer its earliest opportunity to get the NLRB to dismiss the petition.

There are several reasons for which the NLRB will either dismiss or seek withdrawal of a petition for a representation election, including the following:

- The union failed to substantiate to the NLRB's regional office in which the suspicious petition was filed that it had the support of at least 30% of employees in its proposed appropriate unit. As discussed earlier, the 30% "showing of interest" criteria is usually evidenced through the signatures of bargaining unit employees on union authorization cards or informal petitions, which evidence typically is submitted to the regional NLRB office along with a formal "Petition" for an election. The employer's counsel and representatives should be aware that the 30% "showing of interest" NLRB requirement is not a statutorily imposed obligation on the NLRB; rather it is an NLRB guideline, allowing the NLRB much discretion in its use. For example, even assuming that the applicable union is slightly shy of the 30% criteria, the NLRB will permit such union additional time in which to procure more employee signatures in which to satisfy the 30% "showing of interest" requirement. Too, the NLRB does not require any sophisticated authenticity when checking signatures on union authorization cards or other such documents, even when supplied the respective employees' W-4 forms by the employer by which to compare signatures. Again, the NLRB's position is that the 30% "showing of interest" is merely a guideline and to the extent that slightly suspicious discrepancies appear, an election conducted by the NLRB will rectify them.

- The NLRB may lack jurisdiction over the subject employer. Refer to Chapter 1 regarding the jurisdictional requirements of the NLRB.
- The employer is a party to a collective bargaining agreement which has a definite duration of three years or less. This defense to a petition for a representation election is commonly referred to as a "contract bar" defense. The employer's counsel or representative should understand that a petition filed not less than 60 days and not more than 90 days before the contract expires (between 90 and 120 days in the health care industry) or during the period of time between the expiration of an existing labor agreement and the commencement of a new one or after the third year of a contract in excess of three years, will be considered as untimely filed petitions under the "contract bar" criteria, and accordingly dismissed in lieu of the union's withdrawal of same. However, the employer's counsel also should be aware that a labor agreement for an indefinite duration will not "bar" an election for any period; that labor agreements which contain illegal clauses will not, necessarily, preclude an election; or that a labor agreement that does not include those employees covered in the proposed bargaining unit by the petitioner will not bar an election. The employer's counsel should appreciate, also, that whether a certain labor agreement will bar a petition for representation election frequently will turn on delicate facts peculiar to the circumstances at hand and, even though the legal "contract bar" defenses may appear as an applicable defense, factual situations may cause the NLRB to rule otherwise.
- The subject petition is filed within 12 months of the time in which a previous NLRB-conducted representation election was held. The employer's counsel or representative should be aware of this technical standard in which the NLRB will not conduct a representation election within twelve months of the date on which it issued a certification of the results of a previous election and will not permit a new petition by the same union

to be processed until 60 days before the 12-month period and not permit the election to be held until the expiration of the full 12-month period. Also, were a different union to attempt to file a petition during the 12-month period, the new petition would not be processed until the completion of the 12-month period.

- A party to the election files unfair labor practice charges involving or affecting all or some of the employees subject to the proposed election. The employer's counsel should not depend upon this defense very strongly, however, inasmuch as the charging party may file a "request to proceed" with the election. Thus, the "blocking charge" argument for attempting to seek dismissal of a petition may be a very temporary one.
- The unit of employees covered in the petition is an inappropriate bargaining unit. This defense is a most important one and will be covered more in detail in the next chapter of this book.
- The organization or entity seeking to represent the employees in a proposed bargaining unit is not a true labor organization.

The employer's counsel should not rely too heavily on the possibility of the petitioning party's withdrawal of the petition, particularly where the petitioner is a labor organization. Most unions will not withdraw their petitions unless the NLRB informs them, as a courtesy, that in lieu of the union's withdrawal, the NLRB will dismiss the petition, or unless the union's support among the proposed unit of employees has so eroded that an election would be futile for it.

ADVANTAGES AND DISADVANTAGES OF A STIPULATED ELECTION

Assuming that the employer has no defenses by which to convince the NLRB to dismiss the petition for a representation election, or the withdrawal by the petitioner, the employer's counsel has two options remaining: one, voluntarily consent or stipulate to a representation election; or two, assuming the employer's counsel does have some tenable defenses to argue in support of the dismissal of the petition, to defend the employer's position at a representation hearing.

The practice of the NLRB is to notify the employer prior to the setting or commencement of a representation hearing, and attempt to convince the employer to stipulate, or consent to the election in order to avoid the parties having to go through a formal representation hearing, particularly in cases in which there are no apparent issues to argue at such a hearing.

In the event the employer's counsel has no defenses to the petition in terms of getting it dismissed, such as those discussed above, or other issues that may impact upon such an election, then he or she may want to explore with the NLRB agent what such a stipulated agreement would entail. Of course, in the event the employer's counsel has some cogent and convincing arguments for dismissal, he or she would not want to be overly receptive to such a proposal stipulation.

Where there are no issues to resolve or defenses that may cause dismissal or withdrawal, a stipulated agreement may be more advantageous to the employer than deferring the matter to a representation hearing simply because the employer's counsel has a better chance of getting the day of the week and the hours of the day, in which to have the election held than what may be gotten as a result of a hearing. The reason why the employer has some negotiating power to attempt to obtain such strategically important items in the stipulated agreement is that the NLRB does not want to conduct a representation hearing just for the sake of it. This is especially true when there are no issues at stake, and the union (or petitioner) inferentially agrees in filing a petition for a representation election that it is agreeable to hold the election at anytime the NLRB deems proper. Thus, much of the negotiations as to a stipulated agreement, in practice, is carried out more between the NLRB and the employer than between the NLRB and the petitioning union, even though the NLRB will defer to the petitioning union relative to the terms and conditions contained on a proposed stipulated agreement.

Another reason why the employer's counsel should entertain a proposed stipulated election by the NLRB where there are no issues or grounds for dismissal or where the issues can be disposed of through the stipulation, is that it can save the employer an appreciable amount of time and money. It may also save the employer some embarrassment from union propaganda should the employer appear at the hearing and argue issues or defenses that do not have sufficient merit to prevail.

FACTORS TO CONSIDER BEFORE SIGNING A STIPULATED AGREEMENT IN LIEU OF A HEARING

There are several items the employer's counsel would want to include in an NLRB stipulated agreement for a representation election including, among them, the following:

- To have the election conducted on the employer's premises, if at all possible. The NLRB would prefer, in most cases, that the election be held on the employer's premises because the employees can be easily assembled for the purposes of voting. The employer should also want the election held at its premises, rather than at a union hall or some other facility that may symbolize the union's calling or permit undue influence on employees at such location.
- To have the election held during the latter part of the work week, preferably on a Thursday or Friday, and also on a pay day. Most employees are in

a more harmonious mood on such days and seemingly are less resentful toward management.

- To have the election held later in the employees' work shift, especially with respect to the day shift. This permits an opportunity for employees to settle down somewhat, and become less anxious about the voting process. It also permits management to dispel any late rumors or misrepresentations disseminated by the opposition. Such conversations and interactions by management with employees must occur on a one-on-one basis, given the *Peerless Plywood* rule that prohibits a captive audience meeting with employees within twenty-four hours of the election.
- To have the date of the election set far enough ahead in time in order to allow the employer to conduct a winning counter-union campaign during the pre-election period. However, the NLRB has self-imposed timetables in which to conduct representation elections and the NLRB typically will not permit the stipulation to provide for an election period outside the NLRB time targets for an election.
- To have the cut-off date for eligibility of employees to vote after a point in time that the employer would have already hired any additional employees favorable to it.

The most important factor to consider prior to agreeing to a stipulated election is to understand that the NLRB has two different documents (forms) that it uses in such agreements.

One form, typically referred to as a consent form and called an "Agreement for Consent Election" is the form *not* to sign unless the employer's counsel wishes to forfeit and waive the employer's right to appeal any adverse decision to the National Labor Relations Board. When the employer enters into an "Agreement for Consent Election," the employer agrees that the "determination of the regional director shall be final and binding upon any question...."

The other form, typically referred to by seasoned management attorneys as a "Stipulated Agreement," does provide the employer a right to appeal any adverse decision of the applicable regional director to the National Labor Relations Board in Washington, D.C.

Therefore, if the employer's counsel desires to protect the appellate rights of his or her client, the latter form is the one that should be executed rather than the former.

10 Techniques and Tactics in Handling Representation Proceedings

Should the employer's counsel be unsuccessful in obtaining a Board dismissal of the union's petition for a representation election, or not desire to enter into a stipulated election agreement, the NLRB's local regional director will most likely order a representation hearing to determine whether a "question of representation" exists and what, if any, are the issues relating to a question of representation.

A representation hearing is unlike an unfair labor practice hearing in that a representation hearing is considered to be non-adversarial as opposed to a more adversarial unfair labor practice hearing. Also, most representation hearings are heard before a Hearing Officer typically appointed by the regional director in contrast to unfair labor practice cases which are heard before administrative law judges.

A representation hearing is commenced by a regional director serving a notice of hearing on all interested parties. The notice of hearing usually includes an accompanying copy of the representation petition and NLRB forms that outline the procedures for conducting the election, informal settlement methods, and so forth.

The Board attorney or field examiner assigned to conduct the representation hearing is charged with the responsibility of making a complete record of factual information regarding the various issues in question upon which the regional director, and ultimately the Board, can make a proper determination. Thus, the Hearing Officer has the authority to call, examine, and cross-examine witnesses in addition to hearing the testimony of witnesses introduced by interested parties. The Hearing Officer may also receive documentary and other evidence from the interested parties in addition to requesting that other documentary evidence be introduced and received as part of the record.

Although the Board does not require interested parties to comply with technical rules of evidence in developing evidence through the testimony of witnesses, due to the investigatory nature of the hearing, an undue departure from an orderly process in calling and cross-examining witnesses or introducing other evidence may subject the party to a rebuke by the Hearing Officer.

The employer's counsel should also be somewhat familiar with the sequence of events in a representation hearing, such as:

1. The interested parties and respective counsel and representatives note their appearance on an appearance form for the sake of the record.
2. The "formal papers," consisting of such documents as the formal petition for election, the notice of hearing, pre-hearing motions and respective rulings, if any, affidavits of service, and so on are then placed in the record by the assigned Hearing Officer.
3. The Hearing Officer then places any pre-hearing stipulations or factual agreements in the record.
4. Whenever the size or composition of the proposed appropriate bargaining unit is a factual issue, the Hearing Officer will ask the petitioner and other parties to proceed with relative testimony and documents regarding same. The Hearing Officer will develop evidence in other contested issues in the same manner, giving the respective parties an opportunity to call and produce direct testimony and permit the opposing party to confront and cross-examine such witnesses.
5. Upon request, the Hearing Officer will permit the interested parties to engage in oral argument at the conclusion of the hearing.

The employer's counsel or representative who undertakes to represent an employer at such a proceeding may well face the possibility of some other union attempting to intervene and participate in the representation hearing. Such counsel or representative should be knowledgeable regarding the NLRB rules on such Motions to Intervene.

The NLRB rules provide that a motion or request for intervention may be granted only to persons capable of demonstrating an interest in the proceedings.

An employer's counsel or representative may also encounter motions to postpone the hearing and other such related motions prior to, or during, a representation hearing.

Parties to a representation hearing are entitled to subpoena witnesses and testimony in a manner similar to that which was discussed in Chapter 6 relative to unfair labor practice hearings. Such subpoenas are obtained in a representation proceeding by filing a written application with the Hearing Officer if such request is made after the opening of the hearing or with the regional director if such request is made prior to the hearing. In the event that the party against whom the subpoena is issued does not intend to comply with the subpoena and its requirements, he or she must file a petition to revoke such subpoena with the regional director within five working days from the service of the subpoena.

HELPFUL HINTS IN DEFENDING SPECIFIC ISSUES IN A REPRESENTATION HEARING

The employer's counsel or representative should be aware of the issues subject to disposition through a representation hearing, and of those that are not so disposable.

Several issues that may not be determined through the process of a representation hearing include the following:

- The question of whether the petitioning union possesses a "showing of interest" of at least 30% of the eligible voters in the proposed unit. The Board maintains that the determination of the "showing of interest" questions rests completely in the discretion of the applicable regional director.
- The manner or methods employed by the regional director or the Board in determining whether the "showing of interest" criteria has been met.
- The manner or methods employed by the regional director or the Board in evaluating whether an employer's "RM" petition is supported by objective considerations.
- The question of whether union authorization cards or other such documents are valid in terms of how and when they were procured, and whether such cards have been rebuked or are stale, or whether such cards were improperly acquired through supervisory influence.
- Whether unfair labor practice charges by one interested party against the other has merit, unless such matters related to the charge are material to questions concerning representation.
- Whether union security clauses and/or check-off provisions of one or more of the interested party's collective bargaining contracts are valid and enforceable.
- The meaning of a certain contractual provision in a collective bargaining contract of one or more of the interested parties, unless the contract language in question is ambiguous.
- The question of whether, or to what extent, economic strikers have been replaced.

- The question of whether a union maintains discriminatory membership policies.
- Questions concerning membership eligibility requirements of a union.
- Questions relating to allegations that a union violated federal statutes.
- Questions concerning the propriety of a bargaining unit different from that proposed by the union, unless the union has a "showing of interest" in the other such discussed proposed bargaining unit.

On the other hand, the employer's counsel or representative should be most familiar with issues that may be raised in a representation hearing.

Determining Whether the Bargaining Unit Has a Community of Interest

One of the most common issues raised in a representation hearing is whether the bargaining unit proposed by the union, in which bargaining unit the union ostensibly has an adequate "showing of interest," is an appropriate unit for the purpose of conducting a representation election.

The National Labor Relations Board attempts to either qualify or disqualify a proposed bargaining unit under its "community of interest" standards.

Typically, a regional director will consider one or more of the following criteria in evaluating whether the "community of interest" test has been met:

- Similarity of wages and hours of the various employees to be included in the proposed unit
- Commonality of supervision within the proposed unit of employees
- Frequent interchange of work among the employees in question
- Commonality of promotional routes of the subject employees
- The previous collective bargaining history of the employer relative to the proposed unit
- Commonality of rules of conduct and employee relations policies among the employees in the proposed bargaining unit
- The proximity of employees with respect to distance between their various job functions
- Similarity of skills and technical distinctions among the employees proposed to be included in the unit
- Similarity and commonality of working conditions and environmental considerations among the employees in question
- The extent of the union's desire to include or exclude certain employees, or groups of employees

- Commonality of the organizational structure and its impact on the proposed unit

The employer's counsel or representative should also be aware that there are certain statutory restrictions in determining bargaining unit questions. For example, the National Labor Relations Board, as amended, will not permit:

- A bargaining unit to include both professional and nonprofessional employees unless a majority of the professional employees vote in the affirmative to be included in a combined unit
- A bargaining unit of security guards and non-guard employees or a certification of a guard union as a bargaining representative of guard employees if such union either admits non-guard employees to membership or is affiliated directly or indirectly with a union that represents non-guard employees

In addition, the National Labor Relations Act, as amended, forbids the NLRB to find a proposed craft bargaining unit inappropriate on the basis that a different unit has been established by a prior Board decision unless a majority of employees in the proposed bargaining unit vote against separate representation.

Management attorneys and representatives who represent health care clients should be aware that the NLRB, as endorsed by the U.S. Supreme Court, has determined that there may be eight different bargaining units in a hospital or large nursing care home which include units of:

1. Physicians
2. Other professional employees
3. Registered nurses
4. Technical employees
5. Business office clerical employees
6. Non-professional employees
7. Skilled maintenance employees
8. Security guards

In smaller hospitals and health care facilities, an appropriate unit may consist of a combination of professional employees and non-professional employees.

Determining Whether a Multifacility Unit Is an Appropriate Bargaining Unit

Another bargaining unit question that may surface in a representation hearing is whether a bargaining unit containing employees of more than one facility constitutes an appropriate unit. The NLRB will find multifacility units appropriate in the following cases:

- where there is a prior bargaining history relating to combined facilities
- where there is a centralization of labor relations and higher management
- where there is an interchange of jobs among employees at the various facilities in question
- where there is a lack of autonomy at the individual facilities
- where there is a similarity in skills and job functions among employees at the different facilities
- where the geographical distance between the different locations is not so substantial as to cause such a single unit impracticable or infeasible

A similar question that a management attorney or employer representative may face in a representation hearing is whether a proposed bargaining unit consisting of employees from multi-employers is an appropriate one. Again, the NLRB will look to the bargaining history of the proposed unit but, in addition, require the consent of all employers and the union to the appropriateness of such a unit.

Resolving the Issue of Voter Eligibility for Representation Elections

There are several issues other than those that pertain to appropriate bargaining units that are likely to arise in a representation hearing about which an employer's counsel should be intimately familiar, such as the issue of voter eligibility.

Again, the National Labor Relations Act, as amended, specifically excludes certain types of employees from being permitted to vote in a representation election such as agricultural workers, independent contractors, supervisors, governmental employees, airline, and railway employees. In addition, the NLRB has its own policy that excludes those employees who have traditional ties to management, such as:

- close relations of influential managers or owners of the employer's business
- employees who work in a confidential relationship with higher management with respect to labor relations matters
- management-type employees who, although not directly in a supervisory position, nonetheless are perceived to function so closely with higher management members that they are deemed to be managers

The NLRB also disqualifies individuals from voter eligibility who:

- are only irregular part-time employees
- are dual-function employees and who spend such a small portion of their work on bargaining unit work that they have no substantial interest in the conditions of employment in the bargaining unit
- are laid-off permanently and have no reasonable expectation of recall
- are temporary employees and who are not employed during the voter eligibility period or whose tenure is certain and short-lived
- are seasonal employees and who have no reasonable expectation of re-employment
- have been terminated for cause or who have voluntarily quit prior to the election
- are economic strikers and who have been permanently replaced in excess of twelve months after the commencement of the strike
- are new employees and who became employed after the cut-off date establishing the deadline for voter eligibility
- are temporary replacement employees for striking employees

One of the most heated debates the employer's counsel is likely to encounter in a representation hearing is whether an individual is to be considered a supervisor under the statute, and therefore not eligible to vote in a representation election, or, on the other hand, a regular non-supervisory employee and eligible to vote. The NLRB looks to two questions in making such a determination.

1. Does the person have the authority to, or the authority to effectively recommend:

- hire
- fire
- transfer
- suspend
- layoff
- recall
- promote
- assign
- discipline
- adjust grievances
- reward
- direct the work of employees

2. Is the exercise of such authority, to the extent it exists, of such a nature that it requires the use of independent judgment?

A management or supervisory trainee is usually considered as part of management and disqualified from voting in a representation election. However, a "fill-in" supervisor who only occasionally assumes the duties of a regular full-time supervisor typically will be considered an eligible voter.

Resolving Other Representation Issues

The "contract bar" question, as discussed in detail in the preceding chapter, may also become a hotly discussed issue in a representation hearing. Jurisdictional questions, also discussed more fully in the preceding chapter, may abound in a representation hearing.

Another question that may arise in a representation hearing is whether the petitioner is a labor organization. Whenever a well-established and recognized union so petitions, the issue is rather foreclosed, but when some association not usually characterized as a union becomes the petitioner, the employer's counsel or representative may want to investigate and determine whether the issue merits argument.

Another issue that occasionally will surface in a representation hearing is that of an "expanding unit." The NLRB is most reluctant to permit a small percentage of employees to determine the fate of a greater number of employees who will be added at a later date with respect to their bargaining rights. For example, suppose a new manufacturing plant intended to hire 250 employees over a period of one year, but after the first month of business a few of the first employees hired seek out a union which later files a representation election based on five signatures of the original ten employees hired. Most likely the NLRB will not permit the ten employees out of some 250 employees to be hired within the remaining year to disenfranchise the other 240 employees.

TRIAL STRATEGIES AND SAFEGUARDS IN A REPRESENTATION HEARING

The employer's counsel should be as sensitive (or even more so) to the preparation of his or her witnesses in a representation hearing as to preparing them for an unfair labor practice hearing. An employer's counsel or representative who is faced with a representation hearing should read Chapter 5 to gain a better perspective on how to prepare witnesses for trial.

Perhaps the most important item to remember in presenting evidence in a representation hearing is to build a case around documentary evidence, rather than testimonial evidence, not that some testimony from witnesses will not be beneficial.

For example, suppose one of the issues is whether a group of employees who have been laid off are to be considered permanently laid off with no expectancy of recall, and thus not eligible to vote in the election at stake, or to be considered as only temporarily laid-off employees with an expectancy of recall. The employer's counsel and representatives may conclude that the laid-off employees are unhappy and bitter, and accordingly, would vote for the union. Therefore, the employer may want to demonstrate through such documentary evidence, such as recall rights of employees in an employee handbook, exit interview papers, and other such evidence support for the employer's strategic position.

Documentary evidence also is extremely helpful in support of an employer's position that an individual is, or is not, a supervisor by introducing documents to demonstrate more clearly the employer's argument.

The same is true with respect to appropriate bargaining unit issues, expanding unit questions, and so on.

The employer's counsel should also appreciate that the employer has in its possession almost every important document that would be relevant in a representation hearing and, in many instances, the Hearing Officer and the petitioner are obliged to accept such documents at face value.

Another important trial tactic that should be considered by the employer's counsel or representative is to forcefully attack any of the petitioner's evidence that has not been introduced into the proceedings and is not supported by a proper foundation and authorization. In many instances, petitioners will try to introduce documentary evidence without laying a proper foundation through identification, authenticity or authorization, given the fact that many such petitioners are not trained in the law. And even though most Hearing Officers are very lax in determining what evidence they will permit in the record, they do not want the record full of irrelevant and immaterial evidence or evidence that has no foundation to it.

The same tactic should be applied when a petitioner's witness attempts to testify on matters about which he or she has no knowledge. Even the petitioner's representative will frequently attempt to testify about hearsay matters from the counsel table. Such testimony and tactics should receive a quick and forceful response from the employer's counsel.

As with the case of unfair labor practice proceedings, the employer's counsel should cross-check to ensure that all his or her exhibits are properly in the record.

The Hearing Officer will permit the interested parties, or their representative, to present an oral argument at the end of the hearing, unless compelling reasons dictate otherwise, of which such an opportunity should be taken by the employer's counsel. The same is true with respect to filing post-hearing briefs with the Hearing Officer.

PRACTICAL POINTS TO CONSIDER IN HANDLING POST-HEARING PROCEDURES

The employer's counsel and representatives should be familiar with the events that occur after the close of a representation hearing.

First, and soon after the close of the hearing, the Hearing Officer will submit his or her analysis of the issues presented at the hearing and summary of the evidence in the form of a report to the regional director, or to the Board, if the matter has been transferred to the Board.

The regional director has the authority at any time after the close of the representation hearing to transfer the case to the Board, usually when such a case involves some novel or complex question that dictates an expedited answer from the NLRB.

The regional director, or the Board in transferred cases, will then issue a Decision, setting forth the facts of the case, the issues in dispute, the relative positions of the parties, and the determination of the issues. Most such Decisions will either order a dismissal of the petition or the direction of a representation election.

Either party may appeal the regional director's Decision by filing a Request for Review with the Board in Washington, D.C., if such Request is based on at least one of these four grounds:

1. that a substantial question is raised because of the absence of any controlling precedent by the Board, or the regional director departed from existing Board policy on the issue raised
2. that the regional director's Decision relative to a substantial factual issue is clearly erroneous and such finding prejudicially affects the rights of the party so requesting the review
3. that the manner in which the hearing was conducted or any ruling made in connection with the hearing resulted in prejudicial error
4. that there exists compelling reasons for reconsideration of an important Board policy, rule or precedent

In the event the regional director, or the Board in transferred cases, orders the direction of an election, the employer's counsel should comply fully with certain pre-election requirements placed on the employer by the regional director and/or the NLRB.

For example, the employer must submit an original and a copy of an "Excelsior" list to the regional director's office within so many specified days after the Board's order (or within so many specified days following a stipulated or consent agreement). The Excelsior list must contain the names and addresses of the employees eligible to vote in the election. The employer's counsel should be aware that the regional director, in turn, will make a copy of the Excelsior list submitted by the employer, and forward the copy to the petitioner, the union, and all other interested parties in the case. Irrespective of how a union may use its copy of the Excelsior list for campaign purposes against the employer, a failure of the employer to submit the list to the regional director's office in the time period specified could constitute grounds for the election to be set aside and destroy the employer's victory, assuming a victory occurs. Thus, the employer's counsel or representative should make every effort to ensure that all the requirements of the Excelsior list are timely met.

The employer's counsel should also be aware that the regional director will request the employer to post a "Notice of Election" form in conspicuous places in and about the workplace in which eligible voters carry out their job functions, such as on employer bulletin boards. Although the employer is not technically required to display such notices within its workplace, an implied threat of other sanctions, such as the employer's loss of the right to file objections in an election, will typically be sufficient to motivate the employer to comply with the posting standard. The "Notice of Election" poster contains pertinent information about the election details and has, as its purpose, to educate eligible voters on such matters as the day of the election, the hours of the election, the location of the voting place, a sample ballot, and which employees are eligible to vote in the election and which ones are not eligible.

The employer's counsel should attempt to fully cooperate with the regional director's office to ensure that the notice is timely and conspicuously posted throughout the applicable workplace because the failure to do so could give rise to objections to the election, and perhaps, cause the election to be set aside, negating any possible victory for the employer.

11 Stategies in Handling Post-Election Procedures Before the NLRB

A vast majority of representation elections before the NLRB are certification elections in which employees within an appropriate bargaining unit are given the opportunity to vote for or against the petitioning union. Where there is just one petitioning union, the ballot will show two square boxes with a "YES" written at the top of one of the squares and a "NO" written at the top of the other. By marking an "X" or checkmark in the "YES" square, the employee will be deemed to have voted for the union. If the employee marks an "X" or check mark in the "NO" square, he or she will be deemed to have voted against the petitioning union.

Sometimes, two unions will have petitioned the NLRB for a certification election, or one will have petitioned and a second union will have intervened, in whichever case the ballot will consist of three squares or boxes. Over one box will be written the name of one of the unions, over another square will be written the name of the other union. The third square or box will have written over it the word "NEITHER." If the employee marks this with an "X" or check, he or she will have voted for neither union or, in actuality, will have voted against both unions.

To win a certification election, a union must receive a majority of the votes cast by employees, meaning the results of the certification election is determined by a majority of the ballots cast, not by a majority of employees eligible to vote. The union will not be declared the victor and certified as the employees' collective bargaining agent by the NLRB unless it has received a majority of the votes cast, meaning that a petitioning union loses the certification election in the event of a tie vote. Where two unions are listed on the ballot, along with the "NEITHER" square, if a combination of the votes for the two unions constitute a majority of the votes cast but neither union has a majority of its own, the NLRB will hold a "run-off" election in which a "run-off" ballot will provide for a selection between the two choices receiving the largest and second largest number of valid votes cast in the election.

The employer's counsel and representatives should also appreciate that decertification elections are very similar in the form of the ballot, and the determination of the results of the election, as that discussed above with respect to certification elections.

Likewise, the employer's counsel and representatives should be aware of the NLRB rules regarding challenged ballots. Either an employer observer or a union observer may challenge the eligibility of any person to vote in a representation election, for good cause. Observers typically are chosen from the voting unit of employees by the respective employer and union representatives to assist the NLRB agent in the election process.

Such challenges must be made prior to the voter receiving the ballot. The NLRB agent conducting the election has a right to challenge the eligibility of anyone whose name does not appear on the eligibility list. Aside from challenging individuals whose names do not appear on the eligibility list—basically, the Excelsior list—or the names of other persons they know or have reason to believe are not eligible to vote, NLRB agents will not otherwise make challenges on behalf of the parties.

Should an individual be challenged by an observer or the NLRB agent in charge of an election, the challenged party will be given a ballot and instructed to enter the voting booth, mark the ballot, fold the ballot to maintain its secrecy and return to the NLRB agent. The challenged party will then be given a challenged ballot envelope on which there is an identification stub noting the employee's name, and so forth, and the challenged voter will be instructed to place his or her folded ballot in the envelope, seal it, and drop the envelope into the box in which the other ballots have been deposited.

The mechanics of an NLRB certification or decertification election also involve the counting of the ballots at the close of the polls. The employer's counsel and representatives should be aware that the NLRB procedure requires that the ballots be opened and counted as soon as possible after the close of the final polls in the presence of the observers, and typically, other representatives of the employer and the petitioning union(s).

The NLRB agent conducting the election is the only person permitted to touch the ballots, although the election observers will be asked to keep count and tally the ballots as they are counted by the agent in charge.

The general guidelines governing the disposition of the ballots are, as follows:

- an unmarked ballot will not be counted and declared void
- a ballot that does not truly indicate the clear intent of the voter will not be counted and declared void
- a ballot that identifies the voter and destroys the secrecy of the ballot will not be counted and declared void
- a write-in ballot will not be counted and declared void

However, whenever a party disagrees with the NLRB agent's ruling on such a ballot as to whether it is void or valid, to be counted or not, the party can challenge the agent's ruling.

Following the tally of the ballots and the final count, the NLRB agent will execute a tally of ballots form, indicating whether the petitioning union has or has not received a majority of the votes cast, and also indicating whether any challenged ballots are determinative of the final outcome of the election.

HOW TO UNDERSTAND THE ELECTIONEERING GUIDELINES DURING AN NLRB ELECTION

A party to a certification or decertification election has seven days after the tally of ballots has been furnished it in which to file objections to the conduct of the election, or conduct affecting the results of the election. If such a party desires to so object, an original and five copies of the objections must be filed with the respective regional director within the seven-day time limit.

The employer's counsel and representatives should anticipate objections to be filed against the employer if the petitioning union loses the election. Unfortunately, many unions systematically file objections as a strategic measure to attempt to save face in the eyes of the employees who supported the union's efforts, irrespective of the merits or validity of the objections.

The employer's counsel has the responsibility of demonstrating to the NLRB agent who has been assigned to investigate the objections that the employer has not violated any of the NLRB electioneering guidelines.

The employer's counsel, therefore, should know what the NLRB electioneering requirements entail in order to be adequately prepared to defend the employer against such objections, as well as to advise the employer and its management and supervisory members what they can and cannot permissibly say and do prior to and during the pre-election campaign period—that critical period of time in which such objections must have occurred in order to be deemed valid.

The standards and criteria used by the NLRB to determine whether an unfair labor practice has been committed are not the same standards and criteria applied to electioneering conduct to determine whether an alleged objection has sufficient merit to justify voiding the results of the election, setting the results of the election aside, and ordering a rerun election. Thus, objectionable conduct does not need to rise to the level of an unfair labor practice to be declared sufficiently objectionable as to cause an election to be overturned.

On the other hand, conduct and behaviors that are sufficiently heinous to constitute an unfair labor practice by an employer will usually be more than sufficient to establish objectionable conduct in terms of destroying the laboratory conditions in which employees are given a free and untrammeled choice of representatives.

Some of the electioneering standards imposed on employers during the critical period of time leading up to the election proper, the breach of which may constitute objectionable conduct (as well as unfair labor practices in most cases), include the following:

- The ***Peerless Plywood*** Rule. Both employers and unions are prohibited from making speeches on company time to massed assemblies of employees within 24 hours before the scheduled time for conducting an NLRB election.
- The ***Michelm* Rule**. The NLRB forbids electioneering in the voting area and the mere presence of nonvoting union representatives within the vicinity of the polling area may be sufficient grounds to invalidate a union's victory. Employer's counsel and representatives should ensure that supervisors at all levels stay away from the voting areas and the vicinity in which voting employees ingress and egress, because their presence at or near the polling area during the voting period is impermissible, violates the *Michelm* standards, and gives rise to the employer's victory being overturned.
- The ***Sewell Manufacturing*** Rule. The NLRB prohibits both employers and unions from deliberately attempting to overly stress and exacerbate racial feelings and sentiment by irrelevant and inflammatory appeals during the pre-election campaign period.
- ***Invalid Solicitation/Distribution Rules***—The NLRB may also set aside a representation election based on properly timed objections that the employer improperly enforced an invalid "no solicitation/no distribution" rule, or inconsistently and selectively enforced such a policy only when pro-union activity occurred during the pre-campaign period.
- The ***Midland*** Rule. The NLRB has vacillated through the years with respect to what extent a misrepresentation of a material fact during the pre-election campaign period will be sufficient grounds to invalidate an election. The NLRB is likely to vacillate in the future as well, meaning that the employer's counsel should check for the very latest legal decision and revised rule relative to any NLRB issue in question. The NLRB presently regards objectionable only misleading statements and propaganda where a party has used forged documents in its presentation or dissemination of such misrepresentation of material facts.
- ***Improper Employer Favoritism of One Union Over the Other.*** The NLRB may invalidate a representation election where evidence demonstrates that

the employer supported one union over its rival union where two unions are listed on the ballot. Although an employer may suggest that it prefers one union over another—if such be the case—it is impermissible for an employer to do or say more. For example, the NLRB has been known to have invalidated elections in which an employer suggested to its employees that it would deal more generously with one union than with the other.

- ***Employer Threats and Coercion.*** As discussed under the topic of unfair labor practices, it is unlawful for an employer to threaten to take, or actually take, reprisals against employees because of their support of a union. Given the "laboratory conditions" in which a representation election is to be conducted to ensure that employees have a free and untrammeled choice of representative, the NLRB looks most unfavorably upon any action or behavior an employer may take during the pre-election campaign period that may suggest some type of threat against employees were they to select the union as their bargaining agent. For example, such threats that the employer would close its operations, or relocate its business, if the union were to win the election, are classical examples of such unlawful and objectionable conduct on the part of an employer.

- ***Improper Promises and Financial Inducements.*** The NLRB will also invalidate a representation election where evidence shows that the employer granted or promised to grant increased wages and/or benefits to employees as an inducement to vote against the petitioning union(s). An employer does not create objectionable behavior, however, whenever it grants a wage and/or benefit increase during a union campaign when such an increase to employees is in keeping with an established pattern and practice.

- ***Improper Interrogation of Employees.*** The NLRB will also set aside an employer's victory in a representation election where evidence demonstrates that a manager or supervisor has interrogated and questioned an employee, or employees, about union activities, unless such interrogation is of a very outspoken and vocal union supporter.

- ***Improper Surveillance of Union Activities.*** The NLRB will also invalidate and set aside a representation election where an employer spies on union activities, such as attempting to infiltrate a union meeting at a local hotel or at a union hall, or by even suggesting to employees that it knows what goes on at the union meetings, who attends, and so on, as though to give an impression that it is surveying union activities.

There are other miscellaneous reasons for which the NLRB may invalidate a certification or decertification election, many of which are more peculiar to union misconduct than employer conduct, but those discussed above are the most prevalent ones with regard to employer conduct.

The employer's counsel and representatives should also be acutely sensitive to the proposition that an employer's victory may be set aside because of the behavior of some third party who the NLRB regards as an agent of the employer, aside from conduct of supervisors and managers who are always regarded as agents of an employer. For example, in one NLRB case, a town mayor who openly conducted a counter campaign against the union was held to be an agent of the employer and his otherwise lawful activities were imputed to the employer and held to be impermissible under the NLRB electioneering guidelines. An employee who is recruited to "spy" for the employer and charged to carry out covert activities on behalf of the employer may also be held to be an agent of the employer and his or her conduct contributed to the employer.

The employer's counsel and representative should likewise have an understanding of the NLRB agent's responsibilities during an NLRB election and that certain misconduct on his or her part may also constitute grounds for invalidating an election, although the employer or union did nothing improper, themselves. For example, the NLRB has invalidated representation elections in which the NLRB agent gave the appearance, during the election period, of fraternizing with one party to the exclusion of the other, destroying the impartiality policy of the Board. Other such elections have been invalidated where evidence demonstrated that the NLRB agent failed to maintain custody of the ballot box so as to ensure the security and integrity of the ballots. An election may also be invalidated where an NLRB agent arbitrarily denies an employee the right to vote, at least by way of a challenged ballot, or closes the polls too early or while employees are yet in the voting lines to vote.

The employer's counsel may also be benefitted by understanding that an election may be invalidated when either party abuses the processes of the NLRB, such as suggesting to employees that the NLRB and the federal government favors or endorses one side over the other. For example, both employers and unions are prohibited from distributing or posting facsimiles of the official "NOTICE OF ELECTION" poster with an "X" or checkmark within either the "YES" square or the "NO" square on the poster, since an employee may infer that the favorably marking for the "YES" or "NO" was that of the NLRB or the federal government. Thus, such reproductions may take place only to the extent that the party reproduces the official ballot in an unaltered facsimile and clearly marks it as a sample on the face of the ballot.

TECHNIQUES AND TACTICS TO USE WHEN RESPONDING TO OBJECTIONS AND CHALLENGES IN AN NLRB ELECTION

Assuming the employer wins its representation election and the opposing union files objections and/or challenges with the regional director's office within the prescribed time limit, the employer's counsel or representative will be contacted by an NLRB agent who has been assigned to investigate the union's objections and/or challenges.

Request Supporting Evidence for the Objections

Strategically, the employer's counsel or representative should treat an NLRB agent's investigation of objections to the election much like it would with respect to an unfair labor practice investigation and require the NLRB agent to establish that the objectioning union, or unions, have some basis, foundation and supporting evidence to back up the objections.

The employer's counsel and representatives, therefore, should be knowledgeable that the objecting party has only seven days to furnish evidence in support of its objections. Sometimes the NLRB will permit additional time if some evidence is established, but most likely only if some evidence has been presented to establish at least a prima facie case regarding its objections. In the event the objecting party does not submit sufficient evidence to establish a prima facie case in support of its objections within the seven day time limit or there is insufficient evidence to support objections based upon the information furnished the regional director's office, the regional director is not obligated to pursue the investigation and require the employer to furnish supporting documents to overcome such evidence. Should untimely, or insufficient, evidence fail to establish a prima facie case in support of the union's objections, the regional director has the authority and responsibility of overruling the union's objections.

Should the union's evidence establish a prima facie case in support of the union's objections or challenges, the employer's counsel and representatives will have the responsibility of submitting whatever witnesses, documents and information at its disposal to the NLRB agent conducting the investigation that the union's evidence is untrue or irrelevant.

Make Sure All Inequities Are Relevant to the Objections

The employer's counsel and representatives should ensure that the NLRB agent inquires into areas only within the scope of the objections and is not permitted to turn the investigation into a "fishing expedition" for factual information that has no connection or relevance to the union's objections. Therefore, the employer's counsel and representatives should not be timid with respect to inquiring of the NLRB agent how the requested information and documents are relevant and material to the objections in the case. The employer's counsel and representatives should be most sensitive to providing information and documents to the NLRB agent investigating such objections that are not related specifically to the objections because the regional director is permitted to go beyond the scope of the objections if the investigation uncovers other or additional evidence which indicates that the election may have been tainted by way of impermissible electioneering.

Know the Time Frame for Objectionable Conduct

The employer's counsel and representatives should understand the time frame during which objectionable conduct must have occurred in order to be sustainable and sufficient to invalidate an election. Thus, in order to provide a basis by which to invalidate and set aside an election, the alleged misconduct must have occurred after the filing of the petition for an election by the petitioning party and prior to the end of the voting process. In the event of a run-off or rerun election, the time frame during which misconduct must occur in order to sustain objections is that period from the date of the prior election to the end of the voting process in the rerun or run-off election. The employer's counsel and representatives should not take for granted that information outside this time period may not be used to sustain unfair labor practice charges, and perhaps a bargaining order. As previously discussed in Chapters 4 and 5, such information may be used as general background information in such cases.

Handling Challenged Ballots

If challenged ballots are included as part of the objections, or independent thereof, and are sufficient in number to effect the results of the election in that a clear majority or lack of majority cannot be established until such challenges are resolved, then the NLRB agent will conduct an investigation as to the challenges and obtain evidence relative to the issues regarding such challenges. Typically, the challenge to a given ballot is based upon an allegation that the challenged voter was not eligible to vote, for whatever reason. As with objections to the election, frequently it is necessary to defer the resolution of a challenged ballot(s) to a hearing, particularly if material issues of fact are in question.

Preparing for Post-Election Hearings

Once the investigation of the objections and/or challenges has been completed, the regional director either resolves the objections and/or challenges from the administrative record assembled as a result of the investigation or directs that a hearing be commenced in which additional evidence on certain or all issues be taken by a hearing officer.

The NLRB Rules and Regulations, in fact, require a hearing whenever objections and challenges raise substantial and material factual issues and involve credibility questions and are of such a nature that a resolution of such facts cannot properly be concluded on a mere evaluation of the administrative record. Strategically, at any time the employer would be better served through the process of such a hearing rather than some arbitrary decision based upon the administrative investigation alone, the employer's counsel and representatives should insist upon such a hearing, and be properly prepared to take exception if such a hearing is not afforded his or her employer. Even in cases where the employer is defending itself against objections or challenges, a hearing may nonetheless be in the employer's best interest, depending somewhat on the nature of the objections or challenges and the degree that a regional director may rule against the employer's position in the absence of a hearing.

Such post-election hearings are handled much in the same manner as are representation hearings prior to an election. A hearing officer—or in some cases, an administrative law judge—will be assigned to hear the case and develop a record. A hearing of this nature is to be treated as investigatory rather than adversarial. In practice, however, such hearings can become very adversarial and confrontational. The employer's counsel and representative should adhere to much the same trial techniques and tactics discussed in Chapter 5 in representing the employer at a post election hearing on objections and/or challenges.

At the end of the hearing, the hearing officer or administrative law will prepare and serve on the parties a report containing credibility resolutions, findings of fact, conclusions and recommendations regarding the disposition of each issue presented to him or her. Parties have within 14 days of the date of the issuance of the report to file exceptions to it. The employer's counsel and representatives should exercise the employer's right to file such exceptions as to any issue resolved against the employer's position so as to preserve its right and continuity of being able to argue such position through any appellate process.

The hearing officer or administrative law judge's report, and any exceptions to it by the respective parties, is filed with the regional director or with the NLRB, in the event the NLRB has ordered such a hearing.

If filed with the regional director, he or she then prepares a report or supplemental decision, as discussed below.

In the event the election in question was conducted pursuant to a consent election agreement, the parties will have waived their right to appeal the regional director's report on the objections and challenges, and absence, fraud, misconduct, or such a gross mistake on the part of the regional director as to suggest bad faith, the regional director's findings of fact and conclusions will be final with respect to the disposition of the challenged ballot and/or the objections.

An employer preserves its rights to file exceptions to a regional director's report on objections and/or challenges where the election is held pursuant to a stipulated election agreement. As such, the regional director's report contains recommendations to the NLRB, rather than determinations, to which the employer's counsel and representatives not only have the right but should exercise such right and file formal exceptions with the NLRB as to any adverse findings, conclusions or recommendations by the regional director against the employer. Such formal exceptions must be filed with the NLRB in Washington, D.C. within 14 days of the issuance of the regional director's report.

In filing such exceptions to a regional director's report, the employer's counsel should remind the NLRB that the election was conducted pursuant to a stipulated election agreement and the NLRB has a responsibility and duty to review the employer's exceptions from that contractual perspective, rather than merely "rubber stamping" the regional director's findings, conclusions and recommendations. It has been the authors' experience and observation that, sometimes, the NLRB seemingly treats a regional director's report the same in stipulated elections as in consent elections as though the regional director should have the authority to pass upon the final decision in the matter, irrespective of what the parties have signed and to what they have agreed.

In situations in which a regional director of the Board has directed a representation election, in contrast to a consent or stipulated election agreement, the regional director will issue a report on the Objections and/or Challenges, but in addition, a supplemental decision. The report contains the regional director's recommendations as to the resolution and disposition of the objections and/or challenges; the supplemental decision contains his or her determination or final resolution of each issue with respect to the objections and/or challenges. Employers that are parties to such a directed election do not have a right to file exceptions, but may be entitled to file a request for review of the regional director's report and decision. Such a review is somewhat limited and is only available where the employer can establish the following criteria:

- That the regional director's report and decision raises a substantial issue of law or policy because of the absence of or the departure from officially reported NLRB precedent;
- That the regional director's report and decision with respect to one or more substantial factual issue(s) is clearly erroneous, based on the record, and such error prejudicially affects the rights of the party so filing the request;
- That the conduct of hearing on objections and/or challenges, or rulings made in connection with the proceedings, has resulted in prejudicial error against the requesting party; and/or
- That the regional director's report and decision raises compelling reasons for the NLRB to reconsider one or more of its more important rules or policies.

To the extent that an employer is a party to a directed election and has received an unfavorable ruling and determination through a regional director's report and supplemental decision, such as sustaining the union's objections and/or challenges and invalidating the election in which the employer won, the employer's counsel should review closely the above noted ground rules, and conform to them, in filing any such requests for reviews. The employer's counsel and representatives should substantiate the basis upon which the employer's request for review is grounded and distinguish case law and policy decisions that are adverse to its position. The employer's counsel should be mindful that NLRB decisional law is very inconsistent, in many instances, and somewhat tracks the philosophy of the individual Board members. The employer's counsel is challenged to go beyond accepting the rationale of a given Board as to what the law should or should not be and argue a more cogent and rational application of the law.

The employer's counsel should also include in its exceptions and requests for review, and its supporting briefs, as many cases as possible from the federal appellate courts to compliment the employer's position and argument. The NLRB seemingly has a fear of federal appellate cases that are contrary to its policy and philosophy with respect to certain issues.

STRATEGIC STEPS TO FOLLOW IN SEEKING JUDICIAL REVIEW OF POST-ELECTION PROCEEDINGS

In the event the NLRB accepts a regional director's report to invalidate a representation election in which the employer had won—in the sense that the union had not received a majority of the votes cast in the election—the employer and its counsel and representatives are placed in the position of possibly having to technically violate the National Labor Relations Act in order to appeal the NLRB's final decision in setting aside the election and ordering a rerun election.

Strategically, the employer and its counsel should be most reluctant to waive its position that the election in question should not have been invalidated or set aside.

Employer's counsel and representative should understand, however, that a ruling in a representation proceeding is not directly appealable to the federal appellate courts. In order to test a ruling, such as the invalidation of a representation election, an employer must do the following:

1. wait until it is required at some later date to negotiate with the union in question
2. refuse to so negotiate
3. be charged with committing an unfair labor practice charge for such refusal
4. then appeal the unfavorable ruling to the applicable federal court of appeal or respond to the NLRB's petition to enforce its ruling before such federal circuit court of appeals

However, such a circuitous appeal or response to an NLRB appeal to test the NLRB's ruling that a representation election should be set aside may not be necessary if, in a subsequent rerun election, the employer is likewise victorious, and there are no objections or challenges to it.

Assuming, however, that the employer were unsuccessful in a rerun election, for whatever reason, and at some point in time, required to bargain with the union, in order to contest the subsequent certification of the union as its employees' bargaining agent in whatever applicable appropriate unit in question, the employer and its counsel and representative would be forced to take the circuitous path discussed above. Then, the employer's counsel would be able to argue to the applicable circuit court of appeals its contentions regarding the issues in the representation proceedings before the NLRB.

The employer's counsel and representatives should be aware that the courts have permitted NLRB rulings in representation proceedings to be appealed directly to the federal courts with respect to at least two situations:

1. whenever a substantial constitutional issue is raised in the representation proceeding
2. whenever the NLRB rulings or decisions interfere with the federal government's exercise of foreign policy

12 How to Defend Against Strikes and Seek Injunctive Relief in Labor Disputes

The Norris-LaGuardia Act generally prohibits the issuance of injunctions to curtail strikes and work stoppages during a labor dispute. There are several exceptions, however. Should an employer be victimized by some type of labor strike, work stoppage, boycott, or some other form of picketing, its counsel and representatives should know what they may and may not do from a legal perspective to counter the situation.

Some strikes and work stoppages are protected while some are not. Strikes also may be protected, but only within certain limits and guidelines. In many instances, the NLRB and state and federal courts are placed in the position of having to balance the rights of strikers and labor organizations against the rights of employers and the general public.

The employer's counsel and representatives should know that the following strikes are generally treated as unprotected, meaning that they can be enjoined and/or the parties causing or participating in such strikes may be sued for damages they have caused the employer to have suffered:

- Work slowdowns
- Intermittent strikes
- Otherwise lawful strikes that are carried out in an illegal manner, such as by way of mass picketing or the use of violence

- Strikes or work stoppages in violation of no-strike provisions in a labor agreement
- Strikes to further illegal featherbedding
- Strikes to resolve a jurisdictional or work stoppage dispute

Also unprotected are strikes or work stoppages that do not observe a statutorily mandated "cooling-off" period and strikes or work stoppages that are designed to cause or compel a violation of the National Labor Relations Act, as amended, or some other statute or executive order.

Prohibiting Secondary Boycotting

The NLRA, as amended, prohibits labor organizations from engaging in secondary boycotting, the purpose of which is to force a neutral employer to cease doing business with a primary employer, the employer that is the real party to the dispute. A neutral employer, however, is not always protected in its right to enjoin secondary boycotting. It may lose its protection and neutrality status whenever:

- the neutral and primary employers are determined to be but one single employer
- the neutral employer is determined to be an ally of the primary employer
- the neutral employer is engaged in a straight line and integrated operations with the primary employer for the joint benefit of both

The secondary boycotting issue frequently arises in the construction industry in what is frequently referred to as common situs picketing in which at least two employers are engaged in separate jobs on common premises and the union pickets the neutral employer, such as the owner of the premises or the general contractor responsible for the prosecution of all the construction work at the site. The employer's counsel should be most familiar with the "Reserved Gate" standards where the neutral employer may maintain its protection to enjoin picketing at its neutral gate by designating a separate gate for the primary employer(s) being picketed.

The employer's counsel and representatives should also be aware that picketing to enforce "hot cargo" provisions are likely to be interpreted to be secondary boycotting and unlawful except for two statutory exceptions. A "hot cargo" clause in an agreement between an employer and a union that provides an employer will cease to do business or cease buying certain products or services from another who is in a labor dispute with such union is only permitted in the construction industry and the garment industry. The construction industry exception to the "hot cargo" prohibition only applies to work to be performed at the construction site; work performed away from the construction site, such as delivery of materials to and from the construction site, falls outside the statutory protection.

The employer's counsel should also appreciate that what appears to be a "hot cargo" provision, and otherwise illegal, may be interpreted by the NLRB and the courts to be lawful. For example, should the NLRB interpret the purpose of a clause in an agreement between a union and an employer to protect the jobs and work of the primary employees, such clause may be interpreted as legal and not secondary in nature. On the other hand, should the clause be interpreted to achieve union objectives elsewhere, such as with respect to non-contracting, the clause will not likely be interpreted as a legal one.

There are several clauses in labor agreements that the NLRB and the courts regard as outside the "hot cargo" prohibition:

- A work preservation clause in a collective bargaining contract which preserves work for employees in the contracting union will generally be regarded as valid and legal, particularly where the work has been traditionally performed by employees represented by the contracting union and the contracting employer has the power and authority to assign the work to the employees represented by the contracting union. On the other hand, a clause in a labor agreement that seeks to reach out and monopolize additional jobs not historically performed by employees represented by the contracting union will be considered illegal.
- A clause in a labor agreement in which the contracting union seeks to recapture work that, although currently performed by non-unit employees, had been performed historically by employees represented by such union, will generally be considered valid and legal by the NLRB and the courts.
- A clause in a collective bargaining contract in which the contracting employer agrees not to do business with another employer whose labor standards fall below union standards may be valid and legal, unless the intent of the contracting union is to prevent the contracting employer from dealing with non-union employees.

Employers' Rights Under the Norris-LaGuardia Statute

Although the Norris-LaGuardia statute generally forbids the courts to enjoin lawful picketing resulting from work stoppages and strikes, it does not prohibit the courts from enjoining mass picketing in which the employer, its suppliers and employees who desire to come to work are prevented from proper ingress and egress to and from the struck property. The employer's counsel should be properly prepared to show a court that such egress and ingress has been impaired when seeking an injunction to limit pickets at the work site. A plethora of affidavits, photographs, and so forth are usually required by the court as evidence that such a temporary restraining order or injunction is justified.

The Norris-LaGuardia statute does not forbid the enjoining of violence and illegal behavior on the part of union agents and strikers, nor does it forbid the arrest and conviction of strike participants who breach local, state, and federal criminal laws. Should such situations arise, the employer's counsel and representatives should have no qualms in seeking such relief.

In addition, an employer is generally free to discipline or discharge an employee who engages in serious strike misconduct, such as picket line violence, although non threatening verbal abuse is not considered to rise to the level to justify such discipline or discharge.

The Norris-LaGuardia Act does not forbid injunctive relief against repeated, intermittent strikes, and slowdowns, such as employees engaging in a pattern of half work/half strike or some other such ratio.

A work stoppage or strike in breach of a no-strike clause in a collective bargaining contract is generally unprotected, as will be discussed below. Recognitional picketing may or may not be protected, depending on the length of time in which the picketing occurs and other circumstances, as will be discussed below. Likewise, informational and consumer picketing may or may not be protected, depending upon the particular circumstances, facts, and purpose behind the picketing, as will be more fully discussed below.

Employees' Rights During Strikes or Work Stoppages

Aside from those noted exceptions above, most strikes and work stoppages are protected and the individual strike participants may not be disciplined or discharged for their participation in such strikes. Again, the employer's counsel should be ever mindful that much will depend upon the particular facts and circumstances as well as the purpose and objective of such work stoppage.

For example, the NLRB generally considers an employee who engages in a sympathy strike and refuses to cross a picket line maintained by striking employees who are members of a different bargaining unit to be protected, free of reprisal by their employer, if such employees are not subject to a particular collective bargaining contract. In such case, the employer may permanently replace the employee who engages in such a sympathy strike, similar to the replacement of an economic strike, but may not discharge or discipline the employee for so participating in such a sympathy strike. The employer's counsel and representatives should be aware that the federal courts do not always take the same position as the NLRB with respect to sympathy strikers. The federal courts are more inclined to balance the rights of the employer against the rights of the employee in such a situation, meaning that the employer may take such action as discharge in certain limited exceptions. Some courts have overturned NLRB cases and held that an employee may lose such protection when refusing to cross a picket line because of fear or personal reasons, rather than based on principle. One court held an employee who refused to cross a picket line of another employer premises could be discharged if legitimate business reasons required the employee to cross the picket line and the employee's refusal to do so would have injured the employer's business operations.

The employer's counsel and representatives should also keep in mind that an employee's right to engage in a sympathy strike can be waived by his or her bargaining agent in a collective bargaining agreement. Even here, such contract provisions are subject to various interpretations by the NLRB, labor arbitrators, and the courts. Employer's counsel and negotiating teams should draft very clear and specific language respecting such waivers if they want them to hold up under close scrutiny by the Board, as broad no-strike clauses may not be sufficient, in and of themselves, to sustain a position that an employee subject to the labor agreement is forbidden to engage in a sympathy strike.

An individual strike or work stoppage may or may not be protected, again, depending on the facts, circumstances, objectives, and whether the single employee is subject to a collective bargaining agreement.

Generally speaking, an individual employee who is not subject to union representation and a labor agreement is not protected in engaging in an individual work stoppage, irrespective of the purpose of his or her action, unless acting on behalf of more than one employee, so authorized by such collective employees. Even when acting on behalf of two or more employees, and so authorized, the action is not protected unless such activity is for the mutual aid or protection of the applicable group of employees and is a complaint or protest with respect to wages, benefits, and other terms and conditions of employment that are generally regarded mandatory subjects of bargaining in labor agreements.

Where the individual so protesting is subject to a collective bargaining contract and he or she walks off the job or conducts a one-person work stoppage, the language of the labor agreement will control whether the right is contractually protected or not. In the event the labor agreement contains a no-strike clause, the employee may be jeopardizing his or her position with the employer as the employer may well be within its rights to terminate the employment. Where the labor agreement is silent as to such scenarios, if the individual not only walks off the job, but also files a grievance under the collective bargaining agreement, he or she will be deemed to be engaged in protected concerted activity and thus protected from discharge or discipline under the mutual aid or protection clause of the NLRA, as amended.

Unfair labor practice strikers who are engaging in a strike or work stoppage in protest, in part or in whole, over unfair labor practices committed by the employer, in the absence of a labor agreement and language prohibiting strikes during the term of the labor agreement, are protected strikers and have an unconditional right of reinstatement upon their unconditional request to be so reinstated, even if the employer would be required to discharge temporary replacement employees in order to accommodate such strikers.

In contrast, an economic striker—one striking for contract language or proposals—is entitled to reinstatement to his or her former job upon an unconditional request to be so reinstated, but the employer is not required to discharge the permanent replacement employee to so accommodate the economic striker. If such be the case, the economic striker is placed on a preferential hiring list and is entitled to the job if the replacement employee should give up the job at some point in the future, assuming the economic striker did not abandon the right to the job in the interim.

TECHNIQUES AND TACTICS TO ENJOIN WILDCAT STRIKES

The vast majority of labor agreements contain what is frequently entitled a "no-strike" clause, meaning that the contracting union has agreed that the employees it represents in the bargaining unit covered by the contract are forbidden to strike during the duration of the contract, perhaps with the exception to sympathy strikers in certain cases, as discussed above, and certain other very limited situations.

The federal courts for many years held, however, that due to the Norris-LaGuardia prohibition against courts enjoining strikes as a result of labor disputes, that the only relief available to an employer for a union's violation of its no-strike commitment in the contract was to seek monetary damages. However, in the landmark Supreme Court case of *Boys Market, Inc. v. Retail Clerks Union*, the high court ruled that federal courts had the authority and power to enjoin strikes in violation of no-strike provisions in labor agreements provided certain criteria are met.

The employer's counsel whose employer has a contract containing a "no-strike" clause should be adequately prepared to demonstrate to a federal court that the following criteria has been met if he or she wishes to seek a *Boys Market* injunction to curtail a strike in violation of such "no-strike" provision in the labor contract:

- The strike or work stoppage is over a grievance of which both the union and the employer have agreed to arbitrate under the terms and language of the contract.
- The employer is willing and should be ordered by the court to arbitrate the grievance in question as a condition of obtaining the injunction.
- The injunction is warranted under ordinary principles of equity; that is, the employer will suffer irreparable harm in the absence of injunctive relief.

Even where a collective bargaining contract does not contain an explicit "no-strike" clause but does contain a grievance and binding arbitration clause, some courts will grant injunctive relief against a wildcat strike based upon an implied "no-strike" clause in the contract since the courts generally regard an employer's obligation to submit grievances under the contract to binding arbitration as the *quid pro quo* for a union's no-strike commitment.

The employer's counsel should also be aware that where the employer is unable to satisfy the *Boys Market* requirements, or elects a different approach, it may also bring an action for damages against the union for breach of the express or implied contractual no-strike commitment. Where the employer has agreed to submit breaches of the no-strike provision to arbitration, it may be required to do so, rather than pursuing an action through a federal court for monetary damages suffered as a result of a breach of the no-strike provision in the labor agreement.

Frequently, a union will take a position that it neither authorized nor condoned the wildcat strike and any action sought to remedy the damages resulting from the strike must be taken against the participants, rather than the international and/or local union. In such event, the employer's counsel is well advised to obtain as much evidence and proof to show to the court (or arbitrator) that union agents were so involved in the wildcat strike if it wishes to recover.

Should a strike occur in violation of a no-strike clause in a labor agreement, the employer is not without relief against the striking employees. Assuming it can satisfy the *Boys Market* criteria, the employer's counsel may obtain an injunction to enjoin the employees, directly, from further job action and also discharge or discipline such employees to the extent the no-strike clause provides for such.

PRACTICAL TIPS TO FOLLOW IN CURTAILING RECOGNITIONAL PICKETING

Another instance in which an employer's counsel and representatives may wish to seek injunctive relief against a labor organization is that of recognitional picketing.

The secondary boycott provisions of the National Labor Relations Act, as amended, generally forbid a union to induce or encourage employees to engage in a strike or work stoppage with a purpose of attempting to force the employer to recognize or bargain with the union whenever another union has already been certified by the NLRB as the employees' bargaining agent.

In addition, the National Labor Relations Act forbids a union to picket or threaten to picket an employer in an attempt to force the employer to recognize and bargain with it as the bargaining agent of its employees or to force employees to select the union as their bargaining representative if:

- The employer has lawfully recognized another union and the picketing occurs at a time when the question of representation cannot be raised;

- A valid NLRB election has been conducted within the preceding 12 months; or
- The picketing has been occurring for a period in excess of 30 days without a representation petition being filed by the union with the NLRB.

Inasmuch as a union violates the law with respect to improper or untimely recognitional picketing only to the extent that the purpose and object of the picketing is recognitional in nature, the difficult task for the employer's counsel is to present evidence to the NLRB that the union's objective is recognitional, rather than mere informational. The employer's counsel should procure photos of the picket signs, leaflets and other pamphlets handed out in connection with the picketing and such other information, including affidavits of management members who engage in conversations with union representatives, to such extent possible, to provide proof that the union's objective is, in fact, recognitional, rather than informational. Also, the employer's counsel may be required to overcome a union's position that the objective of the picketing was to protest unfair labor practices of the employer and/or to secure reinstatement of certain discharged employees.

In the event of recognitional picketing and assuming the union did not file a representation petition within 30 days from the commencement of the picketing, the employer may file an unfair labor practice against the union and ask the NLRB to seek an injunction in federal court to enjoin the picketing if it does not cease. The employer's counsel should be aware, however, that if the union files a petition within 30 days from the commencement of the picketing, the NLRB will generally permit the picketing to continue, pending the processing of the representation petition. Should the employer file an unfair labor practice regarding the recognitional picketing, the NLRB will seek to cease the picketing and proceed with an expedited election.

POINTS TO CONSIDER IN ADDRESSING HANDBILLING AND OTHER INFORMATIONAL PICKETING

The employer's counsel and representatives should realize that a labor organization typically will take a position that its picketing and handbilling is informational and lawful under the freedom of speech proviso of the U.S. Constitution and the applicable state constitution. The strategy is to convince the NLRB, and the courts, if necessary, that the picketing is merely to advise the consumer and other interested members of the public of the situation and the union's position on the matter.

In fact, a special provision of the National Labor Relations Act, as amended, provides that nothing in the statute forbids picketing and publicity for the purpose of truthfully advising the public and consumers that an employer does not employ members of, or have a contract with, a labor organization, unless an effect of the picketing is to induce an individual employed by any other person in the course of his or her employment not to pick up, deliver, or transport any goods, or not to perform any service as a result. The NLRA, as amended, also provides that consumer boycotting, which advises the public about an employer's substandard wages or benefits, is permissible.

Notwithstanding, a union may be prohibited from practicing such "free speech" on private property. An employer's counsel whose employer may well be subjected to union handbilling, consumer boycotting, and so forth, on the employer's premises should be well aware that the NLRB and the courts apply a balancing test in terms of weighing the interest of the union in exercise of its Section 7 rights under the NLRA, as amended, and the Constitution, against the property rights of the employer. Therefore, the employer or property owner's counsel should understand that each such case is determined by the particular facts within it.

Some of the determining factors, however, include:

- To what extent is the property open to the public
- What restrictions the property owner has imposed on public access to the property
- The size, nature, and location of the property
- The location of the activity to the property
- The manner in which the handbilling or pamphleteering is being conducted
- The alternative accesses to reach the intended audiences of the publicity
- The presence or absence of the primary party targeted at the site of the handbilling
- The type of employer that is being boycotted
- The safety of attempting to handbill and pamphleteer at alternative sites
- The relative additional costs and expenses incurred in attempting to communicate at alternative sites
- The extent to which alternative sites would dilute the effectiveness of the communications
- The right of the neutral property owner or employer not to be enmeshed in a labor dispute with the primary employer

STRATEGIES IN HANDLING JURISDICTIONAL DISPUTES

The employer's counsel and representatives should be aware that their employer may well be made a party to a dispute not directly involving the employer, such as in a jurisdictional or work assignment dispute. In order to best defend an employer against such disputes that so directly affect the operations and success of the employer's business, the employer's counsel should understand the employer's rights and privileges under the National Labor Relations Act and under the NLRB rules and regulations relative to work assignment disputes.

Jurisdictional disputes typically occur when there is a disagreement between two or more unions as to whose members are entitled to the work in question. The employer becomes involved when one or both unions—or perhaps more—attempt to force the employer, owner or general contractor of the work site to assign work to employees represented by one union to the exclusion of the other(s).

The means by which to force an employer to assign work to its members, rather than to members of a rival or competing union, can take the form of a strike, work stoppage, picketing, boycotts, threats, intimidation and other such acts of coercion.

The NLRB will regard such acts of coercion a violation of Section 8(b)(4)(D) and will permit an employer to file an unfair labor practice charge against the union or unions engaged in such conduct.

Whenever the NLRB receives such a charge, it applies very specific and unique procedures, given the nature and impact of jurisdictional or work assignment disputes.

First, the regional director in whose region the charge is filed will assign an agent to determine whether there is reasonable cause to support the charge. Second, assuming reasonable cause is found, the regional director will make a determination as to whether the contesting unions have previously agreed to a voluntary method by which to resolve such a dispute, such as being a signatory to the Impartial Jurisdictional Disputes Board of the Building and Construction Trades Department of the AFL-CIO. However, in the absence of a voluntary method to resolve the dispute, the NLRB will suspend the processing of the Section 8(b)(4)(D) charge and proceed to resolve the dispute through a Section 10(k) proceeding. The NLRB may also seek injunctive relief in a federal district court to enjoin the union's activities under its Section 10(e) powers if it deems such action appropriate under the circumstances.

The employer's counsel and representatives should also understand that the NLRB will not process a Section 8(b)(4)(D) charge or convene a Section 10(k) hearing unless there are two or more groups of employees competing for the same work. Thus, whenever the union's object is recognitional or organizational in nature or it is attempting to apply traditional economic pressure for some other reason, the NLRB will not deem it a sustainable Section 8(b)(4)(D) charge and will refuse to process it further, as such.

Should the NLRB direct that the matter proceed to a Section 10(k) hearing, parties will be given notice of such. Unlike representation hearings, the Hearing Officer's report is submitted to the NLRB and the NLRB makes the final decision, rather than the regional director.

As mandated by the U.S. Supreme Court, the NLRB has the affirmative duty to decide which of two or more groups of employees claiming the work in dispute are entitled to the work.

The employer's counsel and representatives should realize that the employer plays a pivotal role in Section 10(k) hearings, due to the standards and criteria under which such awards are made.

Thus, the employer's counsel should be prepared to take a most active and assertive role in such hearings to ensure the work is assigned to the group of employees it desires.

One of the main criteria used by the NLRB, and the courts, in determining which group of employees should be assigned certain work is the employer's preference as to whom the work should be assigned.

The employer's counsel and representatives should appreciate that the NLRB and the courts look to the efficiency of the employer's business operations in making such awards of disputed work. Who knows more about the efficiency of one's business operations than the employer and its management executives? Thus, the employer's counsel should develop this aspect of its proof to the fullest extent possible when participating in Section 10(k) hearings.

Other factors that the NLRB looks to, aside from employer preference in determining such disputes, in making such rewards, include:

- Custom and tradition
- Company and industry practice
- Safety and skills of the competing groups of employees and the efficient operation of the business
- Certification by the NLRB as to the work in question
- Awards of arbitrators in similar situations
- The impact upon employee job loss
- Collective bargaining agreements on the subject
- Labor management tradition
- Inter-union agreements
- Third-party awards
- Similarity of work previously performed by the competing groups

The employer's position and evidence will impact significantly in Section 10(k) hearings. Employer's counsel and representatives should prepare and preserve their case with such in mind.

13 Techniques and Tactics in Handling Ancillary and Miscellaneous Matters Before the NLRB

The employer's counsel should be fully aware of his or her responsibilities in filing formal pleadings, briefs, and other documents and the service of such instruments upon interested parties in order to avoid procedural errors and prejudice the employer's case or position.

The employer's counsel, or some other representative, who is handling a matter before the National Labor Relations Board on behalf of an employer, such as in filing an answer to a complaint in an unfair labor practice case, should know that he or she is required to serve such papers on the appropriate persons within the NLRB of which the numbers of copies vary given the nature of the case, but also must serve such documents on other parties to the action as well as a copy of such documents on any attorney or representative of the party who has entered a written appearance to the Board.

The employer's counsel or other representative handling a matter before the NLRB on behalf of the employer should preserve proof of its service by the use of registered or certified mail as the return receipt or the registered receipt will serve the employer well if proof of such service later becomes a procedural issue in the case.

The employer's counsel should be aware of the NLRB's policy that timely filing of a document, brief, and so on, with the NLRB, or an applicable regional director, general counsel, administrative law judge, or hearing officer, means that the document must be received by the NLRB or an applicable party before the close of business on the last day of the allowed period. However, the Board will also defer to the date of the postmark of such documents being filed.

For example, any materials postmarked on or after the due date will be rejected by the NLRB as untimely filed. However, the NLRB will consider materials postmarked at least the day before the due date as timely filed, although they are not received by the NLRB, or the designated representative of the NLRB, until after the due date, except for such documents that are statutorily required to be filed by a certain date, such as:

- Petitions for elections
- Election objections and challenges
- Unfair labor practice charges filed pursuant to Section 10 of the National Labor Relations Act, as amended
- Applications for awards and fees as provided under the Equal Access to Justice Act as discussed below
- Petitions to revoke subpoenas

The employer's counsel and other representatives who defend employers in matters before the NLRB should also understand how time is computed in determining the due date relative to filing requirements. Thus, in computing the timetable required by the NLRB in the submission of pleadings, documents, briefs, and so on, the following guidelines should be met:

- Whenever the allowed period of time is less than seven days, Saturdays, Sundays, and any legal holidays that fall within the period *should not be counted.*
- Whenever the allowed period of time is seven days or more, Saturdays, Sundays, and any legal holidays that fall within the time period *should be counted.*
- The day of the particular event that sets the timetable in motion *should not be counted.*
- The day following the day the particular event that sets the timetable in motion *should be counted.*
- The last day of the period of time required by the NLRB *should be counted* if the last day does not fall on a federally recognized holiday.
- The last day of the period of time required by the NLRB *should not be counted* if the last day falls on a federally recognized holiday in which case the day following the holiday must be counted.

The employer's counsel should check the latest NLRB rules and regulations relative to time limits in which documents must be filed and service tendered with respect to each type of NLRB case being handled by the counsel at the time. In most instances, the NLRB will advise in its correspondence to the employer the deadline for filing a responsive pleading. However, the employer's counsel will be well served to check independently the exact filing requirements and follow the time limits as noted in the NLRB rules and regulations as a secondary precaution.

TACTICAL TIPS TO USE WHEN SEEKING REIMBURSEMENT UNDER THE EQUAL ACCESS TO JUSTICE ACT

The employer's counsel should be knowledgeable of another piece of weaponry in its arsenal of defenses when handling a matter before the NLRB. In certain cases, the employer's counsel may be successful in seeking reimbursement for attorneys' fees and litigation expenses of the employer under the Equal Access to Justice Act.

The Equal Access to Justice Act has many limitations. For example, the statute only applies to small businesses, public interest groups, and individual litigants. It does not apply to large corporations. It does provide for eligible parties a recovery of attorneys' fees and other litigation expenses when such party prevails in an administrative or judicial proceeding in which the federal government or one of its agencies is an opposing party. Thus, the applicability of the Equal Access to Justice Act extends far beyond NLRB cases. It is equally applicable in Age Discrimination in Employment Act (ADEA) and other such cases that will be discussed in later chapters of this book.

Another limitation of the Equal Access to Justice Act with respect to NLRB cases is that the statute only applies to unfair labor practice cases and backpay proceedings; it does not apply to representation elections under Section 9 of the National Labor Relations Act, as amended.

A claimant for reimbursement of attorneys' fees and litigation expenses under the Equal Access to Justice Act may not prevail where the federal government or agency can demonstrate to the satisfaction of the administrative law judge hearing the case that its position in the matter was substantially justified and/or other special circumstances make such an award for attorneys' fees and litigation expenses unjust.

As suggested above, the employer's counsel's first obstacle in an Equal Access to Justice claim is to establish that the employer is eligible to receive an award under the statute. Parties eligible to receive Equal Access to Justice claims include:

- The sole owner of an incorporated business who has a net worth of no more than seven million dollars and whose business has no more than 500 employees.

- Partnerships, corporations, associations, units of local government, or other public or private entities whose organizations have a net worth of no more than seven million dollars and no more than 500 employees.

Also eligible to receive awards under the Equal Access of Justice Act are:

- Individuals whose net worth does not exceed two million dollars.
- A charitable or other tax-exempt institution described in Section 501(c)(3) of the Internal Revenue Code and which organization has no more than 500 employees.
- A cooperative association as defined in Section 15(a) of the Agricultural Marketing Act and which association has no more than 500 employees.

Procedural Requirements to Follow in Prosecuting Equal Access to Justice Claims

Should an employer prevail in an unfair labor practice case before the NLRB and be eligible to file a claim for attorneys' fees and litigation expenses under the Equal Access to Justice Act, the employer's counsel has the responsibility of filing an application for such claims with the NLRB in Washington, D.C. Realistically, the employer's counsel should be prepared to expect all sorts of defenses by the General Counsel of the NLRB who has the responsibility of responding to such claims. In many instances, the employer may be required to appeal to the appropriate federal appellate court in order to obtain the recovery that Congress intended.

An administrative law judge who is but an extension of the National Labor Relations Board is not likely to rule that the NLRB and its General Counsel was not substantially justified in issuing an unfair labor practice complaint against the employer. A federal appellate court may be more favorably disposed toward the employer, especially if the employer's counsel can demonstrate that the unfair labor practice charge had no merit or basis but the General Counsel sought to victimize the employer, causing the employer to pay attorneys' fees and other litigation expenses, unnecessarily.

The employer's counsel who desires to seek recovery of attorneys' fees and litigation expenses under the Equal Access to Justice Act must file an application for such within 30 days after entry of the NLRB's final order. The application for such recovery must be signed by the employer's counsel or representative and must be accompanied by written verification, under oath, that the information contained in the application is true.

The General Counsel has the responsibility of filing an answer to the application for reimbursement within 35 days following service of the application.

The NLRB then defers the case to be heard by the administrative law judge who heard the underlying proceeding. Since most Equal Access to Justice awards will be decided on the basis of the documents in the record, an evidentiary hearing is not usually necessary in such cases. Upon the conclusion of the administrative law judge's proceedings, he or she will prepare a decision, including findings of fact and conclusions to which any party to the action may file exceptions to the administrative law judge's decision. Such exceptions are to be filed in the same manner as those used in filing exceptions in unfair labor practice cases. Likewise, procedures for NLRB considerations of the administrative law judge's decision are the same as those used in unfair labor practice cases.

DEFENSIVE TECHNIQUES IN RESPONSE TO A SECTION 10(J) INJUNCTION

The NLRB has the power and authority under Section 10(j) of the National Labor Relations Act, as amended, to seek injunctive relief from an appropriate federal district court in order to prevent delays in the Board's administrative process. In contrast to Section 10(e) injunctions which are mandatory in unfair labor practice charges that involve secondary boycotts and other secondary activities, hot cargo agreements and recognitional and/or organizational picketing, Section 10(j) injunctive steps by the NLRB are discretionary. According to the NLRB case handling manual, the Board considers various factors prior to seeking a Section 10(j) injunction, such as:

- Whether the continuation of the alleged unfair labor practices will result in exceptional and unnecessary hardship on the charging party
- Whether the alleged unfair labor practice is of a continuous and repetitious pattern
- Whether the alleged violations are clear in the unfair labor practice charge
- Whether the alleged unfair labor practice claims involve interference with the conduct of an election or, in some other manner, constitute a clear and flagrant disregard of the NLRB's certification of a bargaining representative
- Whether the alleged unfair labor practices relate to an unusually wide geographic area
- Whether the unfair labor practice case, in question, involves the shutdown of an important business operations, which, in turn, could cause an extraordinary impact on the public interest
- Whether the employees allegedly victimized by the unfair labor practice would suffer such unusual hardship that equitable damages would not remedy such behavior

- Whether the alleged unfair labor practice case has the purpose of creating violence and, if so, is such violence out of control of local authorities to such an extent that a Section 10(j) injunction is dictated

Should the NLRB divert its routine practice, and attempt to seek an injunction under Section 10(j) of the NLRA against an employer, his or her counsel should understand what type cases are, and are not, within the scope of a section 10(j) injunction.

The following categories of unfair labor practice cases against management will normally be considered within the scope of Section 10(j) for which injunctive relief may be sought:

- an employer's withdrawal of recognition from an incumbent union
- an employer's recognition of a union that does not truly represent an uncoerced majority of employees in an appropriate unit
- an employer's refusal to recognize and bargain with a successor union
- an employer's alleged failure to permit employees to engage in protected concerted activity
- an employer's (or union's) refusal to bargain in good faith during labor negotiations
- an employer's attempt to undermine the bargaining representatives' organizing efforts
- an employer's subcontracting out work to adversely affect the working conditions of employees represented by a union
- an employer's interference with the union's organizational campaign, before or after the union obtains majority status
- an employer's attempt to take action to segregate its assets, such as by closing part of or all of its operations

In addition to employer unfair labor practice charges, other unfair labor practice claims may also cause the NLRB to file a Section 10(j) injunction, such as:

- a union's failure to comply with the 60-day notice requirement prior to engaging in a strike against an employer
- a union's failure to give a health care facility a 10-day notice of its intention to strike prior to doing so
- a union's unlawful coercion to achieve unlawful objectives in violation of the National Labor Relations Act, as amended
- a union's (or employer's) retaliation against an employee for filing an unfair labor practice charge, giving testimony or, in some other manner, exercising his or her rights under the NLRB process

The employer's counsel should also be aware that the charging party is not permitted to seek injunctive relief under Section 10(j); only the NLRB has the authority to seek such an injunction. Also, the employer's counsel should realize that a federal district court is not always going to grant an injunction just because the NLRB seeks one. The federal district court may well decide that the NLRB did not establish "reasonable cause" to substantiate grounds for an injunction. The federal district court may well determine that the NLRB should go ahead and decide the case rather than deferring it to the court for a resolution.

II HOW TO DEFEND LABOR ARBITRATION CASES

14 Preliminary Matters in Preparing a Labor Arbitration Case

In defending a labor arbitration case, employers and their representatives, whether in the capacity of human resource professionals or labor relations attorney, must have a fundamental understanding of the Federal Labor Law and its policy encouraging arbitration. Taft-Hartley, Section 203(2) declares that "final adjustment by a method agreed upon by the parties is ... the desirable method for settlement of grievance dispute arising over the application or interpretation of an existing collective bargaining agreement." Thus, the law starts with the idea that arbitration is the preferred method to settle labor controversies. And, although a grievance arbitration clause does not have to be included in any collective bargaining agreement, the overwhelming majority of all collective bargaining agreements signed by an employer include an arbitration clause. It is important for counsel to understand that when binding arbitration is included in a collective bargaining agreement the courts will bend over backwards to find that a grievance submitted by a union is subject to arbitration. This judicial policy favoring arbitration in the resolution of labor disputes was first outlined in three landmark decisions of the U.S. Supreme Court, frequently referred to as the Steel Worker's trilogy.

These decisions established the following propositions favoring court deferral to arbitration:

- The first function of the court should be a determination of whether the party seeking arbitration is making a claim which, on its face, is governed by a collective bargaining agreement

- In making this determination, all doubts as to the coverage of an arbitration clause should be resolved in favor of arbitration
- The court should order arbitration unless it can only be said with positive assurance that the arbitration clause is not susceptible of an interpretation that the arbitration clause covers the asserted dispute
- Courts are to uphold and enforce an arbitrator's award—resulting from an arbitrable issue under a collective bargaining agreement—even though the court's interpretation of the contract would differ from that of the arbitrator's

Thus, counsel for an employer must understand that although arbitration is a matter of contract, and an employer cannot be required to submit to arbitration a dispute which he has not agreed to submit, the employer must be able to point to a specific unequivocal provision in the contract that provides that the matter is not subject to arbitration. And, once an arbitrator renders his or her award, it will be very difficult to reverse the award.

The overwhelming type of arbitration case that is defended by employers involves arbitrators deciding disputes that involve the interpretation or application of an existing contract with its union. This is typically referred to as "rights" arbitration. The arbitrator in this type of case acts as a "judge" to resolve the parties' dispute.

The second type of arbitration concerns the arbitration over terms of a "new" collective bargaining agreement (either the first or a successor). In these instances the parties have failed to arrive at a mutually agreed upon contract and have agreed to submit their differences to a third party arbitrator. Here the arbitrator acts as a "legislator" and is deciding what terms or conditions will be included in the contract. This is typically referred to as "interest" arbitration. As a matter of practice, the arbitration strategies and techniques regarding rights arbitration and interest arbitration are somewhat similar. However, the overwhelming type of arbitration is "rights" arbitration, and the focus of this discussion is on defending a "rights" arbitration case.

Counsel for the employer must understand the concept of arbitrability, both substantive and procedural. The question of whether the underlying dispute between the parties is arbitrable raises the question of substantive arbitrability. Is the grievance pursued by the union one that is within the scope of the arbitration agreement? Thus, it is critical for counsel for the employer to determine whether the subject matter of the grievance is arbitral. For example, some collective bargaining agreements provide that the disciplinary discharge of a probationary employee is not subject to arbitration. Thus, if a probationary employee files a grievance over his discharge, employer's counsel would assert that the matter is not subject to arbitration, i.e., not arbitrable.

In addition to an employer's defense of substantive arbitrability, it is also possible for an employer to raise the issue of procedural arbitrability. Typically, the collective bargaining agreement will set forth certain procedural prerequisites that a union must follow in order for the matter to be properly subject to arbitration. As a result, counsel for the employer must review the contract carefully to determine whether the issue of failure to follow contract procedures can be raised as a defense. However, unlike substantive arbitrability, an employer in the typical case cannot refuse to go to arbitration because the courts have generally held that where the parties are obligated to submit the subject matter of the dispute to arbitration, the "procedural" questions which grow out of the dispute should be left to the arbitrator.

As a practical matter, if employer's counsel can raise (in good faith) either the question of substantive arbitrability or procedural arbitrability, he or she should do so. The question of arbitrability, along with a weak case on its merits, may convince the union to withdraw the grievance or result in a favorable settlement for the company. In addition, in most instances, even though the issue of arbitrability (substantive or procedural) is raised by the company, the company will typically proceed to arbitration, reserving the right to raise the issue of arbitrability before the arbitrator.

TECHNIQUES AND TACTICS IN RESPONDING TO THE DEMAND FOR ARBITRATION

Employer's counsel response to a demand for arbitration is primarily controlled by the collective bargaining agreement (and past practices) between the parties. Although there are many "standardized" clauses in collective bargaining agreements, each collective bargaining agreement is unique; as such, it becomes the key document and must be carefully reviewed. However, as a practical matter, the issues (as mentioned above) of substantive and procedural arbitrability must first be examined once a demand is made for arbitration.

As to substantive arbitrability, employer's counsel should determine whether the subject matter is specifically excluded by either: (1) an exclusion in the arbitration clause; or (2) a specific exclusionary clause.

In every case, the entire agreement should be carefully reviewed. However, the clauses that typically need the most careful scrutiny in this regard are:

- arbitration clause
- exclusionary clauses
- management rights
- "entirety of the agreement" or "zipper" clauses

In addition to exclusionary clauses, counsel for the employer should also review the *definition* of a grievance, set forth in the grievance or arbitration clause. Many times, the definition of a grievance will state that the dispute must be over a violation of a *specific provision* of the collective bargaining agreement. As a result, if the union fails to make a specific allegation, an argument can be made that the matter is not a grievance and, therefore, not substantively arbitrable under the arbitration clause. Although it must be remembered that typically the courts and the NLRB will give a broad reading to the arbitration clause, and, as a result, most employers, as a tactical matter, will proceed to arbitration, but raising as one of its defenses the issue of substantive arbitrability.

The issue of procedural arbitrability, just like substantive arbitrability, is very fact specific. However, employer's counsel must carefully review the procedural requirements set forth in the collective bargaining agreement—typically these requirements (if any) are set forth in the grievance/arbitration clause. The defenses that employer's counsel may be able to assert regarding procedural arbitrability are:

- ***Timeliness.*** Time limitations set forth at each "step" of the grievance procedure must be complied with by the union. This is particularly so if the collective bargaining agreement contains a "time-of-the-essence" clause and a provision that the failure of the union to comply with the grievance time limits will result in forfeiture of the grievance. Thus, employer's counsel must evaluate whether the union has met all time requirements.
- ***Information requirements.*** In addition to timeliness, many collective bargaining agreements provide that a grievance, to be processed, must include specific information, such as:

- date of alleged violation
- date filed
- name of grievant
- a factual statement of the grievance
- specific provisions of the agreement violated
- the specific relief sought

If the union fails to comply with any of the procedural aspects required by the collective bargaining agreement, employer's counsel may assert that the matter is not procedurally arbitrable. However, employer's counsel needs to be aware that although the collective bargaining agreement may specifically set forth certain requirements, an arbitrator may find that the technical requirements have been waived by a past practice. Thus, counsel must review the past practice of the parties regarding the enforcement of time and procedure requirements.

Overall, there are several reasons why employer's counsel should assert, if available, the defense of arbitrability: substantive or procedural. The reasons are:

- The union may decide to withdraw its grievance;
- The defense of non-arbitrability may provide leverage to obtain a favorable settlement;
- In the event that the grievance does go before an arbitrator, the arbitrator in a close case on the merits may find in favor of the union on the arbitrability issue, but decide in favor of the company on the merits of the grievance. As a result, the arbitrator has appeared more reasonable to the union because it ruled in the union's favor on the issue of arbitrability.

In the event that employer's counsel refuses to proceed to arbitration because of alleged non-arbitrability, employer's counsel can expect the union to file an 8(a)5 Unfair Labor Practice Charge asserting that the failure to proceed to arbitration is "bad faith" bargaining on the employer's part, or the union may file a Section 301 lawsuit to compel arbitration. Employer's counsel should not assert the arbitrability issue and refuse to proceed to arbitration unless it is absolutely clear that the matter is not substantively arbitral.

STRATEGIC STEPS FOR SELECTING THE BEST ARBITRATOR FOR THE CASE

Selection Procedure

The selection of the arbitrator and the procedures for selecting the arbitrator will be controlled by the terms of the collective bargaining agreement in effect between the parties. Typically, a collective bargaining agreement will provide that the parties may use an arbitrator that is mutually agreeable or rely upon one of two agencies: Federal Mediation Conciliation Service (FMCS) or the American Arbitration Association (AAA).

Selection by Mutual Agreement

Many collective bargaining agreements provide that an arbitrator(s) is to be selected by mutual agreement. However, in the event that the parties are unable to agree upon an arbitrator, some states allow court appointment of the arbitrator upon application of one of the parties. However, it is important to note that some state statutes have provisions that prohibit court appointment of arbitrators. Thus, the collective bargaining agreement should be reviewed to determine if it provides for a final procedure for selecting the arbitrator to avoid the risk of deadlock. If it does not, counsel should review the law on this issue.

Selection through FMCS or American Arbitration Association

Most collective bargaining agreements provide that one or both parties can request a panel of arbitrators from one of two agencies: FMCS or AAA. These agencies maintain lists of approved arbitrators. Both agencies will submit lists of arbitrators if requested by the parties. The American Arbitration Association charges an administrative fee, whereas the FMCS furnishes a panel without a charge. Thus, the rules and regulations of the Federal Mediation Conciliation regarding its appointment of arbitrators and the American Arbitration Association rules should be reviewed carefully prior to the selection of an arbitrator.

Selecting the Best Arbitrator

Arbitrators come with different backgrounds and experiences. As a result, it is critical that the employer's counsel understand that this step of preparing the case is as important as any other step of preparing a defense in a labor arbitration case. Many times employer's counsel fails to adequately research the arbitrators, resulting in the selection of an arbitrator that from the outset puts the employer's case at a disadvantage.

Thus, the backgrounds of arbitrators must be reviewed. The employer's counsel should take the following steps in reviewing arbitrators:

- Discuss each arbitrator with other lawyers, business associates, and, of course, most importantly, with anyone in the company who may have had any experience with arbitrators. (Clients' memories tend to be very long in this area; and counsel should never subject a client to a hearing before an arbitrator in whom the client has even the slightest doubt.)
- Review the biographical sketch of the arbitrator; look for such information regarding experience, particularly determine whether the arbitrator is a former management advocate or was a former union advocate.
- Research prior awards of the arbitrator on the relevant issue. Such awards are typically available through *Labor Arbitration Reports,* published by Bureau of National Affairs and *Labor Arbitration Rewards*, published by Commerce Clearing House. Additional research information is available from other commercial services:

  Labor Arbitration Information Service (LAIS), published by Labor Relations Press

  computer research service called Instant Computer Arbitration Service (ICAS), also published by Labor Relations Press
- Another looseleaf service, provided exclusively to management representatives, is published by R.C. Simpson, Inc., under the name of Arbitrator

Qualifications Report. The Simpson Service is in looseleaf form which in addition to showing an arbitrator's prior awards, also summarizes the recommendations of management representatives who have arbitrated cases before the particular arbitrator. In addition, the manual provides citations for published awards and can provide unpublished private awards to its subscribers upon request.

It is possible through research, mentioned above, to discern tendencies in arbitrators to rule certain ways in different types of cases.

Once all pertinent information and views have been obtained, employer's counsel will need to rank the panel of arbitrators from best to worst. Typically, the arbitrator determined to be the "best" arbitrator for the particular issue is given a ranking of 1 and the worst is given a ranking of (for example, if there are seven names on the list) a 7. Obviously, the ranking involves judgment after gathering and reviewing all of the available information.

Some helpful hints regarding the ranking of arbitrators are:

Prior awards. If the arbitrator has ruled favorably in a case similar to the employer's case, the arbitrator is likely to rule the same way. Likewise, if the arbitrator has ruled against a company under similar circumstances, that arbitrator is to be avoided.

Quantum of proof. In discharge cases, arbitrators may differ on the quantum of proof required of an employer. Some arbitrators require the employer to sustain a discharge by "preponderance of the evidence," while others may insist on "beyond a reasonable doubt," and some arbitrators insist on "clear and convincing" language. In a discharge case, obviously, an arbitrator who places a greater quantum of proof upon the employer should probably be avoided.

Background of arbitrator. Typically, employer's counsel is going to avoid arbitrators whose background consists of representing unions. However, one of the authors has found that several arbitrators with union backgrounds are very good in contract interpretation cases; but avoids such arbitrators in discharge cases.

Overall experience. Particularly in discharge cases, employer's counsel should view favorably those arbitrators who have practical "hands-on" experience. As a result, professors who have never experienced the real world are typically avoided.

Win/loss ratio. Obviously, an arbitrator who has consistently ruled in favor of management is going to be preferred over an arbitrator who has consistently ruled in favor of unions. However, this factor, like most other factors, cannot be determinative because it's possible that employers in those cases simply had bad cases.

Expertise. In many instances, arbitrators with particular expertise regarding the subject matter of the grievance may be preferred over arbitrators who have less expertise. Because the latter may not fully understand the technical issues, he or she may be swayed by emotional appeal, rather than fact appeal.

To be successful, counsel for the employer must do his or her homework regarding each arbitrator's background.

TECHNIQUES FOR RANKING AND STRIKING THE PANEL OF ARBITRATORS

The ranking procedure itself is typically set forth in the collective bargaining agreement, or the agreement itself may be silent and simply refer to FMCS or AAA procedures. Most, but not all, collective bargaining agreements provide that the union is to "strike" first or that the grieving party is to strike the first name (alternate strike method). It is important that employer's counsel require the union to follow this procedure particularly when obtaining a panel from FMCS with seven names (or any odd number on the list). If an odd number of arbitrators appears on the list, and the union strikes first, by simple arithmetic the company will be left with the choice of the final two names. This provides a slight edge to employer's counsel in selecting the arbitrator. The American Arbitration Association, on the other hand, submits a list of panel of arbitrators to the parties and the parties are then asked to indicate their order of preference on the list. Thus, the mutual first choice is determined by adding the ratings given the panel members whose names remain on the list by both parties.

If after reviewing the panel of arbitrators it's determined that the entire panel should be "thrown out," employer's counsel will have to review the collective bargaining agreement to determine whether a second panel can be selected or requested. Typically, collective bargaining agreements provide that either party may throw out the first panel and request a second. And, if employer's counsel determines that the first panel is not suitable, he or she may want to request a second panel be selected; however, if the collective bargaining agreement does not provide for a follow-up panel, then employer's counsel may simply be confronted with a "bad" panel of arbitrators. Of course, getting a second panel doesn't necessarily guarantee that the new panel will be any better.

Once employer's counsel has reviewed the panel of arbitrators and ranked the panel, the next step is to contact the union representative to "strike" or rank the (FMCS) panel. Before "striking" the panel, employer's counsel, as a preliminary step, should ask the union representatives if any of the arbitrators on the panel:

1. has a close personal friendship or relationship with any union representative
2. was an employee or consultant or independent contractor for the union
3. was ever an attorney for the union

Typically, when researching the panel of arbitrators, this information will generally become available; but, in some instances, particularly if it's on a personal level, employer's counsel will not be aware of such information, and you cannot automatically assume that such information will be brought to the attention of employer's counsel. Therefore, it's important such information be sought at the outset. If such relationship exists, counsel may suggest a new panel be requested or, if the arbitrator was given a negative ranking, insist that the name be removed from the panel before the union's first strike. After the first strike, then the parties alternate until one remains. It is important for employer's counsel to maintain a record of the order of striking for future reference.

HELPFUL HINTS REGARDING ARBITRATION HEARING ARRANGEMENTS AND REQUESTS FOR CONTINUANCES

Once an arbitrator has been selected, the following arrangements should follow:

- Appointment of arbitrator
- Date, time, and place of hearing
- Site selection
- Court reporter

If the arbitrator is one who has been mutually agreed to (or on an FMCS panel), counsel for the employer, with approval from the union, can write direct to the arbitrator advising the arbitrator that he or she has been selected and request available dates from the arbitrator. It is good practice for employer's counsel or representative to make the initial contact to start developing contact and familiarity with the arbitrator. The letter to the arbitrator simply needs to notify him or her of his or her appointment and request hearing dates. In addition, the letter needs to set forth the union representative's full name and address. It is not necessary in this initial letter to set forth a specific time and place. Once the arbitrator responds with available dates, then the time and place of the hearing can be established. In the event that an arbitrator has been selected through the American Arbitration Association, those procedures as set forth in its respective rules will guide the parties in contacting the arbitrator.

Preferably the arbitration will be held at a neutral site, typically a hotel conference room. This way, neither the union nor the company enjoys a psychological advantage. And if held at a neutral site, it is less likely that the union will attempt to call numerous witnesses from the plant in the event that problems arise in the presentation of the union's case. If the parties cannot agree upon the site of the hearing, either the arbitrator or the agency provided for in the collective bargaining agreement may determine the hearing site.

Once the site has been determined, another arrangement that needs to be made prior to the hearing is whether to utilize a stenographic reporter. Generally, employer's counsel prefers to use a stenographic reporter (or at least tape record the hearing) so it can be utilized in drafting a post-hearing brief.

In the event that employer's counsel needs to seek a continuance, he or she should do so at the earliest possible time and will need to demonstrate "good cause" for the continuance or postponement. If cause is shown, continuances are usually granted by an arbitrator. Of course, prior to contacting the arbitrator, counsel for the employer should contact the union representative to determine if the union representative can agree to such continuance or postponement. If no agreement can be reached, employer's counsel should advise the union representative the need to engage in a telephone conference with the arbitrator or that employer's counsel will correspond directly with the arbitrator seeking a continuance.

It is important for employer's counsel to realize that arbitrators are more likely to grant employees and their unions a continuance, as opposed to the employer. Apparently, the difference in approach is based upon the hardship caused employees by delay and the apparent economic resources of most employers. Thus, continuances should not be sought by employer's counsel unless there is good cause for seeking one.

15 Strategic Steps in Preparing for the Arbitration Hearing

One of the most difficult tasks for employer's counsel is that of gathering information and evidence pertinent to the grievance in preparation for the arbitration hearing. Arbitration is a less formal and structured process than litigation, but that is no excuse for casual preparation by employer's counsel. Of course, as the old saying goes, there is no substitute for a good case, but next to the value of having a good case, is the value of thorough preparation. Indeed, good cases are lost by careless preparation. Although there are different types of arbitrations (e.g., discharge/contract interpretation) and the issues will differ from arbitration to arbitration, the following is a checklist to assist counsel in digging for potential information and evidence for an arbitration hearing:

Information- and Evidence-Gathering Checklist

- Grievance
- Company responses
- Discussions, notes, and responses made throughout grievance process (history of grievance meetings)
- Current collective bargaining agreement
- Prior collective bargaining agreement(s)
- Bargaining history
- Company rules and regulations

- Relevant documents
- Site visitation
- Past practices
- Administrative hearings (e.g., unemployment)
- Interview witnesses

To assure that employer's counsel has obtained all information and evidence that may be relevant to an arbitration hearing, it is important that the investigation be centralized. Employer's counsel or a representative must be in charge of the investigation and gathering of information and evidence in preparation for the hearing. Counsel should consider the following as potential sources of information.

Review the Employees Grievance

The first step is to review the grievance filed by the employee (or union). It must also be remembered that in a multistep grievance procedure the union may have made written, as well as oral statements, throughout the course of the grievance procedure. Each of these statements must be carefully reviewed and examined for consistency. It is also important for employer's counsel to remember that written grievances are not written by lawyers and may be merely a summarization; thus, the grievance statement itself may not provide the necessary focus for understanding the issue underlying the grievance.

Review Company Responses

Once a grievance is filed, the company will usually respond both in writing and orally during the grievance procedure. *All* company (and union) responses at each step of the grievance procedure must be reviewed. Typically, after reviewing the grievances and responses, counsel for the employer should be able to discern the issue that will need to be decided by the arbitrator. In addition, as mentioned earlier, another reason to check the grievance papers carefully is to determine whether the union has complied with all procedural requirements set forth in the collective bargaining agreement.

Obtain a History of Grievance Meetings

As noted earlier, many times, due to the shortness of the written grievance, and, in some instances, the brevity of a company's response, employer's counsel may have only a general understanding of the dispute. Counsel should interview company witnesses to determine what was said by the union and its representatives or employees at each step of the grievance procedure, as well as reviewing any notes taken by the company representative present during these grievance steps. Get all information, arrange it in chronological sequence, and review it carefully. This information will undoubtedly shed more light on the issue.

Review the Current Collective Bargaining Agreement

Read the *entire* collective bargaining agreement for relevant (or potentially relevant) provisions. Failure to review the entire agreement is a critical mistake. One article or one section of the collective bargaining agreement cannot be isolated from the remainder of the agreement. Many times other sections or articles of the collective bargaining agreement cast light on the section or article that is the center of dispute. Undoubtedly, the biggest mistake that counsel can make is underestimating the possible interrelationships of all aspects of a collective bargaining agreement. Failure to review the possible interrelationships of the various articles and sections will in the future convince you of its importance.

Read Prior Contracts

Always review the previous contract or contracts. This is particularly so if you have a contract interpretation question; do not rely solely on the present collective bargaining agreement. Go back in time and read prior contracts to see whether there was ever a time when the language now at issue was rewritten, revised, or completely changed. The comparison of a critical clause from contract to contract may have a considerable impact on how one would reasonably interpret the clause in question. Employer's counsel or representative who has not reviewed prior contracts may find to his or her dismay the current language relied upon in the preparation of a case is suddenly weakened or worse—worthless.

Examine the Bargaining History

Closely related to a study of previous labor agreements is an examination of bargaining history regarding the particular articles or section in dispute. Unless the meaning of the clause is patently clear (which is almost never the case), the arbitrators will allow the parties to introduce evidence of bargaining history. In particular, it is helpful if employer's counsel can introduce testimony concerning other versions of the clause that may have been tendered by the union and rejected by the company during negotiations. A persuasive tool is to be able to say to an arbitrator, "Mr. Arbitrator, the union is now trying to get from you what they were unable to extract from the company during bargaining." That's a strong defense!

Review Company Rules and Regulations

Most companies have, apart from the collective bargaining agreement, rules and regulations. These should be carefully reviewed, particularly if the case involves discharge.

Review Relevant Documents

Counsel for the employer must review all documents relevant to the case. For example, if the case involves the termination of an employee, the discharge notice or letter, personnel file, unemployment compensation separation notice, and related documents need to be organized and reviewed. Or, for example, if a grievance concerns the failure to properly pay wages, time cards, pay stubs, and related documents need to be organized and reviewed. In addition, counsel should not overlook the fact that we live in the computer age. Counsel must seek any information that may be stored on computers. The gathering of information and evidence may sound simple; but it is not and counsel for the employer may find out the hard way if he or she does not probe for all relevant information.

Visit the Site

Visiting the site may not be important in some cases (e.g., general contract interpretation disputes) but, in general, the extent that the events occurred in the plant or on the dock or on plant premises, and so on, counsel for the employer should visit the area. During the visit, visualize the events step-by-step that led to the grievance. This will add to counsel's understan, and will greatly assist counsel in direct and cross-examination of witnesses. Thus, a great deal can be learned by visiting the site. In addition, photographs (in order to assist the arbitrator in understanding, for example, some manufacturing process) of the site or machinery should be taken and later introduced at the arbitration hearing.

Review the Company's Past Practices

Counsel for the employer must understand that a favorite argument, frequently advanced by unions to avoid what otherwise appears to be clear contract language contrary to their position, is that the parties have established a past practice that supports the union's position. In preparing for arbitration, you should always make it a point to thoroughly question your client concerning any possible past practices which are contrary to the position you will advance to the arbitrator. Often this questioning is successful in flushing out old side letters, old understandings, or simply prior conduct which could prove embarrassing at the hearing.

For example, assume the company has a rule that sleeping on the job is grounds for immediate discharge, and the grievant was discharged for this offense. Counsel for the employer needs to carefully determine if there has ever been any other instances regarding sleeping on the job. And, to the extent that the employer has discharged other employees for a first offense for sleeping on the job is strong support for the company's case. However, if the union can point to other individuals who were sleeping on the job and were not discharged in the first instance, or worse yet, are still working for the company, this alleged past practice can be very damaging to the employer's case. In addition, there are instances where the tables are turned. That is, the contract language is adverse to the employer, but the employer has always dealt with a certain situation differently than the manner provided for in the contract. Investigation into this past practice and the union's failure to object to similar conduct in the past, may serve to constitute a waiver of the union's right to object over the more recent action of the company. In any event, employer's counsel must be *fully* apprised of all evidence that might arguably constitute a "past practice." In fact, past practice is an extremely important consideration in arbitration hearings. A review of arbitrators' opinions shows that arbitrators, to enforce past practice, will generally consider the following criteria:

- The activity or procedure represents a consistent response to a given set of circumstances.
- It must have occurred a reasonable number of times over a reasonably extended period of time.
- It was expressly or tacitly known to both parties.
- It has had the express or tacit agreement of both parties.

These criteria have been generally accepted and applied by arbitrators. However, while these criteria are generally accepted, it is clear that arbitrators are free to pick and choose among the factors and even to add others. Arbitrators may also consider whether a "working condition" or an employee benefit is involved. For example, some arbitrators allow modifications or changes when basic management functions, such as the direction of the workforce, are at issue. However, benefits which have personal value, and are not directly involved with methods of operating the workforce, generally are considered binding and not subject to modification or change.

Review Records from Related Administrative Hearings (e.g., Unemployment)

In some instances, the arbitration hearing is *not* the first hearing involving the dispute. For example, in a discharge case, the grievant may initially file for unemployment compensation. That hearing is usually conducted prior to an arbitration hearing. Counsel for the employer should obtain any tape recording, transcript, or documents submitted by the grievant or union in these matters. In some instances, other types of hearings (for example, criminal proceedings) may also provide information to the company. For example, if an employee has been discharged for assaulting a fellow employee, it is possible that an assault and battery charge was lodged against the grievant. The court records should be searched to obtain any relevant information or admissions. Needless to say, a search of unemployment records and other court records to the extent available may prove to be a very fruitful source for favorable information to the company.

Interview Witnesses

Generally there are two types of witnesses that employer's counsel may need to interview. Those witnesses who are outside the bargaining unit (clerical, supervisors, management), and those individuals who are within the bargaining unit. Obviously, interviewing witnesses outside the bargaining unit presents an easier task since they are exclusively under the control of the employer and should have no divided loyalties. Listed below are the types of witnesses that counsel may need at the arbitration:

- *Involved witnesses*: Interview, for example, any eyewitnesses to the event; the supervisor who made the decision to terminate, and so on.
- *Explanatory witnesses*: Interview, for example, in a contract interpretation case, the negotiator of the contract to cast light on the meaning of certain contract language.
- *Foundation witnesses*: Interview individuals who may be needed to establish the authenticity of documents, such as time records.
- *Expert witnesses*: Interview and prepare experts, such as safety specialists, writing experts, and so on.

One of the more difficult questions confronting counsel for the employer is whether to interview bargaining unit employee(s) and, ultimately, whether a bargaining unit employee should be used as a witness. Of course, it is inadvisable and should be unnecessary to interview the grievant because during the initial stages of the incident and throughout the grievance procedure, the company should have obtained the grievant's version of events. However, in preparation for the arbitration, it may be necessary for employer's counsel to interview potential witnesses who come from the bargaining unit. Obviously, due to the sensitivity and potential problems of requesting a bargaining unit employee to testify (potentially adverse), care needs to be taken to determine whether this can be avoided. However, if counsel has to interview such witness, counsel should follow these guidelines:

- Always make sure more than one company representative attends the interview so that if a charge of intimidation or coercion is made, there is someone else who can collaborate the truth of the events. In addition, in the event that the bargaining unit employee is called to testify and subsequently changes his or her story, there will be another person to testify of the previous statement. Most arbitrators will allow company witnesses to testify as to the changed version.
- Communicate the purpose of the questioning and emphasize that the company only wants the employee to tell the truth.
- Tell the employee that his or her interview is voluntary.
- Emphasize that there will be no reprisals for not talking with the company, and no favors granted for talking with the company.
- Make sure the questioning occurs in a noncoercive context.
- In those instances where it is determined that an employee may be subjected to harassment, talk with the employee after hours. The employee should be assured that his presence is voluntary and that he may be called as a witness.
- In discussing the possibility of calling an employee as a witness, advise the employee that a subpoena can be issued and that it is the usual procedure of employer's counsel to issue a subpoena so that all involved in the arbitration proceeding will understand that he is testifying pursuant to a subpoena.
- Take detailed notes of the meeting (or have the potential witness handwrite or voluntarily sign an affidavit).

CRITICAL POINTS TO CONSIDER REGARDING SETTLEMENT AND SETTLEMENT DISCUSSIONS

Once information has been gathered and witnesses interviewed, it is important for employer's counsel to make a complete and realistic evaluation of the merits of the company's case. Counsel should analyze both the union's position—its strength, and weaknesses, as well as the company's position—its strengths and weaknesses. Candor and objectivity in making this evaluation are critical. Many times, counsel, particularly if inexperienced, cannot be objective because of a supervisor's or personnel director's personal enthusiasm for pushing the case. This will ultimately result in a disservice both to the company and to counsel (the disservice will be highlighted when the arbitration case is lost). In fact, in almost every arbitration case, counsel should explore the possibility of settlement with company representatives. Counsel for the employer will want to discuss a cost benefit analysis in dollar terms, as well as a cost benefit analysis regarding the principle of the case. In addition, although the union may not have made any settlement overtures previously, it may, just prior to the

Exhibit 15-1
SAMPLE SETTLEMENT AGREEMENT AND RELEASE

This settlement agreement and release is agreed to by company, union local, and grievant. The parties agree as follows:

1. Company agrees to pay to grievant $000.00 less appropriate deductions.
2. Grievant, in consideration of the payment, for himself and his successors, assigns, agents and representatives forever releases company and its agents and representatives from any and all manners of actions, suits, contracts, grievances, arbitrations, claims and demands of any nature at law or in equity, whether known or unknown for damages or losses whatsoever arising from or relating in any manner to the employment relationship (including his termination from the company) between company and grievant.
3. The Union as a duly authorized representative of grievant also agrees to release and completely discharge the company, its agents and representatives from all manners of actions, suits, contracts, grievances, arbitrations, claims and demands of any nature at law or in equity arising from or relating in any manner to grievant's discharge.
4. Grievant will not seek employment in the future with company.
5. The company and the Union agree that this settlement agreement and discussions leading to it will not be used in any manner in any arbitration or any other proceeding of any type, and it is agreed that this settlement agreement and release is entered into for the sole purpose of compromising disputed claims, the validity and existence of which are expressly denied by company.
6. This settlement agreement is confidential and will not be disclosed to anyone by the grievant, union, or company other than for the purpose of enforcing this agreement. (Except the parties may state that the matter has been "settled.")

The undersigned state that they have carefully read each of the above six paragraphs of this agreement and understand and agree with its provisions.

hearing, contact the company to determine whether there is any interest in settlement. Whether the settlement discussions are initiated by a union representative or by employer's counsel, the following points should be considered when discussing settlement:

- Emphasize that the discussions are just that: settlement discussions and, as such, what is said during the settlement discussions will not be used during any arbitration proceeding
- Use this as an opportunity to probe the union's case further, including potential union witnesses
- Emphasize weaknesses in the union's case
- Emphasize that if the case is to be settled, it needs to be settled prior to the company spending any further time and money in preparation, and that if the case is to be settled, hopefully it can be settled before the parties will be required to pay an arbitrator's cancellation fee (many arbitrators now charge cancellation fees if the arbitration is cancelled within a certain number of days—typically 7 to 14 days prior to the scheduled hearing date)

If several grievances are pending, make sure that you discuss each case on its own merits, as opposed to discussing "tradeoff among grievances or arbitrations." A union has the duty to fairly represent each employee and the obligation to review each case on its own merits. As a result, although a number of cases may be dealt with during settlement discussions, it is important that counsel for the employer not inadvertently induce a union into a discussion regarding a trade-off among arbitration cases.

- Determine whether the case can be settled on a nonprecedential basis. The authors have determined that clients are more willing to settle a case, if the settlement cannot be used in any future hearing, including any future arbitration hearing. Thus, a settlement agreement should clearly establish the non-precedential nature of the agreement. Either a short form or a much longer version of the settlement agreement can be used. The authors have used both versions. Exhibit 15-1 illustrates a sample short form version.

PRACTICAL STEPS TO SUCCESSFULLY PREPARE FOR AN ARBITRATION CASE

Preparing an arbitration case is similar in many respects to preparation for a trial. The key differences are significant: arbitration normally involves little, if any, discovery or motion practice. However, the goal in arbitration and litigation are identical: to persuade the judge or arbitrator that your client's position is the correct one. Experienced counsel have probably developed their own techniques to prepare for the hearing. However, the authors have set forth below a preparation checklist, followed by discussion of each point, to guide counsel preparing for an arbitration hearing.

Preparation for Arbitration Hearing Checklist

- Develop chronological history of facts
- Prepare exhibits—joint/company
- Develop theory of case
- Research and review prior arbitration awards
- Draft statement of the issue(s)/submission agreement
- Prepare opening statement
- List potential witnesses
- Prepare direct examination of each witness
- Prepare cross-examination of union witnesses
- Discuss arbitration hearing details with clients/company
- Contact union regarding who will be absent from plant on day of arbitration hearing
- Consider possible evidentiary questions
- Meet with company officials to review key points
- Prepare witnesses to testify
- Contact court reporter

Arbitrators have observed that in many instances cases are lost simply because of lack of preparation. Therefore, counsel must be fully prepared to effectively represent the company. Counsel must do the following:

Develop Chronological History of the Facts

Counsel should develop a chronology of essential occurrences relying on information from both witnesses and documentation. All "facts" and documents should be arranged in chronological order. The chronology should begin with the incident to the filing of the grievance. And, a chronology should be outlined from the filing of the grievance to the filing of the demand for arbitration. This will provide counsel with the necessary background information to prepare the remainder of his or her case.

Prepare Exhibits—Joint/Company

Counsel needs to prepare three copies of each document the company intends to use as exhibits. Counsel should have the original available at the hearing, but should make one copy for the arbitrator, one copy for the company, and one copy for the union. Typically, exhibits that will be submitted jointly will be:

1. Current collective bargaining agreement
2. Grievance
3. Company response

Counsel needs to review all other documents and prepare necessary copies to be introduced at the hearing. In addition, exhibits, such as photographs or unusual or graphics exhibits, must be prepared for introduction at the hearing.

Develop Theory of the Case

Counsel should always prepare a fully developed theory of the case. This is accomplished by reviewing the chronological sequence of events and all documentation, including collective bargaining agreements, past practices, and so on.

Research Prior Arbitration Awards

Counsel should review any prior arbitration awards pertaining to the company or, more broadly, review any prior arbitration awards regarding the same or similar issues published in such publications as *Labor Arbitration Reports* (by BNA) or some other service. Obviously, reviewing these cases will help sharpen counsel's focus on the issue, as well as assist in developing the company's theory of the case. Although counsel must remember that unless an arbitration award is actually interpreting the agreement between the company and the union on the same issue (which is most unlikely), all arbitration awards are of persuasive value only. There is no concept of precedent in labor arbitration. Quite simply, this is because labor arbitration is considered an extension of the collective bargaining process, and, thus, each case must revolve around the particular agreement and relationship between the parties involved in the dispute.

Draft Statement of Issues/Submission Agreement

Typically, at the beginning of any arbitration hearing, an arbitrator will attempt to have the parties stipulate the issue to be decided by the arbitrator. As a result, counsel must give forethought to the exact issue he or she believes the arbitrator should decide. Counsel should draft the issue as narrowly as possible. However, in most instances, union counsel will not agree to a narrowly defined issue, but will only stipulate to an ultimate issue—such as, in a discharge case, whether the grievant was discharged for just cause, and, if not, what is the remedy? In addition, it is good practice for counsel for the employer to draft a submission agreement. Quite simply, draft a statement of the issue to be jointly submitted (signed by both parties) which will be the issue to be decided by the arbitrator. Some contracts may very well require a submission agreement; however, most do not. Even if the contract does not specifically require one, it is good practice for counsel to draft a submission agreement. Of course, any submission agreement submitted to counsel for the employer should be carefully analyzed before signing.

Prepare an Opening Statement

Opening statements are of critical importance, particularly if counsel for the employer in consultation with the company has decided to proceed without a court reporter. It must be remembered that during the testimony phase of the hearing, the arbitrator must simultaneously take notes, rule on points of evidence, admit documents, observe demeanor, and keep order. And, counsel must always remember that the arbitrator knows nothing about the case prior to the beginning of the hearing, and the arbitrator will not be able to understand the overall case through the "piece meal" process of witnesses—that's why the opening statement is so important. The opening statement gives counsel an opportunity to speak directly to the arbitrator at a pace designed to allow the arbitrator to take thorough, clear notes. The opening statement should be brief, but it should give the arbitrator a clear picture of what the case is about and the company's position. Typically, the authors have found that a chronological sequence presentation is very helpful for the arbitrator in understanding the case. Thus, counsel must, prior to the hearing, develop a carefully prepared opening statement.

Develop List of Witnesses

Counsel should have reviewed his or her notes and all other information and evidence to develop a list of witnesses and determine the sequence in which they will be called at the hearing.

Prepare Direct Examination of Witnesses

Counsel should, for example, prepare a file for each witness that includes any document or exhibit that the witness may testify about. In addition, counsel must prepare his or her outline of the direct testimony to be elicited from the witness. The authors cannot stress enough that effort must be put into the development of this outline and the preparation of the witness for the hearing.

Prepare Cross-examination of Adverse Witnesses

In addition to preparing a file on each witness counsel intends to present at the arbitration hearing, counsel must also be prepared to cross-examine each adverse witness. As a result, a "file" on each adverse witness should be opened and any potential documents or cross-examination questions pertaining to this witness should be developed and prepared prior to the arbitration hearing.

Confer with Company Officials About the Final Details

Counsel should consult with company representatives regarding details of the hearing, such as: hotel room, use of a court reporter, and whether post-hearing briefs will not be filed in the case. Companies do not like surprises, particularly when the surprises cost money. As a result, these matters should be reviewed with the company prior to the arbitration hearing.

Contact Union Regarding Employees Who Will Be Absent from Work

Counsel or some company representative should contact a union representative or steward regarding any employee who may be absent from the plant to testify at the arbitration hearing. Obviously, the company has the right to know who will be absent so it can plan its work. Of course, this also is a way to confirm who the potential union witnesses may be at the arbitration hearing.

Prepare for Potential Evidentiary Questions

While rules of evidence (with regard to form and admissibility) are relaxed and not strictly applied in arbitration hearings, most arbitrators will, out of the requirements of a fair hearing, still allow objections to evidence on certain grounds and potentially bar the evidence or prohibit the other side from proceeding in a certain manner. Raising objections, although in most instances overruled by the arbitrator (or allowed admittance for "what they are worth"), serves a useful purpose because it requires the arbitrator to examine the challenged evidence with more skepticism. Thus, as will be discussed later, counsel needs to be aware of certain objections to questions, answers, documents, or other conduct that may occur at the hearing.

Meet with Company Officials Regarding Case.

Prior to the arbitration, counsel should meet with other company representatives to discuss the key points of the case. In this way, in the event that there has been an oversight or a mistake by counsel, it can be corrected prior to the hearing, rather than face the embarrassment of a mistake at the hearing.

Prepare Witnesses to Testify.

Prior to the arbitration hearing, counsel should meet with company witnesses and prepare them for testifying. Counsel should explain what the case is about, where the hearing will be held, and although an arbitration hearing is more informal than the courtroom, the arbitrator is still like a judge with the authority to administer the oath. Counsel at this point has already prepared through review of documents and prior interview, an outline of the questions he will ask the witness. These questions usually begin with general questions regarding background of the individual, to more specific questions regarding the specific events. Counsel should "walk through" each question he intends to ask the witness on direct examination. Then, counsel needs to prepare the witness for every conceivable subject that may arise upon cross-examination. Counsel should actually go through each direct examination and practice cross-examination with his own witness. In this way, the witness will be more confident in his testimony.

Guidelines for witnesses. Furthermore, witnesses need to be instructed to:

- Tell the truth. Explain that you, as counsel, cannot ask leading questions. And the witness is not to volunteer information, but to only answer the question.
- Answer the question as directly and as simply as possible. On cross-examination, to listen to the question very carefully and to hesitate slightly before answering (this gives the witness the opportunity to consider the answer to the question, as well as the opportunity for counsel to raise any potential objection).
- Keep in mind that witnesses always have the right to have the question repeated or to state that they do not understand the question and would like it repeated.
- Answer questions posed by the arbitrator directly and to make eye contact with the arbitrator.
- Remember that if the witness has made a mistake in his testimony, then he has the right to say, for example on cross-examination, that he mis-spoke when he said such and such and that his answer should have been . . .
- Keep in mind that the witness will be put under oath and that he is to tell the truth at the arbitration hearing.

CRITICAL CHECKLIST FOR HANDLING PRE-HEARING MATTERS

Immediately prior to the commencement of the arbitration hearing and usually outside the presence of the arbitrator, counsel for the employer should engage in a pre-hearing discussion with counsel for the union about the following:

- Joint exhibits
- Submission agreement
- Stipulation of facts
- Transcript of hearing
- Filing of post-hearing briefs

Preparing Joint Exhibits

Counsel should discuss with union counsel the possibility of entering into the arbitration record joint exhibits. Typically, counsel for the employer and union will agree that the following are admissible as joint exhibits:

1. collective bargaining agreement
2. grievance
3. company response

Other possible joint exhibits include company's rules and regulations, grievance statement of receipt of rules and regulations, and photographs depicting (if relevant) areas of the workplace.

Preparing a Submission Agreement

Obviously, an important matter to deal with initially is whether the parties can stipulate to a statement of the issue—that is, the precise issue the arbitrator is to decide. This stipulation is what the parties seek an answer to and no other. If the submission agreement can be done in writing, prior to the hearing, this will expedite the hearing and will guide the arbitrator throughout the hearing. If no such written submission agreement can be reached, counsel should explore the possibility of simply an oral stipulation at the commencement of the hearing. If not, then counsel for the employer will simply have to reach an "agreement" with union counsel that the arbitrator will have to decide the issue either at the beginning of the hearing or be left to ultimately determine the issue as he or she sees it at the conclusion of the arbitration.

Stipulating Undisputed Facts

Although stipulations can be fraught with dangers for an advocate, there may be basic facts or procedures that can be agreed upon prior to the commencement of the arbitration. Typically, stipulations would include, for example, that the grievance is properly submitted to the arbitrator, i.e., it is both procedurally and substantively arbitrable.

Deciding How to Use the Transcript

Counsel for the employer should have made a decision whether a transcript will be used. If a transcript is to be used, obviously, the court reporter will be present. However, if not already agreed upon, counsel for the company should discuss with counsel for the union whether the union desires to get a copy of the transcript and, if not controlled by the terms of the collective bargaining agreement, should discuss with counsel for the union the sharing of the cost not only for the copy of the transcript, but also splitting the cost of the court reporter.

Filing Post-Hearing Briefs

Although a discussion of post-hearing briefs can be held until the end of the arbitration hearing, it is a better practice for counsel for the employer to discuss with union counsel that post-hearing briefs will be filed. And the schedule for filing post-hearing briefs should be agreed upon and stipulated either at the beginning of the hearing or at the end of the hearing.

16 Master Strategies in Handling a Case Before an Arbitrator

Arbitration hearings are less formal than courtroom hearings. Often an arbitration simply takes place in a conference room with table and chairs. Present will be the arbitrator, the representatives for the company, the union, and the respective witnesses. In addition, it is, as stated earlier, usually in the company's best interest to have a court reporter (or at least a tape recorder) present. This allows the company to obtain a transcript, which is very useful in preparing a post-hearing brief. In addition, a transcript is also essential in the event that the company decides to appeal an arbitrator's award.

PRE-HEARING CHECKLIST

There are a number of matters that need to be dealt with prior to the actual beginning of the hearing. Set forth below, followed by a more detailed discussion, is a pre-hearing checklist:

- Request for subpoenas
- Joint exhibits
- Submission agreement/Statement of issue
- Stipulations

- Transcript
- Oath for witnesses
- Request to sequester witnesses
- Request to advise witnesses not to discuss testimony
- Burden of Proof Issues

Prior to the actual commencement of the arbitration hearing, a number of preliminary matters should be resolved or at least an attempt should be made to resolve them. Usually, outside the presence of the arbitrator, counsel for the company and counsel for the union consider marking those exhibits that may be introduced as joint exhibits. In addition, a submission agreement should be signed or an attempt made to stipulate as to the statement of issue. Furthermore, counsel for the employer should discuss with union counsel the issue of whether they will want a copy of the transcript and the union obligation (if it's not set forth in the collective bargaining agreement) to pay its share.

Critical Issues to Discuss with Arbitrator

At the commencement of the arbitration hearing the arbitrator will go on the record and typically state the names of the respective parties and ask that the parties sign a list of who will be the representatives and who will be witnesses.

If counsel has decided to call a bargaining unit witness, counsel usually will at least by this time have prepared a subpoena and request that the arbitrator sign for its issuance. Once signed, then the subpoena can be delivered to the employee at the company premises, or typically what occurs is that the employee is asked to be at the hearing room and that he or she will be supplied with a subpoena at that time. In some instances it may be necessary even prior to the commencement of the arbitration hearing to ask an arbitrator to sign and issue a subpoena.

Then either counsel or the arbitrator will ask for joint exhibits. (It should be pointed out that there is no absolute order in which these preliminary issues are discussed with the arbitrator.) Counsel can then submit to the arbitrator those documents that have been marked as joint exhibits.

Next, an attempt should be made to stipulate to certain matters. Obviously, if the parties have reached an agreement or signed a submission agreement, that should be entered in the record as an exhibit or stated for the record. If not, counsel should attempt to narrowly define the issue; failing to reach an agreement then typically agreement will be reached that the arbitrator will frame the issue after reviewing the entire record. In addition, counsel should also inform the arbitrator of any stipulations, e.g., the matter is properly before the arbitrator (procedurally and substantively arbitrable).

Counsel should then request that the witnesses be sworn. The swearing of witnesses is preferred in order to impress upon the witness that he or she must tell the truth. In addition, counsel should request of the arbitrator (and if necessary remind the arbitrator at the appropriate time) that when a witness has concluded his or her testimony, that the witness be reminded not to discuss the testimony with other witnesses who may be sequestered.

In addition, a request should be made of the arbitrator to sequester adverse witnesses. This, of course, ensures that no witness hears the testimony of another witness until each has concluded testifying. Of course, requesting that adverse witnesses be excluded will also result in companies' collaborating witnesses being sequestered, too.

Of course, the union representative has the right to be present, as well as the grievant. In addition, the company has the right to have counsel present and a representative designated by counsel (or some other person whose presence is necessary to the presentation of the case).

In addition, counsel should discuss with the arbitrator the nature of the case, i.e., discipline, contract interpretation, or dual. Counsel should mention the type of case and that with a certain type of case there are certain burdens of going forward and burdens of proof. For example, in contract interpretation cases arbitrators usually adopt a standard that it is the moving party (usually the union who has the responsibility to prove that by preponderance of the evidence that its interpretation of the contract is more likely than not to be the correct one. In a discharge case it is the employer that carries the burden (usually clear and convincing, although some arbitrators require beyond a reasonable doubt, particularly if the matter involves a potential criminal offense) and requires the company to not only proceed, but to carry its proper quantum of proof. In addition, in discharge cases, counsel for the employer often overlooks a critical matter—that the discharge may also turn on contract interpretation. In those instances counsel should point out that although the company may bear the ultimate responsibility for proving that the discharge was proper, if it turns on contract interpretation, the union still must bear its burden of establishing that its interpretation is more likely than not the correct one. For example, an employee is discharged allegedly during the employee's probationary period. The union alleges that the employee was not discharged during the probationary period, but was outside the probationary period and, in any event, the company did not have just cause to discharge the employee. Thus, there may be two issues: (1) whether the employee was or was not a probationary employee, and (2) if he was not a probationary employee, whether the employee was discharged for just cause. Counsel needs to be aware and argue that on the first issue it is the union that bears the burden of proving that its interpretation is the proper one, while only on the second issue the company carries the burden of proving by a preponderance of clear and convincing evidence that the employee was discharged for just cause.

TECHNIQUES AND TACTICS IN PRESENTING THE COMPANY'S CASE TO AN ARBITRATOR

Once the preliminary matters have been resolved, the arbitrator will open the hearing and "go on the record." At this juncture the arbitrator will (after any preliminary remarks and receiving any off-the-record stipulations) ask for opening statements. Typically, it is the moving party who bears the burden of going forward (and giving the initial opening statement). Thus, in a contract interpretation case it is the union that is almost always the moving party and, as a result, carries with it not only the burden of establishing a sufficient quantum of proof, but also carries with it the burden of going forward. However, in discipline/discharge cases, arbitrators (although not required to do so) uniformly require the employer to proceed and justify the discipline meted out with a sufficient quantum of proof. Thus, typically, it will be the employer's counsel who will give the opening statement and proceed with presenting of witnesses in discipline/discharge cases, whereas in contract interpretation cases it is typically the union that will be required to proceed first. Although, it must be remembered that arbitration proceedings are more informal than a court proceeding and the order and burden will ultimately be left to the decision of the arbitrator.

Making the Opening Statement

The hearing will start with an opening statement. It cannot be stressed enough that the opening statement is an extremely important part of a company's case. Remember, during the testimony phase of the hearing, the arbitrator must, in addition to making notes, rule on points of evidence, admit documents, observe demeanor, and keep order. Thus, it is sometimes difficult for the arbitrator to appreciate the full thrust of the advocate's position, as that position emerges through question-and-answer testimony. By contrast, the opening statement gives the advocate an opportunity to speak directly to the arbitrator, at a pace designed to allow the arbitrator to take thorough, clear notes. As a result, opening statements are extremely important. To be effective, an opening statement should:

- Be brief
- Set forth the essential background facts about the company
- Set forth essential facts leading to the grievance
- Set forth the relevant contract clauses and/or rules and regulations on which the party intends to rely
- Be done in a businesslike, straightforward manner avoiding histrionics

Counsel needs to be careful during opening statement so as not to misstate or make claims that will not be supported by the proof during the arbitration hearing. If the arbitrator fails to miss the inconsistency, surely, counsel for the other side will point this out in a closing argument or in post-hearing brief. In addition, in presenting the essential facts, a straightforward, chronological sequence of the facts is one that is most helpful to the arbitrator in understanding the case.

Presenting Witnesses

Typically, counsel for the company will have the opportunity to present his or her witnesses. Each witness will be sworn and then, upon direct examination, questions regarding who, what and when will be asked of the witness. However, in some instances, counsel for the employer may desire to call a bargaining unit employee or even the grievant as an adverse witness. Counsel should consider this approach because it robs the grievant of the opportunity to listen to all witnesses and then shape his or her response to what he has heard. However, many arbitrators will not allow counsel for the employer to call the grievant as the first witness. If counsel decides to call the grievant as the first witness, he or she should be prepared to have the request rejected by the arbitrator. It would certainly appear that the better rule would be to allow the parties to call those witnesses they deem necessary for the presentation of their case, including the right of the company to call as its first witness the grievant. Analogous are those matters before the National Labor Relations Board where counsel for the General Counsel will call the key company witness as part of the development of its case. In addition, counsel for the employer should have interviewed any bargaining unit witness it intends to call as a witness in its case. Because of the pressures of testifying against a fellow bargaining unit employee, many witnesses may not be as candid in their presentation once called to testify (particularly when he or she is sitting across the table from his or her union representative). The interview, of course, has given the company the opportunity to call a company witness to testify that the bargaining unit employee has now changed his story from the story that was given to the company during its interview.

Conducting Direct Examination of Witnesses

Direct examination of witnesses and presentation of those witnesses to the arbitrator is critical to the company's case. Experienced representatives realize that arbitrations are won on the strengths of their case in chief, not on the weaknesses of their opponent's case. Therefore, an effective direct examination that clearly, logically and persuasively sets forth the facts of the company's case will usually have the greatest impact on the outcome of the arbitration. The purpose of direct examination must be kept in mind. It should elicit from the witness, in a clear and logical fashion, the observation and activities of the witness so that the arbitrator can understand and remember the witness's testimony. Typically the first witness is one who can testify to the background of the company, the relevant documents and overview of the events, if possible. Whether this first witness is giving a broad overview, or is giving a narrow slice of the facts, it is critical that the first witness be strong. The very best impression counsel can leave is one created by a strong first witness following an effective opening statement. In addition, the final witness should also be strong, which could include recalling the first witness for additional testimony. Each witness should be asked some general background information regarding himself and his position with the company and then lead into the information he or she may have regarding the particular events or issue to be decided by the arbitrator.

Using Documents and Exhibits

Obviously, if a document has been marked as a joint exhibit, it will, of course, be used without objection during arbitration hearing. Counsel must remember that although he may use copies, under the best evidence rule, he or she must have available the original of the document that he or she attempts to introduce at the hearing. Most arbitrators deal with exhibits in an informal manner. Exhibits can be admitted and, typically, an arbitrator will not require the same formal steps that might be required in a court of law. However, counsel should follow the following procedure:

1. Show the document to the witness and ask the witness to identify the document
2. After identified, mark the exhibit as, "company exhibit number 1" (for example)
3. Provide a copy to the union and the arbitrator and request that the exhibit be received into evidence and marked as "employer exhibit number 1." (Remember, have the original available)

Although the presentation of documents or evidence does not follow this sequence in every case, and although there may be instances where authenticity will be questioned, typically, this procedure is one that will be followed in an arbitration proceeding.

HELPFUL HINTS REGARDING EVIDENTIARY CONSIDERATIONS

The most important thing to remember about testimony before an arbitrator is that observance of the legal rules of evidence is not required absent a contractually adopted rule that evidentiary rules must be followed. However, although not required, arbitrators will use the rules as guidelines and the Federal Mediation Conciliation Service and the American Arbitration Association suggest that the arbitrator should, as a matter of fairness, be the judge of evidentiary matters. For example, the American Arbitration Association's voluntary labor arbitration rules provide as follows:

> The parties may offer such evidence as they desire and shall produce such additional evidence as the arbitrator may deem necessary to an understanding and determination of the dispute.... The arbitrator shall be the judge of the relevancy and materiality of the evidence offered, and conformity to legal rules of evidence shall not be necessary. All evidence shall be taken in the presence of all the arbitrators and all of the parties except where any of the parties is absent, in default, or has waived its right to be present.

Like the American Arbitration Association rules, the Federal Mediation Conciliation has also promulgated rules. The FMCS's rule regarding the admissibility of evidence is less specific and provides in pertinent part:

> All proceedings shall be in conformity with the contractual obligation of the parties.... The conduct of the arbitration proceeding is under the arbitrator's control and the arbitrator's decision is to be based on the evidence and testimony presented at the hearing....

Thus, even though not required, arbitrators (as reflected in the AAA and FMCS rules) require that some modicum of attention be paid to the very basic rules of evidence. For example, it is possible to get most arbitrators to sustain an objection to leading questions of counsel's own witnesses. Gross examples of hearsay are also usually excluded, although most arbitrators are quick to seize upon an argument that even remotely sounds like an exception to the hearsay rule. Arbitrators are particularly fond of telling the parties that they will admit evidence "for what it is worth" preferring to use the rules of evidence not for the purpose of determining admissibility, but rather for the purpose of determining weight (i.e., what it is worth). Therefore, even if the objection will be overruled, it is necessary for counsel to interpose well-founded objections, if for no other reason than to alert the arbitrator that he or she should not give much weight to the testimony that is about to follow.

TECHNIQUES AND TACTICS IN ASSERTING EVIDENTIARY OBJECTIONS

Obviously, as indicated previously, strict rules of evidence are not applicable. However, there are certain evidentiary objections that counsel will commonly encounter, or should make at an arbitration hearing because advocates, particularly those with less experience, may attempt to introduce improper evidence or argument at the hearing. Evidentiary objections to such improper evidence or argument, when well grounded, serve a useful purpose even if overruled, because the arbitrator will be alerted to examine the evidence or argument which has been objected to more closely and may discount it completely or "give it very little worth." The objections described in the following sections are the ones that counsel will commonly encounter or should be prepared to assert at the arbitration hearing. The employer's counsel must not be afraid to assert these but should also be judicious in the use of objections.

Objecting because of a Leading Question

A leading question suggests the answer to the witness. Such questions usually require a yes or no answer. This is generally improper during direct examination and counsel for the employer should immediately object. For example,

> Union Counsel: "Joe, when the foreman was issuing you a written warning, didn't he tell you that he was tired of you filing grievance after grievance?"
>
> Company Counsel: "Objection, Mr. Arbitrator, counsel is leading the witness. Let's hear what the witness has to say, not counsel."

The question that should have been asked is merely, "What did the foreman say to you?"

Many times union counsel tries to lead a witness. Company counsel must be insistent that union counsel not be allowed to lead. Of course, it would be improper for company counsel to lead his or her witnesses. Note, however, that leading questions are generally permissible on preliminary or introductory matters that are not in dispute in order to help facilitate or speed up the process. Such introductory matters may include, for example, a witness' name, address, job title, department, seniority, and relationship to another witness. Remember that this objection only applies on direct examination. Leading questions that require a yes or no answer are permissible and generally the best tactic when conducting cross-examination.

Objecting because Opposing Counsel Is Signaling the Witness

In some instances counsel for the union, either intentionally or inadvertently, after asking a question will shake his or her head in such a manner that it suggests the answer to the witness. Or, if not counsel, some other person in the room may through the shaking of their head or some other method of signaling (for example, by the use of their hands) may try to indicate an answer. Counsel must object to such signaling.

> Union Advocate: after asking a question starts nodding his/her head in such a fashion to indicate yes.
>
> Company Advocate: "Mr. Arbitrator, I object to union counsel's nodding her head in such a manner as to suggest the answer to the witness. I request that counsel be instructed to refrain from such action."

Objecting because the Witness Has Given a Narrative Answer

A narrative answer is objectionable because it allows a witness to inject inadmissible evidence into the arbitration without giving company counsel a reasonable opportunity to make proper objections. Counsel must make sure that the union counsel asks specific questions to which the witness can give reasonably succinct answers. If the company counsel regards the question as objectionable, he should interpose the objection.

> Union Counsel: "Ms. Jones, tell us everything that happened during the week you had the accident with the forklift."
>
> Company Counsel: "Objection, Mr. Arbitrator, the question calls for a narrative answer."

A timely objection will require union counsel to ask specific questions that will break the narrative into specific parts.

Objecting to Questions Calling for the Witness' Opinion

Opinions are generally improper unless the witness has some special expertise. Any question that asks a witness for the witness' opinion or to guess is objectionable. For example:

> Union Advocate: "Joe, as a result of your heart attack, were there any job duties that you were no longer able to perform?"
>
> Company Advocate: "I object to the question. It calls for the witness to express an opinion."

Objecting to Repetitive (Asked and Answered) Questions

Questions and answers previously made by the same party should not be repeated. The objection may be made when union counsel repeats the same question to the same witness, or to additional witnesses asked to testify and answer the same question after others have answered the question, and there is no dispute about the answer.

Typically, union counsel will ask a question and get an answer and then, in an attempt to place an undue emphasis upon the answer, will slightly rephrase the question to elicit the same answer. This is still subject to the same objection, because although the new question may not be identical to the previous question, the new question still calls for the same answer that was previously given by the witness. Under such circumstances, the objection should be made:

> "Objection, Mr. Arbitrator, that question has already been asked and answered."

Objecting to Speculative Questions

Any question that asks the witness to speculate or guess is improper. For example:

> Union Counsel: "Joe, isn't it possible that if the stack of boxes had been back beyond the yellow line that you would have been able to avoid hitting the boxes?"
>
> Company Counsel: "Objection, question calls for speculation on the witness' part."

Objecting to Confusing, Misleading, Ambiguous, Vague, or Unintelligible Questions

A proper question must be specific enough so that a witness can know with some certainty the information being elicited by the questioner. For example (when you're not sure which meeting counsel is referring to):

> Union Advocate: "Who was present at that meeting?"
>
> Company Advocate: "Objection, the question is unclear. Which meeting is counsel referring to?"

Objecting to Questions that Depend on Hearsay

Hearsay is secondary evidence. That is, evidence offered by a witness of what he heard another person say, which is offered to prove the truth of what was said. The classic definition of hearsay is, "A statement, other than one made by the declarant [witness], while testifying at the trial or hearing, offered in evidence to prove the truth of the matter asserted." The hearsay rule and its exceptions, are lengthy and will not be set forth except in its most simplified fashion here. However, counsel for the company can spot the most obvious hearsay problem when a question calls for a witness to testify as to out-of-court statements made by someone else. For example:

> Union Advocate: "Well, Joe, what did your fellow employee Harry tell you about the forklift accident?"

This question (if no exception to the hearsay rule applies, such as admissions by parties) is objectionable.

> Company Counsel: "Objection, Mr. Arbitrator, hearsay."

PRACTICAL POINTS TO CONSIDER FOR CLOSING STATEMENT AND/OR POST-HEARING BRIEFS

At the conclusion of the hearing the arbitrator will give an opportunity for closing arguments. But if post-hearing briefs are to be submitted, it is not likely that a closing argument will be necessary. In fact, counsel for the company should argue that if post-hearing briefs are to be filed, that a closing argument is unnecessary. If union counsel insists on a closing argument, then company counsel, after listening to closing argument, may want to make a brief closing statement by setting forth those aspects favorable to the company's case and pointing out the weaknesses of the union's arguments and adequacy of the union's evidence. However, although certainly not required (and in simple cases even unnecessary), most company advocates will choose to file a post-hearing brief. Unless time limits for filing briefs are set forth in the collective bargaining agreement, the parties may, in discussion with the arbitrator, agree upon any reasonable amount of time. Typically, company counsel will follow the 30/30 rule. That is, 30 days from receipt of the transcript (if one is to be made), the parties will postmark briefs and the arbitrator will render his or her award 30 days after receipt of the briefs. In addition, company counsel should usually request that the arbitrator "cross" the briefs. That is, rather than sending an arbitrator a copy of the brief and sending a copy direct to the union, an original and one copy should be sent to the arbitrator requesting that the arbitrator then supply the opposing party with its brief after the arbitrator has received both company and union briefs. These arrangements should be made on the record and agreement reached on the procedure and time limits for filing briefs.

There is a difference of opinion among advocates as to whether the parties should file a post-hearing brief. The authors recommend that a post-hearing brief be filed. Not only is it possible that the arbitrator has not picked up on every contradiction or inconsistency in the union's testimony, it is possible that only after a careful review of the transcript will company counsel pick up on all weaknesses in the union's position. As a result, most company counsel will make a decision to file a post-hearing brief. A brief should set forth the facts, analyze the pertinent contract provisions, and argue why, based on the facts and pertinent contract provisions, the company should prevail. The biggest mistake (other than mis-statements or errors) is for an advocate to state the facts, re-state the facts, and then repeat the facts. Repeating and stating the facts more than once does not necessarily make your brief more persuasive.

A brief will typically include:

- Cover Page
- Table of Contents
- Introduction
- Statement of the Issue
- Pertinent Contract Provisions
- Burden of Proof Section (If issue is non-disciplinary matter or union has argued in a discipline case a high standard of proof)
- Statement of Background Facts
- Argument Section

- Response to Union Assertions
- Conclusion and Statement of Remedy Requested

Once the brief has been filed and received by company counsel, the union's brief should be carefully reviewed. Typically, company counsel will not find it necessary to respond to a union brief, particularly if the company's brief has (as it should) anticipated the arguments set forth in the union's brief. However, there are instances where the company's brief could not anticipate a gross misstatement in the union's brief, then counsel should file a reply brief.

EVALUATION OF THE AWARD AND APPEAL CONSIDERATIONS

Counsel should carefully review the arbitrator's award immediately upon receipt and ask company representatives to also review the award. Obviously, an award that is favorable to the company will not require a great deal of discussion. However, if the award is adverse, then a decision must be made as to whether an appeal will be made to the courts to review the arbitrator's award. As previously indicated, the courts show great deference to an arbitrator's award. With that in mind, company counsel may want to take a half step by requesting that the arbitrator reconsider his or her award. This is particulasrly so if it appears that the arbitrator has relied upon some statement made by the union in its brief that simply is not supported by the record. In addition, on some occasions the arbitrator has, counsel believes, overlooked a significant argument and counsel may want to request that the arbitrator reconsider. However, it must be remembered that the time for appeal will not be extended because of a request for reconsideration. That is so because of the general rule that once an arbitrator has rendered his or her award, the arbitrator is *functus officio* and has no power to proceed further. (In fact, this general rule appears to be reflected in the arbitrator's code of professional responsibility where it provides: "no clarification or interpretation of an award is permissible without the consent of the parties.") As a result, counsel must be very careful that if he or she intends to file an appeal, to do so within the time limitations from the rendering of the initial award and not from the arbitrator's response to a request for reconsideration. Current court cases will need to be reviewed to determine the time for appeal, although it appears that the courts will apply the most closely analogous state statute of limitations.

III How to Litigate Breaches of Labor and Employment Contracts

17 Strategic Steps to Follow in Litigating Section 301 and Section 303 Lawsuits

Since most collective bargaining contracts contain a grievance-arbitration procedure, providing that disputes arising from a breach of the agreement are subject to arbitration, employers have not been inundated with breach of labor contract lawsuits in federal or state courts through the years. Yet both employers and unions, as well as employees, may file such lawsuits for breach of a labor agreement in certain cases.

Typically, it is the employee, rather than an employer or the union, who files a lawsuit for breach of a labor agreement. In many instances, employees file lawsuits for a breach of a collective bargaining agreement on the grounds that the union and/or the employer has violated the terms of the labor agreement with respect to rates of pay, seniority rights, unpaid wages or benefits, working conditions, and so forth.

The courts require employees to first attempt to exhaust their potential remedies under the grievance and arbitration provision of the labor agreement as a prerequisite to filing such a cause of action, unless the employees can satisfactorily demonstrate to the court that an attempt to exhaust such administrative remedies would be futile, or unless employees can show the court that the union breached its duty to fairly represent the employee's claim under the grievance-arbitration procedure of the bargaining agreement. Employees are also provided a forum through Section 8 of the National Labor Relations Act to seek redress for a union's failure to fairly represent employees in the form of an unfair labor practice charge against the union.

Probably a majority of lawsuits filed by employees against a union and their employer is in the form of a failure to fairly represent cause of action. In such cases, the applicable court must decide two issues:

- did the union violate its duty of fair representation to the plaintiff employee, or employees?
- did the employer's action violate the collective bargaining agreement?

Were the court in such situation to determine that the union did not violate its duty of fair representation, the court would be compelled to dismiss the employee's cause of action because the employer could not be held to have violated the contract unless the union violated its duty of fair representation to the employee(s).

On the other hand, were the court to conclude that the union did violate its duty to fairly represent the employee(s) subject to the contract, the court then would be compelled to determine whether the employer breached the terms and conditions of the contract, such as discharging an employee without just cause.

Given these prerequisites in a failure-to-fairly-represent type lawsuit in which the employer becomes a defendant in addition to the union being a defendant, the employer's counsel has two major defenses and thus should attempt to prove that the union did not fail to fairly represent the employee or employees, in question, and secondly, if such were the case, the employer nonetheless did not violate the terms and conditions of the labor agreement.

Such suits as a failure to fairly represent cause of action are typically brought under Section 301 of the Labor Management Relations Act in the nature of a breach of collective bargaining contract claim. The employer's counsel and representatives should bear in mind that the U.S. Supreme Court has held that the time limit in which an employee may file a Section 301 failure-to-fairly-represent lawsuit is the law in the applicable state in which the action is filed. In a failure to fairly represent a case under Section 301 where the lawsuit does not arise out of a prior arbitration proceeding, different courts apply different statutes of limitations. Some apply the six months time limit used by the NLRB in filing an unfair labor practice under Section 10(b) of the National Labor Relations Act, as amended, while other courts apply the applicable state statutes of limitations. Some apply the personal injury prescriptive statutes; others, the breach of contracts statutes. Given the inconsistencies of the courts in applying statutes of limitations relative to Section 301 failure-to-fairly-represent cases, the employer's counsel and other representatives should research thoroughly the applicable prescriptive period in the state or federal court in which the action is brought and whether such action did, or did not, arise out of a previous arbitration proceeding.

The employer's counsel and other representatives should also appreciate the amount of monetary damages allowable in failure-to-fairly-represent type lawsuits. As a general proposition, the courts limit the applicable employee, or employees, to their actual damages—typically assessed against the employer for violation of the labor agreement for improper discharge, and so on, and attorneys' fees, court costs, and other such litigation expenses against the applicable union for failure to fairly represent. However, a U.S. Supreme Court ruling has suggested the damages awarded to the employee(s) should be apportioned between the employer and the union. The employer's counsel would be well served to check the most recent cases concerning the apportionment of such awards if he or she desires to use such information as part of its defense to such a lawsuit.

The employer's counsel and other representatives should appreciate that the courts typically do not permit punitive damages to be rewarded to an employee-plaintiff who has been successful in a failure-to-fairly-represent lawsuit.

PROCEDURAL CONSIDERATIONS IN LITIGATING SECTION 301 LAWSUITS

Section 301 of the National Labor Relations Act, as amended, provides that causes of action for violations of collective bargaining contracts between an employer and a union, or between unions, or by employees against a union and/or employer, may be brought in any federal district of the United States. In addition, lawsuits to enjoin a strike in violation of a collective bargaining agreement and for resultant damages caused by the strike may be brought under Section 301, as well. Likewise, union lawsuits against employers to enforce an employer's agreement to collect union dues or the failure to pay fringe benefit contributions under the terms and conditions of a collective bargaining contract are examples of lawsuits frequently filed under Section 301.

In most cases, however, whenever a collective bargaining agreement provides for binding arbitration, both the union and employer, as parties to the collective bargaining agreement, are bound by an arbitrator's decision.

Section 301 states that its provisions preempt state laws and regulations over breach of collective bargaining contracts. Thus, the employer's counsel that desires to file a cause of action against a union for breach of a labor agreement must bring such cause of action through Section 301, rather than defer to state laws on the subject. However, the employer's counsel should also note that Section 301 only extends jurisdiction to those employers who fall under the jurisdiction of the National Labor Relations Act. To the extent that Section 301 would not provide jurisdiction in which to prosecute a breach of a labor agreement, a party to the agreement would not be precluded to bring an action for a breach of such labor contract under an applicable state or local law.

The employer's counsel should understand that Section 301 may be the only relief to an employer for a breach of a labor agreement in that many such agreements do not provide that the employer may grieve to final arbitration under the terms of the agreement, only that the union and employees are permitted to grieve to final arbitration under the contract. That does not mean to suggest that some modern collective bargaining contract does not provide an equal right on the part of the employer to the grievance and arbitration mechanism of the contract, but historically, that was not the typical arrangement.

The employer's counsel and representative should review a labor agreement closely if pursuing a breach of collective bargaining contract against a union and/or employees for damages resulting from a wildcat strike in terms of property damages, lost profits, lost customers, and so on, so as to become aware of whether the action should be processed through the grievance and arbitration provisions of the labor agreement or through Section 301.

The employer's counsel should know, also, that the damages to which the employer may be entitled for a breach of a no-strike clause in a labor agreement may be collected only from the union that is a party to the contract, not from individual union members. As a result, the employer may be precluded from recovering any damages whatsoever as in a case where union members engage in a wildcat strike that the union in question neither authorized nor condoned, as the employer may be unable to demonstrate sufficiently to the applicable court that the union was responsible for the strike. Strategically, the employer's counsel should be prepared to use its discovery to show otherwise.

Although most lawsuits filed by employers under Section 301 are for damages resulting from a violation of a no-strike clause by the union and employees, the employer's counsel should appreciate that Section 301 permits the employer to file for other types of violations under the applicable labor agreement as well. For example, should an employer be victimized by an organized slowdown as orchestrated by the union in question, the employer may proceed for lost production and other such damages, if it can substantiate its proof to carry such action.

Should an employer and its counsel wish to pursue a Section 301 lawsuit for breach of a labor agreement, forum shopping may become part of their strategy. If so, the employer's counsel and other representatives should know that Section 301 permits an action under its provisions to be filed either in a state court or a federal district court. Irrespective, however, the provisions of Section 301 are controlling as to the substantive features of the lawsuit as well as most procedural aspects. As discussed earlier, when there is no language controlling the time frame in which a party may bring an action under a federal statute, most courts defer to the state statutes of limitation analogous to the cause of action, meaning that most courts typically regard lawsuits brought under Section 301 by employers against a union for violation of a labor agreement as just that—breach of contract—and attempt to apply the applicable state statute of limitations regarding contract breaches. Since Section 301 is silent as to the timetable in which such an action may be brought, the employer's counsel should be most cautious about filing a timely proceeding since courts vary in their interpretations as to the time limits in which to file such actions with respect to the nature and subject matter of the cause of action as well as with respect to whether state statutes are even controlling in some Section 301 lawsuits.

The employer's counsel and other representatives should also keep in mind that although Section 301 actions typically limit recoverable damages to actual damages such as lost profits, property damages, and so on. The courts have interpreted Section 301 suits not to prohibit the employer from recovering other damages, such as punitive damages for violent conduct occurring as a result of a union's actions.

The employer's counsel should appreciate that the preemption doctrine of the National Labor Relations Act, as amended, is somewhat inapplicable to Section 301 causes of action. In a case in which the defendants' conduct has constituted both a breach of a labor agreement and an unfair labor practice, both the NLRB, with respect to the unfair labor practice charge and the applicable court, with respect to the Section 301 suit, will have jurisdiction to remedy the violation in their own respective jurisdictions.

As discussed in Chapter 12, employers that have binding arbitration clauses to adjudicate violations of a no-strike clause in a labor agreement may also use the injunctive provisions of Section 301 to enjoin wildcat strikes, assuming all the *Boys Market* criteria are met.

Employers may be called upon to defend Section 301 lawsuits, as well as prosecute such causes of actions.

TECHNIQUES AND TACTICS TO USE WHEN LITIGATING SECTION 303 LAWSUITS

The employer's counsel and other representatives should know some of the procedural and substantive features of Section 303 of the Labor Management Relations Act, should their employer be victimized and suffer damages as a result of a union's secondary boycott activities.

In a nutshell, Section 303 provides that a party whose business or property is injured by reason of secondary boycott activities may institute a lawsuit to recover damages for such injuries in any federal district court, subject to the limitations and provisions of Section 301 without satisfying the diversity or "amount in controversy" jurisdictional requirements to bring an action in federal court.

Section 303 lawsuits, being governed by the procedural and substantive guidelines of Section 301 cause of actions, may be brought in either federal or state courts but, in either case, the applicable court must apply the substantive provisions of Section 303, a federal statute. Also, since Section 303 lawsuits are governed by the substantive and procedural provisions of Section 301, the employer's or owner's recovery is limited to the actual damages suffered by such party, unless damages have resulted from violent conduct caused by secondary boycotting, in which case, the employer or owner may seek and recover whatever other damages, such as punitive damages, as are recoverable through the statutes and common law of the state in which the action is brought, or statutes and common law in other states that control such matters.

Although employers may use the injunctive provisions of Section 301 to enjoin unions from violating provisions of a collective bargaining contract, such as seeking an injunction against a wildcat strike in contravention of a no-strike clause—assuming the *Boys Market* and other applicable requirements are met—in addition to a recovery for actual damages under Section 301, employers are not given injunctive rights under Section 303 to enjoin secondary boycotts. The employer has an indirect procedure to procure an injunction against a secondary boycott, however. The employer's counsel or other representative may file, under Section 8(b)(4)(A), (B) and/or (C), an unfair labor practice charge with the NLRB with respect to the secondary boycott and, if the NLRB finds merit in the employer's charge, the NLRB then has the power and authority to apply for injunctive relief under its Section 10 provisions.

HELPFUL HINTS TO CONSIDER IN DEFENDING A BREACH OF A COLLECTIVE BARGAINING AGREEMENT CLAIM

It is the employer that typically assumes the role of plaintiff in Section 301 lawsuits for breach of collective bargaining agreements rather than the union or the employees subject to the agreement. In practical terms, both the union and the employees subject to the contract may seek redress for any breach of the contract by the employer through the grievance and arbitration provisions of the labor agreement, as well as through the unfair labor provisions of the NLRB. Yet, the union and employees that are parties and subject to the provisions of a labor agreement have rights to sue employers for the breach of a labor agreement, assuming certain criteria are met, such as the exhaustion of remedies under the grievance and arbitration provisions of the labor agreement.

Since a union typically has a right to remedy a breach of a labor agreement through the grievance and arbitration provisions of a labor agreement, or through the unfair labor provisions of the National Labor Relations Act, as amended, an employer is not likely to be the defendant in a Section 301 lawsuit by a union to remedy the breach. However, should it become such a defendant, its counsel should be prepared to argue forcefully that the union had not exhausted the grievance and arbitration provisions of the labor agreement and therefore is foreclosed from filing a Section 301 action against the employer.

The employer's counsel and representatives should be alert that unions apparently are attempting to use Section 301 lawsuits more in recent times, not necessarily to recover monetary damages, but rather to enjoin employers from violating the union's fundamental rights and interests under the labor agreement. Assuming that unions are able to overcome an employer's defense to such actions, such as that the union has not exhausted its administrative remedies under the grievance and arbitration provisions of the labor agreement prior to filing the injunctive pleadings under Section 301, the employer's counsel and other representatives should anticipate more injunctions in the future, such as injunctions against the employer's closing or relocating its operations, injunctions against the employer's unilateral implementation of work schedule changes, injunctions against an employer's interference with internal union affairs, and so forth.

As implicitly suggested above, should such injunctions arise, the employer's primary and most meaningful defensive argument would be that the union failed to exhaust its remedies under the grievance and arbitration provisions of the labor agreement and, thus, precluded from filing for injunctive relief.

18 Litigation Strategies in Breach of Written Employment Contract Claims

Although there now are many exceptions to the historic employment-at-will rule that holds an employee without a written employment contract for a fixed duration may be discharged at the will of the employer, which exceptions will be discussed more fully in subsequent chapters, this chapter relates primarily to express written employment contracts for a fixed term. This chapter addresses individual employment contracts as distinguished from collective bargaining contracts that were discussed in the preceding chapter.

EVALUATING ESSENTIAL ELEMENTS OF WRITTEN EMPLOYMENT CONTRACT CLAIMS

Typically, it is the employer that is the defendant, rather than the plaintiff, in breach of individual written employment contracts for a fixed duration. Such individual written employment contracts range from very brief and short agreements involving moderate salaries and benefits for lower and middle management positions to rather comprehensive employment agreements involving complex compensation programs for higher executive members and professional athletes.

Irrespective of the type or length of the written employment contract, its duration, and the salary and benefit arrangements in such documents, the employer's counsel and representatives should understand that for such documents to be enforced, they must contain the essential elements of a contract between the employee and the employer.

Perhaps, the first principle applicable to written employment contracts that should be discussed is that known as the statute-of-frauds. Almost all states have adopted the historic statute-of-frauds principle either as a result of statutory enactment or by way of judicial decisions. The statute-of-frauds principle holds, generally, that any agreement not to be performed within the space of one year from its origin shall not be enforceable unless the agreement has been reduced to a written instrument. There seemingly have been as many exceptions to the statute-of-frauds principle as there have been to the employment-at-will rule. Creative attorneys attempt to get around the statute-of-frauds through such arguments as that the agreement could have been performed within one year, assuming the employer went out of business or the employee died. Many judges, in an effort to find a way to enforce honestly made agreements, frequently accept and adopt such arguments. As will be discussed in subsequent chapters relative to implied employment agreements, judges have been equally as willing to make exceptions to the statute-of-frauds principle in employment agreements.

Some state courts have refused to adopt the many employment-at-will and statute-of-frauds exceptions in employment contract matters and the more resourceful management attorney should fully use these principles in defense of an alleged breach of an oral or implied employment contract in those jurisdictions where such principles are still recognized.

As suggested at the beginning of this chapter, another defense that may be arguable from the employer's perspective in a breach of employment contract is whether the contract is for a specific and fixed term of duration. Since many conservative jurisdictions still maintain that a written employment contract without a fixed term of duration has no more significance than an oral agreement in terms of the employment-at-will doctrine, an employer's counsel may well be remiss not to seek to dismiss a lawsuit on such grounds if the alleged agreement did not contain a fixed period of time during which it would be effective. The employer's counsel and representative should likewise be aware that many courts treat employment contracts for a "lifetime" and contracts for "permanent employment" as contracts of fixed durations and outside the employment-at-will principle.

The employer's counsel and representatives should also be aware of other essential elements of a written employment contract, such as those described in the following sections.

Offer and Acceptance of a Written Employment Agreement

The offer and acceptance essentials with respect to a written employment agreement may well be inferred by the actions of the employer and employee even if the language in the written employment contract does not specifically spell out such terms. Judges also may take judicial notice that employees typically do not work and perform services for an employer unless they expect to be paid for such work and services, and further, that employers do not readily expect employees to work and perform services for the employer without the employer understanding that the employee expects to be paid for such work. Just because an employer makes an offer of employment to a prospective employee does not imply that the employer may not revoke the offer prior to the employee's acceptance of it. The offer may also be deemed to have lapsed after a reasonable period of time without an acceptance by the other party. The employer may also condition the time limit of the offer by stipulating that the offer will terminate upon the occurrence of a certain event or circumstance.

Consideration

Inasmuch as a promise of something beneficial to the other party or detrimental to the party so promising is sufficient consideration to constitute a contract, the amount, or adequacy, of the consideration is not material or relevant in breach of contract cases. As such, since in most employment contractual matters, the employee promises services and the employer promises the employee payment for such services, the question of "consideration" is seldom a major issue in an employment contract dispute.

Mutuality of Assent

The mutuality of assent element of a written employment contract fundamentally means there is a "meeting of the minds" between the employer and the employee as to terms and conditions of the contract into which they have entered. Both parties must share the understanding of what the offer entails. Should the employer's counsel be in a position to demonstrate to an applicable court in a breach of written employment claim that the employee held some secret intent or interpretation not contemplated by the employer and extraneous to what a reasonable person could infer, then a failure of mutuality of assent and/or a failure of mutuality of obligation argument may well prevail as a proper defense to such alleged breach to the effect that there was no contract in the first place.

Pre-existing Duty to Perform

Whenever an individual promises to perform whatever he or she is already legally obligated to perform or to do something he or she is already legally required to do, such a promise does not provide adequate consideration to support another party's promise. Inasmuch as almost any consideration as the basis for a promise will be considered adequate consideration, this defense is not always as successful as one might imagine. Yet, to the extent that such a factual situation would present itself, the employer's counsel and representatives may want to explore its use as a defense in a breach of employment contract claim.

Certainty of Contractual Language.

Vague language and uncertainty in contractual terms such as relates to the time or place of performance, the services to be rendered, the products to be delivered or the monetary remuneration or compensation for such services or products typically causes such a contract to be unenforceable. The employer's counsel, again, should explore the language of a contract carefully to determine whether uncertainty as to the contractual terms will provide on arguable defense to a breach of a written employment claim.

GOOD CAUSE DEFENSES TO ASSERT IN BREACH OF WRITTEN EMPLOYMENT CLAIMS

The employer typically is the defendant in most breach of employment contract claims.

Probably most such claims center upon the employee's dismissal for failure to perform.

The employer and its executive management members should be most careful in formulating the language as to the reason the employee was dismissed from employment, if such will later constitute the basis of the alleged breach.

Most written employment contracts contain a clause with respect to how the contract may be terminated, such as by mutual consent, death of one or more parties, disability, and so forth. Also listed as one of the grounds that will permit the contracting employer to terminate the contract is where the contracting employee is discharged from his or her employment for good or just cause, such as a failure to meet the performance standards of the job so assigned to the employee or for misconduct on the part of the employee.

Since most written employment contracts do not go into great detail and establish as to what specific omission or commission on the part of the employee will be sufficient grounds to dismiss the employee and terminate the written employment agreement, the question or issue as to whether the employer had good or just cause in the dismissal frequently is reserved for a court, jury, or arbitrator to determine. The employer's counsel who drafts such contracts for the employer may want to explore the possibility of including more specific language with respect to what may constitute good or just cause for discharge of the employee, but should use couching and discretionary language to demonstrate that such specifics are just examples and are not all inclusive of all the reasons that may constitute grounds for discharge. Many employers have lost lawsuits and arbitration cases with respect to discharge and disciplinary cases in that some contract or policy stated that certain conduct or behavior would constitute sufficient grounds for disciplinary action or discharge without using caveats within the language to demonstrate that those specific infractions noted were only examples and not exclusive grounds for whatever action to be taken.

Where a written employment contract does not contain specific language as to what constitutes sufficient grounds to discharge an employee and terminate the agreement, judges, juries and arbitrators who may be called on to decide such question, if a claim is processed to such a forum to hear, typically refer to what a labor arbitrator looks to in determining good or just cause. Thus, the employer's counsel should be prepared to defend the case under such traditional standards of just cause, although courts may be somewhat less restrictive than labor arbitrators in using such standards. The employer's counsel should be prepared to meet the most stringent guidelines in preparing its defense to a breach of written employment contract if the basis for termination of the contract centers on the question of "just cause."

The employer's counsel, in order to prepare its good cause defense, should have a clear understanding of what courts and arbitrators look to in determining whether good cause exists.

Asserting Misconduct as Good Cause for Dismissal of an Employee

With respect to misconduct, good cause for dismissal may be defined, generally, as a failure of the employee to perform his or her employment duties in such a manner as an ordinary prudent person would have performed under the same or similar circumstances and conditions. Inasmuch as the question of "good cause" typically is a jury question—a question of fact—should the breach of a written employment agreement proceed to a jury trial, one can only imagine what interpretation a jury might give to "just cause."

The following behaviors describe some of the more recognizable examples of misconduct that juries, as well as courts and arbitrators, acknowledge as going outside the bounds of ordinary prudent behavior.

Dishonesty. Falsification of documents, expense reports, sales sheets, and so on, is one of the more recognizable reasons given to justify grounds for discharging an employee. Given the propensity of employees to sue employers for defamation, employer's management members who have the responsibility of documenting discharge cases where falsification or dishonesty is the grounds for termination should explore language other than that which would accuse the employee of theft or some other criminal act. For example, the management member effecting the discharge may be prudent to state that the employee was discharged for discrepancies for which he or she was unable to adequately justify or explain, rather than a statement to the effect that the employee was discharged for theft, falsification, or dishonesty.

Insubordination. Judges, juries, and arbitrators acknowledge a refusal of an employee to perform a duty or task within the scope of his or her employment duties—and particularly duties and tasks for which the employee has been properly trained and in which previously performed by the employee—to constitute grounds for dismissal unless the refusal or intentional failure to perform is based on unsafe, illegal, or immoral reasons.

Gross Negligence. An employer may also defend a breach of written employment contract resulting from the discharge of the contracting employee on the grounds that the discharge of the employee was based on negligence or gross negligence.

Intentional or Negligent Destruction of Property. Somewhat analogous to gross negligence, noted above, an employer's counsel may assert grounds for the dismissal of the employee, if applicable, upon the fact that the employee destroyed the property of the employer, or perhaps, the property of fellow employees, as a result of his or her negligent and/or intentional behavior.

Intoxication. Although alcohol and drug abuse laws and policies may impact upon a decision as to whether an employee may or should be discharged for intoxication, it has been recognized as a justifiable cause for discharge, historically. Although some laws and policies may require certain rehabilitation measures and/or reasonable accommodation for chronic alcohol or drug abuses, most such laws do not prohibit employers from taking disciplinary action against employees for intoxication on the job.

Disruptive Conduct. Most employers do not condone fighting, fisticuffs, verbal, or physical abuse in the workplace. Just because an employee may have a written employment agreement with the employer, he or she will not be justified by exercising such behavior and such behavior can well be considered to be so outside the bounds of permissible conduct as to give good cause for the dismissal of the employee engaged in such behavior.

Criminal Activity. An employee's intentional behavior that would impute criminal activity to the employer, such as a failure to comply with some regulatory statute, could well justify the employer in the dismissal of the employee and a termination of any existing written employment contract between the employee and the employer. Obviously, theft or embezzlement of the employer's products or property and other related criminal activities against the employer would constitute good cause grounds for dismissal.

Conduct That Endangers the Employer's Interest. Judges, juries, and arbitrators also recognize that an employee's conduct that endangers the employer's reputation and injures the employer's business interest may well serve as a justifiable ground for a just cause dismissal and a termination of a written employment contract between the employee and the employer.

Safety Violations. Certain federal and state laws, such as OSHA, require employers to provide and maintain a safe workplace for employees and others who may be on the employer's property. The employer also has an inherent and common law obligation to implement and maintain safety rules and policies. Given those obligations, employer's managers who discharge employees for safety violations, even to the degree that such dismissal would effectively terminate the employee's written employment contract with the employer, should be in a position to defend their actions, particularly if the employer's counsel can substantiate that the safety policies have been publicized and disseminated to all such employees, that the safety rules are reasonable and proper, and that they have been consistently enforced by the employer.

Defending the Employer's Rationale for Discharging an Employee

As implied before, most employee dismissals fall within two categories: *dismissal for misconduct or dismissal for performance deficiencies.* Whenever an employee's employment is covered in the language of a written employment agreement, and the employee is terminated for failure to meet or comply with the performance standards of his or her job, then the employer's rationale for discharge should be defensible, particularly if such performance standards are reasonable, safe, legal, and moral.

Should an employer's counsel be faced with defending a breach of written employment agreement as a result of an employee's performance problems, most likely the defense will be centered around one or more of the reasons described in the following areas.

Quantity of Work. Here, the employer's position is that the employee did not put in the adequate and sufficient time in which to produce the product or service required by the quantitative performance standards of the job; or if the employee did expend the proper time in which to meet the quantitative standards of the job, the employee's skills were not sufficient to accomplish the task.

Quality of Work. Written employment contracts imply, if no such language in the contract specifically expresses, that the employee subject to the contract will not only perform a sufficient quantity of work, but that the work so performed will be performed in a quality and satisfactory manner.

Disloyalty. Most written employment contracts in today's workplace relate to management, professional, technical and sales positions, all areas in which the employee typically is entrusted with confidential and important information relating to the internal operational and business needs of the organization. Thus, a duty of loyalty is somewhat implied—if not expressed—in written employment contracts.

Other Grounds. There are numerous other grounds, based on misconduct or failure to perform, that may constitute more than good cause grounds to discharge an employee and terminate any existing written employment contract between the employer and the employee, but those discussed above are the most frequent ones that arise.

SETTLEMENT STRATEGIES TO CONSIDER IN BREACH OF WRITTEN EMPLOYMENT CONTRACT CLAIMS

Should the employer's counsel be faced with a breach of a written employment contract lawsuit resulting from the discharge of an employee or based upon some other alleged violation of the contract by the employer—and particularly, if the employer's defenses do not appear to be very promising—the employer's counsel may want to explore settlement of the dispute in order to cut its risk in court, or through arbitration, and also save litigation and legal costs. Should the written employment contract contain provisions for severance compensation, the employer's counsel should examine the provision closely to discern its impact upon settlement and ultimate litigation.

Sometimes when relationships deteriorate to the extent that one party wants to terminate the relationship and the contract, so does the other party, but frequently pride, revenge, and other such emotions impede settlement possibilities.

Should settlement be a viable objective for the employer in a breach of written employment agreement claim or lawsuit, whether to save money or cut risks, the employer's counsel should attempt, as his or her objective, to have the employment contract mutually modified or rescinded to accommodate the terms and conditions of the settlement. Strategically, the employer's counsel should negotiate specific items at issue to reach the desired language for a modification or recision of the contract objective.

As with any negotiations, the employer's approach should be that of a "win-win" strategy, meaning that the employer's counsel who negotiates with the employee and/or his or her representative, should attempt to ascertain what the employee reasonably desires, and then explore whether such desires on the part of the employee are reasonable and rational and the odds of the employee being successful in winning them if the matter proceeded to litigation. The employer's next strategic step would be to consider alternative measures that would provide the employee with the results he or she would like to achieve without being overly burdensome to the employer, perhaps such as not contesting an unemployment compensation claim, agreeing to continue certain benefits that may be critical to the employee for a limited period of time, agreeing to pay for outplacement services for the employee, agreeing to extend the severance pay for an additional, but limited, period of time, agreeing to waive rights to counterclaims, agreeing not to give a negative reference letter, and so on.

Irrespective of the settlement process to achieve, or attempt to achieve, a "win-win" result, three strategic factors should not be overlooked by the employer's counsel:

- if settlement is a desired option of the employer, the employer's counsel or representative should entice the employee and/or his representative to explore settlement negotiations as early as possible once the dispute under the contract arises to ensure that the parties do not become too polarized in the beginning to impede settlement negotiations at a later period during which period of time parties frequently become so adversarial as to foreclose settlement discussions
- attempt to negotiate terms and conditions in the settlement agreement that will encourage, rather than discourage, the employee to find employment elsewhere and get on with his or her life
- the employer should reduce all the terms and conditions of the settlement into a written agreement that is chock-full of caveats, waivers and disclaimers to protect the employer from further liability or exposure of any kind regarding the matter and incorporate such agreement into the mutually modified and rescinded employment contract

Should the employee desire to terminate the written employment contract rather than the employer, the employer certainly would have the edge in attempting to negotiate terms and conditions in the settlement agreement and modifications to the contract that would be more in the employer's interest than vice-versa. Rarely is this the case except with respect to very, very successful intercollegiate football coaches.

PROCEDURAL TECHNIQUES TO EXPLORE WHEN DEFENDING BREACH OF WRITTEN EMPLOYMENT CONTRACT LAWSUITS

Should the employer choose not to settle an alleged breach of a written employment contract or fail in an effort to do so and the matter proceeds to litigation, the employer's counsel should consider various procedural defenses to invoke.

Defer the Dispute to Arbitration

Should the terms of the written employment contract provide that any dispute arising from the agreement be resolved through arbitration and that all parties waive their right to proceed to a court of law for a resolution for an alleged breach, or violation of, the agreement, the employer's counsel may want to attempt to have the matter removed from a court of law and deferred to arbitration by the court in which the legal action is brought by the employee. However, the employer's counsel should be aware that states vary in deferring to arbitration clauses in breach of contract cases. Some states hold that parties to a contract may not waive their legal rights to address an alleged breach of contract in a court of law and, irrespective of the language of the employment agreement, a party to the contract may have his or her "day in court" if the party so chooses. Other states uphold such deferral clauses.

Should an employer's counsel desire to resolve an employment contract through arbitration, he or she should study the law in which state the action is brought, or proposed to be brought, and adjust his or her strategy around such laws.

Whether the employer would be better served through arbitration or through the court system is a question that frequently turns on the philosophy of the respective judge or arbitrator, a factor that the employer's counsel should analyze closely before proceeding in one direction to the exclusion of the other, assuming that the desired alternative is permitted.

Try to Preempt Other Employee Claims Against the Employer

The employer's counsel should also be highly sensitive to preemption questions that may arise in a breach of a written employment agreement lawsuit. For example, the employer's counsel may want to argue that any dispute related to the terms and conditions of the contract must be resolved through the procedures specified within the agreement and that the guidelines for resolving such disputes under the agreement preempts the right of the employee to bring the same claim(s) against the employer through another forum, such as through the Equal Employment Opportunity Commission or some state fair employment practice statute. Some states may well hold that the procedure specified under the written agreement as to the resolution of disputes of any alleged breach of contract relating to the agreement preempts other such claims and provides an exclusive remedy for any breach thereunder.

The employer's counsel should explore carefully what the respective state permits, and does not permit, with respect to such preemption questions. The employer's counsel should appreciate that most state and federal judges will not permit language in a written employment contract to preempt the right of an employee to file a claim of discrimination based upon such protected characteristics as race, sex, national origin, etc., with the federal equal employment opportunity commission or a state fair employment practices commission.

The employer's counsel should address each and every avenue of preemption, whether such preemption is provided through the federal labor policy embodied in the National Labor Relations Act, as amended, the Employee Retirement Income Security Act (ERISA), the Occupational Safety and Health Act, local workers' compensation laws, or some similar federal or state statutes.

The employer's counsel may also want to explore state laws relative to whether an unemployment compensation ruling collaterally estops the employee from bringing up the issue in a subsequent breach of a written employment contract claim.

Establish the Forum for the Hearing or Trial

Another procedural matter that could substantially impact upon the outcome of a breach of a written employment contract claim is the forum in which the matter will be heard or tried, particularly as it relates to the subject of conflicting state and federal laws.

Unfortunately, it is the plaintiff to a breach of a written employment contract, rather than the defending party, that initially determines whether he or she is going to file the lawsuit in a state court or a federal court. Also impacting upon the conflict of laws issue is whether the plaintiff has a right, and/or exercises such right, to file its breach of employment contract claim in the state in which the work was to be performed, the state in which the defendant resides or the state in which the plaintiff resides, or a choice of two or more of such forums.

Assuming the employer is the defendant to a breach of a written employment contract, rather than the plaintiff, the employer's counsel should realize that the employer may have some rights also in determining the court in which the matter will be held, particularly if the case is removable from state to federal court under the federal removal procedures.

The federal removal procedures provide that whenever a lawsuit is filed in a state court, but federal jurisdiction is available either in terms of diversity or provided by statutes and/or the U.S. Constitution, the defending party may choose to remove the action to federal court. Basically, a defendant has a right to remove a cause of action filed in state court when the plaintiff could have originally filed it in federal court.

The federal statutes extend jurisdiction to the federal courts in three major ways:

1. diversity of citizenship
2. statutorily
3. constitutionally

Diversity of citizenship jurisdiction. This may be established to either bring an action in federal court, or to remove an action from state court to federal court, by showing that the defendant is not a resident of the same state as the plaintiff and that the amount of money (or alleged damages) in controversy is in excess of $10,000. Typically, since the employer as a defendant in a breach of a written employment contract claim has its principal place of business, or is incorporated, in a state other than the plaintiff-employee's state of residence and inasmuch as most such breach of contract lawsuits seek more than $10,000 in damages, the employer's counsel may well be in a position to seek removal of an action in state court to a federal court based upon diversity of citizenship.

Jurisdiction by federal statute. The employer's counsel may also be in a position to remove a lawsuit filed in state court to federal court by showing the court that the plaintiff had a right to have filed the original suit in federal court by virtue of a federal statute. Depending on the language embodied in the lawsuit, the plaintiff may be able to establish jurisdiction in federal court by virtue of its claims under such federal statutes and bring its action for breach of a written employment contract, an action limited to a state court's jurisdiction, as part of its federal action under the doctrine of pendant jurisdiction, even though the plaintiff would have been unable to have established jurisdiction in federal court in the absence of the claims under such federal statutes. In like manner, the employer's counsel may be privileged to remove an employee's action filed in state court that contains claims asserted based on alleged violations of federal statutes.

Jurisdiction on the basis of constitutional grounds. This primarily relates to federal or state action, rather than private matters.

Determining whether the employer should remove the lawsuit to federal court. Nonetheless, based upon either diversity of citizenship or federal statutes, or both, most employers are in a position to remove breach of written employment contract lawsuits that are filed in state court to federal court. The more basic question is not whether the employer, as a defendant in such a case, has the right to remove the lawsuit from state court to federal court, but rather whether the employer should exercise its right to do so.

Many practical considerations impact this decision, including:

- the relative philosophies of the courts and the personalities and judicial temperament of the respective judges
- whether the case is to be tried before a jury or not and the type of procedure used in the selection of a jury and the types of jurors likely to be available, the geographical areas from which jurors are selected
- the sentiment of the public and local citizens to the employee and what local prejudices, if any, exist against the employer
- the cost and expenses of trying the case in one court compared to the other and the availability of witnesses and the ease or difficulty of making such witnesses available for trial with respect to one court compared to the other
- the relative discovery procedures and evidentiary considerations compared between the two courts
- the legal decisions by the respective courts as they relate to the issues involved in the case at hand and which forums support the employer's legal contentions
- the waiting time for trial (and appeals) relative to the two courts

- the employer's counsel's experience and comfort level relative to previous trials in state and federal courts

Should the employer's counsel conclude that it would be advantageous to remove a breach of a written employment contract cause of action from state court to federal court, the employer's counsel should be aware that the right to removal will be lost if the lawsuit is not removed within 30 days after the lawsuit is served on the defendant. The employer's counsel should also be aware that the plaintiff will waive its right to demand a jury trial in a removal case to federal court if the plaintiff does not make a formal demand for a jury within ten days of receipt of the petition for removal. Thus, the employer's counsel who is not desirous that the matter be tried before a jury may have an additional advantage in removing a breach of employment contract action from state to federal court in terms that the plaintiff's attorney may overlook the ten-day requirement and forfeit the right to a jury.

Strategically, most management attorneys and employer's counsel believe that it is best to defend an employee's breach of employment contract lawsuit before a judge alone, rather than before a judge and jury inasmuch as the vast majority of juries, being working members of society themselves, have a tendency to be prejudiced against employers, especially "deep pocket" employers. The employer's counsel should also be aware that not all federal statutes through which wrongful discharge or discrimination cases are brought even permit the parties the right of a jury to try the facts of the case. In such cases—assuming the employer's counsel subscribes to the idea that the case is better tried without a jury—the employer's counsel should file whatever pleadings necessary to ensure the matter is not tried before a jury if the court fails to do so on its own. Where the cause of action is of the type that permits a jury to hear and decide the factual issues, the employer's counsel may nonetheless prefer the matter be tried in federal court rather than state court, and exercise its removal rights, inasmuch as a federal jury requires a unanimous verdict where many state court juries do not.

The employer's counsel should also attempt to restrict the employee to a state most favorable to the employer's position should the employee attempt to pursue a cause of action in a state that has questionable jurisdiction over the breach of written employment contract claim. Basically, the considerations noted above with respect to removal cases should dictate the more favorable state in which the employer's counsel should attempt to restrict the employee's cause of action, assuming the employer's counsel has legal authority to achieve such objective. Sometimes the parties, themselves, through the language of the written agreement, specify in what state or states a lawsuit may be filed for breach of the agreement. Should such be the case and the state specified be the most favorable state from the employer's perspective, the employer's counsel should take all necessary steps to ensure the plaintiff is restricted to the specified forum.

PRE-TRIAL STRATEGIES IN BREACH OF WRITTEN EMPLOYMENT CONTRACT LAWSUITS

Check Time Limits for Filing Motions and Pleadings

Once the forum has been selected and finalized, the employer's counsel should check closely as to the time limits in which the employer's answer to the complaint must be filed, assuming that the employer is the defendant in the lawsuit. Also, employer's counsel should ascertain time limits imposed by the rules of the court or applicable statutes in which certain motions and pleadings must be filed.

Analyze the Plaintiff's Claims

As with other lawsuits filed in federal and state courts, as well as claims before an arbitrator, the employer-defendant should study the plaintiff's claims carefully and attempt to have dismissed those claims not permissible due to lack of subject matter jurisdiction, preemption, and so on, or when such claim does not state a cause of action for which relief may be obtained in the court. Certainly, the employer's counsel should attempt to analyze any tort claims within a breach of a written employment contract lawsuit and attempt to have such claims dismissed as early as possible in the lawsuit due to a possible recovery of punitive damages that are permissible under most tort actions. Tort actions in the workplace consist of claims of a breach of a noncontractual obligation on the part of the employer, such as a duty on the part of the employer not to libel or slander the employee, unreasonably invade the employee's privacy, assault or batter the employee, and so forth.

The employer's counsel may need additional information and possible admissions by the plaintiff and/or the plaintiff's witnesses, or other parties, before it will be in a position to seek the dismissal of certain claims alleged in the lawsuit by the plaintiff's counsel. The employer's counsel should not be hesitant in using interrogatories, discovery depositions, and any other discovery mechanism permitted by the court in which the action is brought to position itself to seek the dismissal of as many of the plaintiff's claims and allegations as possible. As a general proposition, the party to an action that exhausts discovery efforts the earliest will be in a better position to support his or her motions and contentions than that of the opposing party.

Respond to the Employee's Complaints and File Responses on Time

The employer's counsel should ensure that all pleadings are properly and timely filed, such as the employer's formal answer to the plaintiff's complaint, the plaintiff's pleading that typically initiates his or her lawsuit. Equally important, the employer's answer should either admit or deny each specific allegation in the plaintiff's complaint, or if the employer-defendant has insufficient knowledge to admit or deny an allegation, it should respond to such an effect but with a statement to the effect, that if required to answer such allegation, would deny the allegation and demand proof of the allegation.

The employer's counsel may want to qualify and expand on its denial or admission to a given allegation in the plaintiff's complaint by asserting its position regarding the allegation to the extent local court rules and controlling laws permit such expansion and amplification. The employer's counsel should ensure that all affirmative defenses to the lawsuit are set forth in the employer's answer inasmuch as some courts hold that such affirmative defenses are waived if not raised in the defendant's answer. For example, if the employer contends that the employment agreement alleged to have been breached by the employer was not in writing and could not have been performed within one year, then the employer's counsel should state the employer's contention regarding its statute of frauds defense to the lawsuit as an affirmative defense. In the same manner, if the employer contends that the employee-plaintiff failed to file its complaint within the proper time limit, then the employer's counsel should assert that the plaintiff failed to comply with the applicable statute of limitations. An employer's contention that the employee-plaintiff failed to mitigate his or her damages by not attempting to find another job is one that must be raised as an affirmative defense in many jurisdictions. A failure to exhaust administrative remedies, failure of consideration in the contract, accord and satisfaction, assumption of risk, contributory negligence, truth and privilege (in a slander case), preemption, collateral estoppel, and similar defenses must be asserted affirmatively in most jurisdictions.

Wrap Up Other Pre-Trial Actions

The employer's counsel should not only ensure that all motions it desires to file are filed and filed timely, but also that other pre-trial matters are exhausted as well, such as the issuance of subpoenas to critical witnesses, pre-trial briefs, stipulations, other traditional pre-trial pleadings, and so on, required by the court and its rules of procedure or required by applicable federal, state, or local statutes governing procedural matters.

TRIAL TECHNIQUES AND TACTICS IN A BREACH OF WRITTEN EMPLOYMENT CONTRACT LAWSUIT

One of the most compelling challenges for the employer's counsel in a breach of employment contract cause of action is to attempt to select the very best jurors possible who will be sympathetic to the employer's case if the plaintiff has demanded a jury to hear the case and the defendant has been unable to have the matter heard without a jury.

Inasmuch as state and local courts have varying rules regarding jury selection, suffice it to say that deciding who should be eliminated from a jury via the defendant's preemptory challenges is akin to a "crap shoot." There is simply no scientific method available to guarantee what a juror will and will not do or decide. However, the employer's counsel, in a breach of a written employment contract lawsuit, should obviously "stock" the jury with individuals who relate to management and management positions, who identify with businesses and entrepreneurship and who do not believe that the "world owes everyone a living."

Just as the selection of jurors in a breach of employment lawsuit can well decide the outcome of the case, so can the nature and scope of jury instructions to the jury. The employer's counsel is challenged to be most creative in drafting proposed jury instructions to the court. The employer's counsel may want to research recent cases in the same or other courts to determine whether there is language in other jury instructions that would be helpful to the defendant's case.

At the trial proper, the employer's counsel should consider having co-counsel at his or her counsel's table to assist in the trial and keep up with essential pleadings, exhibits, and so forth. The employer's counsel should also have a well-mannered, polite, and well-dressed member from management to sit at the defendant's counsel table to help humanize the corporate defendant.

Some of the traditional trial techniques that should be used in breach of a written employment contract claim are the same or similar to those previously discussed in Chapters 5 and 10.

19 Strategic Steps to Follow in Defending Implied Employment Contract Claims Arising from Employee Handbooks and Oral Statements

By the late 1800s, the courts throughout the United States had established and accepted the judicially imposed employment-at-will doctrine, sometimes referred to as the termination-at-will doctrine. The states of Louisiana and California codified the doctrine into statutory form.

The employment-at-will doctrine states that without the benefit of a written employment contract for a fixed duration, or unless some statute or judicial exception provides otherwise, an employee may be terminated at the will of the employer. The employment-at-will concept was based upon the contractual principle that contracts must provide consideration and mutuality of obligation—two of the several essential elements of contracts discussed in the preceding chapter. Since an employee could leave the job anytime he or she desired and thereby end the employment relationship, in the absence of a written employment contract providing a certain term or fixed duration of employment, the courts believed strongly by the end of the 1800s, and for most of the 1900s, that employers should be permitted to terminate an employee's employment at its will and end the employment relationship.

Beginning with such labor and employment laws as the National Labor Relations Act of 1935, judges commenced to recognize statutory exceptions to the employment-at-will principle, meaning that were an employee discharged because of union activities or for exercising his or her right to mutual aid or protection that the employee may be entitled to reinstatement, irrespective of whether there was a written employment contract or not.

The employment-at-will doctrine continued to erode in the 1900s through such federal statutes as the Civil Rights Act of 1964, Title VII, the Age Discrimination in Employment Act of 1967, the Occupational Safety and Health Act of 1970, the Rehabilitation Act of 1973, the Employee Retirement and Income Security Act of 1974, the Pregnancy Act of 1978, the Americans With Disabilities Act of 1990 and so on, either in terms of an outright ban on discriminatory discharge and other employment practices because of certain protected characteristics or activities, or a prohibition of discharge in retaliation for exercising rights provided by such statutes.

Inasmuch as state labor and employment laws typically track federal labor and employment laws, almost all states by now have enacted their own versions of the federal laws mentioned above. Add municipal and local ordinances along with federal, state, and local executive orders prohibiting these types of employment practices and behaviors and one can easily detect a continuing erosion of the at-will principle.

However, aside from such tort claims as libel and slander, assault and battery, state courts, and federal courts applying state laws, uniformly rejected any attempts by employees and their attorneys to encroach upon the employment-at-will standard, from a judicial perspective, until the late 1970s and early 1980s. Since that time period, the trend has been for courts to accept common law exceptions to the employment-at-will based upon every conceivable legal theory imaginable by creative plaintiff attorneys. A combination of statutory and judicial exceptions to the employment-at-will doctrine has caused such an erosion to the standard that there are more exceptions to the "at-will" rule than what remains of it.

One of the first judicial or common law exceptions to the employment-at-will doctrine was that language in an employee handbook, manual, or some similar document may give rise to an implied-in-fact contractual obligation on the part of the employer to fulfill such obligation.

A Michigan court was one of the first in the country to uphold such an exception to the employment-at-will rule.

In the 1980 Michigan case of *Touissiant v. Blue Cross & Blue Shield of Michigan*, a judge held that a provision in an employer's personnel policy manual providing that an employee would be discharged only for good cause could form a contractual obligation on the part of the employer to comply with such provision and, thereby, constitute an implied employment contract.

Other state courts followed suit, thereafter, to such an extent that the vast majority of the states now hold that language in an employee or personnel handbook or manual can create an implied contract, the breach of which may provide a cause of action to an employee who suffers from such a breach.

The *Touissiant* and similar court decisions provided an avenue or basis by which other contractual exceptions to the employment-at-will doctrine followed, such as will be discussed in the next few chapters.

HOW TO RECOGNIZE THE SCOPE OF IMPLIED EMPLOYMENT CONTRACTS ARISING FROM ORAL STATEMENTS AND EMPLOYMENT HANDBOOKS

Employer's counsel and representatives should be aware that state courts—and federal courts applying state laws—have found implied contracts arising from employee handbooks and other such documents.

Specifically, courts have found implied contractual obligations arising from language in employee handbooks where an employer promises that it will follow certain guidelines or steps before discharging an employee, such as adhering to a progressive disciplinary procedure.

An implied contract arising from the language in an employee handbook may exist, or be interpreted to exist, outside the discharge area. Here are some examples:

- ***Vacation or severance pay***—Some courts have held that where an employer promises vacation or severance pay to employees in an employee handbook, that the employer is contractually obligated to comply with its commitment, irrespective that no formally written contract exists on the subject matter.
- ***Promotions***—Other courts have held that where an employer promises employees that it will promote employees under certain specified guidelines in an employee handbook or manual, but fails or refuses to abide by such promises, the employee adversely affected by the employer's omission or commission has a cause of action against the employer for a breach of the implied-in-fact contractual obligations.
- ***Seniority rights***—Similar arguments have been advanced by plaintiff attorneys, and adopted by the courts, with respect to a failure of an employer to honor certain seniority rights it had impliedly promised through the language of a personnel policy manual, a breach of implied promises relating to layoff or recall rights, transfer rights, and so.

In fact, there are few, if any, conceivable employer promises in a personnel handbook relative to employment practices that, if not delivered, could not constitute a breach of an implied employment contract on the part of the employer.

Employer's counsel and representatives should also realize that implied employment contracts may arise from promissory language in applications for employment forms, hiring letters, and many documents other than mere employee handbooks.

PRACTICAL PREVENTIVE MEASURES TO PRECLUDE EMPLOYEE HANDBOOKS AND ORAL STATEMENTS FROM BEING INTERPRETED AS IMPLIED CONTRACTS

Several measures should be considered by employers and their counsel and representatives to fortify themselves against potential breach of implied employment contracts arising from promises in employee handbooks and personnel policy manuals.

Eliminate Promises of Job Security from the Employee Handbook

First, the employer should attempt to either rewrite or modify the employee handbook or similar document in such a way as to eliminate promises of job security, to which it is unwilling to meet. The ultimate precaution by which to avoid a claim of breach of an implied contract in an employee handbook would be to eliminate it altogether and announce to employees that all provisions in prior employee handbooks are null and void and without applicability in the future. Many employers have done so, but such reaction may be a little extreme as employee handbooks do serve several positive purposes, such as fair notice and due process.

Omit Extraneous Information from the Employee Handbook

Second, employers should strip extraneous information from an employee handbook that is covered in other documents, such as in summary plan descriptions.

Clarify that the Employee Handbook Is Not an Employment Contract

Third, employers may want to insert disclaimers and waivers in all such documents to the effect that the handbook does not constitute an employment contract, but is merely a guidebook; further, that such handbook does not modify the employees' "employment-at-will" status, that the employer reserves the right to modify or change any or all such policies or procedures enumerated in the handbook, with or without notice to employees, and that no management or supervisory member has any authority to make any employment agreement or arrangement with any individual to the contrary.

The employer's counsel and representatives should draft such disclaimers, if at all, within keeping with previous judicial decisions recognizing such disclaimers and within keeping with state or local statutes that limit the use or impact of such disclaimers. Employer's counsel and representatives who draft such disclaimers are challenged to use language that protects the employer as much as possible against breach of employment contract lawsuits, but also language that does not paint such a negative environment that employees—and prospective employees—would fear the employer.

Employer's counsel and representatives should understand, additionally, that such disclaimers are not fail-safe defenses to breaches of implied employment contract claims arising from employer promises contained in an employee handbook or personnel manual.

Some courts have begun to permit juries or the trier(s) of facts to determine whether there is other language in an employee handbook that would so dilute the intent and impact of the disclaimer language that no such disclaimer, in reality, exists. It does not take very long for an employer's counsel to conclude how a working person's jury may decide such question if given the discretion to do so by the judge in the case.

Additionally, some judges permit the applicable jury or trier of facts to determine whether certain verbal or written statements made by management and supervisory members so dilute the disclaimer language to the extent of its invalidation.

Such disclaimer language, even if helpful as a defense in a breach of implied employment contract cause of action against an employer, would be inapplicable and ineffective as a defense by the employer in defending a wrongful discharge case based on such legal theories (and recognized exceptions to the "at-will" rule in many jurisdictions) as unlawful terminations caused by violations of public policy considerations, fraud, negligence, or intentional infliction of emotional distress. They may also be ineffective as a defense in lawsuits brought by employees against an employer under such other contractual theories as promissory estoppel, independent consideration, breach of covenant of good faith and fair dealing, oral contracts for fixed durations, and so forth.

The employer's counsel should be mindful that some judges will not permit disclaimer clauses in employee handbooks to modify that which existed at the time of the employee's initial hire, thus making such disclaimers applicable only to those employees hired after the promulgation and dissemination of the disclaimer, especially when the earlier handbook relied upon by employees initially hired under its provisions contained no language permitting the employer to so modify its provisions at a later date.

Thus, the employer's counsel and its representatives should be cautious about relying too heavily upon disclaimer clauses in an employee handbook, applications for employment, and similar and related documents. A close study of the law in the applicable state or states so affecting the lawsuit defended by counsel should be analyzed very carefully by the employer's counsel to discern which, if any, of the above-discussed limitations regarding the use of a disclaimer, as a defense in such case, may apply.

Consider Preparing a Written Employment Agreement with Each Employee

Fourth, due to the limited use of disclaimers in employee handbooks, and the tendancy of the courts to imply contractual obligations on the part of employers from not only the language in such a handbook, but also from verbal statements made by management and supervisory members of an employer, there appears to be a trend by many employers to jump on the offensive and enter into a written employment agreement with each and every employee as to exactly the terms and conditions of his or her employment. Such a written employment contract, if accepted and signed by the employee, could place as many limitations and restrictions on the employment relationship as the employer desired as long as such language did not circumvent the employer's statutory obligations and violate public policy principles and considerations.

PRE-TRIAL GUIDELINES IN DEFENDING LEGAL CLAIMS ARISING OUT OF EMPLOYEE HANDBOOKS AND ORAL STATEMENTS

In any type of claim by an employee that he or she has an actionable cause of action against an employer based upon language in an employee handbook or related document, the employer's counsel's initial defense should be that the employee handbook and the language within it does not constitute a written employment contract for a fixed deduction and, therefore, does not provide an exception to the historic employment-at-will doctrine nor alter the employment-at-will relationship of the employee with the employer; meaning, that the court should dismiss the lawsuit in that the allegations do not provide a basis for a cause of action.

Since the vast majority of states do recognize employee handbooks to constitute some type of implied employment contract, should this first argument fail, in whole or in part, the employer's counsel should then commence to prepare its defensive steps during pre-trial around some, or all, of the following arguments.

Defending an Employee Discharge on the Grounds of Good Cause

Assuming the lawsuit is to be based on a claim for wrongful discharge because the employer allegedly discharged the claimant without cause, contrary to the promises contained in an employee handbook, the employer's counsel would want to prepare its defense during pre-trial based upon the proposition that it did so discharge the employee for good cause. In doing so, the employer's counsel should prepare witnesses and documentary evidence to substantiate that the behavior of the claimant was either so heinous to justify dismissal or was the last of a series of infractions justifying termination in keeping with the employer's progressive disciplinary procedure. In either case, the employer's counsel should likewise prepare witnesses and documentary evidence to substantiate that its discharge and/or progressive disciplinary procedure has been consistently enforced as a means of demonstrating to the court that it had not abandoned its right to so discipline and discharge employees through past practice.

Although it is beyond the scope of this book to analyze each state and its relative position with respect to what extent the courts within the state recognize the *Touissiant* theory, the employer's counsel should be aware that states recognizing the theory differ as to standards of proof and burden of proof with respect to such a case. For example, California Courts, via *Foley*, hold that it is necessary to consider the entire relationship of the parties, including the employee's length of service, statements made by management members, the industry practice regarding the subject matter, as well as the specific personnel policies and practices of the employer, within or without an employee handbook or manual, with respect to adjudicating a *Touissiant* cause of action.

Ohio courts recognize the *Touissiant* theory not from an implied-in-fact contract concept, but rather under the promissory estoppel theory that will be discussed in a later chapter.

Some states hold that oral statements as to job security may constitute an implied-in-fact employment contract just as a statement in an employee handbook.

Defending an Employee Lawsuit Claiming Lack of Good Cause for Termination of Employment

Assuming that an employer's counsel and representatives are called upon to defend their employer against a lawsuit by an employee, claiming that he or she was discharged for lack of "good cause" in breach of the employer's promise of job security in an employee handbook, there are several defensive maneuvers the employer's counsel and representatives should consider.

The employer should argue forcefully, through motion or otherwise, that its "just cause" disclaimer in a handbook—assuming one exists—is valid. Just because the authors suggest that many courts are attempting to neutralize disclaimer clauses in employee handbooks does not mean that they are not accepted and recognized as a valid defense in numerous jurisdictions.

The employer's counsel may also argue, if applicable, that the employee voluntarily resigned from the position and was not terminated. Should this be one of counsel's arguments, he or she should be prepared to show that the employee was not constructively discharged by adverse conditions such as sexual harassment, or other acts of coercion or intimidation, safety or toxic conditions.

Another argument, if applicable, that the employer's counsel would want to advance, and sufficiently prepare during pre-trial, would be that the claimant was either temporarily or permanently laid off, not unlike other employees, and thus the termination was for good cause.

The employer's counsel may also want to take full advantage of motion opportunities, discovery possibilities, and stipulations as discussed throughout previous chapters but particularly noted in Chapters 5 and 10.

As part of its pre-trial strategies in defense of a breach of an implied employment contract claim arising out of an employee handbook, the employer's counsel should take advantage of any removal opportunities the employer may have available.

Also, as discussed in the preceding chapter, the employer's counsel should cross check all its potential affirmative defenses such as whether the employee failed to file the lawsuit within the prescribed statute of limitation, or the failure of the plaintiff to have exhausted administrative remedies, failure to mitigate damages, whether accord and satisfaction bars the action in terms that the matter has been settled or whether the employee has signed waivers to such an effect or the employee has accepted severance pay as full settlement, and so forth.

Most management attorneys typically raise the statute of frauds, also, as an affirmative defense to alleged breaches of oral employment contracts as well as to alleged breaches of statements contained in employee handbooks in that neither constitute a written contract, as technically required by the statute of frauds.

Further, as noted in the preceding chapter, the employer's counsel should ensure that all its pleading by way of answer or motions, be filed timely so as to avoid a potential default judgment.

TRIAL TECHNIQUES AND TACTICS IN DEFENDING BREACH OF IMPLIED CONTRACTS ARISING OUT OF EMPLOYEE HANDBOOKS AND ORAL STATEMENTS

Much has been written about general trial techniques in preceding chapters of this book, especially in Chapters 5, 10, and 18. Refer to these chapters for further edification regarding trial practice in the labor and employment law field.

Specifically, with respect to all phases of both trial as well as to pre-trial techniques and tactics in breach of an implied employment contract arising out of an employee handbook, reread and analyze the preceding chapter with respect to a breach of a written employment contract. The reason for such a review is that, essentially, once a judge permits a lawsuit based upon an alleged breach of implied employment contract to go forward (to be tried before judge and jury or the judge, alone), it really becomes the same type of lawsuit as a breach of a written employment contract.

Assuming the employer's counsel is unsuccessful in his or her motion for dismissal or motion for summary judgment, with respect to the employment-at-will and/or disclaimer arguments, and likewise unsuccessful with respect to other pre-trial motions, the most important challenge for the employer's counsel is to pick a jury most favorable to the employer's philosophy, if a jury trial is provided.

The second challenge is to hope for the assignment of a judge most favorably disposed toward the employer's philosophy, or in the alternative, an appellate tribunal that is so disposed toward the employer's philosophy.

In addition, another most important trial safeguard to consider is to ensure that a trial notebook is prepared, that lead counsel is backed up by co-counsel and paralegals to make sure witnesses are prepared, interrogatories, depositions, and other discovery are indexed and properly typed, that all law cases and legal precedent, both procedural and substantive, are organized for quick and easy access, that all subpoenas are issued (and witnesses accounted for), that all stipulations are in tact, and that all documents and exhibits are likewise organized, indexed and prepared in a manner for quick and easy reference and access.

20 Successful Safeguards in Defending a Breach of an Implied Covenant of Good Faith and Fair Dealing Lawsuit

Along with the development and recognition by various state courts throughout the United States of the *Touissiant* theory—that statements in an employee handbook can create an implied employment contract as discussed in the preceding chapter—came a similar theory, that of the employer's breach of its implied covenant of good faith and fair dealing to employees.

More specifically, the covenant of good faith and fair dealing doctrine is said to forbid the discharge of an employee from his or her employment by reason of bad faith or malice or based upon retaliation.

California was one of the first states to adopt the theory, although limiting its applicability later in the *Foley* decision. The 1980 California case of *Cleary v. American Airlines, Inc.* held that every contract, including oral contracts of employment, contains an implied good faith and fair dealing covenant, requiring that neither the employer nor the employee do anything to deprive the other of the benefits of the agreement.

The covenant of good faith and fair dealing was recognized in the state of Montana in the 1983 case of *Gates v. Life of Montana Insurance Co.*, wherein the Montana courts held that the employer-defendant breached its covenant of good faith and fair dealing to the employee-plaintiff when it discharged the employee without warning or hearing. In much the same way that the *Foley* decision limited the applicability of the covenant of good faith and fair dealing doctrine in California, the Montana Wrongful Discharge from Employment Act of 1987 limited somewhat the applicability of the *Gates* decision in Montana.

In an earlier New Hampshire case, *Monge v. Beebe Rubber Co.*, the New Hampshire Supreme Court held that the employer breached its covenant of good faith and fair dealing when it maliciously discharged a female employee by reason of her failure to date a foreman.

An Alaskan appellate court held that an employee stated a cause of action under the theory of a breach of good faith and fair dealing when he alleged that his employer had suspended him for off-duty drug use based on the results of a urine test conducted two weeks prior to the employer's announcement of a new drug policy.

However, much to the satisfaction of employers throughout the nation, the covenant of good faith and fair dealing doctrine did not gain the same momentum as that of the implied contract arising out of employee handbooks theory.

To the extent that it has been recognized by certain states, and likely to be recognized in other states in the future, its main applicability in the labor and employment law context has been with respect to compensation and benefit matters rather than the loss of job security or wrongful discharge.

For example, in the 1977 Massachusetts case of *Fortune v. National Cash Register Co.*, a Massachusetts court held that the employer had breached its covenant of good faith and fair dealing when it discharged a sales manager for the purpose of not having to pay him a $92,000 sales bonus.

In a New York case, a federal court, applying New York law, held that the court would permit the employee-plaintiff to pursue a claim against the employer to recover earned commissions deprived him under the theory of good faith and fair dealing, but not with respect to a wrongful discharge claim. The Oklahoma Supreme Court held, likewise, that the covenant of good faith and fair dealing theory could be used as a basis to establish a cause of action in a case where an insurance agent allegedly had been deprived of future commissions by reason of his dismissal.

Similarly, an Illinois court held that it would recognize an alleged breach of the covenant of good faith and fair dealing theory as a cause of action only as a basis for awarding damages where employees were dismissed to avoid payment of bonuses, commissions, and other benefits due them.

SPECIAL DEFENSIVE CONCERNS RELATIVE TO THE GOOD FAITH AND FAIR DEALING THEORY

Given the historical background of the good faith and fair dealing doctrine, employers and their attorneys and representatives become faced with two major concerns with respect to its applicability in employment type lawsuits, to the extent of the doctrine being recognized—or likely to be recognized—in certain states.

The first concern is that the use of the doctrine, conceptually, has no limitations. The second is that the courts tend to interpret it as a tort rather than a contract.

Dealing With the Lack of Limitations on the Doctrine of Good Faith and Fair Dealing

There have been few, if any, standards to limit the doctrine's applicability. The term good faith, or rather the absence of good faith, is by definition so subjective that it could be applied to any omission or commission of an employer, irrespective of what is understood between the parties or the relative expectations of the parties to each other. Likewise, the term fair dealing, or the absence of fair dealing, is by definition, also, so subjective that a breach of the fair dealing covenant could conceivably be applied to anything a judge and/or a jury desired, especially a jury without jury instructions to limit its applicability in employment cases.

Perhaps, this subjective feature led many courts to reject the applicability of the theory to employment cases. A review of the cases cited in the preceding subheading provides some insight into the danger of the extension of the good faith and fair dealing doctrine as a basis to establish a cause of action in the employment field.

For example, one case provided that the theory could be used to establish wrongful discharge because the employee had not been given a warning or a hearing. The logical question to follow is: how many private sector employers, especially small businesses, have discharged employees in the past for grievous and heinous conduct without providing such employees a prior warning or hearing. Thus, the employer's counsel should recognize that to the extent that he or she is faced with a lawsuit of this nature and to the extent the state in which the lawsuit is brought permits such a cause of action, one of the most difficult obstacles to overcome is to somehow convince the court that the theory must be used only in conformity with prudent business practices and other objective standards, if at all.

Dealing With the Court's Interpretation of the Doctrine of Good Faith and Fair Dealing

As noted, the second major concern that management attorneys face with respect to the applicability of the good faith and fair dealing doctrine to employment lawsuits is the courts' propensity to interpret the theory to be in the nature of a tort rather than one of contract. Obviously, if the plaintiff's attorney is successful in convincing a court that not only is the theory applicable, but the breach constitutes a tort action rather than a contract action, the plaintiff has an opportunity to recover a judgment for punitive damages in addition to compensatory damages, in contrast to being limited to compensatory damages, alone, if the theory is interpreted as one of contract.

Unfortunately for employers and their counsel and representatives, some courts have so interpreted a breach of the implied covenant of good faith and fair dealing in employment matters as based in tort rather than contract, although the term "covenant" is one historically recognized as contractual as opposed to tortious.

Inasmuch as most juries in the United States are comprised of many working members of society and perhaps do not hold their own employers in such high regard, to permit a jury to reward punitive damages in such a case could be devastating to the small business employer and certainly painful to the larger conglomerates. Irrespective of the "contractual connection" to the theory, some courts have emphasized the absence of good faith to mean malice and bad faith and thus a tort, analogizing the doctrine's applicability in employment lawsuits to its use in bad faith insurance cases where insurance carriers are held to have breached their covenant of good faith and fair dealing in failing to settle a given case properly.

For example, the Nevada Supreme Court, in the 1987 case of *K-Mart Corp. v. Ponsock*, held an employer liable in tort because the employer breached its duty of good faith and fair dealing when it discharged an employee to prevent a full vesting of his pension benefits.

However, it was the California courts, rather than the Nevada courts, that initially caused such an interest among plaintiff lawyers with respect to the use of the covenant of good faith and fair dealing doctrine.

The fact that so many California courts began to hold that not only was an employee permitted to pursue a cause of action under the good faith and fair dealing theory but was entitled to punitive damages, as well, that by the mid-1980's the average jury award in such California cases exceeded $400,000.

The onslaught of wrongful discharge cases in California based upon the good faith and fair dealing theory and the huge awards of punitive damages caused the California Supreme Court to take a close look at the entire spectrum of wrongful discharge litigation in the 1988 California landmark case of *Foley v. Interactive Data Corp.* The California Supreme Court held in the *Foley* decision that only compensatory damages can be awarded where a jury finds an employee to have been discharged for lack of good faith and fair dealing and that punitive damages are not recoverable in such matters.

The *Foley* decision, most likely, has curtailed the extension of punitive damages being awarded in good faith and fair dealing cases in other jurisdictions more than any singular development in the labor and employment field. It may have also curtailed the recognition of the doctrine in other jurisdictions as well.

That does not mean that the pre-*Foley* euphoria is not present in some jurisdictions with respect to the good faith and fair dealing doctrine. It does not mean that jurisdictions that have not previously recognized the doctrine as a valid cause of action will not commence to recognize it in the future.

Thus, the second challenge for employers, and their attorneys and representatives, with respect to the applicability of the doctrine and the interpretation by the courts that such actions are in the nature of tort, rather than contract, is to convince the courts otherwise under the rationale of the court in *Foley*: that the employment relationship is manifestly contractual and that the expansion of the good faith and fair dealing doctrine to include tort damages would involve significant policy judgments affecting social policies and commercial relationships that are best left to the legislature to alter, at all, rather than the courts.

INITIAL TACTICS IN DEFENDING BREACH OF GOOD FAITH AND FAIR DEALING LAWSUITS

Should an employer be faced with a lawsuit based, in whole or in part, upon allegations that it breached its implied covenant of good faith and fair dealing to the employee, the employer's counsel should first determine whether the state in which the lawsuit is filed has recognized the good faith theory as actionable. Numerous states have not recognized the doctrine as a basis by which to proceed in court. If so, the employer's counsel has an obligation to convince the court in such case that not only does the state not recognize the theory as grounds to establish a cause of action, the court should not recognize the theory now or in the future. The employer's counsel would be well served in his or her research to review similar cases in other jurisdictions that have refused to recognize the theory in employment cases and to use the rationale espoused by the courts in such cases in his or her arguments to the court.

On the other hand, if the lawsuit in question is filed in a state that has recognized the good faith and fair dealing doctrine in employment cases, whether limited to compensation matters or to wrongful discharge issues, as well, the employer's counsel should give strong consideration to attempting to move the case to a jurisdiction that has not recognized the doctrine, if such removal is available.

Third, to the extent that the employer's counsel is forced to defend a lawsuit based upon the employer's alleged breach of good faith and fair dealing to the employee, he or she should attempt to persuade the court that the theory should no longer be recognized due to some of the problems associated with it as discussed in the *Foley* decision. In addition, to the extent the court permits applicability of the doctrine to a given case, employer's counsel should argue forcefully that punitive damages should not be recoverable. Equally important, the employer's counsel should impress upon the court that if the court is going to permit the lawsuit to proceed based upon the breach of good faith and fair dealing theory, that the court should limit the applicability of the doctrine to compensation and/or benefit matters and refuse to extend the doctrine to employment practices and/or to discipline and discharge cases. Moreover, the employer's counsel should also, by motion or otherwise, attempt to persuade the court to establish boundaries, standards, and limitations within which proof will be taken and remedies will be awarded and to ensure that such boundaries and standards are sufficiently relative and objective to satisfy both fundamental procedural and substantive due process.

PRE-TRIAL TECHNIQUES IN BREACH OF GOOD FAITH AND FAIR DEALING LAWSUITS

When defending alleged breach of good faith and fair dealing lawsuits in the employment field, most of the various pre-trial techniques discussed in the two preceding chapters (as well as other chapters addressing the subject) are applicable. These techniques include:

- preparing witnesses
- timely filing of pleadings and motions
- exhausting available discovery
- gathering and coordinating documentary evidence
- procuring and issuing subpoenas
- entering into feasible stipulations
- preparing for and attending pre-trial conferences
- preparing an outstanding trial notebook

Specifically, however, there are certain peculiar pre-trial matters that should be addressed by the employer's counsel and representatives in preparation of defending a good faith and fair dealing lawsuit. These are discussed in the following sections.

Limit the Scope of the Lawsuit

First, as alluded to earlier, the employer's counsel should attempt to limit the area of the playing field in a good faith and fair dealing lawsuit, not only with respect to requesting the court to limit the standards and burden of proof, but also by preparing the case in such a manner that the employer's action with respect to the employee was what a fair and reasonable employer would have done under the circumstances. Inasmuch as a good faith and fair dealing lawsuit provides less objective standards within which a judge and jury are permitted to make certain findings and conclusions, an employer's counsel defending such a case must take the initiative and at least convince the jury—hopefully with jury instructions to the same effect—that the "reasonable person," or what is more typically referenced to as the "reasonable man" rule, should apply.

The good faith and fair dealing type of case, particularly with respect to employment matters, is fertile ground. It is up to employer's attorneys to attempt to establish some "reasonable man" standards. That is to say that if an employer must defend such a case, it is up to its counsel to establish that the discharge or compensation practice was, in fact, dealt with in good faith and devoid of malice, bad faith, and/or retaliatory motives.

Show that the Employer Had Just Cause for Discharging the Employee

Once the employer's counsel has been able to establish the reasonable and objective standards in such a case, it is up to him or her to show the court (and jury if a jury case is at hand) that it did, in fact, act in good faith; meaning basically that the employer had "just cause" for the discharge in question or a justifiable position with respect to its decision concerning the disposition of some compensation or benefit practice.

The just cause standards were addressed in Chapter 18. In a nutshell, however, just cause discharge consists of an employer's sensitivity to procedural and substantive due process in the work place. Procedural due process means that the employer is able to show a court that the employee had a fair, reasonable and timely notice of what action the employer would take relative to certain conduct and performance on the part of the employee, or that the rule or policy, if not so previously communicated to the employee, is so commonly recognized in the work place that a reasonable person should have known the violation of which would have resulted in the action so taken against the employee. Procedural due process may also be established through a progressive disciplinary procedure when employees are so advised of the procedure and each step is so communicated and documented that the final step resulting in dismissal comes as no surprise to the employee.

Show that the Employer Followed Due Process

Substantive due process is equally important in defending a good faith and fair dealing lawsuit. Therefore, the employer's counsel and representatives should be able to show the court (and jury, if applicable) that not only did it afford the employee, or employees, in question fair notice, but that it administered and enforced such policies, rules and practices relative to decorum and performance in a fair, reasonable, and consistent manner. To do so, the employer's counsel should be able to demonstrate through verbal testimony and documentary evidence that the policy, practice or rule in question was a reasonable one and necessitated by the business and operational conditions of the organization, that it had consistently been enforced (except when certain mitigating circumstances dictated otherwise, none of which circumstances exist in the present case) and that the employer timely enforced the policy, practice or rule as well, so that no one could have drawn an inference or conclusion that the employer had, for some reason, abandoned the rule, or acquiesced in its lack of enforcement.

TRIAL STRATEGY IN DEFENDING GOOD FAITH AND FAIR DEALING LAWSUITS

General trial strategies and techniques have been covered throughout this book and particularly in Chapters 5, 10, and 18. These chapters provide a general understanding of the pre-trial and trial techniques and tactics that should be employed in defending a breach of good faith and fair dealing lawsuit.

In addition, it might be helpful for an employer's counsel, in a good faith and fair dealing type of lawsuit, to attempt to get the opposing counsel to stipulate to some basic ground rules, as a means to limit liability and potential damages. Most likely, the opposing counsel is not going to agree to any type of stipulation that would prejudice his or her case or reduce any possible award or judgment, but may well agree that certain guidelines would be helpful to both parties so that the trial could be conducted in an orderly and timely manner.

The selection of the jury, if one is provided, and the draw of the judge, and the relative philosophies of both, individually and collectively, will most likely have more impact and significance on the outcome of the case than all the rulings, admissions, and limitations imposed by the court in the trial of the matter.

21 Defensive Strategies to Use in "Promissory Estoppel" and Related Contractual Lawsuits

The three previous chapters have addressed the most common contractual causes of action that have eroded the employment-at-will doctrine. This chapter's scope is to address miscellaneous contractual theories that courts have adopted, to some degree, that further erode the "at-will" rule.

Of the remaining miscellaneous causes of action relative to contractual theories used by plaintiff attorneys to circumvent the employment-at-will relationship of the employee with his or her employer, the "promissory estoppel" theory is the most unique.

The promissory estoppel theory in contract law forbids a party to an agreement to renege on his or her promise to the other, if the latter has reasonably relied and acted upon the promise to his or her detriment. The theory is very similar to that of fraud or misrepresentation, but without the element of intent. Inasmuch as the courts are now so protective of employee rights in the work place, many now recognize and apply the "promissory estoppel" theory in wrongful discharge and other related employment cases even when rejecting some of the other contractual theories such as implied contracts resulting from language in employee handbooks, as discussed in Chapter 19, and the covenant of good faith and fair dealing theory, as discussed in Chapter 20.

PRECEDENT CASES USING THE PROMISSORY ESTOPPEL THEORY

One of the first cases in which the "promissory estoppel" theory was recognized in the employment context was that of *Grouse v. Group Health Plan, Inc.*, in which a Minnesota court held the employer-defendant liable for refusing to fulfill its promise to hire the plaintiff as a pharmacist after the plaintiff resigned from his position with another employer, upon reliance that he had a new job with the defendant, even though the latter had abolished the position in the interim.

The Alaska Supreme Court held that an employer is forbidden to discharge an employee, except for good cause, under the promissory estoppel theory where the employer had verbally promised the employee long-term employment and a definite amount of work upon which the employee had relied.

The employer's counsel and representatives should be acutely aware that the courts are extending the promissory estoppel exception to the employment-at-will doctrine in a variety of factual situations.

For example, a federal judge in the 1986 case of *Burne v. Intermagnetics General Corp.*, applying Connecticut law, permitted a discharged employee to proceed on his legal claim against his former employer where the employee had relied to his detriment upon the employer's promise of job security after sacrificing a job he had held for 23 years with his previous employer.

Similarly, a federal judge in the 1982 case of *Scholtes v. Signal Delivery Service, Inc.*, applying Arkansas law, recognized and applied the promissory estoppel doctrine where an employee had relied to his detriment on his employer's assurances of continued employment by passing over other job opportunities and relocating to a new location at considerable expense, when such assurances were not met.

The Ohio Supreme Court extended the promissory estoppel theory to employee handbooks—rather than applying the implied-in-fact contract theory—by holding that written promises in an employee handbook, when relied upon by employees to their detriment, may form the basis of a promissory estoppel claim in the event the promises are not fulfilled.

One can only imagine how far the courts may extend the promissory estoppel theory in the future in a continual erosion of the historic employment-at-will doctrine.

In addition, most courts that have recognized the promissory estoppel theory as an exception to the employment-at-will doctrine have paid little attention to classic arguments of employers that such a lawsuit is not actionable due to its failure to satisfy the statute of frauds.

From an employer's perspective, the promissory estoppel exception to the "at-will" doctrine could conceivably be as much, or more, dangerous than the good faith and fair dealing exception, given its versatility in application.

HELPFUL HINTS TO APPLY IN DEFENDING "INDEPENDENT CONSIDERATION" LITIGATION

Another increasingly popular exception to the employment-at-will doctrine being advanced by plaintiff lawyers and being met favorably in many courts throughout the various states is that known as the "independent consideration" exception.

Many state courts are now recognizing that an employee may remove himself or herself from an employment-at-will status, and proceed in an actionable lawsuit, under the legal proposition that the employee brought into the employment relationship some consideration above and beyond providing traditional employment services.

As with the promissory estoppel theory, discussed in the preceding section, the potential utilization of this theory by creative plaintiff attorneys and the favorable responsiveness to such theories by pro-employee courts could span the spectrum of employment practices and policies, and especially in the area of discharge or the loss of job security in some form.

To some degree, the application of the "independent consideration" theory to a variety of employment cases has already occurred.

For example, an Iowa court, in the 1973 case of *Collins v. Parsons College*, held an employee may state a cause of action against an employer whenever an employee has furnished consideration independent of his or her regular employment services, such as terminating other employment to accept an offer of permanent employment with the new employer. A North Carolina court held actionable a lawsuit by an employee under the "independent consideration" theory where the employee had relocated from a distant location to accept employment, only to be discharged thereafter for lack of just cause.

The New Jersey Supreme Court recognized the independent consideration exception to the employment-at-will rule in the 1986 case of *Savenson v. Lewis Means, Inc.*, where an employee had submitted his resignation to accept an offer of employment from another employer upon the promise of the employer of lifetime employment and a substantial raise, only to be summarily discharged a few months later, the court holding that his rejection of the other job offer supplied the independent consideration to remove the employee from an at-will status.

Similarly, a federal court, applying Alabama law in the 1987 case of *Hoffman-LaRoche, Inc. v. Campbell*, held that whenever an employee brings the good will and customer contacts from his previous business to his new job, he thereby provides sufficient consideration above and beyond the normal employment services expected of the employee to create an enforceable oral contract of employment.

The employer's counsel and representatives should anticipate that such factual circumstances as those noted in the cases above are merely a tip of the judicial iceberg of what judges may permit in the future to establish some type of consideration independent of regular job duties to remove the employee in question from an employment-at-will status and permit the employee to proceed in his or her lawsuit against the employer.

PRACTICAL POINTS TO CONSIDER IN DEFENDING "PRESUMPTION OF TERM" LAWSUITS

Another legal theory being advanced by plaintiff lawyers to create another exception to the employment-at-will rule is that frequently referred to by the courts as the presumption of term doctrine; meaning, that some courts recognize that an employer's designation of a fixed term in which an employee is to receive compensation will be inferred as his or her fixed term of employment, during which time the employee is removed from the employment-at-will status and during which time the employer may be discharged for good cause only.

The employer's counsel and representatives should readily perceive how an innovative plaintiff attorney could be able to sustain an actionable lawsuit based upon this legal theory were his or her client to have been discharged during the fixed period of time in which the client was to have received certain compensation. A discussion of the following cases provide but a few examples of how this theory is being adopted by state courts, nationwide.

A New York court held in the 1983 case of *Myers v. Coradian Corp.*, that a hiring letter which specified an annual salary constituted an implied contract for a one-year period during which the employee could not be discharged without just cause. Similarly, a North Carolina Appellate Court, in the 1988 case of *Walker v. Goodson Farms, Inc.*, held that a hiring letter specifying a salary for a five-year period of time created an implied contract that the employee would not be discharged except for good cause, thereby removing the employee from an employment-at-will status for the five-year period.

A Texas Appellate Court held that a hiring letter specifying that the newly hired employee would be paid $40,000 per year, plus a percentage of increased sales, constituted an enforceable employment contract for at least a one-year period.

An Arkansas Appellate Court held that a hiring letter to a new employee that he was to receive a $2,500 monthly subsidy for a three-year period created a three-year enforceable employment contract.

The fixed period of time in which an employee is to receive compensation is typically specified in a hiring letter or some similar form of communication. As noted in the cases above, whenever the employer specifies an annual salary, it is inviting this type of lawsuit, not only with respect to the numerous states that have already recognized the "presumption of term" legal theory as an exception to the at-will rule, but also relative to the many courts in other states likely to recognize this exception in the future.

Thus, the employer's counsel's first defensive or, rather preventive, measure to take is to educate the employer and its management members who send out such hiring letters and similar communications as to the potential adverse consequences of specifying compensation and benefits for a fixed period of time.

The scope in which the "presumption of term" theory may be used is not limited to compensation and benefits alone, however. For example, in the 1988 Idaho appellate case of *Holmes v. Union Oil Company*, the court held that an employer's letter to an employee specifying the terms of an 18-month rehabilitation program could constitute an implied employment contract that the employee would not be terminated from his employment during such 18-month period except for just cause, thus removing the employee from his employment-at-will status during such period of time.

PRE-TRIAL TECHNIQUES AND TACTICS IN DEFENDING PROMISSORY ESTOPPEL AND RELATED LITIGATION

The authors have discussed numerous pre-trial and trial techniques and tactics in various chapters throughout this book. The reader should take particular note of pre-trial and trial techniques and tactics discussed in Chapters 17, 18, and 19 relative to various breach of employment contracts, whether explicit or implicit in nature, inasmuch as such techniques and tactics are equally applicable to defending promissory estoppel, independent consideration, and presumption of term type litigation.

Two Ways Employers Can Prevent Lawsuits Based on Promissory Estoppel

The singular most important technique and tactic to use in these types of cases not only during the litigation stage but, rather, at a point in time long before the employer's action that gives rise to an employee's right to even file a cause of action in the first instance is to ensure that both verbal and written communications from the employer to the employee do not contain language that the employee may later use against the employer as a basis for a lawsuit.

To avoid having to defend promissory estoppel, independent consideration and/or presumption of term type lawsuits, here are some of the better preventive measures for the employer to use:

- inundate company communications with a sufficiency of disclaimers and waivers to the employee to such a degree that the "employment-at-will" relationship between the parties is not abridged, and that a court hearing such a case would be disposed to dismiss the employee's action on the basis of such disclaimers and waivers
- Enter into a formal written employment contract, enumerating specifically the terms, conditions, and duration of the employment arrangement

Defense Strategies for Lawsuits Based on Promissory Estoppel

Beyond such preventive measures to obviate the right of an employee to proceed, *ab initio*, the employer's counsel should attempt to convince the court that the theory so advanced by the plaintiff's counsel—whether based on promissory estoppel, independent consideration, and/or presumption of term—is such a departure from the historical employment-at-will doctrine that it should not be permitted by the court, and that if such causes of action are to be permitted, at all, that they should be effected through legislation, rather than through judicial decisions.

And as with previous discussions relative to pre-trial and trial techniques, if the state in which the case has been brought recognizes such an exception to the "at-will" doctrine and the court is disposed to permit the case to proceed to trial, the employer's counsel should attempt to have the case removed or transferred to another state or jurisdiction in which such theory is not recognized, if all other matters are equal and such a move is feasible and possible.

Inasmuch as the promissory estoppel, independent consideration, and presumption of term theories are grounded in the nature of contract law, rather than tort, all other defenses, strategies, techniques, and tactics discussed in the preceding chapters in Part III of this book should be helpful to the employer's counsel and representatives in defending promissory estoppel, independent consideration and presumption of term type lawsuits, as well. In addition, the reader's attention is directed specifically to Chapters 5, 10, and 18 for other pre-trial and trial techniques that may be applied to these types of cases.

22 Litigation Strategies in Breach of Covenants Not to Disclose or Misappropriate "Trade Secret" Claims

The employer's counsel and other representatives have a most important duty to protect their employer against employee misappropriation of proprietary business and information of good will. The employer's right to protect its proprietary business information has developed into the law generically referred to as that of trade secrets.

The law holds that the employee has an implied covenant not to misappropriate business secrets or developments of his or her employer or otherwise infringe upon the employer's ownership of proprietary business information. The employer also may have the benefit of written agreements relative to its trade secrets in which the employee agrees not to misuse, misappropriate or disclose certain business information assembled, developed or patented during the employee's employment, even though the employee may have contributed to the assemblage or development of such property or information.

The employer's counsel and other representatives should first appreciate to what source courts typically refer in defining the scope of what is, and is not, a trade secret. Many courts refer to the *Restatement of Torts, Section 757* for such definition and thus accept that:

> "A trade secret may consist of any formula, pattern, device or compilation of information which is used in one's business, and which gives him an opportunity to obtain an advantage over competitors who do not know or use it. It may be a formula for a chemical compound, a process of manufacturing, treating or preserving materials, a pattern for a machine or other device, or a list of customers."

The employer's counsel and other representatives also should appreciate that their employer is most likely to assume the role of the plaintiff, rather than that of defendant, in a lawsuit for misappropriation or disclosure of some trade secret or other proprietary business interest or information. The lawsuit may be against the employee so misappropriating or disclosing the trade secrets or could possibly extend, in jurisdictions so permitting, to include the employee's new employer who is using the trade secret to its benefit.

The employer's counsel and other representatives also should recognize that although a misappropriation of a trade secret in terms of a breach of an employment contract or a breach of an expressed covenant not to disclose cause of action is one in the nature of a contract, courts apply a variety of legal theories to trade secrets and improper disclosure type cases.

Aside from an actionable claim filed for breach of an express contract not to misappropriate or disclose, an employer may be permitted, in certain jurisdictions, to sue for one or more of the following:

- a breach of an implied-in-fact contract
- breach of a quasi-contract (an action to recover damages for unjust enrichment)
- breach of a confidential relationship
- tortious misappropriation or conversion of a property right
- unfair competition

In addition, the employer may desire to sue under some auxiliary theory such as:

- fraud or misrepresentation
- negligence in the dissemination of such business information
- negligent or intentional infliction of emotional distress resulting from an employee's outrageous conduct in so misappropriating or disclosing such proprietary information and/or trade secrets. These theories assume grounds exist to support such additional counts in a lawsuit, and assuming such legal theories have been recognized as actionable in the jurisdiction in which the lawsuit is brought

Particularly would the employer so victimized by an employee's conduct possess a legal claim against the employee for tortious disloyalty and self-dealing, as discussed more specifically in Chapter 33. Particular causes of action also may be available to an employer against an employee benefiting from misappropriation or disclosure under the tort of unfair competition and/or tortious interference with a contract.

EVALUATING THE ESSENTIAL ELEMENTS OF PROOF IN MISAPPROPRIATION AND DISCLOSURE OF TRADE SECRET CASES

The employer that files a suit against an employee to recover damages for the misappropriation of, or improper disclosure of a trade secret or some other proprietary business information or seeks an injunction against an employee for such conduct, has the burden of proof in such actions.

The law of trade secrets has been developed with a view of balancing the employer's right to protect a business asset against an employee's interest in the pursuit of a livelihood and the right to enjoy the fruits of his or her creative efforts.

The law does not presume that everything an employee learns in his or her previous employment is a trade secret. Thus, on the one hand, courts attempt to protect an employee's right to utilize the knowledge, skill, and experience acquired through former employment, while on the other hand, they do not embrace an employee's attempt to misappropriate his or her employer's proprietary business assets.

The employer's counsel who is called upon to prosecute trade secrets litigation should be aware of the various elements of proof in such a cause of action. These are described in the following sections.

Validating the Existence of a Trade Secret

As suggested above, the courts do not deem everything an employer represents as a trade secret to be a trade secret. The courts require the information alleged to have been misappropriated to contain, or have attached, some degree of uniqueness; otherwise, an employer could contend any confidential disclosure to give rise to liability, no matter how well known or trivial. The courts, for instance, may conclude that some chemical formula developed or discovered by an employer, or some manufacturing or machinery method, because of its scientific uniqueness, qualifies for trade secret status, while rejecting some business list, available to the entire business community, as not rising to trade secret status. Yet, were the business list developed by the employer and contained unique information to its business interest, it may well be judicially interpreted as having trade secret status.

As the court in the 1981 Illinois case of *Lincoln Towers Insurance Agency v. Farrell* concluded, several factors are considered significant in determining the existence of a trade secret, among them:

- the extent to which the alleged trade secrets are known by other employers in the particular industry
- the extent to which the alleged trade secrets are known by the employees in the industry

- the extent to which the employer takes measures to guard the secrecy of the information in question
- the value of alleged trade secrets to both the employer and its competitors
- the amount of time, effort, and money spent by the employer in development of the information or property at issue
- the ease or difficulty in acquiring or duplicating such information

Verifying Ownership of the Trade Secrets

A second element that must be proved by the party filing a misappropriation cause of action is that the plaintiff was the owner of the information forming and constituting the alleged trade secrets. A prior sale by the employer of the alleged trade secret could defeat its misappropriation or disclosure action. Where it is shown that the employer agreed to share ownership with the employee as to an alleged trade secret, the action may be somewhat stymied. Where an employer waived its right to prosecute an action against the employee for misappropriation or disclosure, the employer's lawsuit may suffer an early demise. The most frequently used defense by an employee as to the ownership question is that referred to as *shop rights*. Here, an employee may be able to successfully defend himself or herself against a misappropriation of a trade secret or improper disclosure lawsuit on the grounds that certain inventions and improvements were developed by the employee, even though developed with the employer's materials and/or on the employer's time. However, the courts vary in their decisions as to what degree of shop rights an employee has in a particular invention or improvement and to what extent he or she may be able to use such information outside the employer's business.

Proving the Existence of a Confidential Relationship

In order to sustain a misappropriation of a trade secret lawsuit (or to enjoin such misappropriation), the filing party must be able to show that it had a special relationship with the defendant in which the trade secret was shared in a confidential manner. The relationship may be inferred by the courts between a highly paid employee and the employer or exist in a manner of a written covenant or contract. Proof of the owner's attempt to protect the secrecy is not only an essential part of a plaintiff's proof in terms of establishing the existence of a trade secret, it is also used to establish the confidentiality element of proof, as well.

PRACTICAL TIPS TO CONSIDER WHEN SEEKING TO ENJOIN MISAPPROPRIATION AND UNFAIR DISCLOSURE OF TRADE SECRETS

The employer whose trade secrets are being misappropriated and unfairly disclosed to a competitor—whether by the fact that the employee has commenced its own business in competition with his or her former employer or has become an employee of the employer's competitor—may not be able to sustain its business operations if it has to wait for the process of a formal lawsuit in which to recover damages for the employee's breach of covenant and wrongdoing. In fact, given the financial condition of the employee, a money judgment for the misappropriation and unfair disclosure of its proprietary business interests could be a most hollow one were the employee judgment proof.

As a result, the most expeditious measure available to an employer in such a position is to have its counsel seek to enjoin the employee's misappropriation and disclosure of the information as well as to seek to enjoin its competitor(s)' use of such information. In addition, the employer's counsel could file a lawsuit seeking to recover monetary and other such damages for the injuries it has already sustained, if such can be recoverable, at all.

Therefore, since injunctive relief seemingly is the initial relief sought by employers being victimized by a former employee's misappropriation and disclosure of trade secrets, the employer's counsel should be aware of what courts typically require in order to grant injunctive relief:

- Whether the employer will be able to show on the merits of the case, when tried, a reasonable probability of the existence of a trade secret
- Whether the employer will seek irreparable damages if injunctive relief is denied
- Whether the granting of preliminary injunctive relief will result in even greater damage to the employee and/or the competitor than to the employer
- Whether granting such preliminary injunctive relief is in the best interest of the public

In addition, some courts allude to a need to preserve the status quo in deciding on whether to grant injunctive relief in trade secrets litigation.

The employer's counsel should be most sensitive about the manner and scope in which he or she frames both a petition for a preliminary injunction as well as a petition for a permanent injunction. Pleadings that are not sufficient in scope to cover all possible avenues of misappropriation and unfair disclosure may allow the enjoined party to use a broad range of information not specifically defined in the injunction to circumvent the injunctive process. Therefore, it is better for an employer's counsel filing an action for injunctive relief to err on the side to broaden the scope of the injunction rather than to narrow it.

PITFALLS TO AVOID IN SEEKING SPECIFIC DAMAGES IN TRADE SECRETS LITIGATION

The employer's counsel should be aware that, as with other types of actions, the courts require a party seeking damages for misappropriation and unfair disclosure of trade secrets to establish not only that the damages suffered by the plaintiff were proximately issued by such misappropriation and unfair disclosure, but also, that the damages sought contain a reasonable degree of exactness. This burden of proving damages on the plaintiff's part does not require exactitude of mathematical certainty, but such damages must be based on reasonable estimates.

The employer's counsel should expend all efforts in reviewing the employer's business records, profit and loss sheets, reports, invoices, financial statements, and so forth, by which to provide a reasonable basis to evidence its damages.

Several types of damages may be available to an employer in a misappropriation and unfair disclosure lawsuit:

- ***Compensatory damages***—The employer should seek to recover compensatory damages in an attempt to place itself in the same business position in which it would have been but for the misappropriation and disclosure.
- ***Liquidation damages***—Where the employer is prosecuting its legal claim on grounds that the employee breached an express covenant or contract not to misappropriate or disclose trade secrets and the contractual terms contains a provision for liquidated damages, the employer's counsel should plead same.
- ***Court costs***—Certainly, the employer's counsel should plead for its court costs and related expenditures. Should the law in the state permit, or should the terms of any written agreement between the parties allow, for attorneys' fees, in such a case, a prayer for reasonable attorneys' fees should be added to the employer's prayer for relief.
- ***Punitive damages***—Whether the employer in a trade secrets lawsuit is entitled to punitive damages depends on the nature of the lawsuit filed by it, and the laws of the state in which the lawsuit is brought. Given both considerations, the employer's counsel, now in the role of the plaintiff rather than the defendant, may do some forum shopping so that the cause of action is filed in a jurisdiction most favorable to the employer's cause of action with respect to seeking punitive damages.

Moreover, the employer's counsel should be sensitive to incorporating legal claims in tort, such as a claim of tortious breach of fiduciary duty as discussed in Chapter 33, or misappropriation or conversion of property, along with any claims of breach of an express or implied contract, so as to be in a position to seek punitive damages as well as other damages in its trade secrets litigation against an employee.

PRE-TRIAL AND TRIAL TECHNIQUES AND TACTICS IN TRADE SECRET CAUSES OF ACTION

The employer's counsel who is charged with the responsibility of seeking an injunction against an employee or competitor for disclosing or misappropriating the employer's trade secrets or filing a lawsuit seeking damages suffered as a result, should be most careful in drafting its pleadings.

As suggested earlier, such pleadings for an injunction should be sufficiently broad in coverage not to permit the employee or competitor to use the information in question by way of some loophole in the injunction. On the other hand, neither the injunction, or damage suit should contain theories or allegations that the employer is unable to prove. The employer's counsel should understand that most courts look very unfavorably upon a shotgun approach by a plaintiff attorney that causes the court to spend considerable time in trying to isolate theories and issues that are relevant to provable facts. Not only does the employer's counsel prejudice his or her case before the court and lose considerable credibility in the process, such counsel takes a chance on being subjected to certain sanctions and possibly contempt in some jurisdictions.

The employer's counsel should not only be highly sensitive to the inclusion and exclusion of theories and allegations in his or her pleadings, he or she should likewise be sensitive to discovery opportunities and be the first of the parties to discover through interrogatories, depositions, admissions, and so forth, what the other parties contend and have in their arsenal of defense.

Inasmuch as most management and corporate attorneys are typically defending legal actions against their employer and corporate clients, rather than prosecuting causes of action on their behalf, an employer's counsel must adapt somewhat to a plaintiff's counsel's mind-set and philosophy in prosecuting trade secret litigation, rather than continuing to respond like a typical defendant's counsel. The idea here is to put the defending employee and competitor on the defensive and keep them there. Thus, a proactive mentality should persist rather than a reactive one.

Other matters relative to pre-trial and trial techniques have been addressed in previous chapters, such as Chapters 5, 10, and 18. An employer's counsel who is preparing an injunction and/or lawsuit relative to a cause of action for the misappropriation or unfair disclosure of trade secrets should refer to such information contained in such chapters to checklist and reinforce the relevant techniques and tactics when prosecuting trade secrets litigation.

23 Successful Steps to Follow in Breach of Covenants Not to Compete Causes of Action

The employer's counsel should understand, initially, that many of the strategies and techniques discussed in the preceding chapter on the subject of misappropriation and unfair disclosure of trade secrets are applicable to covenants not to compete litigation as well. That is to say, that the two types of litigation are very similar in that the typically factual situation that gives rise to both causes of action is begun by an employee's breach of his or her express or implied covenant not to take any action that would harm the employer. Also, that in the field of noncompetition litigation, the employer's counsel assumes the role of a plaintiff's attorney rather than that of his or her more frequent role of a defendant's counsel.

There are other similarities, as well. As noted in the preceding chapter, in breach of such covenants as nondisclosure, the employer's initial litigation against the employee most likely would be in the form of an injunction due to the irreparable nature of the damages being suffered by the employer as a result of the employee's breach. The same would hold true in a breach of noncompetition restrictive covenant.

Another similarity between the two types of lawsuits discussed in this and the preceding chapter is the types of various legal theories that may be available to an employer.

For example, an employer may be permitted to file a cause of action against an employee in competition with it based upon an implied-in-fact covenant not to do so. In addition, depending upon the law in the state in which the lawsuit is filed, the employer may have a cause of action against the competing employee based upon a tortious breach of fiduciary duty as discussed in Chapter 33.

The employer may also be permitted in such a factual situation to prosecute a legal claim against the employee for a quasi-contract breach (unjust enrichment) as well as a possible claim of tortious conversion (or misappropriation) of a property right of the employer.

Should the facts suggest, the employer's cause of action could extend to the inclusion of such tort claims as misrepresentation or fraud, negligence, intentional infliction of emotional distress, invasion of privacy, or defamation. The employer's counsel should appreciate that such tort allegations may appear attractive and enticing to incorporate into a noncompetition cause of action, so as to possibly recover punitive damages.

The employer may also possess the right to file certain causes of action against the employer with whom the employee became employed after departing the former employment, the new relationship giving rise to the breach of the employee's covenant not to compete with the former employer. Such suits may be based, if actionable within the jurisdiction in which the suit is filed, upon such legal theories as tortious interference with employment, unfair competition, and so forth.

An employer that does not have the benefit of a written contract with an employee providing a noncompetition covenant may have its most favorable opportunity of sustaining a cause of action against a present employee who is attempting to compete with the employer.

As a general proposition of law, a person acting in a position as a fiduciary of another may not make use of that relationship to benefit his or her own personal interests, except with the full knowledge and consent of the party to whom the fiduciary obligation is owed.

Courts have implied a fiduciary duty of loyalty of an employee to his or her employer; meaning, in part, that an employee must protect the interest of the employer to the detriment of his or her own, if necessary to fulfill the loyalty obligation. The fiduciary duty of loyalty has the effect of prohibiting an employee from competing with the employer during the term of the relationship.

A final preliminary point to address in noncompetition litigation is that a lawsuit to enforce a covenant not to compete, or a petition to enjoin the breach thereof, extends far beyond such agreements between employers and employees. Such business contracts as that of a partnership, franchise, distributorship, independent contractor, sale of business, and transfers of stock, real or personal property type agreements typically contain some form of a noncompetition clause. However, in keeping with the scope of this book, it is the law relative to a covenant not to compete agreement between the employer and the employee that is covered in this chapter.

STATUTORY AND JUDICIAL DETERMINATIONS OF THE REASONABLENESS OF COVENANTS NOT TO COMPETE

Covenants not to compete are not favored by the courts. They are not favored by many state legislators, either. As a result, several states have passed legislation restricting the use of noncompetition agreements.

A California statute prohibits the use of covenants not to compete, in general, with only a handful of narrow exceptions. Other states vary from a veritable ban on the use of noncompetition clauses to a limitation of enforcement of certain types of covenants, rendering them virtually void.

An employer's counsel preparing to file an injunction against an employee in breach of a covenant not to compete, or a lawsuit seeking monetary damages for such a breach, should review the applicable statutes on the subject in the state in which he or she intends to file such litigation to determine what, if any, state statutes limit or ban the enforceability of noncompetition covenants. Even in states where a breach of covenant not to compete lawsuit is prohibited or barred by state statute, the employer wronged by such breach may, nonetheless, be able to pursue some other common law action against the competing employee, such as a suit in the nature of unfair competition or, as noted earlier, a cause of action against the employee for breach of a fiduciary duty or breach of a duty of loyalty.

Verifying the Reasonableness of the Noncompetition Agreement: Three Primary Factors

In states that do permit a cause of action to enforce a covenant not to compete agreement, the employer's counsel should review judicial precedent to determine any judicial restrictions in the prosecution of such legal claims.

In doing so, most likely the employer's counsel will be challenged to show the court that the noncompetition agreement was reasonable in subject matter, time, and territory.

Specifying a Reasonable Territory. First of all, a court may attack the reasonableness of the area in which an employee is not permitted to compete with the employer, after termination of employment. Courts frequently look to the actual threat posed by the employer within the specified area, thus restricting the applicability of the covenant not to compete to the area in which the employee was active while in the employer's employment. However, where an employer is able to show the court that the employee's reputation and influence extend far beyond the geographical area in which the employee worked while in the employ of the employer, the court may extend the area not to compete to be coextensive with the area of the employee's influence.

Specifying Reasonable Time Limits. Second, the courts typically look to the time limitations in which the employee is not permitted to compete in determining whether the noncompetition clause at issue is reasonable. Here, the courts consider several factors in their analysis of time reasonableness, such as the employee's ability to earn a living, the legal consideration given by the employer to the employee in exchange for the covenant, the time remaining in the time restrictions at the time of trial or hearing, and the respective equities between the parties.

Specifying Reasonable Ability of Employee to Earn a Living. Another test of reasonableness by the courts in breach of noncompetition clauses is that of the ability of a former employee to make a living in spite of the covenant. Should an employer's counsel be able to show the court that the employee's ability to transfer job skills to similar employment outside the scope of the restrictive covenant may be sufficient to pass the reasonableness test and keep the applicability and enforcement of the covenant, in tact. On the other hand, should an employee be able to demonstrate to the court that the covenant will force the employee to uproot his or her family and move to a new location to obtain work, because of the terms and conditions imposed by the covenant, may be sufficient to convince the court that the covenant places too much of an undue hardship on the employee to be considered reasonable.

Verifying the Reasonableness of Noncompetition: Twenty Secondary Factors

Courts look to many secondary factors, as well, in applying an overall reasonableness test to a covenant not to compete in noncompetitive litigation. They include:

1. ***The length of employment*** or association with the employer. The employment of an employee for a long period of time may allow an employee an opportunity to establish a more solid relationship with the customer and an opportunity to gain access to confidential information from the customer as a result, thus favoring the reasonableness of the covenant.
2. ***Loss of expenses*** suffered by the employer, such as that incurred through training, and *loss of the employee's unique abilities.*
3. ***The nature and uniqueness of the goods or services*** provided by the employer and whether customers buy such goods and services based upon the personality and good offices of the sales person or on the basis of the quality and price of the goods or services.
4. ***The relative positions of the parties*** at the time in which the covenant was executed. Here, the courts may look to the relative bargaining power of the parties, the attorney or attorneys representing the respective parties, by whom, and the amount paid such attorneys, as well as the general give and take negotiations that went on between the covenantor and covenantee at the time the covenant was executed.
5. ***The prior skill level and experience of the covenantor-employee.*** Typically, the courts tend to be less likely to enforce a covenant not to compete in

which the employee has brought to his or her employment high levels of experience and skill.

6. ***The circumstances under which the employee left his or her employment*** with the employer. For example, if the employee voluntarily left the employment for the purpose of going into competition with the employer, the courts would most likely be more disposed to enforce the covenant than were the employee involuntarily terminated from employment by the employer.

7. ***The employee's animus toward the employer.*** A court would most likely be less favorably impressed with an employee's reasonableness argument were the employee to have destroyed or taken property from the employer at the time of termination. Any such harmful or destructive activity by the employee against the employer prior to or subsequent to the employee's termination may be sufficient for a court to sustain the employer's position that the reasonableness test was met. An employee's stated intentions of breaching the covenant and violating its contractual obligation to the employer may be looked upon with disfavor by a court attempting to determine the reasonableness issue in the case.

8. ***The extent to which a covenant not to compete is executed*** by the parties. A court could well draw as inference that the employee never intended to agree to not compete with the employer if, in fact, he or she failed or refused to sign the agreement. In addition, a court may well be less inclined to grant an employer relief under the terms of the covenant should evidence be presented to demonstrate that the employee deleted the covenant not to compete provision from the employment agreement.

9. ***Deference to professional standards*** or industry practices. This may be considered by some courts in determining the reasonableness of a noncompetition agreement.

10. ***An employer's failure to enforce previous noncompetition covenants.*** A limited number of courts consider this a factor in determining whether a given covenant not to compete is a reasonable one.

11. ***The difficulty of finding a replacement*** for the employee alleged to have breached his or her noncompetition agreement with the employer. This factor is considered by some courts.

12. ***The employee's superior job performance,*** which may demonstrate the unique skill and experience of an employee.

13. ***The peculiar and unique nature of the employer's business*** and how much time an employee devoted in the development of the business information which is being used in the employee's competitive efforts. In the same context, a court may weigh the nature and reputation of the employer in terms of the hard work and effort having gone into building the employer's

business in comparison of the length of time in which the employee was employed.

14. ***The proximity*** of the employee's business location, or his or her employer's business, to the former employer's business location is yet another consideration looked at by some courts in deciding whether a noncompetition covenant is a reasonable one.

15. ***The time the goodwill and other protectable interests came into existence*** in comparison with the alleged breach when determining the reasonableness issue of a noncompetition clause. Some courts insist that the alleged protectable interest of the employer must exist at the time of the formation of the covenant.

16. ***The number of employees remaining*** with the employer, particularly when there has been mass defections within the employment ranks of the employer in determining the reasonableness of a covenant not to compete.

17. ***The motives behind the employer's desire to enforce a given covenant*** not to compete. Courts sometimes consider motive in determining the reasonableness issue in such an agreement where an employer brings an action to enforce a noncompetition for oppressive purposes, such as to make an example out of the covenantor for the benefit of other employees.

18. ***The extent that third parties and the public as a whole may suffer*** should a given covenant not to compete be enforced.

19. ***What an ordinary employee would anticipate*** in entering into a covenant not to compete, particularly one without a sufficiency of education and background to truly understand the potential impact of the terms and conditions of the agreement.

20. ***The "fair play" position of each party*** and their relative attempts to accommodate the other without abolishing or waiving rights under the noncompetition agreement. For example, a court may look more favorably upon an employer in its attempt to enforce a noncompetition agreement against a former employee if the employer attempted to accommodate the employee's effort to make a living, if as a result, the employer would suffer no appreciable loss of goodwill or competitive edge.

PRACTICAL TIPS TO FOLLOW IN EVALUATING AVAILABLE DEFENSES TO NONCOMPETITION LAWSUITS AND INJUNCTIONS

The employer's counsel who is attempting to enforce a covenant not to compete agreement, or to enjoin an employee's breach of such an agreement, should be aware of some of the defenses he or she is likely to encounter in the process.

Although some of the defenses available to an employee and his or her counsel to a noncompetition cause of action have somewhat been discussed—at least, indirectly—in the preceding section relative to reasonableness considerations by the courts, a more specific discussion will be noted here.

Assuming the cause of action advanced by the employer is in the nature of a breach of an express or implied covenant not to compete agreement rather than one grounded upon a breach of an implied fiduciary duty or duty of loyalty, the employer's counsel may encounter the following defenses if supported by sufficient evidence.

1. ***Lack of Consideration.*** As discussed in Chapter 18, consideration in terms of what each party gives up for the promise from the other, is an essential element in the formation of a contractual relationship. Where the employee's counsel can show that there was no *quid pro quo* on the part of the employer in exchange for the employee's covenant not to compete, litigation to enforce such a contract will likely fail.
2. ***Mutual Assent.*** Although a written covenant not to compete may speak for itself in terms that an employee and employer ostensibly have read and understood the terms and conditions of the agreement and had a meeting of the minds as to its coverage, a lawsuit to enforce an implied noncompetition agreement may be defended successfully by the employee and his or her counsel on the basis that the parties never had a "meeting of the minds" of what was and what was not to be covered by the implied contract, to the extent that the court would even permit such a cause of action in the first instance.
3. ***Waiver.*** When an employee's counsel can demonstrate to the court that the employer, by acts of circumstances or words, has relinquished its right to enforce the terms and conditions of a noncompetition agreement, the employee may be successful in procuring the court's dismissal of the action.
4. ***Consent or License.*** Irrespective of language in a written covenant not to compete, an employer may not be permitted to proceed to trial with its noncompetition litigation against the employee if the latter's counsel can sufficiently show the court that the employer consented or granted some express or implied license to the employee to engage in such competition with the employer.
5. ***Statute of Frauds.*** The employee's counsel may advance a defense that the alleged noncompetition is not in writing and, therefore, the employer's suit to enforce such is barred by the statute of frauds, assuming such to be the case.
6. ***Statute of Limitations or Laches.*** The employer's counsel who attempts to enforce a noncompetition obligation on an employee by way of lawsuit or injunction may also be faced with a defensive motion that such litigation is untimely and barred by the prescriptive statutes within the applicable jurisdiction. Should the statute of limitations defense not be available to

the defendant employee, his or her counsel may also advance the argument that the employer had taken such an extraordinary amount of time in filing such an action, that it should be barred by the doctrine of laches.

7. ***A Preemptive Breach of Contract by the Employer.*** An employee also may have a tenable defense to a breach of covenant not to compete agreement should his or her counsel be able to present evidence to the court that the employer breached the terms and conditions of the agreement prior to the employee's alleged breach and should not be permitted to proceed with its action against the employee. For example, suppose an employer reduced the employee's wages, demoted him or her to a lower position or in some other way, either directly or constructively, or terminated the employee without just cause prior to the expiration date of the employment terms. In such event, the employee's counsel may be most successful in arguing that the employer is barred from bringing suit against the employee because it breached its own contract.
8. ***Misrepresentation or Concealment.*** Should an employee's counsel demonstrate to the court that the employer fraudulently induced the employee into signing a noncompetition agreement, the employer would most likely be barred by a court to proceed with its suit to enforce the agreement against the employee.
9. ***Activities Outside the Scope of the Agreement.*** Another argument that an employer's counsel who is attempting to litigate a breach of a noncompetition clause is likely to face is that the competitive activities of the employee fall outside the coverage of the agreement or were never intended to be a part of the agreement.
10. ***Unconscionability.*** Where an employee is able to show a court that he or she signed a covenant not to compete under duress, such as an employer's threat to discharge a long-term employee if he or she refused to sign such an agreement, the court in question may find that the manner in which the contract was consummated was so unconscionable as to bar the employer's action to enforce the agreement.

Additionally, inasmuch as lawsuits to enforce, or petitions to enjoin the breach of restrictive covenants, such as covenants not to compete, are typically referred to as suits in equity, an employee-defendant may seek to bar the action against him or her on the ground that the employer does not enter the court with clean hands.

Although not favorably received by the courts, the employee may advance an argument to the court that the employer should not be able to proceed with its noncompetition litigation because were it to be successful in its legal claim, it would be in violation of state and/or federal anti-trust statutes.

Should the employer file a cause of action against an employee on the grounds the employee breached its fiduciary duty to the employer not to compete or breached its duty of loyalty to the employer by self-dealing, the employee's counsel may have numerous defenses against the employer's actions in addition to those applicable to contract actions noted above.

Although causes of action for a breach of fiduciary obligation will be addressed more fully in Chapter 33 along with the defenses available to such lawsuits, the employer's counsel should appreciate that many courts do not favorably embrace such tort actions and the employee's most likely initial defense to such a lawsuit would be that the employer did not state a legal claim upon which relief may be granted for the court; that is to say, that the court does not recognize such a cause of action within its jurisdiction.

HELPFUL HINTS IN RECOGNIZING REWARDS AND REMEDIES IN COVENANTS NOT TO COMPETE LAWSUITS

Many of the remedies available to employers in lawsuits to expose covenants not to compete agreements are the same or similar to those discussed in the preceding chapter regarding misappropriations of trade secrets.

In addition, an employer's legal claim for breach of noncompetition agreements may extend to the new employer of the employee, or some other entity, receiving the benefit of the breach. Suits against such third parties may lie in the nature of a suit for unfair competition or tortious interference with an employment contract.

The employer's counsel may initially seek to enjoin the employee-defendant (and perhaps his or her employer) from breaching the terms and conditions of the noncompetition agreement on the grounds that the employer is suffering irreparable damages for which a later reward in money damages cannot properly redress. Factors to support the issuance of a preliminary injunction were discussed in the preceding chapter.

Also, as noted in the preceding chapter in its discussion of the breach of covenant not to disclose or misappropriate trade secrets, the authors addressed the types of damages that may be available to a prevailing employer in such a cause of action. Roughly, the same damages are available to an employer that prevails in its noncompetition litigation against an employee (and possibly the employee's new employer).

First, the employer, if successful in its noncompetition lawsuit, would be entitled to compensatory damages so as to place it in the same position as it was before the breach, meaning that it would be entitled to damages suffered as a result of the competition from the employee in terms of lost profits, goodwill, and so forth. The reader should recall from reviewing the previous chapter that proof of such damages must relate to reasonable estimates and exactness, rather than speculation.

Also, to the extent that the covenant not to compete agreement provided for specified liquidated damages, a prevailing employer under such a contract would be entitled to a recovery of the liquidated damages so enumerated in the agreement, unless the court found such damages to be unconscionable or inequitable.

The prevailing employer in a covenant not to compete lawsuit would be entitled to recover its court costs and related expenses. Also, to the extent that the language of the noncompetition agreement provides, and to the extent that such provisions are recognized as enforceable by the court, the prevailing employer may also be entitled to its attorneys' fees.

The employer may also be entitled to a recovery of punitive damages if its counsel is able, and permitted by the court, to incorporate into the noncompetition litigation some tort claims, such as the tort of breach of a fiduciary duty to the employer not to compete or a breach of the duty of loyalty, assuming also that the court in the jurisdiction in which the case is litigated not only recognizes such theories as actionable but that such theories lie in tort and that the employer is successful in such claims.

PRE-TRIAL AND TRIAL SAFEGUARDS IN NONCOMPETITION CAUSES OF ACTION

The employer's counsel should be aware that both state statutes and judicial precedent within the applicable state substantially dictate to what an extent one may enjoin the breach of, or enforce, a covenant not to compete agreement. An employer's counsel that does not review in detail both the statutory and judicial limitations in litigating noncompetition claims may be out of court before they ever begin the prosecution of such claims. Thus, the first safeguard by an employer's counsel to have an opportunity of advancing a covenant not to compete cause of action against an employee is to become comprehensively familiar with the procedural and substantive law on the subject in the state in which he or she intends to seek an injunction or enforcement.

Should either the statutes or judicial precedents in such a state be unfavorable to the employer's position, then, as suggested in many other chapters within this book, forum shopping may be in order by which the employer may seek greener pastures in which to have its legal claims disposed. The employer's counsel should also take note of the remarks in the preceding chapter that he or she should not draft allegations and legal theories into the employer's pleadings that cannot be substantiated and proved.

As was suggested not only in the preceding chapter but in numerous other chapters throughout this book, the employer's counsel should be most familiar with the discovery rules of the court in which the case is tried and take full advantage of them to be sufficiently prepared for trial. In this connection, the employer's strategy should be to strike early with its interrogatories, discovery depositions, and other forms of discovery to isolate the weaknesses of the defendant's position and better define the specific strategies and techniques through which to try the lawsuit.

General pre-trial and trial techniques, tactics, strategies, and safeguards have been exhausted in many of the preceding chapters and do not merit being repeated specifically herein. However, a review of such general techniques and safeguards should be most meaningful and helpful to an employer's counsel and other representatives who are charged with the responsibility of prosecuting a breach of covenant not to compete lawsuit on behalf of his or her employer.

Therefore, the reader's attention is referred to all the preceding chapters in Part III of this book as well as to Chapters 5 and 10 as to general pre-trial and trial techniques.

24 Techniques and Tactics in Defending Post-Termination Entitlements Litigation

The employer's counsel and other representatives should understand that employees have certain residual rights from their employment following their separation from employment, whether voluntary or involuntary, beyond those protected by statute.

The purpose of this chapter is to address specific types of post-termination legal claims: (1) accrued vacation pay; (2) severance pay; (3) accrued wages; and (4) blacklisting and service letter requirements.

The employer's counsel should be aware that some of the other more specific legal claims that may arise as part of post-termination entitlements consist of: both state and federal COBRA rights; unemployment compensation benefits; plant closure notices; workers' compensation benefits; ERISA rights; and social security rights, all of which are covered in later chapters.

SAFEGUARDS IN DEFENDING LAWSUITS FOR VACATION PAY AS A POST-TERMINATION ENTITLEMENT

Several factors impact upon a lawsuit for vacation pay. The employer's counsel should appreciate that his or her defense to such a lawsuit will depend upon, among other factors:

- who brings such action
- in which state the action is brought and the law applicable to vacation pay within such state
- the employer's policy and/or practice regarding the administration of vacation pay
- whether or not there is a written employment contract between the employer and employee that addresses the subject

Should an employer have a written employment agreement (including a collective bargaining contract) covering the subject of vacation pay, especially with respect to what vacation pay is due the employee, if any, upon his or her termination of employment, the employee may well have a cause of action against the employer for breach of contract if such vacation benefits are not paid the employee. Were this the case, the employer's counsel would be required to demonstrate to the court that the employee did not meet the requirements enumerated (or implied) in the employment agreement by which to be entitled to such alleged vacation pay. (Arbitration cases to enforce vacation pay rights of employees subject to the provisions of a labor agreement are covered in Chapter 15.)

Second, short of an express written agreement on the subject matter of vacation pay, many employers promulgate vacation policies through employee handbooks and other such policy manuals. As has been noted in Chapter 19 of this book, many courts interpret such language to create an implied contract and legal obligation on the part of the employer to pay such vacation benefits, irrespective of the employee's at-will status. For example, as noted by the court in the 1985 Tennessee Appellate case of Abbott v. Keelwood Co., terminated employees are entitled to a pro rata share of their annual vacation pay as provided in their company's personnel handbook, irrespective of the termination-at-will status of the employees.

However, the employer's counsel and other representatives should be aware that not all state courts embrace such causes of action that are in contravention of the employment-at-will doctrine. Thus, the employer's counsel is well advised to research the judicial precedent on the question in the state in which such an action is brought against his or her employer and raise the employment-at-will defense if supported by such judicial precedent.

The employer's counsel should be aware that there is much leeway in which a promised vacation pay policy can be interpreted by a court relative to such conditions as whether vacation pay was or was not promised the employee or employees in question, whether the employee did or did not meet the length of service requirements as specified in the employer's policy or employment contract with the employer, and so on. As a result, the employer's counsel and other representatives should prepare their defense to such a cause of action in such a way that the court will interpret and apply the requirements and conditions of the policy or contract terms most favorably to the employer's position.

Several states have some type of statutes that cover the subject matter of vacation pay to employees. In most such instances, the state's payment-of-wages laws either explicitly or implicitly address when and under what conditions vacation pay will be considered as part of the employee's regular wages.

Whenever a state's payment-for-wages law requires the payment of accrued vacation pay to a terminated employee, the employer's counsel may want to argue that the Federal Employee Retirement Income and Security Act of 1974 preempts such a lawsuit. Thus, aside from other such arguments that the state law does not specifically provide for such a cause of action, if supported by the language of the law and legislative history, or that the employee or employees in question did not accrue any such alleged vacation pay in which to meet the accrual requirements, the employer's most meaningful defense may be an ERISA preemptive argument.

Just because an employer's counsel suggests to a state agency that the state law on the subject of vacation pay is preempted by the federal ERISA statute does not guarantee that the state will not test the preemption argument in court, but an assertive employer's attorney may well bluff a state agency whose officials do not want to take that chance and possibly lose its opportunities to continue to enforce the statutory provisions against less astute employers—or rather, employers that have less astute attorneys.

PRACTICAL POINTS TO PONDER WHEN DEFENDING "SEVERANCE PAY" LITIGATION

Many of the same factors discussed above that apply to legal claims for vacation pay equally apply to lawsuits to recover severance pay by terminated employees, or state agencies on their behalf.

Obviously, should an employer have an employment agreement that specifies to what extent and under what conditions employees are to receive severance pay upon their termination from employment, an employee would be permitted by a court to pursue a cause of action against the employer in the event the employer did not meet its contractual obligation upon the employee's termination. The employer's defenses would be similar to those discussed above with respect to vacation pay in terms that the employer's counsel might argue that no written employment contract existed between the parties, or that the contract in question did not explicitly or implicitly provide for severance pay, or that the employee did not meet the requirements and conditions of the contract to be entitled to receive such severance benefits, if such arguments are applicable. Other defensive arguments to breach of written contract lawsuits may be available to the employer's counsel with respect to severance pay litigation, as discussed in Chapter 18. Arbitration cases, and defenses relative to an employer's refusal to pay severance pay as provided under the terms of a collective bargaining agreement, are discussed in Chapter 15.

Should an employee bring a cause of action against an employer for the employer's failure to pay severance pay as promised in an employee handbook or policy manual, the employer's counsel would have the same defenses available as discussed above with respect to vacation pay. Many state courts embrace such actions notwithstanding the employee's terminable-at-will status.

For example, in the 1979 case of *Dulaney Foods, Inc. v. Ayers*, the Virginia Supreme Court held that an employer's circulation of a memorandum to its employees detailing its severance pay policy in its anticipation of a plant closure created a contractually binding obligation upon the employer to pay such severance pay.

The employer's counsel should review closely the judicial precedent in the state in which his or her employer is the defendant in such a lawsuit, because many state courts, just as with vacation pay, have not been willing to encroach upon the employment-at-will doctrine and permit such causes of action to proceed. Assuming, however, that such judicial precedent was not favorable to the employer's position, the employer's counsel would nevertheless want to assert such defensive arguments, as noted earlier, that such employees did not satisfy the requirements and conditions of the employer's statements or policy on the subject by which to be entitled to any such severance pay, if the evidence supports such an argument.

Several states have passed specific statutes requiring employers to pay severance pay to employees upon their termination due to plant closures, and so forth. Some states' payment-for-wages laws either expressly or impliedly treat severance pay as part of wages due employees upon their termination from employment, when the employer has a policy or practice that provides for such severance pay.

As a result, it may be a state agency, rather than an employee, that may prosecute an action against the employer for the payment of severance pay to comply with the statutory provisions. Aside from the arguments that it had no such practice or policy, or that it had abandoned and abolished any such policy or practice, or that the employee(s) in question did not meet the requirements of the policy or practice by which to be entitled to such severance pay, the employer's most significant argument may be that the state law on the subject is preempted by the federal ERISA statute inasmuch as such a severance pay is a benefit covered by the ERISA provisions.

SPECIAL SENSITIVITIES TO BLACKLISTING AND SERVICE LETTER REQUIREMENTS

Blacklisting is some act or conduct on the part of an employer to prevent re-employment of an employee with some other employer. Most states have statutes that forbid blacklisting. Since many of the original state blacklisting laws were designed to prevent employees from securing employment elsewhere because of union activities, the laws are not readily usable inasmuch as the National Labor Relations Board has exclusive jurisdiction over blacklisting cases based on an employee's union activities, at least with respect to employees protected by the National Labor Relations Act.

Many statutory laws against blacklisting are not used because of the numerous common law tort actions even when not preempted by the National Labor Relations Act. As will be discussed in Part IV of this book, plaintiff lawyers prefer to use common law tort actions as a basis of a lawsuit when the employer's actions or conduct provide for such claims as tortious interference with prospective employment or economic advantage, invasion of privacy, defamation, and so forth, because such tort actions provide for a recovery in punitive damages as well as compensatory damages.

Several states also have enacted service letter laws, requiring an employer to tender to a terminated employee a service letter stating such matters as dates of employment, pay, promotions, positions held and reason for termination.

The state of Missouri's service letter law has probably produced as much or more litigation than all the others combined. In contrast to the past, Missouri courts now do not permit an employer to recover in punitive damages when an employer's service letter to an employee states a false reason for termination.

Both blacklisting and service letter laws are limited in usage and in scope due to the employee's available tort actions for violations of them.

POINTS TO CONSIDER WHEN DEFENDING ACCRUED WAGES LAWSUITS

Many state statutes provide for an award of liquidated damages in the event an employer is not paid his or her accrued wages within the time frame specified by the state's wage and hour laws.

The federal Fair Labor and Standards Act also provides that an employee must be paid proper minimum wages and overtime pay. As such, an employee may, in addition to pursuing any claim that he or she may have through state agencies, persuade the federal wage and hour administration to intervene on his or her behalf.

The employer's most tenable defense when faced with a state or federal claim against it for the payment of accrued wages allegedly due an employee who has been terminated is that he or she had not earned such wages, if such argument can be supported by sufficient evidence.

An employer may also be able to argue that the wages so due the employee had been used to repay money owed to the employer as a set-off against other such indebtedness due the employer. The employer's counsel should proceed with extreme caution with respect to such an argument, however, because many state laws prohibit wage deductions to be used to pay for the employee's indebtedness to the employer or for cash shortages, rent, lost equipment, breakage, and so on. Other state statutes provide that only in certain prescribed situations will the employer be permitted to deduct an employee's wages by way of set-off or assignment.

Certainly, an employee could prosecute an action of his or her own if the refusal of the employer to pay accrued wages violated terms and conditions of a written employment agreement between the parties. As was discussed under the preceding subheadings, the employer may be able to argue several contractual defenses to such a cause of action, as well as to advance arguments that the employee in question had not earned such wages.

In addition, an employee may also be able to proceed with a common law action against the employer for breach of an implied contract to pay such wages which action may be permitted by courts in some jurisdictions, irrespective of the employee's at-will status. However, this approach to receiving one's accrued wages is used rarely, if at all, by employees, because of their statutory rights on the subject matter and state and federal agencies' willingness to enforce such rights.

PRE-TRIAL AND TRIAL STRATEGIES IN DEFENDING POST-TERMINATION ENTITLEMENT CAUSES OF ACTION

The employer's initial pre-trial challenge in defending the four types of post-termination entitlement causes of action addressed in the preceding subheadings is to become familiar with the various statutes addressing each such entitlement within the state in which the action is brought against the employer, as well as the ever-developing decisional law within the applicable state.

Inasmuch as the ERISA preemption rulings with respect to post-termination vacation and severance pay are likely to be interpreted differently by various state and federal courts, the employer's counsel faced with defending a cause of action to recover accrued vacation or severance pay by state agencies pursuant to such statutes should update any previous research to ensure an understanding of the current law with respect to the applicable jurisdiction.

The employer's counsel should also be completely familiar with applicable state laws that may limit wage deductions to satisfy an employee's previous assignment, or used as a set-off to repay the employer in some way, as discussed in the preceding subheading relative to the accrued wages.

In addition, as so frequently discussed as a pre-trial strategy, the employer should use the discovery tools and procedures available to it by which to discover the plaintiff's weaknesses and, in turn, use such information to "fine-tune" its case for presentation to the court.

With respect to how more general pre-trial and trial strategies may be used in defending post-termination entitlement lawsuits, the reader's attention is referred to Chapters 5, 10, and 18.

IV How to Defend Wrongful Discharge and Other Tortious Conduct Causes of Action

25 Successful Strategies in Defending Public Policy Discharge Lawsuits

The employer's counsel and other representatives should well appreciate that employee attorneys have carved out other exceptions to the employment-at-will doctrine aside from contractual exceptions discussed in Part III of this book.

Another ever-emerging exception to the at-will doctrine is that a discharge that violates or contravenes some public policy may give rise to an actionable lawsuit. Public policy is a judicial principle that forbids any person or entity to act, by omission or commission, in a way that has a tendency to be injurious to the general public.

Three specific public policy exceptions to the employment-at-will doctrine have been advanced by plaintiff attorneys:

1. unlawful termination for exercising a statutory right
2. unlawful termination for satisfying a public obligation
3. unlawful termination for reporting, or refusing to commit, an unlawful act

The rationale of the various courts that have recognized public policy exceptions to the employment-at-will doctrine is that the fundamental principles of public policy override the employment-at-will doctrine and that employers will not be permitted to invoke the latter in violation of the former, irrespective of an employer's right to otherwise discharge an employee.

The employer's counsel and representatives should be aware, however, that not all courts in the various states have agreed with the concept that public policy considerations should override the historic employment-at-will rule, and further, to the extent that such courts have recognized public policy principles to erode the at-will doctrine, that they have been rather restrictive in their application of the exception.

The degree to what extent the courts in various states have adopted public policy considerations as an exception to the employment-at-will doctrine seemingly turns upon whether the employee's claim is based upon a statutorily or constitutionally protected right. Although some courts have permitted plaintiff attorneys to proceed upon employees' public policy discharge claims even though the public policy advanced by plaintiff was not embodied in a state statue or constitution, the trend of the courts appears to be in the opposite direction.

Some state courts have even reversed their initial acceptance of policy discharge cases based upon some public policy principle not derived from statutory or constitutional provisions. Such is the wrongful discharge developments in the state of California. For example, the court in the 1987 California case of *Dobbs v. Cardiopulmonary Management Services* held that a plaintiff claiming that she had been discharged for refusing to work her shift because her employer had inadequate staffing which, in turn, threatened the health and well being of the patients under her care, was entitled to proceed with her lawsuit due to public policy considerations.

However, in the *Foley v. Interactive Data Corporation* case, a case discussed in detail in Chapter 20, the California Supreme Court held that in order to sustain an actionable public policy discharge lawsuit, the claim must implicate the violation of some fundamental or basic public policy concern, and that exercising some right or disclosing certain information that serves only the interests of the employee, rather than the interests of the public, does not satisfy such standard.

That does not mean that some state courts have not extended the public policy exception to more open-ended claims and accepted the notion that a clear and compelling mandate of public policy, albeit without the benefit of a statutory or constitutionally protected right, is enough to sustain an actionable lawsuit.

Whether a given statute or constitutional provision suggests a basis for a public policy discharge claim is also frequently questioned by the courts. For example, according to the *Foley* court, a statute that states a duty the purpose of which is to benefit a particular employee or employer, or both, as opposed to benefiting the public as a whole, may not be used as a basis to support a public policy cause of action.

The employer's counsel and representatives should also be aware that some state courts accept certain statutory provisions as a basis of permitting a given public policy cause of action to proceed, while denying other public policy claims based on different statutory provisions. In this connection, even courts in the more conservative jurisdictions have been willing to encroach upon the employment-at-will rule where an employee has been discharged or otherwise adversely affected in his or her job due to their refusal to violate some criminal law.

TACTICAL CONSIDERATIONS WHEN DEFENDING AN UNLAWFUL TERMINATION FOR EXERCISING A STATUTORY RIGHT CLAIM

Many state statutes make it unlawful to discharge or take adverse action against an employee for filing a workers' compensation claim. Some states do not yet have such statutory provisions. Many states that have them, presently, did not always have such.

With respect to those states not having such statutory prohibitions against retaliatory discharge for filing a workers' compensation claim, earlier plaintiff attorneys sought to obtain relief through the courts, claiming that since such a retaliatory discharge contravened a fundamentally and statutorily protected right of an employee, that public policy considerations required the court to permit such a claim to proceed, irrespective of the employment-at-will doctrine.

A reading of the earlier cases suggest that the courts summarily dismissed such public policy discharge claims based upon the proposition that it must be up to the legislature to provide such relief rather than the courts, for to do otherwise would encroach upon the employment-at-will doctrine.

However, in the 1970s and 1980s, various state courts commenced to take a closer look at the public policy impact, with respect to such claims.

For example, in the 1973 Indiana case of *Frampton v. Central Indiana Gas Company*, the court held that an employee who had been discharged one month after settling her workers' compensation claim against her employer presented an actionable lawsuit, irrespective of the employment-at-will status of the employee.

Indiana certainly is not the only state in which courts have recognized that a discharge in retaliation for filing a workers' compensation claim provides an exception to the at-will rule. A Florida court in the 1983 case of *Smith v. Piezo Technology & Professional Administrators* held that the discharge of an employee for filing a workers' compensation claim against the employer was so repugnant to public policy that it removed the employee's at-will status. An Illinois court held similarly in the 1978 case of *Kelsey v. Morola, Inc.* The list goes on and on, including among others: Massachusetts in 1980; West Virginia in 1980; Kansas in 1981; New Jersey in 1981; Michigan in 1981; Hawaii in 1983; Nevada in 1984; Washington in 1984; Tennessee in 1984.

The applicability of the exercising a statutory right public policy exception to the at-will principle extends far beyond workers' compensation retaliatory discharges. The employer's counsel and representatives should anticipate that this public policy exception will be advanced in all sorts of legal scenarios by creative and innovative plaintiff attorneys in the future. This becomes even more the case as state legislatures continue to pass statutory prohibitions against retaliatory discharges for filing workers' compensation cases.

More general defenses, techniques, and tactics to consider when defending a public policy discharge lawsuit will be discussed at length below. However, there are some specific tactics relative to defending an "exercising a statutory right" public policy discharge case; these are described in the following sections.

Review the State's Workers' Compensation Law

First, the employer's counsel should ascertain whether there exists a specific non-retaliatory provision within the state's workers' compensation law that forbids such action on the part of the employer. Assuming that the plaintiff's attorney has not brought suit under such statute (or has added the common law public policy claim as pendent to such statutory claim), the employer's counsel should argue that the statutory provision should establish the sole remedy for the employee and that the common law public policy claim should be dismissed by reason of statutory preemption.

Use the Employment-at-Will Rule to Get the Claim Dismissed

Second, assuming there is no such state statute forbidding retaliation against employees' filing workers' compensation cases, or if such, counsel is not successful in getting the public policy claim dismissed under a preemption argument, the employer's counsel should move and argue that the matter be dismissed because it encroaches upon, and contravenes, the historic employment-at-will rule; and in keeping with earlier successful arguments on the subject, if the law should be changed to permit employees to proceed with such actions through the courts within the state, such rights and remedies should be effected by legislation rather than through judicial precedent.

Show That the Employer Discharged the Employee for Just Cause

Last, assuming the employer's counsel is unable to get the public policy claim dismissed or the case transferred or removed to a more favorably judicial climate, the employer's counsel should attempt to prepare the case so as to demonstrate that the discharge (or other actions taken against the claimant) was not in retaliation of the employee's filing a workers' compensation claim or exercising some other statutory right, but such action taken by the employer was for just cause in keeping with past practice and policy.

PRELIMINARY STEPS TO CONSIDER WHEN DEFENDING A "SATISFYING A PUBLIC OBLIGATION" PUBLIC POLICY DISCHARGE CLAIM

A second type of public policy exception to the employment-at-will doctrine that has been recognized and adopted by many state courts throughout the United States is that which is referred to as unlawful discharge for "satisfying a public obligation."

One of the first courts to recognize this type of public policy exception to the at-will rule was an Oregon court in the 1975 case of *Nees v. Hocks* in which the plaintiff alleged she had been discharged by her employer because she had served on jury duty in spite of her employer's request that she ask to be excused from such "public obligation." The Oregon not only permitted the plaintiff employee to proceed to trial on her claim but entered judgment against the employer, holding that employers may not terminate employees on such a socially undesirable motive.

As with workers' compensation legislation, many states have enacted laws that prohibit employers from retaliatory actions against employees who are called upon to serve as jurors. Most states that have not enacted such laws may likely do so in the future. Irrespective, most of the cases that have applied the "satisfying a public obligation" public policy exception to the employment-at-will doctrine have been in the area of wrongful discharge for jury service.

For example, following the *Nees* case, the Pennsylvania case of *Reuther v. Fowler & Williams* in 1978; the Maryland case of *Adler v. American Standard Corporation* in 1981; the Hawaii case of *Parnar v. Americana Hotels* in 1983, all sustained causes of action based upon retaliatory discharges for satisfying a public obligation in serving on a jury.

Many state courts continue to refuse to recognize this public policy exception to the at-will doctrine under the rationale that if the law is to be changed to permit such lawsuits, such changes should emanate from the legislature, not from the courts.

The employer's counsel and other representatives should understand that the "satisfying a public obligation" public policy exception as a basis for a legal claim has been used in more than mere retaliatory discharge for jury service cases.

For example, an Illinois court in the 1981 case of *Palmateer v. International Harvester Co.* permitted a plaintiff to proceed to trial where the plaintiff allegedly had been discharged for providing information to police to be used against a fellow employee, the court holding that there is no public policy more basic and fundamental than one favoring the effective protection of the laws and property of the citizens of the state. Other courts have applied this public policy exception to various factual situations in which a plaintiff has been able to argue and demonstrate that his or her discharge resulted from satisfying some public obligation imposed by the demands of an orderly society.

The employer's counsel should thus be aware that a plethora of such cases are likely to be seen in the future.

Although general techniques and strategies will be discussed below, relative to defending public policy discharge cases, some of the more specific defensive measures that should be entertained by an employer's counsel whose employer is a defendant in a "satisfying a public obligation" public policy discharge case would consist of the following.

The argument that one was discharged for satisfying a public obligation contains much more subjectivity than an argument that one was discharged for exercising a statutory right. Thus, to the extent that an employer's counsel is called on to defend a "satisfying a public obligation" public policy discharge claim, he or she should analyze the plaintiff's pleadings to determine whether the allegations state a reference or connection to some statutory or constitutional provision or merely charge that the employer's action in some way was injurious to the right of certain private parties.

In addition, the employer's counsel should consider employing some of the more specific defensive tactics discussed with respect to defending an "exercising a statutory right" type of public policy discharge claim as was discussed in the preceding subheading.

HELPFUL HINTS TO FOLLOW WHEN DEFENDING A "REFUSAL TO COMMIT OR REPORT" AN UNLAWFUL ACT PUBLIC POLICY DISCHARGE CLAIM

Probably the two public policy discharge cases that have drawn the most interest and have been used most prolifically are claims of unlawful terminations for refusing to commit an unlawful act or reporting an unlawful act.

The reader can more easily identify with the latter in terms of the number of whistleblowing statutes that have been enacted by various state and local legislators through the years. However, it is the former that has received the most notoriety in the courts.

As suggested earlier, even the most conservative judges seem to be highly sensitive to employee claims of being discharged for refusing to commit an unlawful act, as such action is so contrary to fundamental public policy concerns. As a result, most states have recognized and adopted the public policy exception to the employment-at-will doctrine when a discharge is alleged to have occurred as a result of an employee refusing to commit a criminal or some other form of an unlawful act.

Review Precedent Cases

The 1980 California case of *Tameny v. Atlantic Richfield Co.* in which a 15-year employee alleged he had been discharged for refusing to participate in an illegal price-fixing scheme was one of the first such cases. A California court held that an employee suffering damages as a result of such discharge may maintain a cause of action against the employer irrespective of his or her otherwise employment-at-will status.

The 1978 West Virginia case of *Harless v. First National Bank in Fairmont* presented a factual situation in which a West Virginia court held that an employee who was allegedly discharged for refusing to engage in conduct which would have constituted a violation of the West Virginia Consumer Credit and Protection Act could proceed to trial with his cause of action, notwithstanding his employment-at-will status.

The 1980 Connecticut case of *Sheets v. Teddy's Frosted Foods, Inc.* is another such example. Probably the most amusing of such cases is that of *Wagenseller v. Scottsdale Memorial Hospital* in which a nursing services employee alleged she was discharged for her refusal to "moon" fellow employees at a camping retreat with her manager and other staff members, contending that mooning could be considered indecent exposure by law enforcement officers and thus criminal conduct.

The courts have also been highly sensitive to employees who allege they were discharged for reporting certain criminal activity and other such unlawful conduct committed by their employers to proper authorities, or for refusing not to report such activity.

For example, a New Jersey Appellate Court in the 1988 case of *Potter v. Village Bank* held actionable an employee's cause of action alleging that he had been discharged for reporting suspected laundering of drug money by bank officials to the New Jersey Commission of Banking.

Many states now have whistleblowing statutes that forbid the discharge of public and/or private sector employees for blowing-the-whistle on their employers for some criminal or illegal act; yet many states do not. Even in states where such a discharge is forbidden by statute, employees have nonetheless been successful in bringing their common law claims based upon public policy concerns.

For example, a Michigan court ruled actionable an employee's cause of action which alleged he was discharged for reporting patient abuse at a mental hospital even though the employee had a statutory right to proceed with such lawsuit, the court holding that the public policy considerations relative to the matter pre-existed the passage of a subsequently enacted whistleblower statute.

As with legal claims involving discharges for refusing to commit an unlawful act on public policy considerations, most states have recognized that a discharge for reporting unlawful activities or criminal conduct to proper authorities violates such fundamental and basic public policy interests that the employee victimized by such discharge has an actionable claim in a court of law against his or her employer.

How to Defend the Employer

In addition to applying the strategic and tactical defenses discussed in preceding sections, an employer's counsel charged with defending an employer against a refusal to commit, or reporting, a criminal act discharge claim should consider exploring the following defensive steps, as well.

Assuming the state in which the action is brought provides a statutory prohibition as to whistleblowing and the employee's lawsuit alleges that he or she was discharged for reporting an unlawful or criminal act of the employer, the employer's counsel should motion the court that such statutory provisions preempt the filing of the common law public policy discharge cause of action. Assuming that such a "whistleblowing" statute extends to a prohibition of discharge for the refusal to commit an unlawful or criminal act for the employer, or a separate state statute provides such, the employer's counsel should likewise argue that the employee's common law public policy cause of action is so preempted by such statute.

Second, assuming that the employer's counsel is unsuccessful with respect to a preemption argument and must, nonetheless, go forward in the defense of the employee's claim that he or she was discharged for refusing to commit, or reporting of, an unlawful or criminal act, the employer's counsel should look closely at both the judicial and statutory definitions of what constitutes an unlawful or criminal act and what constitutes the reporting of or refusal to commit such an act. Persuasive evidence may also be helpful in clarifying such definitions, assuming an absence of cases on the subject in the state in question. Once such definitions are analyzed and evaluated, the employer's counsel is then challenged to demonstrate to the court that the employer's alleged omission or commission with respect to what led to the employee's discharge does not fall within such definitions.

PRE-TRIAL AND TRIAL TECHNIQUES TO DEFEND PUBLIC POLICY DISCHARGE LAWSUITS

An employer's counsel faced with the challenge to defend his or her employer against a public policy discharge cause of action should expend considerable effort during pre-trial to limit the impact of an adverse decision in two specific ways:

- determine whether the employer is liable, if at all, and if so, to what degree
- if liability is found, determine what type of damages are recoverable.

Much has already been discussed with respect to defending an employer against a public policy discharge case in terms of attempting to get the case dismissed or removed or transferred to a more favorable jurisdiction, all of which may be of assistance to an employer's counsel in seeking to foreclose any liability on the part of his or her employer in such a cause of action. Preemptive maneuvers have already been addressed in this chapter, as well.

Also, preceding sections of this chapter have discussed such defenses as that the employee was discharged for good and just cause.

The employer's counsel should attempt to show the court that the employee's allegations are purely for self-serving purposes and the conduct so alleged, at best, violated some personal and private interests of the employee, rather than any public interests.

Some examples may help to demonstrate the extent to which some plaintiff's counsel go in attempting to sustain a cause of action based upon public policy, some of which contentions have been recognized and others of which have been rejected by the courts. For instance:

- A Pennsylvania court found no public policy violation in the discharge of an employee for constantly complaining to higher management about what the employee thought to be poor supervision of his work area.
- A federal court, applying New Hampshire law, found no public policy violation where employees had been discharged for seeking reimbursements for goods at prices higher than the employees actually paid.
- The Michigan Supreme Court held that an employee discharged for excessive absenteeism due to a work-related injury didn't show any violation of public policy.
- A Wisconsin court rejected a manager's claim of a public policy discharge where he was dismissed because his live-in relationship with a subordinate was causing dissension among other employees.
- A Massachusetts court rejected a store manager's cause of action that he was wrongfully discharged for complaining to his superiors about a fellow manager's filing false damage and shortage claims since his report of such conduct concerned the company's internal operations, rather than some public policy interests.

With respect to the challenge of employer's counsel to reduce or eliminate any liability or adverse judgment in connection with the defense of a public policy discharge lawsuit, he or she should research the law in the state in which the action is brought, and assuming no removal or transfer of the case to a more favorable jurisdiction is available with respect to the employer's interest, said counsel should attempt to convince the court that to the extent that the public policy theory has previously been recognized and adopted in the state to permit a cause of action, it should be limited in its applicability only to those cases in which the plaintiff can demonstrate to the court that some statutory or constitutional provision has been touched by the employer's conduct.

The employer's counsel and other representatives should be aware that many courts, particularly at the lower levels, initially embraced the public policy exception to the employment-at-will doctrine but later had second thoughts and now have reversed their earlier positions on the issue or have had their earlier positions reversed by the appellate courts within their respective states.

For example, the New York Court of Appeals in *Murphy v. American Home Products*, in contrast to earlier reported cases on the public policy exception, rejected a claimant's cause of action that he had been discharged for reporting to higher management what he believed to be certain illegal manipulations of the company's pension fund, the court stating among other things, that "absent a constitutionally impermissible purpose, a statutory prohibition, or an express limitation in the individual contract of employment, an employer's right to terminate an employee at will remains unimpaired."

Thus, the New York High Court, as had previously the California High Court in *Foley*, limited the degree to which it would permit the public policy theory to extend. The second challenge of the employer's counsel and other representatives who are charged with the responsibility of defending a public policy discharge lawsuit, is to evaluate and prepare proper pleadings to argue that, irrespective of the scope of liability and the extent to which the court permits the public policy theory to apply as an exception to the employment-at-will doctrine, any judgment and award permitted by the court should be limited to compensatory damages only and that punitive damages should not be recoverable, whatsoever.

The employer's counsel has a substantial challenge in attempting to convince a court that permits a public policy discharge case to proceed to trial to then limit recovery to compensatory damages alone, rather than to permit a recovery of punitive damages, in that the public policy exception to the employment-at-will doctrine, conceptually, is grounded in tort rather than contract.

The employer's counsel's second challenge during both pre-trial and trial in defending a public policy discharge lawsuit is to convince the court that damages, if any, should not contain any punitive awards. The employer's counsel may find valuable a research of the courts in other jurisdictions that have so limited a recovery to compensatory damages and use such decisions, and the rationale of the courts within the decisions, as persuasive argument to the court at hand.

The employer's counsel should also refer to both pre-trial and trial techniques discussed in previous chapters of this book relative to preparation of witnesses, preparation of documentary and demonstrative evidence, proper preparation of exhibits, and so forth as has been discussed in Chapters 5, 10, and 18.

As a final comment, the employer's counsel and other representatives should be aware that although the scope of this chapter has been limited to a discussion of the public policy exception to the employment-at-will doctrine with respect to discharge cases, courts are now extending the theory to causes of action for less severe disciplinary actions and other adverse employment decisions. Notwithstanding, the same strategies, techniques, tactics, and defensive as discussed through this chapter would likewise apply to public policy claims to address adverse employment decisions less severe than discharge.

26 Safeguards to Employ in Defending "Interference with Employment Relationship" Lawsuits

Seemingly, more and more plaintiff attorneys are incorporating into their wrongful discharge lawsuits an ancillary claim that the employer tortiously and/or maliciously interfered with their client's employment relationship or contract.

Many such claims are used somewhat as a preemptive strategy to prevent a defendant employer from removing an action in a state court to a federal court and, thus, foreclosing the employer's diversity of citizenship argument for removal.

The interference with employment-type lawsuits originated from the 14th-Century Statute of Laborers in England that penalized any person who induced an employee to leave the employment of another or harbored an employee after so leaving. Statutory law on the subject of "unlawful enticement" continues to find its place in American jurisprudence. Indeed, numerous states have enacted such state laws that forbid any person or firm to entice away employees under contract or in the employment of another before the term of employment expires. In such statutes, it is the employer from whom the employee is enticed that has the cause of action against the enticing party rather than the employee, although the employee may, nonetheless, have some common law action against the enticing third party, depending upon his or her employment status at the time of enticement and also depending upon the judicial precedent within the applicable state as to whether a common law action is available to the employee for third party enticement.

Employer's counsel and other representatives who are charged with the responsibility of keeping their employer free from these type lawsuits may readily conclude that the employer could become either a plaintiff or a defendant in a third party interference or unlawful enticement cause of action.

The scope of this chapter relates more to an employee's action against an employer or third party in terms of claims and damages for a tortious interference with an employee's present or future employment, resulting in lost wages, benefits, and/or some economic advantage in the future, rather than an employer's claim against another employer for the latter's unlawful enticement.

Some fundamental limitations and defenses with respect to interference with employment and loss of economic advantage type cases include:

1. inasmuch as the employee's employer is a party to the employment contract with the employee, the employer cannot properly be charged with inducing a breach thereof or interfering with such contract in the capacity of a third party;
2. most jurisdictions do not regard an at-will employee to have proper standing to bring an interference with employment contract cause of action simply because the courts in such jurisdictions do not recognize any formal contractual relationship between the employee and employer with which to interfere. Yet, the trend of the courts to recognize at-will employees' right to bring interference with an employment cause of action is on the increase; and
3. many state statutes, or judicial precedent in lieu of state statutes, protect and insulate supervisors and managers from being charged with an interference of employment contract claim when they are acting as an agent and in the course and scope of their supervisory authority, the rationale for such statutes or common law protection of supervisors and managers in such cases being that since the employer may not be sued for interfering with its own contract with the employee in question, neither can its supervisors and managers who are acting as agents of the employer in carrying out their responsibilities on behalf of the employer, even though their actions may, in some way, cause the employee to suffer damages due to lost wages, benefits, and so forth.

Another aspect of interference with employment-type lawsuits that should be understood by employer's counsel and other representatives is that whenever an employer breaches an enforceable written employment contract with the employee, recoverable damages typically are limited to compensatory damages, such as lost wages and benefits. On the other hand, when an outsider or some third party induces the employer to break the employment contract with the employee, or in some other way interferes with the contracted relationship between the employer and the employee, the employee so victimized by the third party interference will be entitled to not only compensatory damages but also to punitive damages as well, assuming that he or she prevails in the lawsuit, given the fact that an interference with an employment contract constitutes a tort.

HELPFUL HINTS IN RECOGNIZING THE TYPES OF "INTERFERENCE OF EMPLOYMENT" CLAIMS

The employer's counsel and other representatives should appreciate the scope and spectrum within which "interference of employment" causes of action have been advanced.

Case #1: When a Company Entices a Competitor's Employee

Obviously, the typical lawsuit arises in the context of a firm attempting to entice an employee of its competitor to quit his or her employment and become an employee of such firm. In such a scenario, the employer from which the employee is enticed may become either a plaintiff or defendant in a subsequent cause of action, or possibly both.

First, either by virtue of statute or decisional precedent, the employer so losing the services of the employee so enticed from its employment may sue the firm that so enticed the employee on the ground of interference with employment. Assuming that such employer was able to overcome all the potential defenses pleaded against it, it may well be successful in its lawsuit and recover damages.

However, were the employer from whom the employee was enticed, in turn, to interfere with the employee's new employment, causing the employee to lose his or her job as a result, the employee may well be able to proceed with an "interference with employment" cause of action against his or her former employer for loss of economic advantage and other such damages.

Thus, an employer and its counsel must look beyond what the employer may be entitled due to a third person's interference with its employment relationship with a given employee; it must also foresee how its actions may, in turn, interfere with the employee's rights, as well. For example, in the 1983 West Virginia case of *Torbett v. Wheeling Dollar Savings & Trust Co.*, the court held that a bank employee who voluntarily terminated her employment with an employer with whom she had entered into an employment contract, restricting her employment with any other bank within a 25-mile radius upon her resignation, was not only entitled to a declaratory judgment that the restrictive covenant was unreasonable but also could amend her complaint against the employer and sue her former employer for tortious interference with her employment on grounds that the restrictive covenant had prevented her from obtaining other employment.

Case #2: When a Former Employer Interferes with an Employee's Current Employment

A similar case also demonstrates the necessity of management attorneys to be ever sensitive to the possibility of an employee filing some type of interference of employment lawsuit against his or her former employer for post-separation conduct on the part of the employer. It is the 1977 South Carolina case of *Webster v. Holly Hill Lumber Co.*, in which the court held that an employee, who had been discharged by his new employer after the new employer had received an unsolicited telephone call from the former employer stating to the new employer that the employee had a workers' compensation claim pending against it for a back injury, had an actionable claim against the former employer for tortious interference with employment.

Case #3: When a Third Party Induces an Employer to Fire an Employee

Another typical case in which the interference of employment legal theory is frequently advanced by plaintiff attorneys is whenever a third party induces an employer to fire an employee who has an enforceable contract with the employer for a fixed term.

For example, in the 1987 Massachusetts case of *Malhoit v. Liberty Bank and Trust Co.*, the court held a bank president personally liable in tort for interfering with an employee's opportunity with another employer by maliciously fabricating charges of misconduct in an attempt to get her discharged.

A Georgia court held in the 1988 case of *Favors v. Alco Manufacturing Co.*, that an employee who was allegedly discharged for rebuffing the sexual advances of a union shop steward could proceed with her lawsuit against him for tortious interference with employment.

A creditor may likewise become a defendant in a tortious interference with employment lawsuit if by and through its actions an employer dismisses an employee, particularly where the creditor is not justified in terms of business necessity. The creditor's privilege to interfere with an employee's employment, aside from the process of judicial imposed garnishments or attachments of income, has been narrowly construed by the courts. For example, in the 1971 Alaska case of *Long v. Newby*, the court sustained an employee's interference with an employment cause of action against a hospital's bill collector who made good on his threat to get the employee discharged from her employment if she did not pay her bill, especially in view of the employee's legitimate protest over the validity of the alleged indebtedness.

A customer may become a defendant in a tortious interference with employment cause of action, as well, particularly if the customer does not have a justifiable business connection with the employer sufficiently to justify his or her actions toward the employee, or such actions of the customer is carried out maliciously. For instance, in an earlier Pennsylvania case, a court held that an insurance carrier could be sued in an interference with employment cause of action by an employee who had been dismissed as a result of the insurance company's threats to cancel its insurance with her employer if she was not so discharged.

Professional regulatory agents may also be subjected to defending interference with employment type lawsuits. The question with respect to whether such a claim is sustainable turns upon whether the agency is acting within its scope to establish and maintain standards within keeping with its licensing authority or goes outside such bounds. In one case on the subject, the court permitted a former employee of a savings and loan association that had been implicated in misuse of funds to proceed with her interference with employment cause of action against a state banking official who had conveyed to her prospective employer what he knew about the situation and, although the employee had not been implicated in any misuse of funds, that he, nonetheless, recommended she not be hired by such employer.

Case #4: When Fellow or Former Employees Are Named as Party Defendants

One of the more popular types of third party interference with employment lawsuits is that in which fellow or former employees are named as party defendants.

The employer's counsel and representatives should appreciate that the courts do not extend the same privilege with respect to employees and their interactions with fellow employees as they do with supervisors who serve as agents of the employer, especially when such supervisors act within the scope of their supervisory authority. Moreover, some courts permit interference with employment actions against fellow or former employees even when the person prosecuting the lawsuit was terminable at the will of the employer.

Several cases illustrate the trend of employees' propensity to sue fellow or former employees for tortiously interfering with their employment. For example, a Washington appellate court in the 1988 case of *Eserhut v. Heister* permitted an employee to proceed on his claim against former co-workers where he was forced to resign his position because of their harassment of him. In the 1987 Oregon case of *Lewis v. Oregon Beauty Supply Co.*, a court held that an employee, who was allegedly discharged for complaining to her supervisor about his son's continuous harassment of her after she had broken off her relationship with the son, stated an actionable interference with employment lawsuit against the supervisor's son, the supervisor's son also being a fellow employee at the time of her dismissal.

The employer's counsel and other representatives should well appreciate that an interference with employment by an employee against a fellow or former employee, or employees, does not necessarily remove the employer from being involved in some way. Aside from whatever morale problems may persist from the lawsuit within the employer's workplace, the employer may be brought into the suit in some way, perhaps as a co-conspirator with employees in such a cause of action, or a third party defendant in some other manner.

Case #5: When a Company Interferes with a Former Employee's Unemployment Compensation

Interference with employment lawsuits may arise in cases other than those that involve discharge. For instance, a federal district court, applying Virginia law, held in the 1986 case of *Welch v. Kennedy Piggly Wiggly Stores, Inc.*, that an employee could proceed with his lawsuit against his employer on the ground of tortious interference with economic opportunity where the employer had hired a polygrapher to conduct a lie detector examination and falsified the results thereof in order to deny the employee unemployment compensation.

PECULIAR DEFENSES TO ADVANCE IN "INTERFERENCE OF EMPLOYMENT" CAUSES OF ACTION

An employer's counsel who is called upon to defend an interference of employment type lawsuit against the employer should evaluate the various defenses that he or she may attempt to use, if applicable to the specific cause of action, given the facts and circumstances, and if available as a defense in the jurisdiction in which the action is brought. Employer's counsel who are charged with prosecuting an unlawful enticement or interference with employment lawsuit against an employer that has enticed an employee from the employer should be aware of such defenses, as well, and prepare his or her case in such a manner to overcome such defenses.

From a defensive perspective, however, the employer's counsel should first seek to ascertain the true employment relationship with the employer, and what, if any, written contracts of employment exist between the parties.

Defense #1: The Employee Is a Terminable-at-Will Employee

Assuming the employee bringing the lawsuit against the employer is a terminable-at-will employee and thus free to leave his or her employment at any time desired, then such a defense should be espoused. Such argument may not always be relevant as a defense, however, as some courts have ruled that a third party's interference with an employee's present employment relationship, or prospective relationship, is nonetheless actionable irrespective of his or her at-will status.

Defense #2: The Employer Is Not a Proper Party to the Lawsuit

Should the employer be the defendant in an interference with employment action by an employee who has a written employment agreement with the employer, the employer's primary defense would be that it is not a proper party to the suit because it is impossible for it to have interfered, as a third party, with its own contract.

Defense #3: The Employer Had Privilege and Justification

One of the most useful defenses in an interference with employment type cause of action is that of privilege and justification. For example, suppose an employer is sued by a former employer of an employee who has commenced working for the employer on the grounds that the employer-defendant maliciously and tortiously enticed the employee from the former employer and interfered with its employment relationship with the employee. Aside from the defensive argument noted above, the defendant's counsel may argue that the employer so sued had a business privilege of attempting to hire the best employees it could possibly find. This privilege of competition may be impaired, however, were the employer-plaintiff able to demonstrate and show the court in such case that the motive of the later employer was not to hire the best employees possible, but rather, that it hired the employee in question so as to procure its customers list and attempt to raid its customer base.

Defense #4: The Employer Had Privilege of Self-Protection

A similar defense that an employer-defendant may want to advance in an interference with employment lawsuit is that of the privilege of self-protection; that is, it acted in the manner it did, not to interfere with the employee's employment, but rather to protect its own business interest.

An example of the privilege of self-protection is reflected in the 1976 Oklahoma case of *Del State Bank v. Salmon*, in which the court held a bank that had made substantial loans was privileged to exercise its influence over the company to seek the removal of the president of the company when the bank ran into financial difficulties, jeopardizing the bank's loans to the company, especially where the bank believed that the company's financial condition resulted from the poor performance of the company's president.

Defense #5: The Employer Had Managerial Privilege

As has been suggested earlier, another defense that an employer's counsel may find beneficial, especially as it relates to supervisors and managers being named as defendants in interference with employment type lawsuits, is that of managerial privilege; that is, when supervisors are acting within the scope of their supervisory authority as an agent of the employer, their actions with respect to an employee is the same as that of the employer and since the employer cannot be held to have interfered with its own contract with the employee, neither may its supervisors or managers.

Notwithstanding the managerial privilege as a justifiable defense, it can easily be lost if a management member acts outside his or her scope of authority. For example, the court in the 1985 Illinois case of Powers v. Delnor Hospital held that a supervisor may be liable for tortious interference with an employee's prospective employment if he knowingly gave a false reason for termination to a prospective employer. Similarly, a Michigan court held in the 1985 case of Stack v. Marcum that a supervisor can be held personally liable for a tortious interference with an employee's employment when acting on his own behalf and for his own benefit in discharging an employee. Too, a District of Columbia court ruled that a supervisor could be found personally liable for intentionally interfering with an employee's contractual relationship where the supervisor engaged in a malicious pattern of conduct to bring about the employee's dismissal.

Defense #6: The Employer Had Other Privileges

Another defense that an employer may want to advance in an interference with employment type lawsuit is that the action on its part that allegedly caused the plaintiff in question to suffer was privileged in some other way, such as a customer's right to demand quality services or products from a supplier or retailer of such, or a creditor's right to ensure that a debt is properly paid, or an employee's freedom of speech and association.

Defense #7: The Employer's Action Was Not the Proximate Cause of the Employee's Discharge

An additional defense that the defending employer may want to present to the court and/or jury in an interference with employment type of lawsuit, if applicable and relevant, is that the defendant's action was not the proximate cause of the discharge or other adverse consequence suffered by the plaintiff, in that the same injury or harm to the plaintiff would have occurred with or without the alleged interference of the defendant.

PRE-TRIAL AND TRIAL TECHNIQUES TO CONTEMPLATE WHEN DEFENDING AN "INTERFERENCE WITH EMPLOYMENT" LAWSUIT

The most significant pre-trial maneuvers that a defendant's counsel should explore in an interference with employment type lawsuit is an exhaustive investigation into the facts of the case from which proper legal arguments can be prepared to either attempt to get the action dismissed or substantially limited. As has been suggested in earlier chapters, an employer's counsel is bordering on "de facto" malpractice when he or she does not take advantage of every discovery tool available to obtain each and every fact that is relevant to the trial of the case and discern the respective positions and issues as to each and every party to the cause of action. Defending an interference with employment lawsuit deserves no less.

As to other pre-trial and trial techniques in an interference with employment type lawsuit, the employer's counsel should exhaust his or her efforts in researching all legal precedent within the jurisdiction in which the action is filed so as to ascertain all defenses available, as well as to exhaust favorable persuasive decisions in other jurisdictions and incorporate such favorable decisions in its motions and pleadings to the court.

The reader's attention is referred to Chapters 5, 10, and 18 to review general pre-trial and trial techniques, tactics, and strategies that may be utilized with respect to defending interference with employment type lawsuits.

27 Successful Strategies in Defending Invasion of Employment Privacy Lawsuits

One of the first significant arguments to espouse that an invasion upon one's right of privacy should give rise to a cause of action in tort was that of Samuel Warren and Louis Brandeis in their famous 1890 *Harvard Law Review* article entitled "The Right of Privacy."

The Warren and Brandeis law review article followed one of the earliest reported cases on the common law cause of action for the invasion of privacy. It was the 1881 case of *DeMay v. Roberts* in which the Michigan High Court affirmed a tort action against a medical doctor who permitted a single male with no medical background or training to be present during a childbirth by the plaintiff.

Courts gradually began to recognize a common law cause of action for the invasion upon the privacy of another in the first half of the twentieth century, but the decisions took on a variety of rationale and were somewhat fragmented relative to structure and continuity. This seemingly led Professor William Prosser to suggest in a 1960 article entitled "Privacy" that the primary right of privacy should be separated into four categories that were later adopted by the *Restatement (Second) of Torts* in 1977. This four-part analysis of a common law right of privacy consists of the following:

1. Appropriation of one's name or likeness, sometimes referred to as the "right of publicity"

2. Unreasonable intrusion upon the solitude or seclusion of another
3. Publicity or disclosure that unreasonably places a person in a false light before the public
4. Unreasonable publication or disclosure of private facts about another

During the same period of time in which the various courts began to recognize a private cause of action for an invasion upon one's privacy, many states began to enact statutes and constitutional amendments to protect the right of privacy, as well. During this same period of time, also, the courts began interpreting then-existing statutes and constitutions in a more favorable light relative to privacy rights.

For example, in the 1987 case of *O'Conner v. Ortega*, the United States Supreme Court addressed the question of whether an employer's search of a state employee's desk, without prior notice or approval and while the employee was away on vacation, violated the employee's constitutional protection against unreasonable search and seizure. The court's decision is somewhat instructional not only by way of precedent in constitutional law but also as to common law causes of action for invasion of privacy law because it attempted to strike a balance of the employer's right to meet its business interests against the employee's right of privacy against abusive intrusions. The U.S. Supreme Court adopted the *Ortega* standard that a search by a federal, state, or municipal employer (involving state action) of an employee's office must be justified from the inception in terms of "probable cause" of work-related misconduct or necessary for a justifiable work-related purpose, must not be excessively intrusive, and the methods used to accomplish the search must relate to its objective. Although the *Ortega* decision applies only to public sector employees, such as federal, state or municipal, given its constitutional basis, many state courts are interpreting state constitutions and statutes similarly, particularly state laws that extend privacy protection to private sector as well as public sector employees.

For example, the Alaskan constitution states that the "right of the people to privacy is recognized and should not be abridged" and applies to both private and public sector employees.

In addition, the Arizona, California, Florida, Hawaii, Illinois, Louisiana, Montana, South Carolina, and Washington constitutions recognize certain constitutional rights of privacy for private citizens without the necessity of state action.

State statutes that limit the right of employers to invade upon an employee's right of privacy are too numerous to even attempt to address within the scope of this book, but they continue to grow in numbers each year, not only with respect to privacy against unreasonable disclosure of employee's personnel and work records (and the employees' right of access to review such records), but also in terms of limiting drug and alcohol testing, aids testing, polygraph testing, and so forth.

HELPFUL HINTS IN EVALUATING THE VARIOUS TYPES OF WORKPLACE PRIVACY LAWSUITS

It would appear that the ever-emerging common law rights of privacy in the workplace, as well as the developing state statutes on the subject, has caused plaintiff attorneys to explore further how they may incorporate additional claims of privacy invasion into their lawsuits against employers.

The employer's counsel and other representatives should appreciate that plaintiff attorneys' attempts to use invasion of privacy claims in their lawsuits against employers serve several purposes, the most significant of which is that the elements in proving a common law action for invasion of privacy are not as numerous and difficult as are the elements of proof in many other tort actions incorporated into such law suits. For example, a plaintiff may have difficulty establishing a lawsuit based on defamation by the employer should the employer be able to show that the statements or publication made against the plaintiff were truthful — truth constituting a defense to slander and libel type lawsuit. However, since truth is not a defense to an invasion of privacy cause of action, the plaintiff may nonetheless be successful in its secondary claim that the employer tortiously interfered with the plaintiff's privacy by "public disclosure of private facts" or publicizing or disclosing information that placed the plaintiff "in a false light before the public."

Generally speaking, the four-part analysis of common law causes of action for invasion of privacy may be helpful in numerating the various types of litigation to which employers and their counsel may be exposed.

Claims of Intrusion Upon Seclusion

First, an intrusion upon seclusion invasion claim could arise from many types of workplace situations. For example, suppose a male manager called a female employee into his private office, locked the door, commenced to ask the employee about her sex life, insisted that she engage in sexual acts with him, threatened to discharge her if she didn't, and carried out his threat upon her refusal to answer his questions or submit to his proposals. Aside from sexual harassment and other such claims against the employer (and the manager) for the manager's conduct, the employee may be able to incorporate into any private cause of action against the employer (and manager) an invasion of privacy allegation based upon the intrusion about her sex life. This, indeed, was part of the alleged facts presented to the court in the 1983 Alabama case of *Phillips v. Smalley Maintenance Services, Inc.*, in which the court held that such intrusive, coercive, and repetitive inquiries with respect to private matters of no relevance to the employee's employment provided a sufficient basis to support a private invasion of privacy cause of action against the employer.

Thus, the employer's counsel should be aware that the intrusion upon seclusion type of invasion of privacy type lawsuit typically arises in the context of employer tests and inquiries of prospective and current employees. Such intrusions are deemed actionable in many courts, such as in the *Phillips* court irrespective of whether the intruding party was able to obtain any information from his or her inquiries. However, most courts require that the inquiry or question be considered highly offensive to a reasonable person, such as was evidenced in the *Phillips* case.

The intrusion of seclusion invasion of privacy type action does not require the element of publication as is required by other invasion claims. For example, in the 1976 case of *Venars v. Young*, the third federal circuit court of appeals held that an employee's claim that his employer had opened and read mail, without the employee's approval or authorization, which mail had been delivered to the employee's workplace but nonetheless addressed to the employee and marked personal, constituted an actionable invasion of privacy claim, the court concluding that opening and reading private mail without approval is as intrusive as wiretapping.

Claims of Unreasonable Publication or Disclosure of Private Facts

Second, the "unreasonable publication or disclosure of private facts" invasion of privacy theory also is likely to be used more prolifically in the future, especially with respect to the disclosure of such medical conditions as AIDS, criminal records, and so on. As noted earlier, truth is not a defense to a cause of action based upon unreasonable disclosure of private facts.

The dissemination of one's medical or psychiatric records may, perhaps, be used to support an unreasonable disclosure of private facts. However, the courts require that the publication be highly offensive, applying a "reasonableness" test, and disclosed to the public. Although the term "public" has been interpreted to be anyone without a business need to know such information, where the employer is able to show the court that the disclosure was limited to individuals who had a legitimate need to know the information, the "public" test is not met.

Claims of Placing the Employee in an Unfavorable Light Before the Public

The publication of a matter to "place one in an unfavorable light before the public" invasion type cause of action is somewhat analogous to the tort of slander or libel. However, in defamation cases the information publicized must be false in order to sustain a cause of action. On the other hand, although widespread publicity of defamation is not an essential element to sustain a slander or libel suit, it is an essential ingredient to establish a *false light* claim.

Perhaps a good example of a false light invasion of privacy action could be that of an employer's disclosure to the media of the reasons for one's dismissal, particularly if communicated in such a way and manner to cause the employee to suffer mental anguish and emotional distress and not in keeping with what a reasonable person would have done under the circumstances.

Claims of Unreasonable Appropriation of a Name or Likeness

The fourth category of invasion of privacy type lawsuits—unreasonable appropriation of a name or likeness—can best be illustrated in the employment context where an employer uses an employee's name or photograph to promote the employer's business in some way without the employee's consent. The employee in such a situation, may also have a legal claim against the employer for infringement of property or contractual rights.

The employer's counsel should appreciate that many employers photograph employees in workplace settings and use such in employer newspapers, handbooks, and so on. Many courts find no invasion of privacy associated with the use of employees' names and photographs in such manner since they made no objection to their photographs being taken for such purpose and their consent may, therefore, be inferred.

Other Claims of Invasion of Privacy Actions

The types of invasion of privacy actions based on state statutes vary, depending on:

- unlawful disclosure of personnel or medical records in violation of state privacy laws
- a failure of the employer to disclose hazardous or toxic conditions
- unlawful disclosure of credit information
- unlawful use of lie detector tests
- use of random drug testing in violation of a state statute
- unlawful requirements for AIDS testing in violation of state statute
- unlawful use (or manner of use) of detectives and "observers"
- unlawful use of electronic surveillance or wiretapping
- unreasonable or unlawful search of an employee's person or property or workplace

The list could go on and on, and continues to increase.

TECHNIQUES AND TACTICS IN APPLYING PECULIAR DEFENSES TO "INVASION OF PRIVACY" LAWSUITS

Many employers properly justify to the courts and successfully defend a policy of inquiring into, or regulating, the off-duty conduct of employees who, in the absence of the employment relationship, could be considered highly offensive and intrusive by a reasonable person.

Defense #1: Justifiable Business Reason

The employer, particularly governmental employers such as police departments, may well sustain its position that it had a justifiable business reason for having such a policy or taking certain action in keeping with the policy. For example, in the 1983 case of *Baron v. Meloni*, a federal district court in New York ruled that a police officer failed to sustain an invasion of privacy against his police department when he was discharged for continuing to associate with the spouse of a reputed mobster.

The employer's defense of its off-duty policy that could otherwise constitute an unreasonable invasion of privacy may be based on an attempt to avoid conflicts of interest, in both the private and public sector, as illustrated in the 1986 case of *Salazar v. Furr's, Inc.*, in which a federal district judge in New Mexico held that the dismissal of an employee due to being married to an employee of a competitor did not violate state or common law. The employer's counsel should be aware, however, that the trend is more in the opposite direction in terms of the courts' protection of employees' rights to off-duty activities.

The employer may also invoke the defense of a legitimate business interest with respect to a policy or practice that may otherwise appear unreasonably intrusive. For example, an employer—particularly a private sector employer—whose business operations involve high safety risk may be able to defend a random drug test where such random drug testing may not be justified in purely an office atmosphere where sensitivity to safety matters are essentially non-existent.

Defense #2: Disclosure of Information Because of Need to Know

The employer may also justify its disclosure of information about an employee, that could otherwise be interpreted as unreasonable, on the basis of the need to know by fellow employees, the employer and its management members, or society.

Defense #3: Employee Consent or Waiver

The employer may defend itself against an invasion of privacy lawsuit, especially one based upon "appropriation of the name or likeness of another," where it is able to show the court that the employee consented to such appropriation. Inferred consent may be established to defeat such a legal claim by the employee.

Similarly, the employer may be able to defend itself against an invasion of privacy cause of action by proving that the employee had granted the employer a license for the use of his or her likeness or name.

Although a consent or waiver may be used as a defense in an appropriation type case, many courts reject them as a defense to an intrusion upon seclusion claim, especially when a court determines that the nature of the intrusion of the employer exceeds the advanced consent and/or license of the employee.

Defense #4: Employer Had a Qualified Privilege

Some employers have successfully argued that a "qualified privilege" to make a statement in good faith about a subject in which the person to whom it is communicated has an interest in receiving the information should be correspondingly extended to invasion of privacy actions.

Other employers have been successful in advancing a "qualified privilege" to protect its own legitimate interests as a defense to an invasion of privacy cause of action, particular in those workplaces where the industry practice is to monitor phone calls, conduct time and motion studies, and use video of employees at work as a means of training and improving productivity and quality.

Defense #5: Information Was Not Made Public

Also, as alluded to in the preceding section, the employer may be successful in showing that the disclosed information in question was not disclosed to the "public" and thus not an invasion in terms of attempting to place the employee in an unfavorable light before the public.

Defense #6: Information Was Not Private

An employer may also want to advance the defense that the information so disclosed was not a private fact about the employee (or individual) who has brought the lawsuit against the employer but one of common knowledge to the public.

Defense #7: Disclosure of Information Was Required by Law

Employers have been upheld by the courts in defense of an invasion of privacy lawsuit where their duty to disclose information was required by law. For example, in the 1986 case of *Davis v. Monsanto*, a federal district court in the state of Washington held that Monsanto's disclosure to a union that it had received information from a mental health professional that it was believed the plaintiff was lethally dangerous to himself and those around him because of his exposure to potentially dangerous chemicals was absolutely privileged in that the company was required by law to provide a safe workplace.

An employer may be able to justify its inquiries of an applicant or employee with respect to certain criminal connections, and so on, depending on the law or the subject in the state in which the inquiry is made, based upon the employer's legitimate interest to protect itself against a negligent hiring or retention claim.

Defense #8: The Employee Suffered No Damages or Harm

An employer may also be successful in a defensive argument, that irrespective of an alleged intrusion, that the employee has suffered no damages or harm as a result. For example, even though the employer may be found liable for the appropriation of the likeness of one of its employees because it published his or her photograph in a promotional brochure, the employee nonetheless has the burden to show that he or she has suffered damages as a result. The employer's counsel should not overly rely on an absence of damages argument, however. Usually, a combination of a liberal judge and a liberal jury can derive at some otherwise inconceivable monetary damages, particularly in terms of punitive damages which is permitted in invasion of privacy lawsuits.

The employer's defense that the employee suffered no harm or damages as a result of the employer's disclosure, intrusion, or appropriation may best be augmented by an argument that the employer's action was not outrageous or offensive when applying the reasonableness or prudent person rule to it.

Defense #9: The Employee Waived the Right to Claim Invasion of Privacy

An employer may also advance a defense to an invasion of privacy action that the employee, explicitly or implicitly, waived his or her right to advance such a legal claim in terms of such waivers being covered in conditions of employment at the time of hire or conditions of continuing employment, thereafter. An employee may waive his or her right to assert a legal claim against an employer for alleged unreasonable disclosure when the employee had previously disclosed the same information to the same parties or to the public.

Defense #10: Absence of Physical Intrusion in an Intrusion-Upon-Seclusion Claim

An employer may also be successful in some jurisdictions when establishing that there was no physical intrusion by which to establish an intrusion upon seclusion invasion cause of action. As noted earlier, many courts do not require physical intrusion, *per se*, to establish such a claim, such as the court in *Venars v. Young*, noted in the preceding subheading.

PRE-TRIAL AND TRIAL STRATEGIES TO USE IN DEFENDING "INVASION OF PRIVACY" LEGAL CLAIMS

The first item of business for the employer's counsel in pre-trial preparation to defend an "invasion of privacy" lawsuit is to ascertain whether the plaintiff has an actionable lawsuit. The employer's counsel should not be intimidated by an invasion of privacy action simply because the courts in many states have recognized an individual's private right to bring such a cause of action in a limited number of cases.

Should legal precedent be on the side of the employer in terms of the refusal of the courts within the state to embrace an invasion cause of action, the employer's counsel should ensure that the employer's motion to dismiss, motion for summary judgment or some similar pleading to get rid of the case has a well-researched and written memoranda of law or brief to back its position.

The employer's counsel should be equally zealous in attempting to dismiss a cause of action based upon some statutory or constitutional claim relative to privacy rights. Again, courts in various states have interpreted such statutes and constitutions very narrowly and, should the employer find itself defending an invasion of privacy legal claim based on statutory or constitutional provisions within such a state, the employer's counsel should attempt to take advantage of the court's philosophy and prior rulings and precedents on the matter.

Should the employer reside in a state whose judicial precedent has not been so favorably disposed toward the defendants' position in an invasion of privacy cause of action or its counsel was unable to sustain the employer's pleadings that the case should be dismissed or limited with respect to liability and/or damages, the employer's counsel may want to explore the possibility of attempting to procure the transfer or removal of the case to a jurisdiction more favorably disposed to the employer's position, if such is available, feasible, and practical in terms of time, talent, and costs.

In addition, either by motion or by way of formal answer and/or affirmative defenses, the employer's counsel should review the peculiar defenses available in invasion of privacy lawsuits in various jurisdictions, as discussed in the preceding subheading, and take full advantage of arguing any such applicable defenses on behalf of the defending employer.

In this connection, the employer's counsel should exhort its various privileges as a defense to an invasion of privacy legal claim, especially the absolute privilege to comply with some statutory obligation. In many instances, there appears to be an attempt by courts to balance the legitimate interests of the employer against the privacy rights of the employee, but when some statutory provision or regulatory agency requires an employer to take certain action, report or disclose certain tests, no longer is there a balancing act to consider; the employer's legal obligation to comply overcomes any right of privacy by the employee "to be left alone."

The employer's counsel should also explore, as part of his or her pre-trial preparation, any and all preemption, exhaustion of remedies, statute of limitations, and other such affirmative defenses to an invasion of privacy claim.

As has been discussed in so many previous chapters, the employer's counsel would be substantially remiss if he or she does not expend the necessary time and effort to properly prepare witnesses, prepare documentary and demonstrative evidence, and attend to other pre-trial matters.

Obviously, all efforts should be made by the employer's counsel to take full advantage of all reasonable discovery available to the defendant, to expend sufficient time and effort to exhaust all pertinent research on the subject matter as well as to procure and issue all necessary subpoenas desired by the defendant's counsel in defense of the invasion of privacy litigation.

Should the situation arise and appear worth exploring, the employer's counsel may want to test settlement avenues, especially if counsel evaluates its chances to win the case as somewhat unfavorable.

As has been discussed in previous chapters, as well, time and attention to such matters as stipulations with opposing counsel, coordination of exhibits for easy reference and access, and arranging to have the available co-counsel in more comprehensive invasion of privacy cases may be beneficial to the employer's counsel.

Relative to trial techniques in an invasion of privacy cause of action, the most important challenge of the employer's counsel is to attempt to select the best jury possible, if the matter is tried before a jury.

The employer's counsel certainly should take all actions necessary to ensure the record of the trial proceedings is clear, intact, and contains all matters of evidence, pleadings and arguments made to the court and/or jury during the trial of the case for proper preservation of the record in case such is needed for appellate purposes.

The techniques and strategies to be used in the art of direct and cross-examination of witnesses, as has previously been discussed in Chapter 5, should be likewise applicable in defending invasion of privacy actions.

28 Successful Strategies in Defending Defamation in the Workplace Litigation

Defamation in the workplace lawsuits have been on the increase for some time. Their continuing emergence seemingly tracks the ever-developing wrongful discharge litigation throughout the nation. Indeed, many plaintiff attorneys attempt to weave defamation claims into wrongful discharge actions if there is a trace of slander or libel associated with the unlawful termination allegations in a given lawsuit.

Defamation in the workplace lawsuits may arise in a variety of ways in the employment context:

- Previous employers make defamatory references to prospective employers about a given plaintiff—this is a major source of slander and libel lawsuits in the workplace.
- A member of management makes a slanderous statement to other management members, employees or individuals outside the organization who have no need to know such information. Since management members, including supervisors, are considered to be agents of the employer, defamatory statements made by managers and supervisors to individuals who have no legitimate business interest in knowing such information, is imputed to the employer and subjects the employer to potential liability.

Another way in which a manager or supervisor's defamatory remarks may be imputed to the employer is where the manager or supervisor loses his or her communication privilege by making such statements in a malicious manner.

Some courts permit the person so defamed to not only file a cause of action against the employer, but also against the manager or supervisor making such a slanderous remark, or publishing a libelous statement, on the basis that he or she went outside the scope of the supervisory function by such action and conduct.

The employer's counsel and other representatives should be aware that anyone can be sued for slander or libel, including an employee bringing a lawsuit against a fellow employee on the grounds of defamation. Although an employer and its counsel may be involved to some degree in such an employee's defamation cause of action against a fellow employee in terms of dissension in the workplace as a result, the employer usually has no liability in such an action. The one exception to such a proposition would be in the context that the employer had some statutory or common law duty to attempt to cease and desist the employee activity, such as with respect to various employment harassment and discrimination laws.

However, the scope of this chapter is to limit the discussion of the law of workplace defamation to those circumstances and factual situations in which the employer becomes the primary defendant as a result of slanderous and/or libelous statements made by its supervisors and managers.

Defamation exists in two forms: either by way of *slander*, which consists of defamation through speech, or *libel*, which consists of defamation by written publication. Moreover, the law regards either a spoken or written statement defamatory if the statement tends to harm the reputation of another so as to lower the person in the eyes of the community or to cause third persons to deter from associating or dealing with that person.

Most workplace defamation is considered *per se* defamation in that the alleged slander or libel includes false statements that affect the aggrieved employee's job or profession and, thus, presumed to be defamatory. An employee is not required to prove special or actual damages in order to recover a judgment from an employer when there is personal, or *per se*, defamation because of the subject matter, such as false statements as to why an employee was discharged.

An employee bringing a defamation cause of action against his or her employer is required to prove four essential elements in order to prevail in the lawsuit. The employee must prove:

1. That some defamatory communication existed regarding himself or herself.
2. That the alleged defamatory statement was "published" by the employer to a third person.
3. That the person to whom the defamatory communication was allegedly published understood the communication to have been about the employee bringing the cause of action.
4. That the employee-plaintiff suffered actual harm as a proximate result of the published communication, unless the communication was defamatory *per se*.

PRACTICAL FACTORS TO CONSIDER WHEN INVOKING THE "COMMUNICATIONS PRIVILEGE"

An employer that is able to convince a court that the alleged defamatory communications in a given slander or libel cause of action were privileged becomes immune from liability as a result.

There are various kinds of communications that are considered privileged under the law, giving rise to a defense that the communications are immune from liability. For example, statements by witnesses in judicial or administrative proceedings that might otherwise give rise to a defamatory cause of action are considered privileged and precludes such an action against the publisher of the remarks. A more commonly known communication privilege is that which exists between spouses to protect the sanctity of the marital relationship, thus preventing a communication by one to the other from being used in a subsequent action by a third party for slander or libel. Both communication privileges noted above are considered absolute privileges and immunizes the communicators from liability irrespective of its truth or maliciousness.

Although some authorities maintain what a supervisor or manager says about an employee in a grievance or arbitration proceeding is absolute privilege due to the judicial proceedings, most communications made about employees by supervisors and managers do enjoy some level of qualified privilege, although not always an absolute privilege. Most such statements, at best, enjoy what is termed a qualified privilege, meaning that the supervisor or manager in question can easily lose the privilege if he or she goes outside certain bounds.

A supervisor or manager may have a qualified privilege to make or publish certain statements about an employee (or fellow manager) provided certain conditions and requirements are met. In general terms, a supervisor or manager has a qualified privilege to make certain statements about an employee when the statements are made in good faith and communicated only to those individuals who have a legitimate right to know the information. In this context, a supervisor's statement to a fellow manager about an employee's job performance may be qualifiedly privileged, assuming that both the supervisor reciting and receiving the information had some connection or association with the employee's performance. Likewise, a statement by one management member to another as to the reason why a certain employee was discharged may be privileged, in a qualified sense, inasmuch as supervisors and managers have a legitimate interest in this type of information.

Reviewing the Precedent Cases

A brief discussion of some cases on the point may be instructive as to the way in which the manager's "qualified privilege" has been sustained as a defense in defamation in workplace lawsuits.

- The Washington Supreme Court ruled that an employer was not liable for defamation by placing a letter in an employee's file which stated the reason for his discharge since the employer had a qualified privilege to take such action on the belief that the information was true and correct and that it had an interest in preserving the instrument for that effort.
- A Tennessee court in the 1985 case of *Andrews v. Hagood* held that an employer had a qualified privilege to circulate a written memo to company managers regarding an alleged theft by the employee-plaintiff.
- A Pennsylvania court held that an employer had a privilege to discuss the conduct of employees among management, such as a memorandum to management members about customer complaints about a discharged employee.

Losing the Qualified Privilege

A supervisor may lose his or her qualified privilege to make statements about employees, which statements might otherwise be regarded as defamatory, in one or both of two specific ways:

1. when the communications are made to individuals who have no legitimate business reason for knowing the information
2. when the communications are made in bad faith and/or with malice

Statements to prospective employers may be considered qualifiedly privileged by the courts, immunizing the statements, and the employer whose supervisor published such statements, from liability. The rationale for the qualified privilege attached to reference statements made by a management member of the former employee to a prospective employer is that prospective employers have a legitimate interest in obtaining information as to the employee's past work history and suitability to the prospective job. However, should a prior supervisor disclose such information about the employee in question to a prospective employer in bad faith or in a malicious manner, the court may conclude that the supervisor lost his or her qualified privilege.

In more specific terms, the qualified privilege, when applied to employee references, may be lost and a cause of action for defamation may exist in the event:

1. The information given was not in response to the inquiries of the prospective employer;
2. The management member responding to the prospective employer's inquiries did not believe the truth of what he or she was reporting;
3. The information was being communicated to someone in the prospective employer's employment who had no legitimate need to know the information so communicated;

4. The information was made available to the other party for a purpose extraneous to the privilege;
5. The information was given in bad faith and not for a legitimate purpose; and/or
6. The management member had no reasonable grounds for believing the information being reported to the prospective employer.

In addition, there is some judicial support to hold employers liable for defaming former employees even when the employer has said nothing defamatory to the prospective employer or some other third party. This type of cause of action is based on the precept that where an individual is discharged for some reason other than the actual reason, he or she, in turn, in future interviews, has a duty to republish the false information to the prospective employer, thus satisfying the "publishing" element of a defamation claim. This "self-slander" theory was immortalized in the 1986 Minnesota case of *Lewis v. Equitable Life Assurance Society of the U.S.*, where the Supreme Court of Minnesota ruled actionable a lawsuit in which four employees who were discharged for refusing to falsify accurate expense reports, but which discharges were listed as for "gross insubordination" in their employment records, were forced to admit in later job applications the false reason for their dismissals—that of "gross insubordination"—the court holding that since the plaintiffs were forced to republish a defamatory statement by the previous employer, they could proceed to trial with their defamation lawsuit against the former employer, even though the former employer never made any false statements to the prospective employer, itself.

Since the most prevalent defamation lawsuit in the employment arena is that in connection with some statement made in an employer reference, the employer's counsel should be aware that the law does permit the employer to give a prospective employer information about a former employee, even though somewhat defamatory on its face if it can show that the communication either helps the employer protect its own interests or aids the prospective employer who has an "important interest" in such matters.

PITFALLS TO AVOID WHEN DEFENDING MALICIOUS DEFAMATION CLAIMS

Aside from losing its qualified communications privilege for certain particular reasons as discussed above, such as communicating the information to someone who had no legitimate reason to know, an employer's qualified privilege may also be lost when an employer's supervisor or other management member communicates or publishes some defamatory statement with a malicious intent, even though such statement would otherwise have been immune from liability because of the employer's privilege.

Whenever an employer demonstrates to a court that it communicated what otherwise may have appeared as a defamatory statement on its face to a third party based upon an important interest, and the communication, therefore, privileged, the burden of proof then shifts to the employee-plaintiff to show that the privilege was lost because of the employer's malicious motives in communicating the information.

The law regards a malicious motive in this context to be one designed to injure the employee. More generally, malice typically is regarded as an intent to cause ill will, spite, envy, or revenge. Other words have likewise been used to describe malice, such as hatred, animosity, acrimony, vindictiveness, and so forth.

Thus, an employee who has brought a defamation cause of action against an employer may demonstrate a malicious motive on the part of the employer by way to overcome the employer's "qualified privilege" by demonstrating the presence of such factors as the employer's:

1. Reckless disregard of the injury to the employee;
2. Knowledge that the statement was untrue;
3. Use of the statement or communications in such a way as to perpetuate its adverse impact upon the employee;
4. Bad faith motive in disseminating the communications;
5. Indifference to the potential results that could be regarded as willfully wrong;
6. Unnecessary repetition of the statement without any legitimate reason;
7. Pretentious use of the statement to harm and injure the employee; and/or
8. Communications of the statement through improper channels or media with the intent that it would be disseminated to those who had no legitimate interest to know its content.

Reviewing Precedent Cases

The employer's counsel and other representatives should be aware that the courts are permitting employees great latitude in proving the element of malice to deprive the employer of its qualified privilege defense in workplace defamation lawsuits. For example:

- A federal district court, applying Virginia law in the 1978 case of *Griffith v. Electrolux Corp.*, held that an employer was liable in defamation for false and malicious statements made by its representatives to customers that the plaintiff sales agent had been discharged for theft, cheating customers, and selling stolen property.

- The Vermont Supreme Court similarly held in the 1983 case of *Lent v. Huntoon* that an employer was liable in defamation for making false statements to customers that the plaintiff had stolen money from the employer, had a criminal record, and was untrustworthy and incompetent.
- A Texas court in the 1984 case of *Frank B. Hall & Co., Inc. v. Buck* held that an employee was entitled to money damages from an employer because of the employer's derogatory statements to other employees in the organization and prospective employers of the plaintiff as to the reasons for his discharge from employment.
- A court in the 1983 Oregon case of *Benassi v. Georgia Pacific* held that an employer lost its qualified privilege in a defamation suit where a management member announced to a large group of employees that another manager had a drinking problem and was found drunk and misbehaving.
- The Nebraska Supreme Court in the 1986 case of *Hennis v. O'Connor*, held that an employer lost its qualified communication privilege where one of its management members made false and malicious statements to employees and customers accusing the plaintiff, a former discharged employee, of stealing company property.

STRATEGIES IN USING SPECIFIC DEFENSES TO DEFAMATION IN THE WORKPLACE LITIGATION

Although several defenses to an employee's defamation lawsuit have been discussed above, this section discusses the various defenses available to an employer, subject to such litigation.

Defense #1: Argue the Employer's Communications Privilege

The employer's most beneficial defense is to argue the employer's communications privilege in an attempt to rid itself of the litigation at an early stage. Should the employer be able to demonstrate that it had an absolute privilege with respect to the alleged defamatory statements at issue in the lawsuit, all the better. Therefore, the employer's counsel should investigate the case to determine in what setting or forum the alleged defamatory remarks were stated or published. In the event that such statements were made in some administrative proceeding such as in an unemployment hearing, a workers' compensation trial, a labor arbitration case, or in a more formal lawsuit, the employer's assertion of an "absolute privilege" should be summarily sustained by the court, obviating the employee's claims of defamation.

Defense #2: Demonstrate Justifiable Business Purpose

The employer's counsel should be equally as zealous in his or her attempt to demonstrate to the court that the alleged defamatory remarks in question were made to only persons having a justifiable business purpose and "imputed interest" in knowing such information to support the employer's qualified privilege argument.

Defense #3: Argue that the Manager Was Not Acting as an Agent of the Company

The employer's counsel may also want to defend a defamation claim against its employer on the grounds that the manager or supervisor so accused of making the alleged defamatory statement made such a statement outside his or her capacity as a member and agent of the employer, and without any express, implied, apparent, or ostensible authority of the employer to do so. Several factors, however, may dictate that this argument not be used, such as an inference on the part of other managers that the employer will not back and support their supervisory decisions in the future and the resultant dampening of supervisory morale, or that some statutory or decisional law on the subject would run so contrary to the employer's position that the argument would be futile.

Defense #4: Argue that the Statements Were Not Published

The employer's counsel should avail himself or herself of the argument that the alleged defamatory statements were never so published by the employer or its management or supervisory members, if he or she has the evidence to support such argument, inasmuch as the plaintiff has a duty to prove that the defendant to a defamation cause of action "published" the defamation communication, either by the spoken word (slander) or the written word (libel). Nonetheless, should the employee's theory maintain that he or she was forced to republish what an employer had falsely written in its personnel file as to the reason for discharge and such theory was embraced by the court — as was the case in Minnesota, noted earlier — the employer's counsel would then be obligated to show that no such false reason for termination was ever so recorded by the employer or communicated to the employee that would impose an obligation on the part of the employee to republish the information to a prospective employer.

Defense #5: Assert that the Published Information Was Not Defamatory

The employer's counsel should also assert the defense that the information so published was not defamatory and thus no defamatory statement existed by which to support a cause of action by the employee, assuming the employer's counsel can present evidence to the court that such remarks could have in no way caused harm to the reputation of the employee.

Defense #6: Argue for the Truth of the Information

Truth is said to be the purest defense to a defamation cause of action in that it serves as an absolute defense. Thus, the employer's counsel should use the defense of "truth" to the extent that evidence will support such. In some instances, there are nuances and subjective statements made in the context of communicating the reason for a former employee's discharge. The employer's counsel is challenged to present the subjective, as well as the objective, aspects of the employer's statements to prove the truth of the communications so alleged to have been false. For example, an employer's manager, in responding to some inquiry by a prospective employer of a former employee, may couch his or her response in the form of an opinion, rather than a statement of fact. Just because someone communicates a statement in the form of an opinion does not guarantee that a court or jury will not interpret such statement to be a statement of fact, but the argument that it was merely an opinion should serve as a tenable defense to a workplace slander or libel suit to some degree.

Defense #7: Assert Mistaken Identity

Mistaken identity may be advanced as a defense to a defamation cause of action, if evidence supports such argument, in terms that the alleged defamatory remarks were made in reference to someone other than the plaintiff. Here, the employer's position, if provable, would be that the published statements or communications were about some employee, or former employee, other than the party filing the defamation action. Should both the employer's manager and the prospective employer's manager both testify that the alleged defamatory remarks were not made in reference or with regard to the plaintiff, then an essential element of proof to support his or her defamation claim is missing.

Defense #8: Argue that the Information Was Not Provided to a Third Party

Another defense that may be advanced by an employer's counsel in a defamation action, as alluded to previously, is that the alleged defamatory remarks were never published to a third person. This argument could be most relevant, and, hopefully, successful, where an employee files a defamation cause of action, alleging that he or she was slandered by a defamatory statement made by one manager to another manager. Since managers, especially when serving in the capacity as managers, are presumed to be an agent of the employer, the employer's argument that one manager's remark to another manager, whether defamatory or not, is no more than an employer talking to itself, and the employee bringing such an action has failed to show that the alleged defamatory statement was communicated to a person other than the employer or the employee.

Defense #9: Assert that the Employee Suffered No Harm, Injury, or Damages

Another defensive tactic that may be advanced by an employer's counsel in defense of a slander or libel action is that the employee suffered no harm, injury, or damages as a result of the alleged defamatory communications. For example, suppose an employer communicated some malicious and false statements about a former discharged employee to a prospective employer. Should the prospective employer nonetheless hire the employee, in spite of the defamatory statements, in the same manner for the same position and at the same rate of pay as it would have hired the employee had the former employer made complimentary remarks in response to the prospective employer's inquiry, what damages would the employee be able to show? Here, nonetheless, depending on the law or the jurisdiction in which the lawsuit is pursued, the employee may be entitled to certain damages based on *per se* or presumed defamation, as noted earlier.

PRE-TRIAL AND TRIAL SAFEGUARDS IN DEFENDING A WORKPLACE DEFAMATION LAWSUIT

First, the employer's counsel should ascertain the specific law in the state in which the lawsuit is brought regarding which defenses must be pleaded affirmatively in the employer's answer to the plaintiff's defamation action. For example, the defense of "truth" to a slander or libel action must be pleaded as an affirmative defense in many states.

Many states require that the defense of a qualified or absolute communication privilege be asserted as an affirmative defense in a defamation lawsuit. There are many other traditional defenses available to a defendant to all types of suits, including defamation actions, that most state courts require to be pleaded, affirmatively, such as the statute of limitations, laches, set-off, accord and satisfaction, exhaustion of administrative remedies, mitigation of damages, and so forth. Should such traditional defenses apply to a defamation action, at hand, the employer's counsel should ensure that his or her answer not only contain such defenses but that the defenses are pleaded in the form and manner required by local and state court rules.

A second safeguard to employ in defending a defamation action is to attempt to limit the amount of damages awarded to a plaintiff, assuming an absence of sufficient defenses to overcome liability. A prevailing plaintiff in a slander or libel claim is entitled to recover compensatory damages.

In cases of defamation *per se*, as discussed earlier, general damages need not be proved. Such presumed or general damages are awarded whenever the defamation impairs the reputation of the plaintiff in spite of an absence of any pecuniary loss. Whenever a court (or jury) finds defamation, *per se*, the trier of fact may consider several factors in deciding its reward to a plaintiff, including the character of the publication, the probable effect of the defamatory statements on the plaintiff's reputation, the length or duration of the communications, and the area in which the defamatory statements were communicated or published. Should a court permit an award based upon presumed defamation, the employer's counsel should attempt to argue to the court the absence of an adverse effect on the plaintiff's reputation as well as an absence of any ill-will or malicious motive on the part of the employer in making such statements so as to limit the *per se* damages to the extent possible.

The employer's counsel should be most sensitive in its pre-trial efforts to remove all elements of malice from any alleged defamatory statements as part of its defense, inasmuch as whenever a plaintiff proves malicious defamation, he or she is entitled to a special award of punitive damages. Punitive damages are those in excess of what actual, special, or general damages may be recovered by a prevailing party, the purpose of which is to serve as a signal and an example to deter others from similar behaviors. Inasmuch as "working persons" jurors are rewarding inordinate sums of monetary damages on behalf of employees at the expense of employers across the country when allowed to do so by the courts, the employer's counsel should argue that the employer should not be victimized by an unrealistic and unreasonable punitive reward to the plaintiff.

An employer's attorney should also use the experience of defending a defamation action to take some preventive measures with respect to the employer's policies and practices regarding what, when, how, and to whom statements may be made to prospective employers, employees, customers, and third parties about employees.

In addition to the pre-trial safeguards noted above relative to the peculiarities associated with defamation in the workplace cases, an employer's counsel faced with defending a defamation lawsuit on behalf of his or her employer may want to review some of the techniques, tactics, and strategies discussed in other tort cases throughout Part IV of this book.

Other general pre-trial and trial strategies and safeguards relative to all types of labor and employment litigations are covered in Chapters 5, 10, and 18.

29 Strategic Steps to Follow When Defending an Intentional Infliction of Emotional Distress Lawsuit

Another tortious action an employee may have against an employer is that commonly known as a suit for mental distress and more specifically addressed as an action for intentional or negligent infliction of emotional distress. This cause of action has also been alluded to as the "tort of outrage."

In the early development of the intentional infliction of emotional distress cause of action, the courts required that the plaintiff suffer some type of physical trauma caused by the defendant in order to prevail. Most modern courts do not require a physical trauma connection as a necessary element of proof in a mental distress lawsuit, particularly in employment matters.

Most courts now recognize that a person, such as an employer, may be found liable for the tort of infliction of emotional distress where the defendant's conduct is so outrageous and extreme that it shocks the conscious of a reasonable person. A defendant may also be liable for any bodily harm caused by a defendant's outrageous action, although bodily harm, as noted above, is not a necessary part of the plaintiff's proof.

The employer's counsel should realize that not all courts have recognized and embraced the "mental distress" theory as an actionable cause in the employment context. Many courts have adopted the theory. However, even those courts that recognize mental distress lawsuits vary as to what they require with respect to standards and burden of proof. Generally, the courts that recognize the mental distress theory as a basis for a legal claim require two fundamental conditions to exist:

- that the defendant's conduct be so outrageous in character and so extreme in degree as to go beyond all possible grounds of decency
- that the plaintiff suffer severe emotional pain and distress as a result

Reviewing the Precedent Cases

The courts do not regard minor insults and indignities as sufficiently outrageous to sustain a mental distress cause of action. Neither do hurt feelings suffice in proving that the employer's conduct was outrageous.

For example, in the 1983 Montana case of *Gates v. Life of Montana Ins. Co.*, a court rejected an employee's mental distress cause of action based upon her assertion that she was "rather disturbed" and "kind of shocked" as a result of her discharge.

An Ohio court rejected an employee "mental distress" lawsuit based on the employee's testimony that she had been given conflicting reports by two supervisors as to the reason for her demotion.

Although a discharge, or some other adverse action taken by an employer against an employee, standing alone, may not be sufficient grounds upon which to support an infliction of emotional distress action, the manner in which the employment decision is communicated to an employee may serve to support a mental distress legal claim. The 1986 case of *Meierer v. E.I. DuPont de Nemours & Co.* illustrates the point, in which a federal court, applying South Carolina law, permitted an emloyee's mental distress claim to proceed to trial where the employee alleged that her supervisor, in the process of discharging her, accused her of stealing company records, yelled at her, pounded his fists, and ordered her out of the plant. In another federal district court case, applying Massachusetts law, a federal court awarded an employee $125,000 in damages based on his claim that he suffered humiliation and mental distress as a result of being observed urinating for the purpose of a drug test, the results of which led to his discharge.

Indeed, several mental distress cases based on the manner in which the plaintiff was discharged have become judicial classics, one of the most famous of which is the 1976 Massachusetts case of *Agis v. Howard Johnson Co.* in which the plaintiff's discharge resulted when the employer, in an attempt to detect an unknown thief in its restaurant and convince the culprit to confess, arbitrarily commenced firing one waitress a day in alphabetical order, starting with the plaintiff.

The employer's counsel should be aware that the courts look at the relative positions of the employer and employee in determining whether the elements necessary to sustain an infliction of emotional distress cause of action are present. The tendency of the courts, in doing so, is to consider the power and authority the employer has over the employee to affect its interests and any knowledge the employer may have of the employee's peculiar susceptibility to mental distress.

An illustrative case in point is the 1987 case of *Nash v. AT&T Nassau Metals* in which a South Carolina appellate court permitted a discharged employee to proceed on his mental distress action against an employer that caused him to lose his insurance benefits while knowing his psychiatric condition made him more susceptible to such distressful circumstances. A Georgia court held actionable an employee's intentional infliction of emotional distress cause of action where her employer, by detaining and questioning her about a matter for some five hours, prevented her from taking medication necessary to her health.

The employer's counsel and other representatives should be aware, in addition, that plaintiff attorneys customarily incorporate an action for mental distress in their wrongful discharge and other employment tort claims in support of the primary claims. Plaintiff attorneys, also, attempt to use the concept of the infliction of emotional distress theory as a tort action in addition to a contract action in order to seek punitive damages.

A plaintiff's attorney may plead the same allegations in an action for retaliatory discharge in violation of public policy as he or she pleads in an action for infliction of emotional distress. The same or similar allegations may be advanced in a lawsuit for defamation on the one hand and infliction of emotional distress on the other. Few cases plead infliction of emotional distress as the sole basis of an employee's lawsuit.

PRACTICAL TIPS IN EVALUATING FORMS OF BEHAVIOR THAT CONSTITUTE ACTIONABLE MENTAL DISTRESS IN THE WORKPLACE

There appears to be several types of behavior that the courts regard as peculiarly suitable for an actionable infliction of emotional distress claim.

Harassment on the Basis of National Origin, Race, Religion, Age, Gender, or Disability

One of the most prevalent forms of behavior upon which the courts look most disfavorably with respect to a mental distress cause of action is that of national origin, racial, or sexual harassment. Although federal laws, as well as most state laws, forbid harassment associated with such characteristics as sex, race, age, religion, handicap, or national origin, an employee subjected to these forms of harassment in the workplace may also pursue a separate, independent, and private mental distress cause of action in many states. For example:

- In the 1983 Georgia case of *Cummings v. Walsh Construction Company*, the court held that an employee could proceed in her mental distress action against her employer whose manager repeated demands for sexual favors, and intimidated and threatened employees into sexual relations.

- A court in the 1981 District of Columbia case of *Rogers v. Loews L'Enfant Plaza Hotel* held an employee's infliction of emotional distress lawsuit actionable where management members had made insulting, demeaning, and threatening remarks to employees as well as the use of abrasive language to female employees.
- A Washington state court found an employer liable for the infliction of emotional distress where a manager's constant ridicule of a Mexican-American employee caused him to suffer mental distress.

The courts find racial slurs and harassment equally or more offensive and proper grounds for an actionable mental distress case.

For example, in the 1977 Washington case of *Contreras v. Crown Zellerback Corp.*, the court recognized that racial harassment provides grounds on which to base a mental distress cause of action. Racial slurs and discrimination were some of the factors that led a court in the 1982 California case of *Agarwol v. Johnson* to sustain the plaintiff's mental distress lawsuit.

With the passage of statutes like the Americans With Disabilities Act, the Rehabilitation Act of 1973 and the various state handicap laws, plaintiff lawyers are likely to continue filing infliction of emotional distress actions based upon harassment of disabled and handicapped employees, particularly where a plaintiff alleges that his or her benefits were denied on the basis of disability. Other forms of on-the-job harassment may be found by an applicable court to give rise to an actionable infliction of emotional distress claim.

Mental Distress Due to Retaliatory Discharge of an Employee

Aside from harassment as a form of behavior that may constitute an actionable mental distress suit, courts recognize that retaliatory discharges may also provide grounds for a mental distress action, even though an employee subjected to a retaliatory discharge may pursue other lawsuits such as an action for wrongful discharge in violation of public policy.

The manner in which an employee is discharged and the physical or mental condition of the employee at the time the discharge is communicated to an employee may be considered so outrageous by a court of law as to sustain a mental distress cause of action.

For example, in the 1985 case of *McCarthy v. KFC Corp.*, a Kentucky court held actionable an employee's mental distress claim against her employer where she had been required to work long hours which led to her becoming seriously ill, resulting in her subsequent discharge after which her employer continued to harass her throughout her unemployment compensation proceedings.

A Massachusetts court held that an employee could proceed with an intentional infliction of emotional distress action where his employer had undertaken and systematically harassed the employee over a period of time to force him to resign.

An Oregon court in the 1983 case of *Smithson v. Nordstrom* held actionable an employee's intentional infliction of emotional distress claim where an employee who had been accused of theft, was held and interrogated for a long period of time, induced to sign a confession, and then discharged.

Emotional Distress Claims Due to an Employer's Outrageous Conduct

Emotional distress claims based upon outrageous conduct relative to employment decisions less than discharge may also be actionable in some courts by an employee suffering severe emotional distress.

For example, a Virginia court held an employer liable for a claim of intentional infliction of emotional distress where it had fabricated false evidence to deprive an employee of unemployment compensation, causing the employee to suffer mental pain and distress. Another example is the 1984 case of *Fory v. Smithkline Beckman Corp.* in which a Pennsylvania court allowed an infliction of emotional distress to proceed against her employer for the employer's intentional creation of an oppressive work atmosphere by repeatedly denying promotional opportunities to her. The 1990 case of *King v. Brooks* is also illustrative of the point in which an Alaskan court held actionable an employee's cause of action for mental distress where a manager carried out a two-year private vendetta against the employee that consisted, among other things, of altering and making false accusations about the employee's job performance records.

TECHNIQUES AND TACTICS IN USING SPECIFIC DEFENSES TO AN "EMOTIONAL DISTRESS" LAWSUIT

Courts have recognized various hybrids of the historic mental distress type of lawsuit. In an employment context, courts have distinguished emotional distress on the basis of whether the employer's conduct was intentional or negligent, the latter raised by creative plaintiff attorneys who apparently felt the element of intent or malice was either absent or weak in the given case.

The *Restatement (Second) of Torts* on the subject suggests that the conduct on the part of the employer that allegedly caused the plaintiff to have suffered severe emotional distress must have not only been extreme and outrageous but also intentional or reckless.

Attempt to Have the Case Dismissed

Irrespective of whether a court recognizes negligence as a substitute for intent to carry this peculiar element of proof in an "emotional distress" case, the employer's counsel should take the following actions:

- prepare evidence, if available, to demonstrate that the element of intent and/or negligence was not present in the employment decision or interaction with the employee
- be prepared in a proper manner to overcome any allegations and arguments that the employer's conduct was extreme or outrageous
- attempt to demonstrate to the court that the employee could not have suffered any unusual or abnormal sensitivities as a result of the employer's behavior

In other words, the first three specific defenses that the employer's counsel should employ in its answer and preparation for trial to rid itself of, and win, the lawsuit is to show and demonstrate to the court that the essential elements of proof in the intentional infliction of emotional distress action brought against his or her employer are not present.

Use Preemption to Dismiss the Case

An equally prevalent argument by management attorneys in defending emotional distress cases by which to attempt a dismissal of the action at an early stage is that of preemption. For example, if the employee's emotional distress claim is based on alleged sexual harassment, the employer's counsel should move to dismiss the action on the ground that there are specific statutes providing the claimant with a right of action which statutes preempt his or her private action based on the intentional infliction of emotional distress claim. The same argument would hold true where the employee's intentional infliction of emotional distress is based on a retaliatory discharge, provided that some federal or state statute grants the employee a private statutory right of action.

One of the most prevalent—and sometimes successful—preemptive arguments in the defense to an intentional infliction of emotional distress lawsuit is that the applicable state workers' compensation law preempts the action in that the workers' compensation statute provides for the exclusive remedy available to the employee for injuries suffered in the workplace, including those associated with mental pain and distress.

The employer's counsel should be aware that the courts in many states do not give much deference to preemption arguments in "emotional distress" cases, yet many of the more conservative courts do, especially those that have been reluctant to recognize an intentional infliction of emotional distress action where there is no presence of physical trauma.

Argue that the Mental Distress Is Not Imputable to the Employer

Certainly the employer's counsel may advance many other arguments and defenses to overcome a mental distress lawsuit, many of which were discussed in the preceding chapter regarding defamation in the workplace. For example, where the behavior of a supervisor gives rise to a mental distress claim and the behavior occurred outside the course and scope of the supervisor's authority, the employer's counsel might advance the argument that such behavior is not imputable to the employer. The employer's counsel would be in a more favorable light with the court with respect to this argument where the employer is able to show the court that all supervisors and managers have been trained and counseled about the behaviors expected of them with respect to administering employment policies and the behavior of the supervisor fell outside the guidelines.

Invoke a Proximate Cause Defense

The employer's counsel and other representatives may want to invoke a "proximate cause" defense and argue that the emotional distress and pain suffered by the employee-defendant, to the extent of its existence, were not caused by the employer's conduct but caused by something extraneous and outside the bounds of the employment relationship.

Show that the Employer's Actions Were Reasonable and Justified

The employer's counsel may be successful, also, in procuring the dismissal of an intentional infliction of emotional distress cause of action against his or her employer where it can be shown that the employer was acting within the industry standards and the action taken against the employee, and the manner in which the action was taken, was within the industry norms, and thus reasonable and justified. This argument should specifically be advanced by employer-defendants in a negligent infliction of emotional distress case in that the employer exercised the ordinary care toward the employee that a reasonable employer would have exercised under the circumstances.

Additionally, the employer's counsel may be successful in advancing an argument that no reasonable employer could possibly foresee that its actions with respect to the employee could have caused the employee to suffer mental distress and pain. Here, the thrust of the employer's argument is that the employer had no knowledge of any peculiar medical or psychological conditions of the employee that would have created a heightened sensitivity to the employer's conduct.

Other General Defenses

The employer's counsel may want to refer to other defenses available to defendants of wrongful discharge and other employment tort cases that have been discussed throughout Part IV of this book and, again, particularly to those defenses discussed in the preceding chapter about defamation inasmuch as many of the defenses noted there are common to those that should be advanced when defending "emotional distress" cases.

Other general defenses should be evaluated by the employer's counsel to discern what applicability they may have with respect of an intentional infliction of emotional distress action, such as exhaustion of internal remedies as provided by a collective bargaining contract (and the preemptive qualities associated therewith) or to what extent has the employee-plaintiff attempted to mitigate his or her damages.

PRE-TRIAL AND TRIAL STRATEGIES IN "EMOTIONAL DISTRESS LITIGATION"

The employer's counsel should appreciate that intentional and negligent infliction of emotional distress lawsuits are in the nature of tort and permit an employee-plaintiff a recovery in punitive damages as well as compensatory damages—both types of damages having been discussed in the two preceding chapters as well as other chapters in Part IV of this book.

The employer's counsel must prepare his or her case in the best way possible to reduce the amount of damages available to the employee should the employee prevail in the lawsuit.

The first order of business, aside from seeking an early dismissal of the case through one or more of the defenses noted in the preceding subheading, is for the employer's counsel to exhaust all efforts through discovery by which to be in a position to limit not only the potential compensatory damages that may be recoverable by the employee, such as lost wages and benefits, but likewise to limit any punitive damages that the trier of facts (judge or jury) may be inclined to award the employee.

As noted in the preceding chapter, one of the most important pre-trial safeguards is to research the substantive and procedural law in the state in which the emotional distress lawsuit is brought and take full advantage of all affirmative defenses available to the defendant and to ensure they are pleaded in the proper form and manner as the court rules dictate. The employer's counsel may want to refer to the preceding chapter for additional recommendations regarding a discussion of available affirmative defenses in a tort action.

The employer's counsel should also be most careful with respect to courtroom behavior and demeanor during the trial of an "emotional distress" cause of action. The employer's counsel should caution his or her witnesses to present themselves in a polite and courteous manner to all in attendance at such a trial, including the employee-plaintiff and his or her attorney.

The employer's counsel should appreciate that a seasoned plaintiff's attorney will attempt to cross-examine supervisors and managers in such a way as to cause them to "lose their cool" and display behaviors that would help confirm the allegations in the employee's pleadings that the supervisor or manager displayed similar behaviors toward the plaintiff, giving rise to the plaintiff claim that he or she suffered mental pain and distress.

Other pre-trial and trial techniques and tactics of a more general nature have been discussed in previous chapters and, indeed, throughout this book, such as in Chapters 5, 10, 18, and 27.

30 Techniques and Tactics to Use When Defending Assault and Battery and Related Workplace Causes of Action

Certain conduct committed by an individual against another may constitute criminal conduct as well as a basis for a civil action in tort. Some of these behaviors may be exhibited in the workplace as well as outside the workplace and, if committed by a supervisor or manager against an employee or fellow manager, could subject the supervisor's employer to liability in tort.

An employee also could commit some act against an employer that could constitute a crime, punishable by law, but also one that could give rise to a tort action by the employer against the employee. An example here would be where an employer brings a tortious action against an employee for conversion of property after an employee has been arrested for theft against the employer.

It is the scope of this chapter, however, to focus on certain supervisory quasi-criminal conduct against employees such as that of assault and battery, false imprisonment, false arrest, and/or malicious prosecution rather than employer causes of action against employees.

Assault and battery within the workplace typically arises as a basis for a civil action by an employee against an employer. Assault and battery, although separate actions, are usually considered together both with respect to civil actions as well as criminal actions in that when one is present, so is the other, usually. In legal terms, an assault is the threat of an intent to inflict immediate injury on another person; battery is the act of inflicting injury to another person.

Generally speaking, an employer is liable for assault and battery committed by its supervisors and managers against employees, whether related to sexual harassment or otherwise. The courts usually do not extend the same liability on employers for injuries suffered by an employee as a result of an assault and battery by a fellow employee, perhaps with the exception of an employee's cause of action against an employer for negligently hiring a certain employee (or negligently retaining such an employee).

An action by an employee against an employer for the tort of false imprisonment typically arises out of circumstances surrounding an employer's investigation and/or interview of an employee accused of some type of misconduct (such as theft) or for some other such reason that led to his or her discharge. Such conduct on the part of the employer also could possibly serve as grounds to support an intentional infliction of emotional distress type action, particularly if the length of time in which the employee was detained greatly interfered with some special need or interest, such as the taking of medication.

A false arrest or malicious prosecution action usually arises, at least in the employment context, where an employer swears out a warrant or report against an employee, charging the employee of theft, selling illegal drugs, etc., and maliciously encourages the local authorities to prosecute a criminal action against the employee, only to find out later that the accused party was absolutely innocent and the employer's investigation of the matter was so hastily and arbitrarily conducted, that the attorney general's office would not have even pursued the matter to trial.

SPECIFIC SCENARIOS IN WHICH QUASI-CRIMINAL LITIGATION MAY ARISE IN THE WORKPLACE

Sexual Harassment

As suggested earlier, most assault and battery causes of actions against employers arise when a supervisor assaults and batters an employee in a sexual harassment manner, particularly touching or fondling another person without any express or implied consent. The courts have held that touching is regarded as intentional in the law, even though the touching may not have been intended to harm another.

The law regards the employer to be liable for sexual assault and battery committed by one or more of its supervisors if the sexual offense is committed while the supervisor was acting in the scope and course of his employment.

False Imprisonment

Regarding false imprisonment cases, one of the primary elements of proof is that the imprisonment was established by actual force or by an express or implied threat of force. The courts sometimes infer a force or threat of force where an innocent person is restrained in such a way that the person confesses to some act or conduct which he or she did not admit.

As was cited in the 1930 California case of *Vandiveer v. Charters*, the court stated:

> "The restraint constituting false imprisonment may arise out of acts, words, gestures or the like, which induce a reasonable apprehension that force will be used if the plaintiff does not submit, and it is sufficient if they operate upon the will of the person threatened, and result in the reasonable fear of personal difficulties or personal injuries .... A voluntary display of force, intended to deprive plaintiff of his liberty, even without laying hands on plaintiff, has been held sufficient, but there is no legal wrong unless the detention was involuntary in the sense of being contrary to the will of the plaintiff."

In the *Vandiveer* case, the California court held an employer to be liable to an employee in damages for false imprisonment where the employer called an employee into a room for questioning about a theft, accused the employee of the theft, threatened the employee with arrest, implied that there was an officer on the scene, and told the employee that she had three minutes to sign a confession or be taken to jail. The court concluded that the three minutes in which she was given to sign a confession or be sent to jail was a sufficient period of time in restraint of her personal liberty to constitute a false imprisonment.

Most likely, it was the manner in which the employer approached its investigation in the *Vandiveer* case, rather than the time of the alleged false imprisonment, that so offended the conscious of the court. That is to say, that the court would have been equally as receptive to an action for intentional infliction of emotional distress on the part of the employee for the employer's outrageous conduct as it would have been with respect to a false imprisonment cause of action.

Indeed, most courts do permit employers some type of implied privilege to detain and restrain an employee in its investigation of pilferage or theft, although such employers must take extreme caution in doing so in order to avoid liability associated with other torts discussed in the various chapters in Part IV of this book such as invasion of privacy, defamation, outrage, and torts discussed within this chapter such as assault and battery and false arrest.

For example, the Massachusetts Supreme Court in the 1987 case of *Foley v. Polaroid Corp.* rejected an employee's false imprisonment civil action even though his employer had confined him to an office for several hours while being questioned by a security officer about sexual assault charges alleged against him by a co-employee.

False Arrest

An excellent example of how an employer may become a defendant in a false arrest and malicious civil action is presented through the facts discussed by the North Carolina Supreme Court in the 1984 case of *Jones v. Gwynne* where the court upheld a judgment of $300,000 in compensatory and punitive damages to a former manager against an employer that had falsely accused the manager of stealing money from a cash register and sought the district attorney to prosecute the manager on criminal charges, such charges of which were later dropped by the district attorney general, the court concluding that the jury awarding the $300,000 judgment to the manager had sufficient evidence before them to find that the employer's cursory investigation of the theft charges showed a reckless and wanton disregard of the manager's civil rights.

PRACTICAL TIPS TO FOLLOW IN ASSESSING SPECIFIC DEFENSES IN QUASI-CRIMINAL TORT ACTIONS IN THE WORKPLACE

Defense on the Basis of Preemption

A management attorney's first defense to a quasi-criminal tort action against his or her employer-client is that of preemption, especially an argument that the workers' compensation laws of the state in which the action is brought provides the exclusive remedy to an employee for tort injuries occurring during the course and in the scope of an employee's employment. Other preemption arguments may also be available to the employer's counsel in terms that other statutes may provide exclusive private rights of action to an employee-plaintiff who allegedly was a victim of some criminal behavior by an employer's supervisor.

The degree to which courts may be receptive to a preemption defense depends directly upon the statutory and decisional laws within the state that address the question.

The employer's counsel and other representatives should not be overly optimistic about a preemption defense to such tort actions as assault and battery, false imprisonment, false arrest, however, especially in states such as California, as the courts in California have held that the exclusive provisions of the state's workers' compensation statute does not insulate an employer from becoming liable for assault and battery.

Some state courts may be more receptive to an employer's preemption argument where an assault and battery claim is based on bodily injuries resulting from fisticuffs or some other physical altercation, especially where the employee-plaintiff was an equally willing participant with the supervisor-manager in the physical altercation, discounting the poor judgment of the supervisor in such circumstance.

Defense on the Grounds of Employee Consent

An employer's counsel may well use the argument that the employee-plaintiff consented to the physical altercation as a defense to the employee's assault and battery civil action against the employer. It would appear that the defense of consent would be available to the employer in such a situation irrespective of the employer's preemption defense based on the exclusivity of workers' compensation. Certainly to the extent that an employer's preemption argument fails, the employer's counsel should heighten his or her argument that the employee-plaintiff consented to the alleged assault and battery by participating in the physical interchange.

The consent argument is particularly applicable to certain assault and battery lawsuits involving alleged sexual harassment and physical contact of a sexual nature.

The defense of consent may not be so available to the employer's counsel with respect to assault and battery based upon sexual harassment and physical contact of a sexual nature where the supervisor's behavior is unilateral and there is no evidence available to the employer's counsel that the behavior was welcome or desired by the employee-plaintiff.

The defense of consent with respect to a physical altercation between two or more non-supervisory employees also may be advanced by an employer who becomes a defendant in a subsequent assault and battery action arising out of such altercation. Here, however, an employer's defensive argument that the employee-plaintiff's exclusive remedy is under workers' compensation should prevail, inasmuch as the employee allegedly assailing the employee-plaintiff is not an agent of the employer in that he or she has no supervisory authority.

The defense of consent, or implied consent, should likewise be advanced, where applicable, as a defense to a false imprisonment tort action by an employee against an employer, especially where an employee is an at-will employee and is being detained in the course and scope of his or her employment, inasmuch as either the employer or employee may terminate the relationship at its will and, thus, foreclose any such alleged false detention or imprisonment. Should there be some written or enforceable implied employment contract between the employee-plaintiff and the employer, the employer's defense to a false imprisonment lawsuit may well be that the terms and conditions of the contract are controlling and that the employee's civil action against the employer, if at all, lies in one based on a breach of contract, not one based upon false imprisonment.

Defense on the Basis of the Employer's Implied Privilege

A defensive argument similar to that of consent, or implied consent, that may be advanced by an employer's counsel in defense of an assault and battery, or false imprisonment action against the employer is that the employer had an implied privilege to take the action it took to protect its proprietary property and business interests, especially with respect to such actions arising from investigations and interviews related to theft or drug abuse cases.

Defense on the Grounds of the Employer's Self-Defense

In addition to the specific defenses noted above with respect to an assault and battery action against an employer, an employer's counsel may be well served in advancing the defense of self-defense. For example, should an irate employee take upon himself or herself to attempt to physically assault a supervisor—for whatever reason—the supervisor's attempt to defend himself or herself against some physical bodily injuries should create an early demise of the employee's assault and battery civil action against either one or both the supervisor and his or her employer.

Defense on the Grounds of Lack of Intent

Inasmuch as the element of "intent" is an essential one in quasi-criminal civil actions such as assault and battery, false imprisonment, false arrest, etc., where an employer's counsel can demonstrate to the court that such element is lacking, an employer may well prevail in such an action brought against it by an employee.

For example, suppose a supervisor, in a heated verbal interaction with an employee about the employee's poor performance, quality, or behavior, accidentally brush against the employee, or place his or her hand on the employee's person as part of the counseling or corrective session. An employer's defense to an employee's assault and battery action against an employer for the physical contact arising out of the counseling interaction could be that the physical contact was not one "intended" to inflict injury on the employee.

Suppose a police officer came upon the property of an employer and arrested an employee because of some warrant sworn out by some person other than someone in management and supervision of the employer. The employer may have several defenses to a subsequent false arrest action against it arising from the employee's arrest on the employer's premises, but one such defense could be that it was not the intent or the desire of the employer that the employee be arrested, irrespective of the legitimacy or falsity of the arrest.

Defense on the Basis of No Proximate Cause

Another specific defense that may be available to an employer that becomes a defendant in an assault and battery civil action is that the alleged assault and battery by the employer's manager or supervisor, in question, was not the proximate cause of any physical injuries suffered by the employee-plaintiff.

This argument is particularly applicable where there are no "real" physical injuries to an employee-plaintiff or where the employer can demonstrate to the court (and/or jury) that to the extent that the plaintiff suffered any physical injuries, they were the result of some action or activity extraneous to any physical interactions between the employee and the manager or supervisor who was alleged to have caused them. For example, the facts may show that any injuries suffered were self-inflicted or occurred at a point in time other than during the time of the alleged assault and battery.

The employer's counsel should appreciate that the "absence of proximate cause" as to the injuries suffered by an employee-plaintiff may be helpful in decreasing a monetary judgment by a jury to an employee. In such a case, however, the employee may nonetheless be entitled to punitive damages and other related type damages if he or she can show that an assault and/or battery occurred at the hands of an employer's agent. For that reason, the "absence of proximate" cause argument is not very relevant in defending false imprisonment and false arrest civil actions where, typically, no physical injuries result from the alleged wrong.

Other Defense Strategies

In addition to some of the specific defenses somewhat indigenous to quasi-criminal civil actions by employees against employers, the employer's counsel and other representatives may want to review defenses noted in other chapters in Part IV of this book relating to other tort actions, such as an argument that the employer acted within business "norms" with respect to its actions and behaviors toward an employee-plaintiff, that the employee failed to mitigate his or her damages, or failed to take reasonable care in protecting against further injury.

PRE-TRIAL AND TRIAL SAFEGUARDS WHEN DEFENDING ASSAULT AND BATTERY AND RELATED WORKPLACE LAWSUITS

The first precaution for an employer's counsel to take during the pre-trial period of defending a quasi-criminal tort action, such as assault and battery, is to research thoroughly not only the statutory and decisional law within the state with respect to both substantive and procedural aspects so that he or she can take full advantage of some of the defenses discussed in the preceding subheading on the subject, such as a workers' compensation preemption argument, but also to specifically ensure that all such possible defenses are addressed by timely and proper motions and answer and included in the form and manner required by the rules of the court in which the action is brought.

Particularly should the employer's counsel research the procedural law in the state in which the action is being defended and raise all of the affirmative defenses available to the employer in the form and manner prescribed by the court. The measure as to what defenses must be pleaded affirmatively and in what form and manner they must be pleaded vary from state to state. Typically, however, such defenses as that the plaintiff did not file his or her pleadings within the period required by the applicable statute of limitation must be pleaded affirmatively. So must set-offs, accord, and satisfaction. The failure of the plaintiff to exhaust his or her administrative remedies (such as through collective bargaining contracts), or failure to mitigate his or her damages also constitute affirmative defenses.

As an additional pre-trial safeguard, the employer's counsel should research any specific statutory laws governing the types and limitations of damages recoverable in assault and battery civil actions and other such quasi-criminal tort actions, and prepare the employer's lawsuit in such a manner to decrease any recoverable damages.

As to the more general pre-trial and trial techniques and tactics that the authors discuss in defending labor and employment lawsuits, the reader's attention is referred to the many chapters throughout the book that address them, and specifically to Chapters 5, 10, 18, and 27.

31 Strategies and Techniques in Defending Fraudulent Misrepresentation in the Workplace Lawsuits

The theory of fraud as a basis of a cause of action in tort is a judicial sibling of the theory of promissory estoppel—discussed in Chapter 21—as a basis of a cause of action in contract.

The main distinction of the two lies in the proposition that to prove a fraud cause of action, the plaintiff must demonstrate to the court, in addition to the fact that the defendant promised something to the plaintiff upon which the plaintiff relied after which the defendant reneged on the promise to the plaintiff's detriment (the essential elements in a promissory estoppel action), that the defendant *intended* to cause such detriment to the plaintiff. That is to say, that should an employee be able to prove to a court all the essential elements necessary to prevail in a promissory estoppel lawsuit and, in addition, have sufficient evidence to show the court that the defendant intended to cause the resultant detriment to the plaintiff, the employee's attorney will have two theories to advance in its lawsuit against the employer-defendant, one based on contract (promissory estoppel) but another based in tort (fraud), the latter of which provides for a recovery of punitive damages.

In a nutshell, five essential elements must be established in order for a plaintiff to sustain a fraud action:

1. Misrepresenting or concealing a material fact;
2. Having knowledge of the falsity of the misrepresentation;

3. Intentionally inducing the other party to rely upon the misrepresentation or concealment;
4. Causing the other party to justifiably rely upon the misrepresentation or concealment; and
5. Resulting in some harm or injury to the other person.

The employer's counsel and other representatives will readily discern that the heart of a fraud action is the concept of misrepresentation, meaning that lawyers and judges typically substitute the word "misrepresentation" for the word "fraud," or combine the two to coin a term, "fraudulent misrepresentation," which sounds more ominous, if nonetheless redundant. The authors choose to use the term fraudulent misrepresentation to distinguish it from that of negligent misrepresentation which is discussed below.

A cause of action based on the theory of fraud frequently is referred to as an action in tort for deceit.

Whenever a misrepresentation action is couched in the language of a tort for fraud or a tort for deceit, intent is considered by the courts to be an essential element of proof. However, plaintiff attorneys have now advanced a slight twist to the classical fraudulent misrepresentation case. Where there is an absence, or perceived absence, of intent on the part of the employer, plaintiff attorneys are now suggesting that the defendant may have nonetheless failed to exercise reasonable care in misrepresenting a material fact to the plaintiff and, therefore, the defendant is liable to the plaintiff for negligent misrepresentation. For instance, a Connecticut court held that statements made by an employer to the plaintiff that negligently misled the employee about her job status could serve as a basis for an actionable negligent misrepresentation claim.

TYPICAL SITUATIONS FROM WHICH FRAUDULENT MISREPRESENTATION ACTIONS ORIGINATE

The employer's counsel and other representatives should appreciate that most fraudulent misrepresentation cases in the employment context relate to that of job security in terms of a refusal to hire or wrongful discharge. Yet, employee-plaintiffs frequently have used the tort of fraud to prosecute a cause of action against an employer where the employer allegedly had deceived the employee with respect to other employment decisions less than that of hire and fire.

Some examples of various employment situations out of which employees have advanced the fraudulent misrepresentation theory as a basis to proceed with a lawsuit against their employers may be instructive in better understanding fraud in the workplace.

One such example is found in the 1987 case of *Albrant v. Sterling Furniture Company*, where an Oregon appellate court held actionable an employee's wrongful discharge that she had been fraudulently induced to abandon her former employment because of the employer's misrepresentations to her about the amount of hours and commissions to which she would be entitled in her new employment.

A slight variation with respect to misrepresentation as to job security is found in the 1988 case of *Shebar v. Sanyo Business Systems Corporation* in which the New Jersey Supreme Court upheld the right of an employee to proceed with his claim that his employer had fraudulently and maliciously interfered with his prospective employment when it breached its verbal promise of lifetime job security if he turned down another job offer. This case illustrates how overlapping tort actions may be used in the employment context because the employee's action here is based on a combination of two separate tort theories: fraudulent misrepresentation and tortious interference with prospective employment.

A Florida court in the 1986 case of *Telesphere International, Inc. v. Scollin* upheld a lower court's decision that an employer was liable for its fraudulent failure to inform an employee at the time of hire that his job was tentative in that the developmental product on which he would be working was in danger of being abandoned by the employer. Here, the court implied that the employer had embellished its promise of job security by withholding essential facts relating to the expected length of the job.

One of the most interesting cases that depicts how fraud actions are used in the employment context, and one that should be reviewed by management attorneys who are called upon to advise clients about the use of permanent replacement employees during an economic strike, is the 1985 Idaho case of *Verway v. Blinkcoe Packing Co.* in which the Idaho Court of Appeals sustained a cause of action based on the tort theory of fraud where the employee-plaintiffs were induced to replace striking employees by the employer's representations that the work would be permanent, after which the plaintiffs were discharged when the strike was settled and the employer returned strikers to their former jobs.

A similar case with respect to the tort of fraud is the 1989 case of *Windfield v. Groen Div., Dover Corp.*, in which the Fifth Federal Court of Appeals remanded a case back to a lower court where an employee union activist had filed a lawsuit against his employer alleging that he had been discharged shortly after a union had lost an NLRB representative election at his employer's plant, when prior to the election he had been given a written guarantee by his employer that he would not be fired if the union lost, the court ruling further that the employee's fraudulent misrepresentation action against the employer was not preempted by the National Labor Relations Act, as amended.

STRATEGIC STEPS TO FOLLOW WHEN EVALUATING SPECIFIC DEFENSES TO FRAUDULENT MISREPRESENTATION CAUSES OF ACTION

Many fraud claims arising from employment decisions, and permitted by the courts to proceed to trial, are based upon the idea that even though the employer's statement to the prospective or current employee was couched in terms of a prediction, projection or opinion, falling short of a technical misrepresentation of a material fact, that due to the unique relationship between the employer and employee, the court should nonetheless infer that the "existing facts" rule is satisfied because the prediction, projection or opinion constitutes an implied misrepresentation of fact.

Convince the Court to Refuse to Erode the Common Law Elements of Proof

The employer's counsel who is charged with the responsibility of defending his or her employer against a fraudulent misrepresentation case brought by a prospective, current or former employee first should attempt to convince the court to refuse to erode the common law elements of proof, especially in permitting a fraud action to proceed unless the employee-plaintiff can demonstrate that the employer misrepresented a material fact, rather than having made some passing projection, prediction or opinion about a job opportunity. A case in point is the 1974 case of *Senec v. L.M. Berry Co.*, in which a Louisiana appellate court held that where there is no identifiable representation of fact, promise, or concealed fact, the plaintiff will not be allowed to proceed with his or her fraud cause of action. However, all courts have not bought into the idea that the traditional requirements to prove a fraud case should not be compromised just because the action is based on a claim arising out of a workplace situation.

Argue that an Action Is Not Available to an Employment-at-Will Employee

Another defense, in addition to the "existing facts" defense, noted above, is that an action of fraud should not be available to an employment-at-will employee. Inasmuch as either party may terminate the employment relationship at any time, the employee cannot establish that he or she reasonably relied upon the employer's prediction, projection or opinion, or some other employer communication to the employee-plaintiff.

The employee-plaintiff must be able to demonstrate to a court that his or her reliance upon the employer's promise was reasonable. Where a reasonable person would doubt the sincerity with which the employer made the promise to an employee or the equivocal manner in which it was made, the court may find that the employee did not carry his or her burden of proof as to the reliance element. Also, where the employee knew, or should have known, that the person making the promise did not have authority to make such promise, his or her fraud action should fail.

More specifically, if an employer has a lawful right to dismiss an at-will employee at any time it desires, unless in violation of some statutory right of the employee, how could an employee reasonably assert that he or she relied upon some passing projection by the employer to the contrary, especially when such alleged promises were not reduced to writing?

The First Federal Circuit Court of Appeals in the 1986 case of *Broussard v. CACI, Inc.*, in applying Maine law, seemed to strike that judicial note where it upheld a lower court's decision that an employer's failure to specify its at-will policy to an employee, who was later discharged, could not serve as sufficient grounds for a fraudulent misrepresentation cause of action.

Defend on the Grounds of Absence of Intent

The employer's counsel should also consider, if applicable, an absence of intent defense to a fraud case against the employer, as an addition to, and in complimentary of, the "absence of a misrepresentation of a material fact" and the "absence of the recipient's reliance upon the alleged misrepresentation of a material fact argument," as discussed above.

As discussed in various preceding chapters relative to tort actions against employers in which the element of "intent" is an essential one of proof, the courts may imply intent even when no actual intent can be shown. Yet, where an employer is able to demonstrate that any statement made by it to an employer was made in good faith and one out of which it could not foresee any possible harm or injury to the plaintiff, it should be able to argue an "absence of intent." For example, the First Federal First Circuit Court of Appeals in the 1969 case of *Doody v. John Sexton & Co.* upheld a lower court decision which found that the employer's argument that it was only kidding at the time it made certain statements to the plaintiff about the job in question was enough to establish that there was no "intent" to perform at the time the statements were made.

The employer's counsel should also be aware that some jurisdictions require the statement or promise allegedly made to induce the employee to take certain action must be a part of some scheme on the part of the employer in order to prove the element of "intent" in a fraud action. This scheme or device requirement to prove "intent" calls for the employee-plaintiff to demonstrate to the court that the employer possessed some ulterior motive—such as to eliminate the employee as a competitor, to obtain the benefit of the employee's good will—as its purpose for making the promise to the employee. The employer's counsel may well want to advance to the court, also, that the material fact allegedly relied upon by the employer that caused him or her to suffer harm was not a misrepresentation at all, but one that the employer believed to be true at the time the representation was made to the employer. The suggestion here is that both the elements of "intent" and "misrepresentation" are so closely connected that the employer's argument to the court, if demonstrated by evidence, is that where there is no presence of intent, there can be no misrepresentation and where there is no presence of misrepresentation, there can be no intent to misrepresent.

Defend on the Grounds of No Proximate Cause

Another defense that emanates from an analysis of the requirements necessary to prove a fraudulent misrepresentation case is that the employer's alleged misrepresentation is not what induced the employee to take whatever action he or she took that proximately caused a suffering of harm, but that some extraneous action on the part of the employee proximately caused the alleged harm. This argument may be advanced where the employee procured a better job at a higher rate of pay subsequent to his or her termination of employment with the employer-defendant, or where the employee-plaintiff could have secured such a better and higher paying position and breached his or her duty to mitigate damages in a failure to do so.

Other Defenses Against Fraudulent Misrepresentation

In addition to the specific defenses enumerated above relative to employee fraudulent misrepresentation claims against an employer, the employer's counsel and other representatives should review other general defenses that are applicable to most tort actions—although not always recognized by the courts in certain jurisdictions—such as where an employee's tort action is preempted by some statutory right of action provided the employee, where the employee's action is preempted by his or her rights under the grievance and arbitration provisions of a collective bargaining contract, where the employee has failed to exhaust the administrative remedies available to him or her, where a previous decision on the same facts collaterally estops the employee from proceeding with the tort action at hand, where the alleged promise or misrepresentation in question was made to someone other than the employee-plaintiff, and so on.

The employer's counsel should review the various subheadings relating to specific defenses in other tort actions covered in Part IV of this book. The employer's counsel can use these subheadings somewhat as a checklist, to determine if he or she has taken advantage of some of the many defenses associated with tort actions when preparing to defend against a fraudulent misrepresentation claim.

PRE-TRIAL AND TRIAL TECHNIQUES TO USE WHEN DEFENDING A FRAUDULENT MISREPRESENTATION CAUSE OF ACTION

Research the Decisional Developments of Previous Fraud Cases

Given the fact that many states have been reluctant to recognize a fraud action arising out of employment decisions, especially the employee-plaintiff employment-at-will relationship with the employer, the employer's counsel should first research the decisional developments of fraud cases in the state in which the action is brought as part of his or her pre-trial efforts to defend a fraudulent misrepresentation case. Second, counsel should attempt to research the developing decisions in other states whose courts have taken a very conservative approach in permitting fraud in the workplace lawsuits to proceed to trial and use such decisions as persuasive authority to convince the applicable court that the case in question is not one that should proceed to trial, based upon whatever judicial rationale that is advanced in the persuasive decisions.

Research the Statutory Law

In addition, the employer's counsel should research the statutory law within the state to determine to what extent the state law addresses and/or provides any private action to a plaintiff with respect to a fraudulent wrongdoing, and in turn, assert as a defense and argue that the statutory provisions provide the only right of action available to the employee-plaintiff.

Review the Rules of the Court and Applicable Jurisdiction

As suggested in previous chapters, the employer's counsel should review closely the rules of the court and the applicable jurisdiction in which the action is brought and being defended. Should such procedural rules permit a removal, or by some means, an opportunity for the employer's counsel to transfer the case to a court or jurisdiction whose judicial philosophy is more in tune with the employer's position, then counsel should explore proceeding in that direction, assuming other factors do not dictate otherwise.

Ensure Compliance with the Rules of the Court

As part of the employer's pre-trial and trial checklist, the employer's counsel should ensure that his or her answer and other pleadings conform and comply with the rules of the applicable court and jurisdiction and that all affirmative defenses such as that of prescription, mitigation, set off, accord and satisfaction, exhaustion of remedies, and other affirmative defenses be pleaded properly.

Exhaust All Discovery Opportunities

An employer's counsel should not be reticent in exhausting all discovery opportunities that may be available to him or her when defending an employer-client against an employee's fraudulent misrepresentation lawsuit. The employer's counsel may want to approach discovery more by way of face-to-face deposition, rather than by interrogatories, however, so that it can seek spontaneous responses from the employee-plaintiff and other witnesses to important questions relating to the absence of the essential elements of proof in a fraud case. For instance, the employer's counsel may be able to cross-examine an employee-plaintiff in a face-to-face discovery deposition in a way that the employee may readily reveal that he or she never truly believed or relied upon what the employer had allegedly promised.

Review the Relevant Statutory and Decisional Law

As part of the employer counsel's pre-trial preparations when defending a fraud case, a review of the statutory and decisional law within the court's jurisdiction is essential in order to determine to what extent a recovery of punitive damages are available to a plaintiff. Thus, the employer's counsel's efforts should be directed toward eliminating or limiting an award of such damages. If the employer's counsel is unable to eliminate an award of damages, he or she should seek to limit the damages.

Many other pre-trial and trial techniques relative to not only the defense of tort actions, as discussed in Part IV of this book, but to the defense of numerous other types of labor and employment lawsuits typically brought against employers, have been discussed throughout this book. The reader's attention is directed to them as well as to the pre-trial and trial subheadings throughout this book, specifically to Chapters 5, 10, 18, and 27.

32 Strategies and Tactics in Defending Negligent Hiring and Retention Causes of Action

The idea of an employee bringing a negligence tort action against an employer in the employment context was considered to be completely antithetical to what was provided him or her through the exclusivity of workers' compensation legislation during most of the twentieth century.

Courts looked jaundicely upon such actions because the purpose of workers' compensation was to provide employees an exclusive remedy for workplace injuries, based upon the concept of strict liability. Workers' compensation laws were enacted, in effect, to displace negligent causes of action in the workplace and to overcome such traditional employer defenses to negligent actions as that of assumption of risk and contributory negligence.

Thus, one can only imagine the ire of employers and management attorneys when courts began to hold that the exclusivity of remedies traditionally provided to employees through the workers' compensation laws did not apply in certain cases in which an employer is sued for negligence by employees.

One of the most discussed cases in which a court recognized a negligence action by an employee against an employer in modern times was the 1982 Michigan case of *Chamberlain v. Bissell, Inc.* in which a Michigan court held that the employer-defendant had a duty of ordinary and reasonable cause to the employee-plaintiff to inform him at the time of his last performance evaluation that he was about to be discharged if certain matters where not corrected in the employee's performance.

Understanding Tort Negligence

Therefore, even though this chapter is mostly devoted to the coverage of employees' and third parties' lawsuits against employers based upon the employer's negligent hiring or detention of a given employee who, in turn, causes harm or injuries to others, it should be recognized that other employee types of negligent actions have been brought against employers as well, such as that of negligent misrepresentation which was discussed in the preceding chapter.

The tort of negligence is the failure or omission to do something which an ordinarily prudent person would have done under the circumstances, or the doing of something that an ordinarily prudent person would not have done in such a situation.

In order for a plaintiff, including employee-plaintiffs, to prevail in a negligence cause of action against another, he or she must be able to establish the four essential elements of negligence:

1. Some duty or obligation recognized by law which obligates a person to comply with certain standards of conduct in order to protect other persons against unreasonable risks
2. A failure on the part of the person, so obligated, to comply with the required standard
3. A reasonably close causal connection between the obligor's failure to comply to the required standard and the proximate cause of the harm or injury to the other person; and
4. An actual loss or damage resulting to the other person

Employers traditionally have been held liable for negligent acts of their managers and supervisors, as well as employees, to third parties, under the doctrine of "respondent superior," when such negligent acts occurred during the course and scope of their employment. However, now both third parties, as well as employees, have commenced to sue employers for negligent and criminal acts committed by employees outside the course and scope of their employment on the basis that the employer did not exercise due care in hiring an employee who has a history of, or proclivity to, commit such criminal or negligent conduct (negligent hiring) or that the employer did not exercise due care in retaining an employee who had such a history or proclivity towards violence and criminal conduct (negligent detention). The courts justify third party actions against employers for negligently hiring or retaining an employee having a history or proclivity to commit criminal conduct on the basis that the four elements of tort are satisfied; that is, the employer has a duty to protect its customers and visitors from injuries caused by employees whom the employer knew or should have known posed a risk of harm to others, and to do otherwise would have deprived a third party victim from recovery at all.

Courts now are extending this doctrine by permitting employees to file negligent actions against employers for negligent hiring and negligent detention.

In the typical negligent hiring cause of action, the plaintiff seeks to show the court that the employer was negligent in selecting an applicant for hire by its failure to contact the applicant's former employers, to check the applicant's criminal record with state and federal authorities, to verify that the applicant possessed the necessary licenses and certificates required in the job, and so forth, when such an investigation and inquiry would have shown that the applicant had a criminal background, a violent nature, or was in some other way unsuitable for the job.

An employer's counsel can readily acknowledge that an employer is placed in the classical catch-22 position when, on the one hand, many states prohibit police departments to provide employers with certain criminal records of prospective employees and previous employers will not provide information about former employees, while, on the other hand, the courts (and juries) hold employers liable for their negligence in not obtaining such information prior to hiring an applicant with a criminal background or violent past. Predictably, this is an area in which state and/or federal legislators will provide employers with some protection in the future.

That does not mean to suggest that courts in all the states have recognized the tort of negligent hiring or, if so adopted the theory, have not placed certain restrictions and qualifications so as to protect employers from a lose-lose situation; yet, in many states, there exists an area of undefined territory in which such abuses can take place.

In the typical negligent retention (or negligent supervision) cause of action, the plaintiff seeks to prove that the employer failed to conduct an investigation, failed to timely and properly discipline or failed to discharge an employee once the employer became aware, or should have been aware, of the employee's criminal or violent behaviors or lack of suitability for the job, the failure of which subsequently resulted in the employee causing some harm or injury to the plaintiff.

UNIQUE ILLUSTRATIONS OF NEGLIGENT HIRING AND RETENTION CAUSES OF ACTIONS

Employment situations out of which negligent hiring causes of action arise are sometimes bizarre. Some examples of negligent hiring cases may be illustrative of the extent of their coverage.

Third Party Causes of Action

Some of the earlier cases relate to third party negligent hiring causes of action against employers, perhaps more than that of employee lawsuits against employers on the basis of a negligent hiring claim. For instance, in the 1985 Maryland case of *Cramer v. Housing Opportunities Commission*, a Maryland court held that a tenant of a housing project who was raped by a housing inspector could proceed against the inspector's employer for negligently hiring the inspector where the employer allegedly had failed to inquire into the inspector's fitness for the job, had not contacted any previous employers for reference checks, and did not attempt to verify any information on the inspector's application for employment, and thus failed to learn that the inspector had been convicted of robbery, assault and burglary, and at the time of hire, was under indictment for rape.

In the 1985 case of *Toney v. Casey's General Stores*, the Iowa Supreme Court held actionable a negligent hiring cause of action by a customer of a cable television company against the company for its failure to investigate the criminal record of one of its installers who raped the plaintiff-customer after entering her apartment with the keys he had been given by the employer-defendant.

Similarly, in the 1983 Michigan case of *Burch v. A&G Associates, Inc.*, a Michigan Appellate Court permitted a cab passenger to proceed with his negligent hiring cause of action against a cab company whose driver, apparently displeased with the amount of tip he received from the passenger-plaintiff, jumped from his cab, beat the passenger with an iron bar, pulled off the passenger's trousers and drove off with the trousers and their contents, where the plaintiff alleged that the cab company knew or should have known of the driver's violent and dangerous propensities when it hired him. A California court in the 1983 case of *Underwriters Insurance Co. v. Purdue* approved the negligent hiring theory where the plaintiff, a bottling company employee, while in the process of making a delivery to a liquor store, became involved in an argument with a store clerk during which verbal exchange the clerk pulled a gun and shot the plaintiff, in which cause of action the plaintiff contended that the employer of the clerk had negligently hired the clerk when knowing that he was a violent person and unfit for a position that required constant interactions with customers and delivery persons.

Employee Lawsuits Claiming Negligent Hiring

The employer's counsel should appreciate, too, that courts apparently are just as enthusiastic in embracing employee negligent hiring lawsuits against their own employers.

For instance, in the 1984 case of *Athas v. Hill*, a Maryland Appellate Court held actionable an employee's negligent hiring claim against his employer as a result of being stabbed by a co-worker, the plaintiff contending that the employer had breached its duty of due diligence by selecting the co-worker for employment when it knew or should have known the co-worker's propensity for violent behavior.

Negligent Retention Causes of Action

The employer's counsel should be aware, also, that negligent retention causes of action are on the increase. One of the earliest cases in which a court upheld the tort theory of negligent retention against an employer was the 1928 California case of *Sullivan v. People's Ice Corp.*, where an ice salesman, while driving an ice wagon along his designated route, was attacked by another ice salesman who worked for a competitor ice company and who apparently was attempting to discourage the former from working the route, all of which resulted in the ice salesman bringing a negligent retention cause of action against the competitor based on the continued employment of its employee who attacked the plaintiff.

The employer's counsel should appreciate that many of the injuries caused by an employee, negligently retained in the employment of the employer, result from customer altercations with employees in restaurants, bars, and so forth.

For example, in the 1988 Massachusetts case of *Foster v. Loft, Inc.*, a Massachusetts Appellate Court permitted a bar customer to proceed with his negligent retention cause of action against a bar owner whose bartender, after hearing the plaintiff complain about his drink, leaped over the bar and punched the plaintiff and them punched out another customer, fracturing his cheek bone in the process, where the bar owner had retained the bartender after having previously been advised by local police that the bartender had a criminal record. A similarly factual situation was found in the 1985 California case of *Greenfield v. Spectrum Inv. Corp.*, in which a California court held actionable a customer's negligent retention cause of action against a Budget rental car agency whose agent ran from behind the counter, struck the plaintiff on the back of the head, hit him and kicked him with "judo chops" after an argument with the plaintiff about a security deposit, where the facts demonstrated that despite the agency's knowledge of the agent's previous problems with customers and a fight off its premises, it still continued to keep him employed.

As with negligent hiring claims, the courts permit employees to sue their employers for the negligent retention of fellow employees who previously engaged in behavior for which they should not have been retained. For instance, in the 1983 Georgia case of *Cox v. Bruno*, a Georgia Appellate Court upheld an employee's negligent retention action against her employer where despite her supervisor's having made obscene comments and gestures to her, having made sexual advances to her and at one time having dropped his trousers in her presence, the employer continued to retain the supervisor, even though previously having received similar reports about his behavior from other female employees.

SIGNIFICANT DEFENSES TO NEGLIGENT HIRING AND RETENTION LAWSUITS

Move to Dismiss

The employer's initial approach in defending an employee's negligent hiring or retention lawsuit against his or her employer is to motion the court that the action should be dismissed on the grounds that the workers' compensation statute of the state provides the exclusive remedy available for employee injuries occurring while during the course and scope of the employee's employment and thus the employee's cause of action is foreclosed by the workers' compensation exclusivity provisions.

Show the Employer's Inability to Investigate the Employee's Background

Second, an employer's defense should focus upon the employer's inability to carry out any duty to investigate the background of a prospective employee's criminal history, propensity toward violent behavior, or lack of suitability for the job in question based on one or more of the following, if applicable:

1. That the laws of the state make if unlawful to check the criminal records of applicants or employees;
2. Former employers would not provide any such information about the applicant, although the information was requested; and/or,
3. Such requests cannot be made without subjecting the employer with charges of discrimination in that applicants rejected or dismissed because of such behavior may charge that they are being discriminated based upon their protected characteristics, rather than upon some objective reason, or that to make such requests and act upon them could also subject the employer to charges that the employer's action has a disparate and discriminatory impact upon a certain class of employees because of their protected characteristics.

Obviously, the first two of the three defensive arguments discussed above are likely to receive a higher degree of receptivity than the last but the last one has merit, as well, particularly to those employers who take great pains in making sure that their pre-employment inquiries and investigations do not discriminate against any person because of his or her protected characteristics or against any class of employees because of their protected characteristics.

A secondary defensive argument to that noted above is that were an employer to make inquiries into a prospective or current employee's past with respect to criminal conduct or a penchant toward violent behavior, the employer could be subjecting itself to an invasion of privacy or some similar tortious cause of action.

Argue No Grounds for Employer Negligence

Aside from the preemption argument relative to workers' compensation statutes and the argument that it is impossible to carry out any implied duty of care in making investigations about the criminal background of previous violent behaviors of applicants, and possibly current employees, the employer's counsel should analyze its potential defenses to a negligent hiring or retention lawsuit by evaluating whether the plaintiff's lawsuit contains the essential elements to prove a negligence case, specifically:

1. Does the employer have a duty to the plaintiff which requires it to investigate the background of an applicant to determine his or her propensity toward criminal conduct?
2. Did the employer do everything it could to conform to the standard of duty required?
3. Was there a reasonably close causal connection between the employer's failure to conform to the standard of duty required and the proximate cause of the injuries or harm suffered by the plaintiff?
4. Did the plaintiff suffer any actual loss or damage resulting to his or her interests?

Aside from these specific arguments, the employer's counsel should analyze other defenses discussed in the previous chapters in Part IV of this book regarding general defenses to tort cases as well as chapters in other parts of the book relative to general defenses to all types of labor and employment lawsuits, particularly those defenses that require affirmative pleadings.

PRE-TRIAL AND TRIAL TECHNIQUES AND SAFEGUARDS IN DEFENDING NEGLIGENT HIRING AND RETENTION CAUSES OF ACTION

Review the Decisional Developments Regarding Negligence

The employer's counsel should seek, as part of his or her pre-trial strategies, to review the decisional developments on the subject of negligence, particularly that of negligent hiring and negligent retention within the state in which the action is being defended as well as the law in other state courts whose decisions may be used as persuasive authority in support of the employer's position.

Special attention should be given to the catch-22 defense discussed earlier in terms of attempting to convince the court, as a matter of law, that the employer does not enjoy the capacity to satisfy the standard of care required of it to avoid negligent hiring and negligent retention legal claims because of countervailing statutes of the state and extraneous policies and practices over which it has no control. Here, the employer's counsel should preliminarily attempt to get his or her employer-client dismissed from the case on the legal question of capacity, rather than to permit the case to go forward on its merits.

Seek to Limit Damages

The employer's counsel, as part and parcel of its pre-trial preparations, should attempt to seek to limit the damages that may be recoverable by the plaintiff, assuming that he or she is unsuccessful in getting the action dismissed on the basis of various defenses already noted, or is unsuccessful in prevailing on the merits of the matter if it proceeds through trial. The employer counsel's efforts in attempting to limit the amount of damages can be aided by timely and sound discovery methods to define the presence or absence of any causal connection between the employer's failure to satisfy its duty to investigate the background of its employee's background with respect to his or her ability to do the job or penchant for criminal or violent behavior and the alleged resultant injuries suffered by the plaintiff. Here, the employer should attempt to discover any other sources of causal connection to decrease its liability and the amount of damages to the plaintiff.

Determine the Extent of the Plaintiff's Injuries

Likewise, in an attempt to limit the employer's damages to the plaintiff, the employer counsel's pre-trial discovery should include thorough inquiries into the exact nature and extent of the plaintiff's injuries, so as to curtail any propensity on the part of the plaintiff to embellish his or her damage claims.

Show the Employer's Attempts to Investigate the Employee's Background

The employer's counsel should prepare his or her oral and documentary evidence in a manner to convince the court and jury that the employer took all possible measures to investigate the employee's background who allegedly caused the plaintiff to suffer injuries. Here, the employer's counsel should prepare his or her evidence for presentation to the court and jury in a proper manner to convince them that a thorough investigation was made to ensure that the employee in question possessed all necessary licenses and certificates required of the position held.

Other Defense Strategies

Aside from some of the pre-trial safeguards discussed above, the employer's counsel should draw heavily upon pre-trial techniques and strategies discussed in previous chapters in Part IV of this book regarding tort actions in the workplace.

Also, the employer's counsel may want to refer to pre-trial and trial strategies covered throughout this book with respect to defending labor and employment lawsuits, and specifically to Chapters 5, 10, 18, and 27.

33 Successful Strategies in Winning a Breach of Fiduciary Duty Lawsuit

In most all tort actions in the employment context, and as noted and discussed in all the preceding chapters in Part IV of this book with the possible exception of the tortious interference with an employment contract or prospective employment, it is the employer who is the defendant, rather than the plaintiff.

And just as in a breach of covenant not to compete or a breach of covenant not to disclose or misappropriate cause of action as was discussed in Part III of this book, the employer assumes the role of the plaintiff in a breach of the fiduciary duty cause of action against an employee.

The distinguishing characteristic between a breach of a covenant not to disclose and misappropriate and/or a breach of a covenant not to compete and a breach of duty of loyalty or some other fiduciary duty to the employer, lies in the fact that the former causes of action are based in contract, and breach of the fiduciary duty lies in tort.

The reason the employer becomes the plaintiff in such a cause of action is that the employee is the party who typically breaches his or her covenant to the employer by going into competition or disclosing or misappropriating trade secrets, not the employer, and it is the employee who typically fails to conform to his or her duty to remain loyal to the employer, rather than vice-versa.

Thus, the employer's counsel must take on the role as plaintiff's counsel in an action against an employee for the breach of his or her fiduciary obligations to the employer. Even though, strategically, an employer may be in a more tenable position of proving a breach of covenant not to compete or disclose, particularly if it has a written document which contains such covenants, many employer's counsel incorporate into a breach of covenant type action also a breach of fiduciary duty cause of action in attempt to seek a recovery of punitive damages as well as compensatory damages—punitive damages being available in tort actions, but not available in contract actions.

The breach of a duty of fiduciary obligation is more significant to an employer's counsel, however, where there is no written covenant not to compete or disclose. In the absence of some written covenant not to compete or disclose, the employer's counsel may be limited to an independent cause of action for the tortious breach of fiduciary duty, solely. If so, the employer's counsel should be aware that not all courts embrace such tort actions, and those who do are very reluctant to become too enthusiastic toward the idea of permitting an employer relief under the theory.

That is not to suggest that an employer may not prevail in a breach of a fiduciary duty cause of action against an employee. There are many reported cases where employer-plaintiffs have been most successful in such lawsuits.

For example, in the 1983 case of *Poe v. IBM*, a federal district court, applying California law, held that an employer was justified in discharging a staff member for a breach of the duty of loyalty where the employee had placed a newspaper ad seeking capital for his new business that would have been in direct competition with the employer's business. Although the case related to the employer's use of the theory of disloyalty in the context of defending an unlawful termination claim, it has been used in numerous other jurisdictions as a basis for an employer's cause of action against an employee.

How to Use the Tort of Fiduciary Breach

Employers and their counsel probably do not use the tort of fiduciary breach as much as they should, probably because they are unfamiliar with its existence or the proper manner in which to use it.

The employer's counsel should realize that in addition to using the breach of a fiduciary duty as a basis for a cause of action against an employee, he or she may want to use it, as it was used in the California case, as a defensive tool or, alternatively, use it as a basis for a counterclaim against an employee in a wrongful discharge action.

Also, some employers combine a breach of duty of loyalty action with one based on unfair competition as a means of getting their case before the court.

The employer's counsel also may seek to use a breach of duty of loyalty theory as a basis for a petition to enjoin an employee from so engaging in competitive conduct or disclosing or misappropriating trade secrets where there is no written covenant to protect the employer's interest, contractually. As noted in the Colorado case of *Kandt v. Evans*, an employee's common law duty of loyalty to his or her employer forbids him or her from soliciting customers for a new business venture while in the employment of the employer and also prohibits him or her from soliciting co-workers to join in the new business during such time of employment.

As noted earlier, in the chapter discussing covenants not to compete, a breach of a fiduciary duty cause of action provides a slight advantage over a covenant not to compete in that once a possible breach of a fiduciary duty is established to the court's satisfaction, the burden of proof shifts to the employee-defendant, which is not the case in covenants not to compete causes of action in which the burden of proof continues to lie with the employer-plaintiff.

EVALUATING ESSENTIAL FIDUCIARY DUTIES APPLICABLE TO DISLOYALTY LITIGATION

There are many types of common law breaches of fiduciary duty just as there are many types of relationships in which fiduciary duties attach. A fiduciary relationship may exist whenever there is an imposition of trust and confidence by one party on the fidelity and integrity of the other party. Thus, fiduciary relationships exist between partners, joint venturers, principals and agents, stock holders, and corporate officers.

Fiduciary relationships exist between employers and employees and it is within the scope of this chapter to discuss under what circumstances an employee is deemed to have breached his or her common law duty of loyalty to the employer.

As a general proposition, any person acting in the capacity of a fiduciary to another may not take advantage of his or her fiduciary relationship for the benefit of his or her own personal interest without the full knowledge and consent of the other party to whom the fiduciary duty is owed.

The same holds true when a fiduciary relationship is formed between an employer and an employee; that is, until the employment relationship is terminated, the employee must prefer the interest of his or her employer to his or her own.

Thus, an employee must actively promote the interest of his or her employer during the existence of the employment relationship. An employee, therefore, may not compete with his or her employer during the time of employment, without the full knowledge and consent of the employer.

In addition, an employee who stands in a fiduciary relationship with the employer has an affirmative duty to inform the employer of any matters significant to their ongoing fiduciary relationship. For example, in the 1972 case of *Lowndes Products Co. v. Brower*, a South Carolina court found that a plant manager had breached his fiduciary duty to the employer when, upon learning that other key employees were going to leave the company, he joined in their defection without informing the employer as to what was occurring.

An employee is forbidden to use deceptive or coercive tactics and schemes to take advantage of a party with whom he or she enjoys a fiduciary relationship. Thus, many courts hold that any inventions which an employee develops while occupying a fiduciary relationship with an employer and which invention relates to the occupation of the employer must be turned over and assigned to the employer for its benefit.

As a general rule, the fiduciary duties end with the termination of the relationship between an employer and an employee. However, in some cases, the employee's fiduciary duty to the employer may continue to exist after the relationship is terminated.

For example, in the 1973 Second Circuit Court of Appeals case of *Abbott Thinlite Corp. v. Redmont*, the court found that the employee had a residual fiduciary obligation to his former employer not to exploit projects for which he had procured for his former employer in which the former employer would have made substantial profits but for the employee's attempt to compete after the termination of the fiduciary relationship.

SIGNIFICANT DEFENSES AND REMEDIES IN BREACH OF FIDUCIARY DUTY LAWSUITS

The remedies available to an employer who prevails in a breach of a fiduciary duty cause of action against an employee includes a recovery in punitive damages, as well as a recovery of compensatory damages. The employer may be able to recover for lost profit or lost sales caused by the employee's breach of his or her fiduciary duties to the employer.

The essential elements of proof necessary to establish a breach of a covenant not to disclose or misappropriate a trade secret are the same elements that are necessary to establish a breach of fiduciary duty cause of action for disclosing or misappropriating trade secrets, with the exception that with respect to the latter, there is no existence of a written contract or agreement in which the employee so covenants. The reader may recall that such elements as the *existence of a trade secret*, the *ownership of the trade secrets*, and the *existence of a confidential relationship* were key elements of proof in breaches of covenants not to compete, disclose or misappropriate as was discussed in Chapters 22 and 23. Inasmuch as the courts apply the same essential elements of proof in a breach of a fiduciary duty cause of action as it does in a breach of covenant not to compete, not to disclose or misappropriate, the employer should review Chapters 22 and 23 in his or her preparations to prosecute a breach of duty of loyalty lawsuit against an employee.

The employer's counsel should be prepared to overcome any defenses that the employee is likely to assert in a breach of a duty of loyalty cause of action.

For example, an employee may attempt to show that he or she had the employer's permission or consent in whatever action he or she took that formed the basis of the employer's lawsuit against the employee.

The employer's counsel should be prepared to withstand an employee's argument that the employer had abandoned its right to a trade secret and, thus, the employee had a perfect right to use the information in any way he or she wished without being liable for a breach of a fiduciary obligation.

Inasmuch as a breach of a fiduciary duty is, essentially, the same as a breach of covenant not to disclose or misappropriate a trade secret, or a breach of covenant not to compete, the primary distinction being that a breach of covenant cause of action lies in contract where as a breach of fiduciary duty cause of action lies in tort, the employer must be prepared to persevere against the types of defenses available to the plaintiff in a breach of covenant not to disclose or misappropriate "trade secrets" as was discussed in Chapter 22 and a breach of covenant not to compete as was discussed in Chapter 23.

Therefore, the employer's counsel should review other defenses so discussed in Chapter 22 and Chapter 23 in attempting to anticipate the defenses the employee's counsel is likely to assert against an employer's breach of duty of loyalty cause of action.

PRE-TRIAL AND TRIAL TECHNIQUES IN WINNING A BREACH OF FIDUCIARY DUTY CAUSE OF ACTION

The employer's counsel should be ever-conscious that his or her role, just as the employer's, has changed from that of typically defending an action in the labor and employment field, to that of prosecuting an action against an employee.

Therefore, the first pre-trial technique is to become as assertive and zealous as the more traditional plaintiff's lawyer and seek to discover as much of the employee's cause as possible through the use of depositions and interrogatories as early in the lawsuit as possible.

The employer's counsel, in prosecuting breach of fiduciary causes of action against an employee, should research thoroughly the applicable decisional law within the state in which he or she chooses to bring the action to determine any limitations, restrictions or rights to bring such a cause of action within the court's jurisdiction.

Since the employer's action is one based in tort, the employer's counsel may desire to review some of the more prevalent defenses used in such actions in order that he or she can adequately prepare the case to overcome specific defenses unique to tort cases as discussed throughout Part IV of this book.

The employer's counsel should not only prepare his or her breach of fiduciary duty cause of action in the proper form and manner to ensure that the employer-client will prevail upon the merits of the case, but, in addition, be entitled to a sizeable money judgment as a result of the employee's breach of its duty of loyalty to the employer. Plaintiff attorneys seemingly spend as much or more of their preparation time with respect to proving damages in a tort action as they do with respect to proving disability. The employer's counsel in the role of a plaintiff's role probably should do no less.

In addition to the pre-trial techniques noted above with respect to prosecuting a cause of action based on the employee's breach of his or her duty of loyalty to the employer, the employer's counsel may want to review the pre-trial techniques discussed with regard to covenants not to disclose or misappropriate "trade secrets" found in Chapter 22, and pre-trial techniques with respect to covenants not to compete found in Chapter 23.

More general pre-trial and trial techniques and tactics relative to labor and employment lawsuits are discussed throughout this book, but the reader's attention is referred specifically to Chapters 5, 10, 18, and 27.

V How to Defend Employment Discrimination Cases (Race, Sex, Religion, Age, National Origin, Handicap, and Veteran)

34 What Management Representatives Should Know About Federal EEOC Policy

Most charges of discrimination allege violations of Title VII of the Civil Rights Act of 1964, as amended (42 USC §§ 2000e—2000e-17, 1974; and Civil Rights Act of 1991). Title VII prohibits discrimination in the terms or conditions of employment on the basis of sex, race, color, national origin, or religion. The EEOC also enforces the Age Discrimination in Employment Act of 1967 (ADEA) (29 USC §§ 621—634 Z (1967 & Supp. 1982) and the Equal Pay Act of 1963 (29 USC § 206 (1938 & Supp. 1977). The ADEA prohibits discrimination in the terms and conditions of employment on the basis of age. The EPA prohibits sex-based compensations differentials for work requiring equal skill, effort, and responsibility.

Most charges of discrimination stem from instances of discharge, failure to hire, or failure to promote, but virtually any aspect of employment may be challenged as discriminatory. Prohibited discrimination also includes an employer's tolerating harassment of or an environment hostile to members of a protected category of employees. Each anti-discrimination statute also prohibits retaliation by an employer against anybody who files an EEOC charge or cooperates with the investigation of a charge. Also prohibited is retaliation against an employee for opposing actions the employee believes to be illegal discrimination, whether or not the employee actually files an official charge of discrimination. The most common forms of protected opposition activities include filing grievances through an employer's internal grievance procedure and complaints to management or outside parties. However, protected opposition activity is not limited. Most any activity that the employer understands to be in protest of alleged illegal discrimination is protected, so long as the employee continues to perform his job duties competently and does not disrupt the employment environment to the extent that other employees are prevented from performing their job duties.

Beginning July 1992, the EEOC will also enforce the Americans With Disabilities Act of 1991. Currently, discrimination on the basis of disability or perceived disability is monitored by the U.S. Department of Labor's Office of Federal Contract Compliance Programs (OFCCP).

Most states have now enacted their own anti-discrimination statutes and established their own fair employment practices agencies. Usually these state laws prohibit all types of discrimination prohibited by the combination of federal acts, and sometimes prohibit discrimination for reasons not prohibited by federal laws, such as discrimination because of marital status or AIDS. State charges are investigated in the same manner as EEOC charges. References in these pages to "the EEOC" should be read to mean the appropriate state fair employment practices agency when a state charge is involved.

The EEOC has developed work-sharing agreements with most state agencies to avoid duplication of efforts. Work-sharing agreements ordinarily provide for simultaneous filings with the EEOC and the state agency, so that a charge filed with one agency is filed with both. The charge will be investigated by the agency designated under the work-sharing agreement. In most cases this will be the EEOC, which has much greater staffing than most state agencies. If the charge alleges discrimination on a basis not prohibited by both state and federal statutes, the charge will be investigated by the agency with jurisdiction over the discrimination alleged. In cases of dual jurisdiction, the EEOC will retain the right to do its own investigation after a state agency completes its investigation. However, it rarely decides to do this.

FUNCTION OF THE EQUAL EMPLOYMENT OPPORTUNITY COMMISSION

The Equal Employment Opportunity Commission consists of a Chairman, Vice-Chairman, and three other members appointed by the President of the United States for five-year terms. The President also appoints a General Counsel (for a four-year term) who is responsible for litigation.

There are 22 EEOC district offices, each headed by a district director. Under each district director is a legal staff (headed by a regional attorney) and an enforcement staff. In addition, there are 37 EEOC area offices, each a sub-element of a district office. Area offices usually are staffed with enforcement personnel only and are limited to investigative and voluntary compliance activities.

The EEOC is charged with preventing any person from engaging in any employment practice made unlawful by Title VII, the ADEA, or the EPA. It receives written charges of discrimination against labor organizations, employment agencies, and joint labor-management apprentice programs as well as against employers. The EEOC will also investigate charges filed against governmental agencies, although these charges are litigated when appropriate by the Justice Department rather than by the EEOC.

EEOC charges may be filed by an individual, an organization, or by a member of the Commission. A charge may allege discrimination against one or more specific individuals or systemic discrimination against a class of employees protected either by Title VII, the ADEA, or the EPA. They may seek both monetary damages and injunctive relief, including preliminary injunctions.

The EEOC has the power to order access to evidence and to pay witness and mileage fees. If it determines that there is reasonable cause to believe that a charge is true, it must attempt to remedy the discrimination through informal methods of conciliation, conference, and persuasion. If it is not able to remedy the discrimination through persuasion, it may bring suit in an appropriate U.S. District Court at any time once 30 days have passed after the charge was filed. If it decides not to bring suit on a charge, it issues a right to sue letter giving the charging party 90 days in which to bring his or her own suit. The EEOC may intervene in a suit brought by a charging party, and a charging party may intervene in a suit brought by the EEOC.

The EEOC is also authorized to conduct research and pay for research conducted by state fair employment practice agencies, issue procedural regulations and written interpretations, and to assist employers and unions whose employees refuse to cooperate in effecting federal anti-discrimination provisions.

The EEOC may also issue written interpretations or opinions at the request of employers concerning particular situations. Reliance upon an EEOC opinion letter is a complete defense to a charge of discrimination in which the challenged action was sanctioned by the letter. Employers should *beware that* they are relying upon an official opinion letter or information published in the Federal Register, however. An official opinion letter is entitled "Opinion Letter" and signed by the General Counsel. They may be obtained by writing the Chairman, Equal Employment Opportunity Commission, Washington, D.C., and stating the name and address of the requestor and other interested parties, all the known relevant facts, and the reasons why the opinion should be issued.

JURISDICTION OF THE EQUAL EMPLOYMENT OPPORTUNITY COMMISSION

Title VII outlaws employment discrimination by employers, unions, employment agencies, or joint labor-management committees. The overwhelming majority of charges are filed against employers. Title VII provides that a civil action may be brought against a respondent "named in the charge," which has been interpreted differently by different courts. The issue arises when a charging party names a subsidiary in a charge and later files suit against the parent company or the respondent plus individually named officers or management. Some circuits hold that failure to name the party in the charge is a jurisdictional defect and dismiss the suit, while others allow the suit to proceed so long as the defendants had actual notice of the charge that was filed or where the subsidiary's activities are so closely related to the parent's as to establish an agency or integrated enterprise.

Title VII covers all employers with fifteen or more employees. It prohibits discriminatory employment practices concerning every term or condition of employment, including recruitment, hiring, job classifications, transfer, promotion, compensation, and termination.

UNDERSTANDING CRITICAL DIFFERENCES BETWEEN TITLE VII, STATE ACTS, ADEA AND EPA

The primary substantive differences between state fair employment practices statutes and Title VII is that an employer must have 15 employees before the EEOC has jurisdiction, while state acts may require as few as five; Title VII limits monetary damages to backpay plus attorney fees and costs (albeit with a liberal definition of backpay) while state acts often allow compensation for humiliation and mental distress in addition to backpay, attorney fees, and costs; and, state acts often prohibit discrimination for reasons not prohibited by federal anti-discrimination statutes, such as discrimination because of marital status or AIDS. Procedural differences are that state acts sometimes do not require an administrative charge be filed by an adversely affected individual prior to the individual's filing a lawsuit, whereas a timely filed charge with the EEOC is a prerequisite for discrimination litigation in federal court; and, court dates currently are more available in state courts than in many federal district courts due to criminal cases repeatedly bumping civil trials off of federal court dockets.

There are two major differences between Title VII actions and ADEA or EPA charges. One is that a charging party may recover liquidated damages in addition to backpay, attorney fees, and costs in successful litigation of ADEA and EPA charges. The amount of liquidated damages is a sum equal to the amount of backpay. Until the passage of the 1991 Civil Rights Act, Title VII plaintiffs were limited to recovering backpay, albeit liberally defined. Since passage of the Civil Rights Act of 1991, however, Title VII plaintiffs may now recover compensatory and punitive damages. However, the 1991 Act places dollar limitations (14 to 101 employees $50,000 ceiling; 200 to 501 employees $200,000 ceiling; 500 or more employees $300,000 ceiling).

Second, there is a definite statute of limitations for filing suit for an alleged ADEA/EPA violation, this being two years from the date when a reasonable charging party should have been aware of the discrimination. Title VII charges must be filed with the EEOC within 300 days of the charging party's becoming aware of the alleged discrimination in states with a fair employment practices agency. In states without fair employment practices agencies, the charging party has only 180 days to file a charge. If a Title VII charge is not timely filed, the EEOC does not have jurisdiction and the charging party's only recourse is to the state agency (provided there is one and the state statute of limitations has not also run).

So long as a Title VII charge is timely filed, there is no statute of limitation for filing suit. The EEOC may take as long as it requires to investigate a charge and decide whether to litigate. If the EEOC decides against litigation, charging parties have 90 days from the date of notice of the EEOC's decision in which to file their own lawsuits. The 1991 Civil Rights Act has added a provision to the ADEA that provides that a charge filed with the Commission that is dismissed or the proceedings of the Commission are otherwise terminated by the Commission, the Commission has the obligation to notify the person aggrieved. Then the aggrieved person has 90 days after the date of the receipt of such notice of dismissal or termination of the proceedings.

Charging parties have the same time limit for filing an ADEA or EPA charge as for a Title VII charge, and are barred from filing their own lawsuits should they fail to file a timely charge with the EEOC. However, a charging party's failure to timely file an ADEA or EPA charge does not deprive the EEOC of jurisdiction or prevent it from filing suit on the charge, so long as the charge and suit are filed within the two years statute of limitations.

There used to be a third major difference, this being that plaintiffs had the right to a jury trial in ADEA and EPA cases, but not in Title VII cases. Juries are much more likely to rule in plaintiff's favor than a judge (80% to 20%, according to one study) and may be more liberal in calculating plaintiff's damages. The Civil Rights Act of 1991 changed the law to give Title VII complainants (who seek compensatory or punitive damages) rights to jury trials, though.

AN ANALYSIS OF BURDEN OF PROOF REQUIREMENTS UNDER EEO LAW (DISPARATE TREATMENT AND DISPARATE IMPACT)

Most claims involve charges of disparate treatment against an individual member of one of the protected classifications. Except for a minor variation for charges alleging religious discrimination, the analysis of any disparate treatment charge is the same, whatever the discrimination alleged.

The analysis was enunciated by the U.S. Supreme Court in the cases of *McDonnell Douglas v. Green* (411 U.S. 792 (1973) and *Burdine v. Texas Board of Education* (450 U.S. 248 (1981). These were Title VII cases, but most courts apply the same analysis to ADEA and EPA cases.

The charging party first must establish a prima facie case by showing that:

- the charging party belongs to a protected class
- that the charging party was qualified for a job he or she applied for (or held, in termination cases)
- the charging party was rejected (or fired) under circumstances that give rise to an inference of discrimination
- the employer continued to seek to fill the position after rejecting (or firing) the charging party

Many published decisions make a point of stating that the degree of proof necessary to establish a prima facie case is not onerous. Circumstances that give rise to an inference of discrimination include statements by the employer's decision-makers indicating prejudice against the protected class; an employer's history of hiring nonmembers of a protected class with similar qualifications to rejected protected class members; or, a statistical disparity in the percent of protected class members in the employer's work force or the charging party's job classification versus the availability within the geographical area of protected class members with the specified qualifications for such jobs.

Rebutting the Case on the Grounds of Nondiscrimination

Once a prima facie case is made, the employer may rebut it by articulating a legitimate, nondiscriminatory reason for its decision. In so doing, the employer must provide enough details that the charging party has a reasonable opportunity to prove the employer's articulated reasons are pretextual. If the charging party can prove by a preponderance of the evidence that the employer's articulated reasons are a pretext, there is a presumption that the pretext is to mask a discriminatory motive. The employer has a last chance to limit liability by showing that its real motive, although not originally stated, was not discriminatory, or that the employer would have made the same decision even if it had not improperly considered the protected characteristic when making its decision.

Prior to the 1991 Civil Rights amendments, the courts held that once the employers established that they would have made the same decision, absent the discriminatory motive, employers were to prevail. However, the 1991 amendments provide that any intentional discrimination will be considered unlawful, even if the employer would have taken the same action without the discriminatory motive. However, in those instances where the employer can establish that the same employment action would have been taken, the court "shall not award damages or issue an order requiring any admission, reinstatement, hiring, promotion, or payment." But, Section 107 of the Act does provide that in those instances a court may "grant declaratory relief, injunctive relief and award attorneys' fees and costs."

Even if an employer does not intentionally discriminate, it still can be liable under Title VII if an otherwise neutral policy has a disparate impact on members of a protected class. If an employer's policy has this effect, prior to the 1991 Act, the employer escapes liability if it showed a business justification and the charging party cannot show an alternate policy will meet the employer's legitimate business need without causing the adverse impact on the protected group. However, with the enactment of the 1991 Civil Rights Act employers now confront a heavier burden. The Act at Section 105 requires the employer to "demonstrate that the challenged practice is job related for the position in question and consistent with business necessity."

Defending Charges of Religious Discrimination

Charges of religious discrimination involve a question of fact not present in other discrimination charges. Employers are required to make reasonable efforts to accommodate the religious beliefs of employees that are known to the employer when the employees are hired or become known afterward. There are few hard and fast rules as to what constitutes reasonable efforts, but the burden is on the employer, not the employee, to make every reasonable attempt to find an arrangement that will work.

Defending Sexual Harassment Cases

Two different fact situations constitute prima facie cases of sexual harassment. One category is *quid pro quo* cases, where charging parties experience adverse employment actions because they won't go along with a superior's unwelcome requests for sexual favors. The other category is hostile environment cases, where unwelcome verbal or physical harassment so disturb an employee emotionally as to significantly degrade the work atmosphere. Whether the harassment has this effect is determined from the viewpoint of the victim, not those doing the harassing. Employers are strictly liable for quid pro quo situations, but must be shown to have been aware of the harassment and taken no corrective action to be liable for permitting a hostile environment.

Race plaintiffs may also prevail on hostile environment theories.

35 Strategies in Defending EEOC Cases (Race, Sex, Religion, Age, National Origin, Handicap, and Veteran)

Often, the first notice an employer has of an EEOC charge of discrimination is receipt of the charge, along with a lengthy list of requests for information from the employer's files. The charge states in broad terms the charging party's potential cause of action, but usually contains very few details as to the actions by the respondent employer alleged to constitute discrimination.

INVESTIGATING THE CHARGE OF DISCRIMINATION

An employer's first step upon receiving notice of a charge of discrimination must be to investigate the underlying facts. The investigation should be conducted with two purposes in mind:

- to obtain sufficient information to allow the respondent to make an objective decision whether to settle the charge
- to become thoroughly familiar with all the available documents and witness testimony so that the company states reasons for its challenged actions that are supported by existing evidence

If the company's investigation indicates that improper actions were taken, the company should initiate corrective measures and negotiate a settlement earlier rather than later.

If the company determines to defend rather than settle a charge, not having to amend its reasons for the challenged actions once they are articulated is of crucial importance.

A company should not entrust its own investigation of a charge to just anybody. The best choice to conduct the investigation is someone experienced in employment discrimination. The advantages of an attorney's conducting the investigation is that attorney-client and attorney work product privileges attach to the statements taken from witnesses and other documents prepared during the investigation. The advantage of the attorney's being from outside the organization is that, having played no role in the challenged action, he or she can assess the evidence without emotion and make objective recommendations. Whoever does the investigation should be impartial and knowledgeable of the sort of statements by management that are regarded by the EEOC as indicating prejudice against protected groups of employees. The company should never assign the investigation to a member of its management who was a participant in the challenged action.

Should the company not be able to pay outside counsel to handle the administrative stage of a charge, there are less expensive ways to attach attorney work product and attorney-client privileges to the documents produced during the company's investigation. The persons investigating the charge can work under the direction of company's in-house counsel, if the company has such. The company also can retain counsel simply to advise the company in conducting its investigation and review the results. Under either of these approaches, all documents prepared by the individuals investigating the charge should be addressed to the attorney for review.

If the company does not have an attorney involved during the investigation, the documents prepared in the process of the investigation are subject to discovery. Under these circumstances, the company should make sure that its investigation documents contain no admissions or other harmful statements that later may prove helpful to the charging party's case.

As soon as the company decides who will serve as its representative during the charge investigation, that person should send a letter of representation to the EEOC contact whose name appears on the notice of the charge. The letter should request that all communications from the EEOC be sent to the representative. The letter should also request that the EEOC not contact individual employees without first advising the representative.

INVESTIGATING SOURCES OF INFORMATION

There are three immediate sources of information to be investigated: the employer's records; witnesses and others with first-hand knowledge of the facts; and, the EEOC itself. The EEOC will be the most useful at the beginning of the investigation, and the company's representative should telephone the EEOC representative named on the notice of charge as soon as the letter of representation has had time to reach the EEOC.

Some company representatives believe it is better to put off contacting the EEOC for some time. They argue this allows the company more time to investigate the charge, and that the passage of time allows some of the emotion that usually accompanies a charge to subside. However, the EEOC will almost always be liberal in allowing the company as much time as needed to investigate the charge and prepare its response. Moreover, the EEOC possesses information about the charging party's allegations not otherwise available to the company that it should know when conducting its own investigation. This is particularly true when the company has suspicions about the motives of the individuals who made the challenged decisions.

The charging party filled out an intake questionnaire and signed an affidavit when he or she filed the charge. Each of these documents contain specific details that are not mentioned on the charge sent to the employer. The EEOC will not turn over these documents to the company, but it usually will read the statements on them to the company's representative. By phoning the EEOC contact before conducting its own investigation, the company can learn all the facts known to the EEOC at that time without the EEOC expecting any information in exchange.

Along with the details in the charging party's affidavit and intake questionnaire, the company should ask the EEOC contact what the charging party's monetary damages are to that point, whether the charging party seeks reinstatement, and whether the charging party is currently working.

REVIEWING COMPANY RECORDS TO DETERMINE REASONS FOR THE DISCRIMINATION CHARGE

After learning what it can from the EEOC contact, the company should review its own files and interview its own management to learn the official reasons for the complained of actions. When the charge complains of a discharge, the company usually will already have conducted an investigation and have much information compiled.

Compiling all of the relevant documents from its files may be a time-consuming process, and should begin as soon as the company knows enough about the charge to identify what documents are relevant. The company must identify all of its policies, guidelines, and training programs relevant to the charge. It must review how information about each was communicated to employees. It must assemble all documents from prior instances where the company took comparable actions to that challenged in the charge. It is imperative that the company be thoroughly familiar with the information contained in these documents before it articulates any reason for the challenged action to the EEOC. Both state and federal anti-discrimination statutes require a company with notice of a charge to retain all documents in its possession that may be relevant.

Records relevant to a failure to hire charge include:

- applications for employment and resumés
- notes from pre-employment interviews
- the company's personnel policies regarding recruiting, hiring, and interviews
- job advertisements
- communications with governmental and private employment agencies
- notes regarding employment decisions

Records relevant to discharge cases include:

- production records prepared during the normal course of business that show the actual work output of the charging party and other employees who performed similar jobs
- disciplinary records
- the documentation made at the time the challenged discharge occurred
- the documentation made at the time of other discharges for similar reasons
- job descriptions
- performance evaluations
- posted work rules
- personnel policies regarding disciplinary action and discharge
- employee handbooks
- collective bargaining agreements

The personnel files maintained by the company on the charging party and other employees who may be comparatives are relevant regardless of the type charge.

INTERVIEWING WITNESSES TO THE ALLEGED DISCRIMINATION

The next logical step in the company's investigation after interviewing the members of management who were involved in the challenged action is to interview nonmanagement employees who may be witnesses or have knowledge about the alleged discrimination. However, the company must exercise some caution in this so as not to generate additional charges of discrimination against itself.

It is a violation of any anti-discrimination act to retaliate against any employee for participating in the filing or investigation of a charge of discrimination. This is true whether or not the charge is determined to have merit. Retaliation for participation in a charge is not permissible even if an employee makes statements that are not true, even if the employee knows the statements to be untrue and defamatory and makes them out of malice.

Employers should consider carefully what information is to be gained by interviewing employees who may have poor work or disciplinary histories or otherwise are likely candidates for future disciplinary action. Employees whose statements corroborate charge allegations may well claim retaliation if the employer later takes disciplinary action against them. It is an especially bitter finding when the EEOC issues a no-cause determination on the original allegations in a charge but finds cause to believe one or more employees were retaliated against for cooperating with the EEOC's investigation of a charge.

This is not to say that such employees should not be interviewed by the company. It is especially important for the company to obtain signed statements from employees whose testimony supports charge allegations. This will aid the company both in accurately evaluating the likelihood of a cause finding and in impeaching these witnesses' later testimony should they add or change details.

CRITICAL CONSIDERATIONS REGARDING SETTLEMENT FOR A DISCRIMINATION CHARGE

The immediate purpose of the company's investigation is to obtain sufficient information to decide early whether to settle the charge or defend it. If the employer learns the charge may have merit or there is substantial evidence in support of the charge allegations, negotiating an early settlement is the percentage move. However, employers should not succumb to the temptation of buying their way out cheap from meritless charges. News of settlements quickly become known on the shop floor, encouraging other employees to file charges. This is true whether or not the settlement agreement includes a confidentiality clause. Employers should not bring this upon themselves simply not to bother with investigating and defending a charge.

Charges supported by evidence should be settled early. As fervently as a company wants to believe its motives were not discriminatory, the EEOC rarely will "no-cause" a charge supported by any amount of probative evidence. (This space is reserved for readers' editorial thoughts as to the probative value of the EEOC's evidence the last time it found cause on a charge filed against them.) It is most cost-effective to settle before even preparing a position statement.

Companies often react emotionally to charges to the point they will not consider settlement. Procrastination in facing up to the need to settle a charge when the allegations are supported by credible evidence only causes backpay (including pre-judgment interest) to run. When sufficient time passes for companies to unemotionally assess the merits of settlement, they usually decide, after incurring thousands of dollars in legal expenses and much aggravation among its work force, to settle charges supported by evidence (at much greater out-of-pocket dollars than would have been the case had reality been faced at the outset).

Representatives for employers caught up in the machismo of defending a charge have a difficult task in persuading them that it is in their best interests to settle a charge regardless of their personal feelings. Settlement recommendations while counsel's emotions are boiling can affect a relationship with the company. Pointing out that attorneys are the real winners when a company wants to defend charges to the death may help counsel bring up the subject of settlement under such circumstances.

There are two other reasons why settlement should be attempted earlier rather than later when there are problems with the company's defense. One is that it is often possible to settle for less than full relief early on. This is easiest to do by negotiating settlement directly with the charging party. The EEOC usually will not object to direct negotiations between respondent and the charging party early in the processing of a charge. Respondent should discuss protocol with the EEOC prior to initiating direct settlement discussions with the charging party, though.

The charging party often will agree to settle the charge for less than full backpay. A charging party will also often agree to waive reinstatement, which sometimes is more important to the company than the monetary damages. The more time the EEOC puts in investigating a charge, the more involved in settlement negotiations it will insist on becoming. The EEOC is much less likely than charging party to accept a settlement offer of less than full relief or to waive reinstatement.

The other compelling reason why settling early is advisable is the possibility that the EEOC may find other actions by the company that it believes also were discriminatory. If the company does not believe the challenged action was discriminatory, it is possible that it took similar actions earlier. If the EEOC finds other situations where it believes a company acted discriminatorily, it can seek relief for any aggrieved employee or applicant for employment it identifies, whether or not the individuals ever filed charges. The EEOC may go back as far as two years prior to the filing of the charge it is investigating in seeking remedies. Companies who know they have skeletons in their closets from the past several years are particularly well-advised to consider settlement rather than open their records to EEOC review.

ASSESSMENT AND ASSERTION OF JURISDICTIONAL DEFENSES

Counsel's evaluation begins with an examination of the charge itself. Although the face of a charge usually contains little information about the facts alleged to constitute discrimination, it sometimes indicates possible defenses to the charge.

There are procedural requirements a charge must fulfill in order for the EEOC (or state fair employment practices agency) to assert jurisdiction:

- A charge must be signed, dated and notarized, and filed within 300 days (180 days in states without fair employment practice agencies) of the alleged discrimination.
- The charge must name the proper employer as respondent, and the respondent must be an employer as defined in the appropriate statute. To be "an employer" under federal anti-discrimination statutes, the company must have 15 employees during at least twenty weeks in the calendar year. Owners and shareholders who take no part in the employer's daily activities are not considered employees. State anti-discrimination statutes may require as few as five employees for the state fair employment practices agency to have jurisdiction.
- The employer must have received notice of the charge of discrimination within ten days of its having been filed with the EEOC.

Courts are very liberal in deciding that a charge complies with these procedural prerequisites, frequently stating that Congress did not intend them to be technicalities to defeat legitimate charges of discrimination. Because of this, attempting to defeat a charge on a procedural deficiency is usually an exercise in futility. Such defenses should be pursued whenever they present themselves, but an employer who puts off settling a charge on the hope of prevailing on a procedural technicality is not well-advised.

Arguing that the Charge Is Not Signed, Dated, or Notarized

A charge that is not signed, dated, or notarized may be "perfected" by the charging party. The charge then relates back to the filing of the original, unperfected charge. A perfected charge is deemed filed within the proper filing period so long as the imperfect original charge was.

Arguing that the Charge Was Not Filed on Time

Charges that appear on their faces not to have been timely filed may be ruled timely under a theory of equitable estoppel. If the charging party was misled by the company so that the charging party was not aware of the discriminatory nature of the company's action, the period for filing a charge is extended to 300 (or 180) days from the date on which a reasonable charging party should have been aware of the discrimination. Equitable estoppel may arise when an employer attempts to spare the sensitivities of a discharged employee and does not tell the employee the true reason for the employer's action. (For example, when an employer discharges an employee for unsatisfactory performance, but tells the employee it is a reduction in force, the period for filing a charge of discrimination begins when the employee learns that he or she was replaced and nobody else was reduced.)

The company need not have actually said anything misleading to the charging party before equitable tolling is invoked. An allegation of misleading statements by a charging party creates an issue of fact. Both the EEOC and courts will tend to favor the charging party's account so that the charge may be decided on its merits rather than on a procedural technicality. The moral here for employers is to always give employees the correct reasons in writing for adverse actions. Of course, once the charge is received it's too late to worry about that. The filing period may also be extended by a continuing violation. This term refers to a series of actions by an employer over a period of time that, considered together, constitute an overall course of discriminatory conduct or maintenance of a discriminatory system. So long as one of the actions takes place or the system is in effect within the filing period, the charge is timely filed. Some federal circuit courts also regard failure to award promotions as continuing violations, with a new violation occurring every time the passed-over employee receives a paycheck. However, an employer is liable for damages on continuing violations only for the period of time beginning two years prior to the date the charge is finally filed.

Arguing that the Company Has Less than the Required Number of Employees

One jurisdictional defense that sometimes wins is when the company has less than the number of employees required for jurisdiction. However, if the employer is a corporation with sister corporations under the same officers, management, and owners, the collective corporations may be regarded as one employer and their employees combined for the purpose of determining jurisdiction.

Arguing that the Alleged Discrimination Occurred During Prior Business Ownership

Another sometimes successful jurisdictional defense is that the company is a purchaser without notice of a business where an alleged offense occurred under prior ownership. The crucial issue of fact is whether company had notice of the charge at the time of the purchase. Usually purchase agreements provide that the purchaser has purchased the assets of the prior owner and those liabilities and potential liabilities set out in the agreement. In the absence of other proof that it had actual knowledge, company usually escapes liability for the alleged discrimination if the charge is not listed in the purchase agreement.

A purchaser will be held liable for an act of discrimination that occurred under prior ownership if the purchaser is found to be a successor corporation. This may be the case if the purchaser keeps relatively intact the business operation, work force, and management of the prior owner.

Arguing that the Defendant Is Not the Responsible Employer

Another situation that arises is when an employee of a temporary services provider files a charge alleging discrimination or harassment while working an assignment on the premises of another employer. The customer-employer may be tempted to defend on the grounds it is not the charging party's employer. The test usually used by the EEOC and courts is the "economic realities" test. If the customer-employer directed the work and was ultimately responsible for the wages of the charging party, it is liable for discrimination against the charging party that occurs during the assignment on its premises.

The temporary agency may successfully defend against liability in the above situations with the argument that it is not the responsible employer.

PRACTICAL POINTS TO PONDER IN ASSESSING THE MERITS OF THE CHARGE

The essence of discrimination is different treatment. The company must state a legitimate, nondiscriminatory reason why it took the challenged action. When it cannot prove nondiscriminatory motives, it has a second defense which may limit liability if it can prove it would have taken the same action regardless of the charging party's being a member of the protected class. This second defense, that the employer would have made the same decision regardless of discriminatory factor, now goes to the question of remedy and not to the question of whether there is a violation. The 1991 Civil Rights Act provides limited relief in these instances (Section 107).

The best evidence to support the company's articulated reasons for the challenged actions are documented instances of similar actions being taken with comparative employees who were not members of the protected class, and an absence of documented instances where non-protected class members received more favorable treatment. Even if the company can show that comparatives received similar treatment, evidence that other comparatives received more favorable treatment will likely result in a cause finding.

Other evidence almost certain to result in a cause finding are statements by the company's decision-makers indicating prejudice against a protected class of employees or against the charging party because of membership in a protected class, witnessed by employees not parties to the charge. Statistical disparities are also probative, although explainable.

In failure to hire cases, the company should determine whether its records show that it hired members of the protected class in the same percentages as exist in the respondent's applicant flow.

A history of arbitrary handling of promotions, hiring, or disciplinary actions will raise the EEOC's suspicions, even if the evidence doesn't clearly show discrimination. However, an arbitrary reason not prohibited by Title VII, the ADEA, the EPA, or a state anti-discrimination act is a defense if not contradicted by evidence. For example, a management official terminated the charging party simply out of dislike or malice. Respondents are reluctant to defend charges with this sort of reason because such reasons often run afoul of internal personnel policies, grievance procedures, or collective bargaining agreements. If the respondent's evidence does not support another nondiscriminatory motive, though, this can be a successful way out. One possible snafu with this approach is that the EEOC may decide prejudice was the basis for the management official's animosity.

Assessing the Employer's Exposure to the Discrimination Charge: Backpay, Relief, and Damages

In assessing its exposure in a charge, the respondent should consider not only for backpay liability, interest and injunctive relief, but will now under the 1991 Civil Rights Act also have to assess its exposure to compensatory and/or punitive damages. Compensatory damages are awardable only in those cases of intentional discrimination. In addition, punitive damages is recoverable against private employers, but only when the employer has acted with "malice or reckless indifference" to a complaining party's rights. (The Civil Rights Act places dollar limitations as explained earlier on these damages.) The respondent can escape a court injunction by settling the charge early in the conciliation period. The EEOC will usually insist on an injunction to settle a case after suit is filed. Unless the respondent's behavior during or before the investigation was egregious, however, the injunction usually requires no more than that respondent obey the law. Sometimes reporting compliance is required of the respondent for a period of time after the charge is settled. This sometimes can be negotiated by the respondent. Respondents can also negotiate out-of-court settlements in some cases. The EEOC's policy is to operate in plain view and it is reluctant to settle out of court, but it will if it has a particularly bad set of facts. The respondent should also consider reinstatement of the charging party. This also can usually be negotiated out of settlement terms.

Backpay that the respondent may be liable for includes fringe benefits not paid to the charging party, including health insurance premiums not paid, medical bills not paid by insurance because the charging party could not afford to pay premiums after being discharged, expenditures in moving to obtain employment, profit sharing proceeds, contributions to pension funds, and interest on lost wages. Interest begins to run on lost wages from the date of the alleged discrimination. An offer of reinstatement stops backpay from running in all but the most egregious cases.

Sometimes the charging party may bear so much ill will toward the employer that an offer will be refused even though the charging party has not found comparable work. At that point, the charging party is voluntarily unemployed and the employer's liability is tolled. The employer should not offer reinstatement simply as a ploy to beat a despised employee out of damages, however. Since declining an offer of reinstatement also disqualifies an employee from receiving unemployment benefits, should somebody inform the local department of employment security, an unemployed charging party will accept an offer of reinstatement even if he or she would prefer living on unemployment benefits to returning to work for the employer.

Another important consideration is whether the charging party wants to settle the case administratively or, with the assistance of an attorney, is pursuing the administrative proceeding only for free discovery.

36 Techniques and Tactics in Responding to an EEOC Charge

The object of submitting a position statement to the EEOC is to convince the EEOC contact to "no-cause" the charge without the necessity of an on-site investigation. For respondent to accomplish this, it is crucial that its position statement have two features: it must be accurate, and it must articulate reasons for the challenged action that may not be interpreted as discriminatory.

ENSURING THE ACCURACY OF THE POSITION STATEMENT TO THE EEOC

The respondent should be sure that there is evidence to support every fact asserted in the position statement. Even more important, respondent must be sure that the available evidence does not disprove any fact asserted in the position statement. If the EEOC discovers during its subsequent investigation that facts stated in respondent's position statement are not true, it will regard the statements as pretextual. This by itself can result in a finding of cause.

Charging parties win cases by showing respondents' stated reasons for challenged actions are pretextual. If the respondent states reasons for an action in its official response that it later must amend because of evidence uncovered during the EEOC's investigation, the respondent should not expect the EEOC to display great understanding of the circumstances that caused the mistake.

ARTICULATING NONDISCRIMINATORY REASONS FOR THE CHALLENGED ACTION

The second essential feature of respondent's statement of position is that it must articulate reasons for the challenged action that may not be interpreted as discriminatory. This sounds obvious enough, but if the preparer of the position statement does not understand that certain neutrally-worded statements may be considered proxies for discriminatory motives, respondent runs the risk of providing evidence of discrimination on its own letterhead. For example, the statement that a charging party was not recalled because respondent believed he or she "would have a negative attitude after filing the charge" is evidence of retaliation by respondent because of the charge. Statements that a charging party is being replaced because respondent "needs some young blood" or because charging party "doesn't cover as much ground as he used to" are evidence that the charging party's age was a factor in the action. Such evidence out of respondent's own mouth is virtually impossible to rebut, no matter how knowledgeable are counsel who respondent may bring in later.

The statement of position should specifically address all of the allegations made by the charging party. Failing to address one or more allegations may lead the EEOC to conclude these allegations are true. Conclusory statements such as "respondent hired the best qualified applicant" or that the protected characteristic "was absolutely not a factor" in respondent's decision, without any rationale or supporting facts and details, have virtually no persuasive effect with the EEOC.

PROVIDING ALL INFORMATION REQUESTED BY THE EEOC

Some management representatives don't believe they should provide the EEOC any more information than what the EEOC forces them to. They treat an investigation as they would a lawsuit and try to put the minimum amount of information on the table. They theorize that since the EEOC will not permit the employer to view the affidavits of the charging party and witnesses—in some cases the EEOC will hold confidential even the identity of the witnesses—why should the employer provide unlimited access to an EEOC investigator to dig up evidence against it. This is particularly so if the employer believes the charge to be unfounded and the allegations of the charging party demonstrably untrue.

The drawback to this approach is that failure to provide all the information requested by the EEOC is likely to guarantee an on-site inspection. On-site inspections are fraught with bad possibilities for the company. When the EEOC does an on-site, its investigators talk to numerous witnesses in private and may ask to review all the employer's personnel files and other documents related to employment histories, such as past job bids, disciplinary actions, and the like. If the investigator does not approve of an action taken against another employee any time up to two years prior to the filing of the charge, the action may result in a finding of cause. This is so even if the investigator learns that every allegation by the charging party was a bald-faced lie and issues a finding of no cause as to the charging party.

The course most likely to avoid an on-site is to provide the investigator with all information needed to justify closing a file without the necessity of the investigator's leaving the office. The respondent may find the investigator quite willing to be convinced that a charge has no merit, for reasons that will be discussed in the next section.

Providing the EEOC with everything in its first requests for information may be a daunting, time-consuming task for an employer, with much of the information requested not having obvious probative value. Respondents may well resent the time spent assembling stacks of documents of dubious probative value from various work areas that may have been long ago stored in several different areas. This is particularly so if the respondent believes the charge being investigated to be frivolous. Respondents usually may whittle down the task by phoning the investigator and discussing the need for each item of evidence in light of the actual allegations in the charge. Such conversations often result in the investigator's agreeing to dispense with certain requests, at least for the time being. Respondents should consider supplying all the information the investigator does not agree to waive, however, regardless of the time involved. The investigator can subpoena information that is not voluntarily provided, so the respondent is going to have to provide it sooner or later. If the investigator insists that certain information be provided, chances are it is because the investigator's supervisor will not approve the charge being closed without the information having been considered.

Stonewalling is ultimately futile, because the EEOC can administratively subpoena whatever information it believes it must have to properly evaluate the charge. Stonewalling is also counterproductive to respondent's goal of an early no-cause determination because it creates distrust of respondent by the EEOC. The EEOC expects each respondent to deny discrimination. Unless the investigator believes respondent to have been truthful about the facts, however, the respondent's denial will be treated skeptically. Along with misrepresentation and concealment of facts, stonewalling is almost guaranteed to create mistrust of respondent by the EEOC.

Preparing the Position Statement: Format and Content

The respondent should always submit a statement of position in narrative form, incorporating respondent's answers to the EEOC's requests for information. Whether respondent should also answer the EEOC's requests for information item by item depends in large part upon how clearly each item is addressed in the narrative. When answering a particular request for information, respondents should carefully consider how the requested information fits into the issues of the charge. Respondents should also consider that it is easier for an EEOC investigator to no-cause a thick file than a thin file that may appear not to have been thoroughly pursued.

The position statement should incorporate the information requested by the EEOC into the bigger picture of the respondent's business operation. The position statement should describe:

- the charging party's role with respondent
- the business purpose behind the policy or action challenged in the charge
- all the evidence respondent believes exonerates its motives for the challenged action, whether or not it was requested by the EEOC. The respondent should never count on the EEOC investigator locating the pertinent facts in respondent's favor among the mass of documents submitted in response to information requests.

The position statement narrative should begin with the facts about which there is no dispute or which can be established definitely by existing evidence. One reason to begin the narrative with a description of respondent's business operations and a brief history of the company is that neither the charging party nor the EEOC should be able to disagree with what is said. The uncontested facts should be presented in journalistic language, not argumentatively. The idea is to create a "halo effect," to word each statement so uncontroversially that a reader cannot but agree with each statement. As the reader agrees with one statement after another, the document develops credibility. Hopefully, the credibility will continue to build until the point when the narrative must address the points in contest, at which point the credibility carries over and respondent's explanations are accepted.

In preparing its statement, respondent should keep in mind that the essence of discrimination is different treatment. The respondent must explain why it took the challenged actions, and show that it would have made the same decisions even if the charging party was not a member of a protected classification. The most convincing evidence for respondent's position is instances where similar actions were taken with comparative employees who are not members of the protected category. Not quite as convincing but always worth mentioning are statistics showing respondent's good history with employees in the protected classification. All documented instances of misconduct or substandard performance by the charging party should also be mentioned.

How to handle "bad facts" in a position statement can be a dilemma. The respondent would like to simply ignore information that appears to support the charge allegations rather than respondent's defenses. However, if the bad information is known by employees in non-management positions, it is always possible the EEOC will learn of it even if respondent does not mention it. If the EEOC learns of it without respondent mentioning it, the EEOC may give a skeptical ear when respondent then tries to explain the bad facts. On the other hand, when respondent provides information about bad facts along with an explanation, it risks the EEOC's forming its own conclusions about the facts and rejecting respondent's explanation. This is particularly a likelihood if respondent's explanation is legalistic. EEOC investigators generally are not attorneys and well may fail to recognize the rightness of a statement of position that relies heavily on case law.

Since concealed evidence almost invariably comes to light sooner or later, whether to disclose bad evidence voluntarily must be judged in light of the respondent's possible explanations in the event the EEOC asks why the information was not disclosed initially. If the respondent can shrug off the failure to disclose with a statement it did not believe the information significant, it may be wise not to volunteer the bad information. If the information obviously has major probative value, however, such an explanation is not believable. A respondent who attempts it loses credibility, its most valuable asset in dealing with the EEOC. In these cases, respondent is best advised to address the bad facts in its statement and explain why they don't mean the respondent in fact discriminated. Even if the respondent's best explanation is legal to an extent that it is over the investigator's head, it is worth making if it might make sense to an EEOC attorney. Virtually all charges are reviewed by EEOC attorneys prior to findings of cause being issued.

The respondent's reasons for the challenged action may be subjective or arbitrary without being illegally discriminatory. The successful applicant's having been hired because he was the plant manager's son-in-law may run afoul of respondent's own personnel policies and cause dissension among respondent's work force. This is a reason other than discrimination against members of a protected classification, however, and a defense to a charge of discrimination. Asserting that the applicant was selected because of superior qualifications, when the real reason was nepotism or cronyism, opens the possibility that evidence will refute the qualifications defense. Even if respondent then argues that nepotism was the real reason for the challenged action, the EEOC likely will regard respondent's initial qualifications argument as having been a pretext for illegal discrimination.

Respondents should not be too eager to raise cronyism as a defense, however. Employees become more irritated over favoritism and arbitrary treatment than anything else they see in the workplace. Employers who advertise that such are facts of life in their operations are rolling out the welcome mat to union organizers. Most employers would regard beating an EEOC charge at the expense of gaining a union to be winning the battle while losing the war.

One exception to the recommendation of full and speedy disclosures of information to the EEOC is when respondent has reason to believe the charging party intends to retain private counsel and initiate a personal lawsuit, and is just using the administrative proceeding for free early discovery. If respondent stalls under these circumstances, the charging party may lose patience and request a right to sue letter.

TECHNIQUES AND STRATEGIES IN INVESTIGATING BACKGROUND INFORMATION

Investigate the Discrimination Charge

In order to draft a position statement that does more good than harm, respondent must complete its own investigation of the charge before it provides the EEOC anything in writing. The investigation begins with interviewing all management personnel with knowledge of the facts underlying the charge and learning what information the EEOC contact has about the charging party's allegations.

Review All Relevant Documents

Next, respondent should assemble and review all documents requested in the EEOC's requests for information, and any others respondent has that may shed light on the charge allegations. Along with documents in its own files, respondent should obtain any statements charging parties make to outside agencies about their employment with respondent. Unemployment hearings offer respondent an early opportunity to pin the charging party down to a story, and respondents should always attend scheduled unemployment hearings of discharged employees. If the employee later files a charge of discrimination, a transcript of the unemployment hearing may prove invaluable in impeaching the charging party's statements to the EEOC.

Investigate Other Employment Actions that Might Be Challenged as Discriminatory

Along with specific allegations made in the charge, respondent's investigation should seek to discover any other employment actions which the EEOC might deem challengeable. Such situations increase respondent's potential liability, since the EEOC can issue a determination of cause based on any facts it learns during its investigation of a charge. This is true even if the EEOC finds no cause on all the allegations made by the charging party. Defending even a meritless charge may not be wise if respondent has skeletons in its closets. A history of questionable employment actions for which the respondent has not previously been called to task is reason for respondent to adjust its equation for when settlement of a charge makes economic sense.

Interview Witnesses Objectively

The respondent's representative should remain objective when speaking with management witnesses, particularly those who participated in the challenged actions. Some may be defensive and attempt to cover up evidence if they believe the outcome of the charge could have personal repercussions for them. To make a determination as to the credibility of management's witnesses, respondent's representative should interview them without letting them know how much he/she already knows. How forthcoming they are under circumstances when they believe they are speaking with somebody with limited knowledge of the matter is an indicator of the extent to which they should be trusted. Among other things, they should be pressed to produce all documents they have related to the challenged action and for the names of all persons, management or otherwise, who may have knowledge of the facts underlying the charge.

Each witness identified should be interviewed in turn. During the course of each witness interview, respondent's representative should obtain a signed statement from the witness. Even when a witness claims to have no knowledge of any facts underlying the charge, the witness should be asked to sign a statement to that effect. Non-management employees often will tell respondent they know nothing, then later give testimony to the EEOC that is hostile to respondent's position. Their signed statements that they know nothing about the charge are invaluable in impeaching their testimony when this occurs.

The respondent should interview all witnesses before it submits its position statement or any responses to the EEOC's requests for information. There are several reasons for this:

- It prevents witnesses who may be hostile to respondent from knowing what respondent's evidence shows and being able to tailor their statements accordingly.
- It provides for witnesses to sign statements before they have heard what the EEOC investigator considers important. Once witnesses have been educated by the EEOC investigator, their statements are more likely to include details harmful to respondent's position.
- It prevents EEOC investigators from typically writing witnesses' statements for the witnesses to sign, which they typically do. In so doing, they paraphrase what each witness says, sanctions in ways that favor the charging party. Previous statements in the witnesses' own words are a powerful tool by which respondent may impeach EEOC-drafted statements in witness affidavits.
- It enables the respondent to offer the statements to the EEOC when the investigator expresses interest in speaking with the witnesses. If respondent cannot offer such statements, the investigator will request an on-site for the purpose of interviewing the witnesses. (Unfortunately, the investigator may request an on-site even if respondent offers statements from the employees

the investigator desires to speak with. However, nothing ventured, nothing gained.)

Other reasons why respondent should interview witnesses early rather than late are because their recollections become faulty with time, and because their testimony may become more hostile to the respondent should their employment later be terminated.

The respondent's representative should personally interview each witness either alone or with only one other management representative as a witness. Witnesses generally will speak more openly under those circumstances. If a witness makes statements to the representative that respondent does not believe to be truthful, the witness can be interviewed a second time with management present. However, respondent should be careful that no witness is retaliated against for any statements made during the investigation, even if respondent determines that statements were not truthful or made in good faith.

If the charging party is a member of a collective bargaining unit, respondent may want to speak with the charging party's union steward about the charge allegations. Union representatives can be a valuable source of information about witnesses who might be unknown to management. Union representatives usually will cooperate with an employer's investigation of an EEOC charge. (Respondents should be advised that union representatives will also cooperate with the EEOC's investigation, including telling the EEOC about their conversations with respondent concerning the charge.) Most union contracts contain anti-discrimination clauses. If the union has not filed a grievance alleging discrimination in behalf of the charging party, the union likely is not sympathetic with the charge. The union representative may have been offended by the charging party's pursuing the issue with the EEOC instead of through the union grievance procedure, or the charging party may have gone to the EEOC only after being advised by a union representative that the allegations of discrimination were not well-founded. The union leadership's stature among voting members is diminished when members obtain relief through the EEOC that the union could not obtain for them.

If the union did file a grievance alleging discrimination against the charging party, the employer can obtain information from the union representative in the course of processing the grievance.

INTERVIEWING WITNESSES THE COMPANY KNOWS ARE LIKELY CANDIDATES FOR FUTURE DISCIPLINE

As discussed previously, an exception possibly should be made about interviewing all witnesses when a potential witness is regarded by the company as a likely candidate for future disciplinary action. In these cases, respondent should consider carefully the potential value of the witness's testimony. If the likely probative value of what may be learned from such an employee is not substantial, the employee should not be interviewed. This reduces the probability of a charge of retaliation if the employee later is terminated or receives disciplinary action. (This is especially true if the EEOC has interviewed the witness first. No evidence is worse for a respondent in a retaliation charge than for the charging party to testify that respondent interrogated him about what he told the EEOC investigator shortly prior to terminating him.)

There are no rules regarding any warnings a witness must be given before being interviewed, such as the *Johnnie's Poultry* warnings that must be given to an employee when an employer is investigating an unfair labor practice charge. However, it is advisable to give the employee the option of not making a statement. Nothing hurts a respondent's cause more in the eyes of the EEOC than when a witness repudiates a statement respondent has provided the EEOC or asserts that the statement was coerced by respondent. If respondent explains that it is simply seeking to learn the facts from those individuals with first-hand knowledge, that there will be no repercussions to the witness for whatever he or she says, and that respondent will be interviewing all potential witnesses and not just the particular individual, most employees will willingly tell respondent what they know.

If the charging party has remained employed with respondent, respondent should not interview him or her without the EEOC being present. Doing so only strengthens allegations of retaliation should the charging party later receive disciplinary action or be discharged.

37 Techniques and Tactics in Dealing with EEOC Investigators

A common misperception by respondents is to regard EEOC investigators as "the gummint," monolithic, inflexible and impractical. In fact, the EEOC investigator is an individual person with a supervisor looking over his or her shoulder rather than with a monolithic "gummint." The investigator assigned to investigate a charge may well have doubts about the charge's merits early on. In any given year, only between 4–5% of all EEOC charges filed result in findings of cause (another 15-20% are settled prior to a determination being issued), and the most rabid investigators become skeptical of charging parties as they gain time on the job.

HELPFUL HINTS IN DEALING WITH EEOC INVESTIGATIONS

An investigator's doubts about a charge's merit will not excuse the investigator from investigating the charge or respondent from cooperating with the EEOC's investigation, however. The investigator still must answer to a supervisor. The most common recourse taken by charging parties who are upset about no-cause findings by the EEOC is to write their congressmen, who routinely follow up such complaints with the EEOC. EEOC supervisors know not to approve an investigator's closing a file until all practical investigative steps have been taken. Nonetheless, an investigator with doubts about the charge is a valuable potential ally of respondent's, if respondent doesn't screw it up by misrepresenting facts or some such thing to cause mistrust.

In many EEOC offices, investigators have goals regarding the number of charge files they are expected to close each year. The goals may be high. There is much less time and effort involved for the investigator to close a file with a no-cause finding than with a finding of cause. The investigator may have additional pressure to close a file if the charge is at least 270 days old and the end of a fiscal year or fiscal quarter is approaching. For charges this old, well-advised respondents will be sure that the EEOC has all the information needed to justify a no-cause recommendation well before the EEOC's fiscal year ends on September 30.

Don't Provide Too Much Information

Respondents should not provide too much information in efforts to be cooperative, however. Their responses should not stray beyond the issues presented by the charge allegations, and they should not discuss departments, work areas, or employees not directly involved in the charge. Each subject a respondent brings up potentially expands the EEOC's investigation. The EEOC may issue findings of cause based on any information it learns, even information going beyond the scope of the original charge allegations. Counsel should not turn over any information until first reviewing it and determining how it fits into the company's defenses.

Request an EEOC Attorney, If Necessary

EEOC investigators are not attorneys, and usually do not solicit legal help during the investigation of a charge unless they experience a problem. Respondents should keep this in mind when defending a charge and argue their cases in terms of the facts rather than the language in legal opinions. If respondent has only legal defenses to a particular charge, it should ask the investigator to involve an EEOC attorney in the investigation.

The respondent can coerce the involvement of an EEOC attorney by not responding to requests for information and forcing the investigator to issue a subpoena. Doing this will likely strain respondent's relationship with the investigator, but may be worthwhile if the investigator is being unreasonable or respondent's defense involves fine distinctions in published legal opinions.

Cultivate a Personal Relationship with the EEOC Investigator

Respondents should cultivate personal relationships with the EEOC representatives assigned to their charges, both investigators and their supervisors. The supervisor often sends the EEOC's initial information requests personally, and may not assign an investigator to the charge until respondent provides some of the requested information. A phone call early in the proceedings gives the respondent an opportunity to discuss the charge directly with the EEOC supervisor. Respondent should always take advantage of this opportunity. Along with asking for the details about the charge on the charging party's affidavit and intake questionnaire (discussed earlier), respondent should inquire into what relief the EEOC is seeking, whether the charging party is currently employed, who the charging party named as comparatives, and whether respondent may attempt to negotiate a settlement of the charge directly with the charging party. If the charging party waited over 300 days to file the charge (180 days in non-deferral states), respondent should ask about the date of the challenged action, when the charging party became aware of it, and the EEOC's theory of why the charge is not untimely. If the allegations of the charge seem weak, respondent should ask if the EEOC has a prima facie case.

If respondent believes it has a jurisdictional defense, that defense should be raised and supporting information offered before respondent provides any information about the facts underlying the charge allegations.

Whenever speaking with the EEOC, respondents should assume that some of their employees are informing the charging party about any visible steps taken in charge investigations. Respondents may be sure that a charging party is passing along to the EEOC any information received.

Deflect Inquiries for Information Before Submitting the Position Statement

If respondent is pressed for information by the EEOC prior to submitting an official position statement, such inquiries should be deflected by stating that respondent has not yet learned enough to form any conclusions. EEOC enforcement personnel routinely make notes during every phone conversation with respondent. The respondent wants to present its position in writing after a full investigation and consideration of all known evidence, not state it off the cuff over the phone.

Offer to Reinstate the Employee

In situations where the charging party has found employment elsewhere comparable to what he or she had or sought with the respondent, respondent may cut off the running of backpay by offering to reinstate the employee. Charging parties usually will elect to stay with their new employers rather than return to respondent where the employment atmosphere may be strained. Once the charging party declines reinstatement, the running of backpay stops even if the charging party's new employment subsequently ends. If the charging party has not declined reinstatement, backpay begins to accumulate anew for every period of unemployment the charging party experiences until the charge is finally resolved.

Communicate Often with the EEOC Investigator

After respondent submits its position statement, an EEOC investigator will be assigned to the charge. The investigator can be a great source of information for the respondent, and should be called by respondent every week or two. The excuse for calling can be that backpay is running and respondent is anxious to have a determination on the charge. The investigator may be under pressure to close a stack of older charges and not inclined to aggressively pursue the charge against respondent right away. The respondent will not learn much when this is the situation, but should call the investigator anyway to establish and maintain a personal relationship. These situations give the respondent opportunities to appeal to the sympathy of the investigator about the hardship to respondent caused by the charge. This is not a spurious lament. If the charging party remains unemployed, respondent's financial exposure continues to increase during periods of inactivity by the EEOC, and respondent's work force and management may be working under considerable additional tension because of the charge.

Provide Information as Soon as Possible

Once the investigator begins working the charge, respondent should contact him about whether he has any questions or needs any additional information. If so, the information should be provided as soon as possible. If respondent is located close to the EEOC office, respondent should offer to deliver the information directly to the investigator. Otherwise, the information should be placed in the mail at once. The object in doing this again is to not give the investigator any reason to believe he needs to do an on-site. If the EEOC requests huge quantities of documents and cannot be negotiated down, respondent may be tempted to ask the investigator to come to respondent's facility to review them. Unless respondent's work force mirrors the local population in terms of race, gender, and age, and respondent is absolutely confident of every personnel decision it has made for the past several years, it is better for respondent to take the mountain to the investigator than to invite the investigator in.

If the EEOC investigator requests to speak personally with witnesses, respondents should offer to bring them to the EEOC office or to set up interviews in the office of its own attorney. There is no requirement that the EEOC's interviews with employees be conducted on-site.

Determine Whether the EEOC Has Doubts About the Charge

Respondents should miss no opportunity to press the investigator about whether the EEOC has a prima facie case. If the investigator does not respond strongly, chances are the EEOC has doubts about the merits of the charge. If respondent keeps the investigator talking long enough, it usually can learn the reasons for the EEOC's doubts.

Once discovered, these doubts should be fed with any additional information respondent can find. The respondent may send a letter with supplemental information to the EEOC at any time after submitting its original position statement.

Verify the Charging Party's Background Information

A tactic that frequently benefits respondents when charges involve failures to hire or discharges of short-term employees is to verify each item of information on a charging party's resumé and application for employment with respondent. Many applicants for employment exaggerate statements on their employment applications or resumés about their education, prior work experience, previous salaries, or dates of service with prior employers. A thorough investigation generally will uncover several false or exaggerated items by the charging party. Bringing these items to the attention of the investigator will undermine the investigator's confidence in the charging party's credibility, which significantly increases the chances of a no-cause determination on the charge.

Try to Prevent an On-Site Investigation by the EEOC

After reviewing respondent's position statement, the EEOC supervisor will direct the investigator to verify the statements in it and the allegations of the charging party. This requires the investigator to obtain statements from all persons named as witnesses by the charging party or identified by the investigator from information provided as likely to have first-hand knowledge of facts. The EEOC's preferred method of doing this is through an on-site inspection.

To persuade an investigator not to conduct an on-site, the respondent must provide the investigator all the information required to substantiate the lack of disparate treatment toward the charging party. This includes all documents mentioned by the charging party and access to employees named by the charging party as having knowledge relevant to the charge. If the charge resulted from a disciplinary action, the investigator will need to review prior disciplinary actions for years back and the personnel files of employees who received (or who did not receive) earlier disciplinary actions. If the charge results from a failure to promote, the investigator will review prior job postings and the personnel files of those who did and did not receive prior promotions. If the charge regards a failure to hire, prior applications and applicant flow summaries are mandatory review material for the investigator. The investigator will also review the employee handbook and all relevant personnel policies and procedures.

Emphasize Exculpatory Evidence

The investigator must review the above evidence in order to justify a recommendation of no cause, so the respondent should raise no protest to providing this much. The respondent should bring to the investigator's attention all exculpatory evidence the investigator does not specifically request. Particularly persuasive are non-management eyewitnesses who believe the charging party's allegations are not true. The respondent should insist that the investigator speak with these employees as well as the charging party's witnesses.

Should the respondent not learn of any favorable non-management witnesses during its investigation, respondent should carefully substantiate each detail in the statements of its decision-makers with available documentary evidence. The failure to find favorable non-management witnesses should caution respondent to examine critically the veracity of the statements of the challenged decision-makers, particularly if there also are few available supporting documents. When a challenged action was based on purely subjective criteria and judgments, the chances of a cause finding increase.

Respondents should consider whether defending a charge is cost-effective when the underlying proof amounts to a swearing contest. If the EEOC determines the charging party to be credible, it will resolve conflicts in the testimonies of witnesses in favor of the charging party. Litigation costs are considerable even if the respondent ultimately prevails, and the EEOC in the past has made some incredible judgments about the credibility of charging parties.

TECHNIQUES AND TACTICS IN HANDLING ON-SITE INSPECTIONS

Despite a respondent's full cooperation, the EEOC may decide to conduct an on-site inspection as part of its investigation of a charge. Some investigators simply enjoy getting out of their offices, and an on-site inspection is an excuse to do so.

Ask the EEOC to Describe the Scope of the Investigation

If an on-site is insisted upon, respondents should limit the scope of such by asking the EEOC to identify the goals of the investigation, who is to be interviewed, and the jobs and work areas it desires to observe. Respondents should not agree to a time for the on-site until the EEOC has provided this information. Respondents should walk the route the EEOC will take during the investigation to ensure that all required notices are posted and that the proper records are in the proper files. The respondent should object if the EEOC attempts to expand its inspection beyond what it has identified once it is on the respondent's premises.

Attend Interviews of Employees by the EEOC

An on-site investigation will include the EEOC's interviewing privately any number of the employer's employees. The charging party will have given the EEOC the names of certain of the respondent's employees to speak with. The respondent may be assured that these names will include possible malcontents among its work force. If any of these employees complain of problems similar to those alleged by charging party, there is a good chance the EEOC will issue a finding of cause. The respondent should insist that the EEOC also interview favorable witnesses named by the respondent while on-site. This not only balances unfavorable testimony, but takes up time the EEOC might otherwise use to view the premises and identify other employees it desires to speak with.

The respondent's representative should attend interviews of management employees and agents whose statements can be binding upon the respondent. Respondents have no right to sit in the EEOC's interviews with non-management employees, however, nor will respondents be provided copies of statements rank and file witnesses have signed. Respondents should ask that management be interviewed first. The EEOC investigator may forget to ask the respondent's representative to leave when the interviews move on to rank-and-file employees.

Prepare Statements to the EEOC

The respondent's decision-makers should be prepared as for a deposition before they give statements to the EEOC. Relevant documents should be reviewed with them and ambiguities discussed. The processes which resulted in the challenged actions should be examined from step one through their conclusions. It is crucial that management not volunteer information or make statements to the EEOC that may be indicative of bias against members of protected classifications. It is equally crucial that their statements not seem to contradict the statements in respondent's position statement. EEOC investigators are not attorneys, and their investigations are rarely conducted with an attorney's thoroughness. If they hear incriminating statements from the respondent's decision-makers, they often will ignore other evidence and regard the respondent's position as pretextual. Respondents can guard against this to an extent by bringing out all its exculpatory evidence, but bad statements by respondent's management usually will result in findings of cause.

First-line supervisors can be difficult to prepare, regardless of how much time is spent with them. Because of the propensity of some foremen to talk first before thinking, respondents generally are well-advised to determine whether the EEOC considers it essential to speak with first-line supervisors before offering them as witnesses.

The investigator may review any number of the respondent's records and files. The respondent should have offered to bring all relevant documents to the investigator's office to avoid the on-site, but sometimes the EEOC requests so many documents that small and mid-sized employers are overwhelmed by the task of assembling them all.

If the EEOC asks management witnesses to sign statements, the witnesses should insist on preparing statements in their own words. They should not sign statements drafted by the EEOC investigator.

Discourage Tours of Work Areas

The investigator also will want to look around. The respondent should attempt to discourage this, although not to the point of refusing the investigator's request to see a particular area. Respondents definitely should not encourage tours of work areas the EEOC has not requested to see. If the charge alleges race discrimination and the investigator sees only caucasian faces in the office, this will buttress the charge in the investigator's mind. If he sees women only in clerical positions, or hears inappropriate remarks made to women, even in kidding, this will buttress charges of sex discrimination or sexual harassment. The investigator will be an impeachment witness in subsequent litigation as to statements made by the employer's witnesses, and a possible eyewitness as to a hostile atmosphere.

The respondent should offer the EEOC an office to use while on-site. The office should be located near the entrance of the respondent's facility, without a good view of the respondent's work force. Most employers' personnel offices are so located and are logical locations. While on-site, EEOC investigators should be escorted everywhere, even to restrooms and the cafeteria. This reduces the chances of impromptu interviews with the respondent's employees.

HELPFUL HINTS IN HANDLING A FACT-FINDING CONFERENCE

As the EEOC investigation progresses, the investigator has the option of scheduling a fact-finding conference. This conference, usually held in the EEOC's offices, is conducted by the EEOC and attended by the charging party and the company representative. These conferences are not mandatory. In addition, although both the employer and the charging party may have their attorney in attendance, the attorney's role is advisory. The EEOC will ask questions of each party. The answers to the questions may determine whether or not the EEOC issues a finding of cause on the charge. This gives the company its first chance to propose questions directly to the charging party, and respondents may convince the EEOC that it need not conduct on-site inspections.

The fact-finding conference is a setting which provides EEOC investigators a unique opportunity to serve as mediators, a major role of the EEOC in charge investigations. It is a role that many investigators enjoy more than they do their role as cop. They get satisfaction in helping disputants resolve their differences, and they get credited with closed files when the parties settle. Respondents may receive active help in concluding inexpensive settlements from investigators wearing their mediator hats, particularly if the respondent has gained the investigator's trust. Respondents should be receptive to such efforts and accept what advantage they provide. Flexibility by respondents on a few minor points greatly assists investigators in bringing about resolutions. Investigators usually will go along with most any settlement the parties agree to, at least early in the investigation.

Respondents should bring their proof to the fact-finding conferences, so that the charging parties may be confronted with it in front of the EEOC. Charging parties who have made up allegations may become nonplussed when statements they have made are discredited by respondents' documentary evidence. No better place for this to happen than in front of the EEOC investigator. Respondents should have their documents organized point by point that they desire to demonstrate, just as they would organize their receipts were they going to an IRS audit. They should prepare lists of questions to be asked the charging party by the investigator. Spokesmen for respondents should participate as actively as the EEOC will permit, and should attempt to focus the conference on the weaknesses of the charging party's position.

Respondents should decide who their spokesmen will be at the conferences, and other attendees should allow the spokesman to do the talking. Respondents should not allow the EEOC investigator decide who will speak. If other attendees may best answer certain questions, they should wait before answering until the spokesman turns the question over to them. Respondents' attendees must be careful to maintain their discipline, because the informal setting can lull people into statements that have not been thought all the way through.

Respondents should prepare each conference attendee as if for deposition, and decide in advance of the conference which attendee will answer questions about particular aspects of the charge. To better accomplish this, a respondent should prepare its conference attendees as a group as well as individually. Responses at the conference should be succinct and address the questions that are asked. When responding, respondents should not volunteer information unrelated to the particular question asked.

PRACTICAL POINTS TO CONSIDER FOR DELAYING A RESPONSE

Although cooperating with the EEOC is appropriate in the majority of charges, there are times when it may be better for respondents to delay. As mentioned above, delaying is appropriate when the charging party is known to have retained an attorney and is planning to sue regardless of the outcome of the administrative proceedings. When a particular EEOC representative is being unreasonably burdensome, delaying by respondent results in the charge file being temporarily assigned to an attorney for the issuance of an administrative subpoena. This provides the respondent a different contact to talk to, and one who understands the legal significance of requested items.

Another situation where delaying may benefit a respondent is if it has laid off protected age group employees during the past couple of years who have not filed charges, and is not sure how sound its defense was had they filed charges. Although the time period for them to file charges may have passed, the EEOC can still find cause in their behalf and seek relief for them so long as the statute of limitations for filing suit has not also passed. If there are but a few months to run on the statute of limitations, respondent may stall its way out of potential litigation by putting the EEOC off until those final months have run.

To maximize the length of time the EEOC will tolerate its delaying, a respondent should request as many extensions of time in preparing its position statements as the EEOC will grant, which may be a surprisingly large number. Until the charge is 200 days old, the EEOC will usually go along with requests for time extensions.

UNDERSTANDING THE CONCILIATION REQUIREMENTS OF THE EEOC

If the EEOC issues a finding of cause, it is required to attempt to settle the charge through a formal conciliation agreement. Failure by the EEOC to do so is a potential defense to a subsequent lawsuit brought by the EEOC. However, any effort by the EEOC will usually be deemed by courts as adequate. The EEOC usually will not accept a conciliation agreement offering less than full relief, and courts will not regard its failure to compromise on this point to be unreasonable. Respondents should focus conciliation arguments on reducing the calculations of backpay rather than attempt to persuade the EEOC to accept less than full relief. The EEOC will bargain with respondents as to how the amount of backpay should be calculated, and may agree to reductions when charging parties' efforts to secure other employment and mitigate damages have been less than demonstrably diligent.

If a charge is not settled with a conciliation agreement, the EEOC's Office of General Counsel in Washington, D.C. must approve the charge for litigation. The respondent's position statement is among the documents reviewed by the OGC in deciding whether a charge should be litigated. Other than its position statement, a respondent has no input into the OGC's decision-making process, and respondents should be sure their position statements contain all the information the respondents want considered when this decision is being made. If not, respondents should submit supplemental statements before the conciliation process is terminated.

If conciliation is unsuccessful, the EEOC may do one of three things:

1. File on behalf of the EEOC a federal complaint against the company;
2. Refer the matter to the United States Attorney General's office who has the discretion to file a civil action; or
3. Issue a right to sue letter to the charging party. The charging party then has 90 days within which to file a federal complaint.

38 Strategies in Litigating Employment Discrimination Cases

There are several differences between discrimination litigation and litigation of other types of cases. One major difference is that the defendant-employer may be sued by either the aggrieved individual or the EEOC. Who the plaintiff is will affect the employer's defense strategy. If the charging party is the plaintiff, the employer enjoys the advantage in resources typical of litigation between a large defendant versus an individual plaintiff. If the EEOC is the plaintiff, however, defendant is confronted by an adversary supported by the full resources of the federal government. An aggressive defense including extensive discovery and numerous motions can be effective in wearing down an attorney representing the charging party. This is particularly true if the attorney is from a small law office, which is often the case. Such tactics against the EEOC only run up the defendant's own legal expenses, however. The EEOC seldom cares how much time its attorneys spend on a particular case. They are on salary and must be kept busy doing something. However, defendants' potential liability is less when the EEOC is the plaintiff due to the fact that it is not awarded attorney fees when it prevails in trial. Awards of attorney fees increase substantially the amounts of judgments awarded to individual plaintiffs. In addition, the 1991 Civil Rights Act allows the court to award expert fees.

Another difference between discrimination litigation and other types is that there are always documents to be discovered in discrimination cases. The EEOC's investigative file contains all the evidence known by the plaintiff to exist. The defendant should always propound a request for production of the investigative file soon after being served with the complaint. The file will contain not only documentary evidence, but the names of witnesses whose testimony the plaintiff will rely upon. The file will also contain statements by these witnesses that may be invaluable in impeaching their courtroom testimony. The file may also reveal witnesses who do not support the plaintiff's version of the facts.

A large percentage of discrimination cases distill down to the word of the charging party versus the word of the defendant's decision-maker. Preparation of defendant's witnesses for deposition and trial testimony therefore is even more crucial than is ordinarily the case in lawsuits. If defendant's witnesses are credible, plaintiff does not carry the burden of proof based on his or her testimony standing alone. Defendants should spend whatever amount of time is necessary to ensure that their witnesses give testimony consistent with the available documents and the testimony of its other witnesses.

The EEOC considers uncorroborated testimony by a charging party who it finds to be credible to be sufficient evidence to support a charge. The EEOC routinely does nothing in the way of background checks on charging parties and tends to find most any charging party to be credible. Many suits are thus brought by the EEOC without sufficient evidence to carry its burden of proof. The only way defendants may lose such suits is if its witnesses give confused or inconsistent testimony that causes the trier of fact to deem them not to be credible.

DEFENSE GOALS IN DISCRIMINATION LITIGATION

Defendants should have two goals in discrimination litigation. One is to have the complaint dismissed on a motion for summary judgment. This is particularly true since the enactment of the Civil Rights Act of 1991, which gives plaintiffs the right to a jury trial and to seek compensatory and punitive damages. Juries are notoriously sympathetic to individual plaintiffs taking on goliath defendants, and defendants should endeavor to have cases disposed of without having to trust juries to render justice.

Second, defendants should seek awards of their costs and attorney fees against plaintiffs, particularly when being sued by the EEOC. Courts are often reluctant to award fees against charging parties suing on their own, as such awards have a chilling effect on the willingness of attorneys to take such cases. If a case is patently without merit, however, a court may make such an award. In any event, it costs defendant nothing to ask. The EEOC is composed of bureaucrats who, having decided to litigate a charge, are extremely reluctant to admit to having made a mistake as the case proceeds to trial litigation. Because the EEOC is not incurring attorney fees, it feels little pressure to drop a case regardless of what evidence comes out against its position. Virtually the only way for defendants to pressure the EEOC to drop a lawsuit is to gear its defense toward obtaining an award of attorney fees. Fortunately for defendants, many federal judges have now heard enough ill-considered suits brought by the EEOC that awards of attorney fees are becoming more frequent.

To strengthen a claim for attorney fees at the conclusion of a case, defendants should propound early discovery to the EEOC to pin it down as to the evidence it relied upon in deciding to file suit. Defendants should also bring to the EEOC's attention—in writing—any evidence that clearly refutes the allegations of discrimination made by the charging party, and invite the EEOC to nonsuit the case.

Awards of attorney fees in discrimination cases are at the discretion of the court. Courts will usually award fees to charging parties who win at trial, but not always. Awards of attorney fees to successful defendants are usually made only when the court believes the case to have been so without merit as not to have been in good faith. The EEOC will not be awarded attorney fees simply for prevailing at trial, but may be awarded some fees as sanctions against defendants for failure to comply with discovery or for asserting frivolous defenses (such as bogus statute of limitations arguments).

Advantages of Delays in Discrimination Litigation

The passage of time generally works to the advantage of the defendant in discrimination litigation. Charging parties tend to have unpleasant personality characteristics. This is why they were discharged or not hired in the first place. This is exacerbated by the emotions accompanying the belief of having been done wrong and frustration over delays in getting to trial. Their attorneys catch the brunt of charging parties' unpleasantness, since they are the ones having the most contact with them. As a case drags on, the defendant rarely will be incorrect in assuming that the charging party's attorney is becoming thoroughly put out with the charging party. This is particularly true if discovery has turned up evidence that conflicts with key elements with a charging party's version of what occurred. Defendants may benefit from this in a major way if it results in opposing attorneys not spending sufficient time with charging parties to properly prepare them for deposition or trial.

The downside to a lawsuit's being strung out is that the defendant's potential liability increases with the passage of time. Also, if employees of the defendant are terminated before a case goes to trial, there is a greater chance of their giving testimony harmful to the defendant than was the case when they were employed. How soon a case goes to trial may be out of the parties' hands, however. Since passage of legislation that guarantees criminal defendants the right to speedy trials, civil cases frequently are bumped off of federal court dockets by criminal trials. This is a particular problem in metropolitan areas with large numbers of drug cases. Defendants who desire to go to trial quickly because of mounting liability should complete discovery and be prepared for trial in time for their first trial settings. Should they be bumped, they should inform the court they are ready for trial whenever an opening may develop on the court's docket.

Counsel should also at the outside of litigation determine whether insurance coverage is available to his or her client. Although such lawsuits may not be covered, it is critical for counsel to review the insurance policy or policies to determine steps that must be followed to protect his or her client's interest. At least, counsel should notify the insurance company that a lawsuit has been filed and counsel's position regarding whether there is or is not coverage.

STRATEGIC DISCOVERY STEPS TO FOLLOW AFTER RECEIPT OF THE LAWSUIT

The heaviest burden in discovery falls upon charging parties rather than defendants. Defendants usually know what has occurred by the time suit is filed, while charging parties' information may consist largely of hearsay and rumors. Charging parties have to obtain the evidence necessary to establish their cause of action, while defendants should focus their discovery on winning motions for summary judgment and awards of attorney fees.

Request All Documents Related to Plaintiff's Complaint

Defendants should propound written interrogatories and requests for production of documents inquiring about every fact or document known to the plaintiff to support the allegations in its complaint. If the responses are skimpy, the foundation is laid for a motion for attorney fees after the case is decided in favor of the defendant. Defendants' interrogatories should ask charging parties to state with specificity why they contend discrimination occurred. Charging parties should also be requested to turn over any documents or tape recordings related to the case, including any personal notes or diaries they may have been keeping.

Avoid Turning Over Defense Documents to Plaintiff

Discovery in discrimination cases tends to be document-intensive as opposed to discovery in other types of litigation. Defendants should not simply turn its files over to charging parties, particularly when the charging party is represented by a private attorney. Charging parties often seek documents containing trade secrets or other sensitive information. Defendants may seek protective orders from the court to avoid turning such information over. Even if the court ultimately rules the information must be provided, the charging party's attorney has been required to spend time fighting the motion that he or she would have preferred to spend on something else.

As mentioned earlier, defendants should request production of the EEOC's investigative file early on. If the EEOC is the plaintiff, this is done by a formal request for production of documents under Rule 34 of the Federal Rules of Civil Procedure. If the charging party is suing in his or her own behalf, the investigative file may be obtained from the EEOC through a written request under the Freedom of Information Act.

Taking the Plaintiff's Deposition

When taking the charging party's deposition, the defendant wants to get the charging party to agree to the defendant's version of critical facts, to admit having no competent proof that discrimination occurred, to obtain admissions that will support a later motion for summary judgment, and to obtain information that may be used either to impeach the charging party's credibility or to show that the defendant would have discharged or not hired the charging party regardless of any discrimination that may have occurred. The deposition is also an opportunity for the defendant to judge the charging party's effectiveness as a trial witness. The deposition should be lengthy, as charging parties tend to give answers more damaging to their positions after they get tired. Defendants should take charging party depositions only after receiving the charging party's theory of the case in responses to interrogatories, and after completing their own investigations into the facts and the background of the charging party.

Besides the allegations of the complaint and the underlying charge of discrimination, charging parties should be asked in deposition about the following:

- every item of information they wrote on their applications for employment and resumés they submitted to defendants, particularly about their prior work experience and education
- any work experience that they did not mention on their employment applications
- the names of their supervisors at their prior places of employment
- the names of all witnesses with any knowledge about the allegations in the complaint and the underlying charge of discrimination
- prior participation in legal proceedings and whether they have ever had criminal charges brought against them
- whether they have ever been deposed before
- whether they have ever declared bankruptcy
- whether they have ever defaulted on a student loan
- their earnings and efforts to obtain employment since the alleged discrimination by the defendant

Investigate the Plaintiff's Responses to the Deposition Questions

Defendants should investigate each response by a charging party to these questions. If a charging party gives an untruthful response while under oath at deposition, the defendant may use it to impeach the charging party's credibility at trial. If the charging party turns out to have fudged information on an application for employment with the defendant, the defendant may argue that charging party is not entitled to any damages even if discrimination occurred. (This is the *Summers* defense and will be discussed in more detail in the next section.)

Should a charging party state responses known by the defendant to be untruthful, the defendant should ask the charging party to provide more details. The defendant should not challenge the credibility of the charging party during the deposition, however. Once the charging party has been pinned down to a story, the defendant can wait until trial to prove the untruthfulness of the charging party's answers. The charging party should be asked whether he or she has been drinking or taking medication or other drugs prior to being deposed. If defendants fail to ask this question, charging parties can explain in trial that their untruthful deposition answers were because drugs had impaired their memories. Defendants should not waive the charging party's signature on the deposition. It is more difficult for the charging party to explain away deposition answers if he or she subsequently reads and signs the deposition.

Charging parties should be asked who they spoke with and what documents they reviewed in preparation for their depositions. All documents used to refresh their memories are discoverable, even if otherwise nondiscoverable because of attorney-client or attorney work product privileges. Also, when the defendant impeaches a charging party's trial testimony by showing it is inconsistent with the charging party's deposition testimony, the charging party often will attempt to attribute the inconsistencies to the difference in preparation for the deposition versus preparation for trial. By establishing on the record what the charging party did in preparation for the deposition, the defendant can take this explanation away from the charging party. Defendants should also serve the charging party with a subpoena to bring to the deposition all notes and documents related to the case. Otherwise, the charging party may claim an inability to recall the answers to key questions in deposition, then give very detailed answers to these same questions in trial.

Charging parties should be asked to produce their income tax returns to substantiate claims of lost earnings. Many charging parties become extremely nervous about having to provide their tax returns. The EEOC is also put on the spot, should it turn out that a charging party did not file tax returns or did not report all their income. As a sister agency to the IRS, it is inappropriate for the EEOC to assist a charging party in any way in failing to pay the proper amount of income tax.

Keep Up with Meetings with Plaintiff's Attorney

Defendants have the right to attend all conversations between a charging party's attorney and members of its own management or any other agent whose statements can be binding upon it. Should a defendant learn that charging party has contacted such employees or ex-employees without notice to the defendant, the defendant should file an ethics complaint with the bar association to which the charging party's attorney belongs.

Keep Informed of Plaintiff's Expert Witnesses

Defendants should also propound interrogatories to learn of any expert witnesses the charging party intends to call. Experts are often used to interpret statistics and the charging party's efforts at mitigating damages. Defendants should depose any experts a charging party intends to use, and should consider using expert testimony themselves to challenge the testimony of the charging party's experts.

UNDERSTANDING THE FIVE CLASSES OF DISCRIMINATION CLAIMS AND EVIDENTIARY PRINCIPLES REGARDING EACH CLASS

There are five classes of discrimination claims:

- disparate treatment
- adverse impact
- perpetuation of past discrimination
- failure to make reasonable accommodations
- retaliation

Disparate treatment is by far the most frequently asserted, with retaliation being the second most frequent. Failure to accommodate currently applies only to charges based on religion or disability. Adverse impact and perpetuation of past discrimination are theories upon which major litigation has been based in the past, but the number of these type cases has greatly fallen off in recent years.

Disparate Treatment Claims

Disparate treatment occurs when an employer treats some employees or applicants for employment less favorably than others because of race, gender, age, or any other characteristic protected by anti-discrimination legislation. To prove a case, a charging party must establish that the defendant acted with a discriminatory motive. Discriminatory motive can be proved directly (where the defendant has stated that the protected characteristic was a reason for the challenged action) or inferred from the fact of different treatment to similarly situated individuals. Statistical evidence is also relevant, although statistics alone is not sufficient to prove disparate treatment.

Direct evidence has the most probative value in proving disparate treatment, although most employers have now been educated to the point that direct evidence seldom is available to a charging party. Direct evidence includes statements indicating bias against the charging party's protected class by the defendant's management who took the action challenged, either in documents or orally. The statements may be blatant slurs against the protected class or the charging party because of the protected characteristic, or more subtle statements that nonetheless indicate stereotyped views of the protected class. A manager's statement that women are not strong enough to hold a particular job is direct evidence of sex discrimination, as is an employer's policy of requiring women to wear short skirts but having no dress code for males. However, statements of bias by officials who had no say in the challenged employment decision are not direct evidence (although they still are admissible as evidence as to what the employer's policies actually are, and thus a very bad thing).

The evidence most frequently used to show disparate treatment is comparative evidence, where the treatment of individuals of the protected race, gender, and so on is compared with treatment accorded individuals not of the protected class. If black employees are discharged for a first offense of fighting while white employees are only suspended, it is reasonable to infer that the difference in treatment is due to the race of the individuals involved. This presumption may be rebutted by the employer, but the burden of proof shifts to the employer once different treatment is shown.

Similarly situated employees does not necessarily mean identically situated employees. If black employees are discharged for a first offense of fighting and no white employees have ever been involved in a fight on employer's premises, evidence of the discipline meted out to white employees for a first offense of stealing, drinking on the job, or other violations for which discharge may be appropriate for a first offense may be considered. The more instances of similarly situated individuals that are shown, the more probative the comparative evidence becomes. The defendant may rebut the charging party's comparative evidence either by showing the comparatives were not actually similarly situated, or by showing other comparatives did receive similar treatment as the charging party.

Statistics are probative when the incidence of selection of members of a protected class are two standard deviations or more in variance from the selection rate of non-protected class members. Statistics are potent evidence when combined with statements by defendant's management indicating bias against the protected class. The charging party's statistics may be challenged by showing that the sample used is too small to be meaningful (if changing one or two individual situations eliminates the variance) or by showing that an inappropriate sample was used. A defendant may also use statistics to rebut an inference of disparate treatment created by a charging party's comparative evidence, whether or not the charging party introduces statistical evidence.

Proving that the chosen employee is better qualified than the charging party is a defense to a hiring or promotion charge, regardless of the other evidence. So is showing that a hiring decision was made because of an affirmative action policy adopted to remedy past discrimination, or in accordance with a collective bargaining agreement's seniority system, or an act of simple nepotism or cronyism. (Note—while favoritism based on kinship or friendship is a defense to an EEOC charge, it is also the equivalent to an engraved invitation to union organizers.) A defense for when an employer has admittedly discriminated against a protected class is to show that not having the protected characteristic is a *bona fide* requirement of the job, such as when a modeling job specifies a male model. (Race discrimination may not be defended as a *bona fide* occupational qualification.)

The Supreme Court stated in *Price Waterhouse v. Hopkins* that the employer's motives are determined by what the employer's motives actually were when it made the challenged decision. However, there is a line of cases that hold that after-acquired information of misconduct by the charging party is relevant to the question of whether the charging party incurred an "injury" that entitles him or her to damages. Most of these cases quote the Tenth Circuit case of *Summers v. State Farm Insurance Co.*, 804 F.2d 700 (10th Cir. 1988), which pre-dates *Price Waterhouse*, so there is a question about these rulings. Nonetheless, if a defendant learns of significant falsifications by charging party on an employment application such that the defendant can argue it would not have hired charging party had it known the truth, it is worth arguing that the charging party is entitled to no relief regardless of whether discrimination occurred. This is why defendants should investigate a charging party's background thoroughly. As mentioned earlier in mixed motive cases, prior to the 1991 Civil Rights Act an employer could avoid liability in cases even when the court found discrimination if the employer could prove that it would have made the same decision even had it not considered the protected characteristic. Section 107 of the 1991 Civil Rights Act provides that if the charging party shows that one of the prohibited factors was a motivating factor, then an unlawful employment practice is established even if other lawful factors also motivated the company's decision. In those instances in which an employer can demonstrate the same action would have been taken even absent the discriminatory motive, the court may not award damages or require reinstatement, hiring, or promotion. However, the court may grant declaratory relief, injunctive relief (with certain exceptions) and attorneys' fees and costs demonstrated to be directly attributable pursuant to a claim of unlawful discrimination under Section 703 of the Civil Rights Act.

Adverse Impact Claims

Adverse impact cases are proved when the charging party shows that an employment policy, although worded neutrally, nonetheless weeds out members of a protected class. Classic examples are height and weight requirements, which invariably screen out a disproportionate percent of women applicants. Employers may defend these charges by demonstrating "that the challenged practice is job related for the position in question and consistent with business necessity." (See §105 - 1991 Civil Rights Act.) To do so, they must show an actual relationship between the requirement and the job performed. This is typically done by having the job validated by an industrial psychologist.

Perpetuation of Past Discrimination Claims

Perpetuation of past discrimination occurs when an employer admittedly discriminated before such became illegal, then adopted a facially neutral policy that continues to exclude the protected class. One example is when an employer once refused to hire black employees and now accepts employment referrals only from current employees. Employers can defend this type charge by showing business necessity for the current policy. Collectively bargained seniority systems that pre-date Title VII (July 2, 1965) have been ruled by the Supreme Court not to be violations of Title VII, even when they perpetuate past discrimination.

Claims of Failure to Make Reasonable Accommodations

Accommodation cases are unique in that they require an affirmative obligation on the part of an employer to accommodate an employee's religious beliefs, and generally arise when the employee needs to miss work for religious observances. Employers may defend these charges by showing that accommodating the employee's religious beliefs would pose an undue hardship on the employer. An undue hardship is where the accommodation would impose more than a *de minimis* cost on the employer. What is a *de minimis* cost is determined by the size of the employer and nature of the business operation on a case-by-case basis. The burden is on the employer to attempt accommodation. It is not a defense that the employee was not able to suggest an accommodation acceptable to the employer. It is an undue hardship on the employer if a suggested accommodation would require it to violate a seniority system in a collective bargaining agreement.

The Americans With Disabilities Act also requires reasonable accommodation for individuals with physical or mental disabilities. The act becomes effective for many employers in July, 1992, and what is a reasonable accommodation is far from worked out at this time. Again, the size of the employer and the cost of the accommodation will determine the reasonableness of an accommodation.

AN ANALYSIS OF DAMAGES AND JURY TRIALS UNDER THE 1991 CIVIL RIGHTS ACT

Section 102 of the 1991 Civil Rights Act expands the possible award of compensatory and punitive damages to include not only racial or ethnic bias, but also to those individuals who suffer intentional discrimination on account of sex, religion, and disability under Title VII, ADA, and Section 501 of the 1973 Rehabilitation Act. However, compensatory damages may be awarded only in cases of intentional discrimination. Furthermore, punitive damages can be awarded, but only when the employer is found to have acted with "malice or reckless indifference to" the complainant's rights.

In addition, there are dollar limitations that each individual complaining party can be awarded. The law provides that such awards shall not exceed, for each complaining party—in the case of a respondent

- who has more than 14 and fewer than 101 employees in each of twenty or more calendar weeks in the current or preceding year, $50,000;
- who has more than 100 and fewer than 201 employees in each of twenty or more calendar weeks in the current or preceding year, $100,000;
- who has more than 200 and fewer than 501 employees in each of twenty or more calendar weeks in the current or preceding calendar year, $200,000; and
- who has more than 500 employees in each of 20 or more calendar weeks in the current or preceding year, $300,000.

Furthermore, in the event that a complaining party seeks compensatory or punitive damages, the party may then demand a trial by jury; however, the court is not permitted to inform the jury of the dollar limitations set forth in the Act. Thus, the stakes are now higher and in difficult cases settlement may want to be explored earlier rather than later.

STRATEGIES TO MINIMIZE EXPOSURE IN DIFFICULT CASES

Counsel for the employer will want to consider the possibility of settlement. However, there are instances in which the complaining party has either refused settlement or whose settlement expectations are extremely high—and this of course will occur more frequently under the 1991 Civil Rights Act. Counsel should consider the following:

Offer of Judgment. The Federal Rules of Civil Procedure, Rule 68 provide some leverage for an employer faced with a difficult case. Rule 68 basically provides that any party "at any time more than ten days before the trial begins to allow a judgment to be taken against" the company for "specified money or other terms." A rejected offer is not admissible at trial, but "if the judgment finally obtained by the offeree is not more favorable than the offer, the offeree must pay the cost incurred after making the offer."

The use of Rule 68 may exert additional pressure on the plaintiff to consider settlement discussions seriously.

Unconditional Offers of Reinstatement. Counsel may also want to consider the use of an unconditional offer of reinstatement. In those instances where an unconditional offer is made to a complaining party, the failure of the complaining party to accept the offer will cut off backpay liability. However, the offer is unconditional. That is, the employee may choose to come back to work and continue to pursue the lawsuit against the company. Typically, in these instances to effectuate an unconditional offer, the employer or employer's counsel needs to write the employee making the unconditional offer to come back to work. The offer must be unconditional and offer the same or substantially the same job that the employee left, at the salary and benefit level which the complaining party would have been making had he or she remained employed by the employer.

39 Strategic Steps to Follow in Preventing and Defending Sexual Harassment Claims

Sexual (and racial) harassment in the workplace is recognized as "unlawful discrimination." In fact, numerous studies have shown that both minorities and women have suffered from harassment. For example, one survey found that 88% of more than 9,000 female respondents reported having personally experienced sexual harassment on the job. Since that time, the composition of the work force has changed significantly, increasing risk of sexual harassment. Both sexual and racial harassment can constitute violations of law.

Title VII of the 1964 Civil Rights Act prohibits discrimination on account of sex. Although this statute is typically applied to traditional forms of discrimination, it has also been interpreted by the courts to apply to sexual harassment, i.e., conditioning an employee's job status on submission to sexual advances. These types of cases establish a traditional theory of sexual harassment: quid pro quo, that is, sexual favors for job status. In addition to the quid pro quo type of discrimination the legal system also protects an employee against a hostile or offensive work environment. This notion that Title VII affords employees protection against these types of environments originated in the context of racial and ethnic epitaphs.

EEOC DEFINITIONS OF SEXUAL HARASSMENT

In 1980, the Equal Employment Opportunity Commission (EEOC) issued guidelines on discrimination because of sex, 29 C.F.R. Section 1604.11, which set forth definitions of sexual harassment. The guidelines provide in pertinent part that harassment on the basis of sex is a violation of Sec. 703 of Title VII. Unwelcome sexual advances, requests for sexual favors, and other verbal or physical conduct of a sexual nature constitute sexual harassment when:

1. submission to such conduct is made either explicitly or implicitly a term or condition of an individual's employment,
2. submission to or rejection of such conduct by an individual is used as the basis for employment decisions affecting such individual, or
3. such conduct has the purpose or effect of unreasonably interfering with an individual's work performance or creating an intimidating, hostile, or offensive working environment.

The EEOC guidelines also state that, in determining whether alleged conduct constitutes sexual harassment, the Commission will look at the record as a whole and at the totality of the circumstances such as the nature of the sexual advances and the context in which the alleged incidents occurred. The determination of the legality of a particular action will be made from the facts, on a case-by-case basis.

Traditionally, sexual harassment has consisted of an aggressor making sexual demands on a victim in return for economic gain, such as a promotion or raise, or with the threat of economic loss, such as a demotion or firing (play or pay). In an unanimous decision, the Supreme Court in *Meritor Savings Bank v. Vinson*, 40 FEP cases 1822, 106 S. Ct. 2399 (1986) held that sexual harassment is a violation of individual rights whether or not the threat of economic loss exists. Indeed, the court held that,

> sexual harassment which creates a hostile or offensive environment for members of one sex, is every bit the arbitrary barrier to sexual equality at the workplace that racial harassment is to racial equality. Surely a requirement that a man or a woman run a gauntlet of sexual abuse in return for the privilege of being allowed to work by making a living can be as demeaning and disconcerting as the harshest of racial epitaphs.

The court went on to state that not all workplace conduct may be described as harassment. Rather, the court said, for sexual harassment to be actionable, it must be *sufficiently severe or pervasive* to alter the condition of the employee's employment and create an abusive working environment.

Until recently, the "reasonable person" standard was used in determining whether a particular incident was considered to be sexual harassment. Cases are now redefining the definition of sexual harassment and as a result the "reasonable person" standard is becoming the "reasonable woman" standard. In the case of *Robinson v. Jacksonville Shipyards*, 136 LRRM 2920, 760 F. Supp. 1486 (1991), the court used the "reasonable woman" standard to determine whether an atmosphere of sexual harassment was present in the working environment.

UNDERSTANDING THE PLAINTIFF'S ELEMENTS OF PROOF IN A SEXUAL HARASSMENT CASE

The Sixth Circuit Court of Appeals has established five elements that a plaintiff must show in order to prevail in a Title VII offensive work environment sexual harassment action. *Rabidue v. Osceola Refining Company*, 42 FEP cases 637 (6th Cir. 1986). These are listed below, followed by a brief discussion of each element.

- **The employee was a member of a protected class.**

  This can be established by either a man or a woman.

- **The employee was subjected to "unwelcome" sexual harassment.**

  In *Vinson* the Supreme Court held that sexually related conduct in which the complainant's participation was "voluntary" could still be "unwelcome" and the basis for Title VII liability. Specifically, the court stated that "voluntary" submission to sex-related conduct, which the court defined as "in the sense that complainant was not forced to participate against her will" does not constitute a defense to a sexual harassment suit brought under Title VII. The court explained: "While the question whether particular conduct was indeed unwelcome, presents difficult problems of proof and turns largely on credibility determinations committed to the trier of fact, the district court in this case erroneously focused on the 'voluntariness' of respondent's participation in the claimed sexual episodes. The correct inquiry is whether the respondent by her conduct indicated that the alleged sexual advances were unwelcome, not whether her actual participation in sexual intercourse was voluntary."

  Thus, the focus in a sexual harassment claim is on whether the complainant's conduct indicated that the alleged sexual advances were unwelcome, not on whether the actual participation in sexual relations was "voluntary."

- **The sexual harassment was based upon sex.**

  It is possible that Title VII would not be applicable to cases where a supervisor sexually harasses employees of both sexes or where non-directed sexual conduct creates a hostile environment equally offensive to men and women. In addition, homosexual harassment has been held to be cognizable under Title VII. In *Wright v. Methodist Youth Services*, 511 F. Supp. 307 (N.D. Ill. 1981), the court held that a male employee's claim that he was terminated for refusing the homosexual advances of his supervisor, stated a claim under Title VII, because the claim involved "an alleged demand of a male employee that would not be directed to a female."

- **The charged sexual harassment had the effect of unreasonably interfering with the plaintiff's work performance and creating an intimidating,**

hostile, or offensive working environment that affected seriously the psychological well-being of the plaintiff.

The *Vinson* court, in adopting the position enunciated in the EEOC guidelines, indicated that in a hostile environment case, as opposed to a quid pro quo case, the harassment must be sufficiently severe and persistent as to affect the average employee's work performance or create an "intimidating, hostile, or offensive working environment." This standard, however, may be easier to articulate than to apply. One court held that "Regular, almost daily exposure to sexual terms over the course of six to seven months, is, by any definition, a concerted pattern of continuous harassment which pollutes a working environment."

- **Since Title VII provides a cause of action against the "employer," it is essential to examine the issue of employer vicarious responsibility for the action of its employees.**

As the court indicated in *Vinson,* the extent of employer liability traditionally has turned on two factors:

a. Whether the challenged conduct was undertaken by a supervisor or a co-employee, and

b. Whether the plaintiff is alleging quid pro quo or hostile environment harassment.

In *Vinson,* the Supreme Court rejected the position taken by the D.C. Circuit that employers should automatically be liable for all forms of supervisory harassment. The court held that the determination of employer liability is to be made on a case-by-case basis, applying general agency principles. Thus, this question is still open. Some courts take the position regarding supervisors in quid pro quo cases, that the employer is strictly liable for all acts of supervisors, regardless of knowledge. As to non-supervisors, the general rule is that an employer is liable only when it has actual or constructive knowledge of the harassment and fails to take "immediate and appropriate" corrective action.

SIGNIFICANT DEFENSES IN SEXUAL HARASSMENT CASES AND EMPLOYER RESPONSES TO AVOID

The court in *Rabidue* addressed the issue of burden of proof and "defenses." The court stated "in considering an order of proof to implement the resolution of Title VII sexually hostile working environment controversies, this court has reviewed the procedure enunciated in *McDonnel Douglas Corporation* . . . and has concluded that the order of proof and procedures enunciated therein are not readily adaptable to developing the proofs and defenses in this type of Title VII action." It would appear that the most effective and efficient procedural format would implement the traditional practice of placing the ultimate burden of proof by preponderance of the evidence upon the claimant followed by a proffer of defense and an opportunity for a plaintiff's rebuttal. Counsel for the employer may have available the following defenses:

- The events alleged did not take place.
- The events were isolated—that is, in view of the totality of the circumstances, there was no hostile or abusive working environment.

In *Highlander*, 42 FEP cases 658, the court stated that in passing upon the question, the court is directed to adopt the prospective of a *reasonable person's reaction* to a similar environment under similar or like circumstances to determine if the defendant's conduct would have interfered with the work performance and would have seriously effected the psychological well-being of that characterized individual.

In addition, even if a reasonable person may have been so offended, the court went on to state that the trier of fact is also required *"to determine if the plaintiff was actually offended by the defendant's conduct* and suffered some degree of injury as a result of her exposure to the work environment."

- That the claimant was aware of the prevailing work environment. This defense, although available, is obviously the weakest defense.
- The employee welcomed the acts. Courts have restricted evidence of plaintiff's past sexual history or misconduct for impeachment or to show "welcomeness". But, speech or dress in the workplace has been found relevant.
- Failure to complain promptly or use grievance procedure is a possible defense or will at least undermine credibility.
- The employer did not know and had no reason to know.
- Prompt and appropriate remedial action.
- Demonstrating that plaintiff was discharged for legitimate reason. Although an employer may have other valid reasons for discharge, the 1991 Civil Rights Act provides that if harassment is proven the court may prohibit such action in the future.

The following is a list of employer responses to avoid:

- The Ostrich Approach. Does not work.
- "I don't know who to believe—so everybody involved take a polygraph." Polygraphs are highly regulated by law. See Chapter 49 on polygraphs.
- "He has pictures—Go through his desk and locker." Some courts hold that employees who have a reasonable expectation of privacy (e.g., lockers where the employees supplied locks) and the employer searches the locker and its contents without permission constitutes an intentional invasion of privacy supporting an award of damages.

- "I'll turn you over to the police if you don't sign a confession and resign." This approach poses several problems, the most serious of which is whether a state extortion statute may be applicable.
- "I'll hire an undercover agent." Employers have a conditional privilege regarding reporting events in the workplace. But again, each state law will need to be consulted regarding invasion of privacy claims.

Thus, an employer's best defense is to have a well-publicized policy in force, immediately investigate the claim, and take appropriate action.

PRACTICAL STEPS TO AVOID OR MINIMIZE LIABILITY IN SEXUAL HARASSMENT CASES

The EEOC has stated that prevention is the best tool for preventing sexual harassment. In fact, the Equal Employment Opportunity Commission in its rules and regulations state:

> "Prevention is the best tool for the elimination of sexual harassment. An employer should take all steps necessary to prevent sexual harassment from occurring, such as affirmatively raising the subject, expressing strong disapproval, developing appropriate sanctions, informing employees of their right to raise and how to raise the issue of harassment under Title VII, and developing methods to sensitize all concerned."

While the Supreme Court in *Vinson* "decline[d] the parties' invitation to issue a definitive rule on employer liability" and "reject[ed] it, the petitioner's view that the mere existence of a grievance procedure on a policy against discrimination, coupled with (an employee's) failure to invoke that procedure, must insulate (an employer) from liability." The *Vinson* decision leaves no doubt about the importance of having an explicit sexual harassment policy and a clearly defined grievance procedure. In *Vinson*, the court rejected the argument that management was free of liability because (1) it had a policy against harassment and a grievance system for complaints, and (2) the employee who claimed she was harassed never used a grievance procedure. The Supreme Court stated that the bank's "general non-discrimination policy" (1) did not address sexual harassment specifically, and thus did not put on notice employees as to their employer's interest in correcting this sort of discrimination, and (2) the grievance procedure apparently required the employee to complain first to a supervisor, who in the *Vinson* case also was the alleged harasser. Thus, even though the existence of a policy, the employer's failure to invoke the grievance procedure does not afford an employer freedom from liability. The Supreme Court commented that an employer would have a "substantially stronger argument" that it should be insulated from liability "if its procedures were better calculated to encourage victims of harassment to come forward."

The Supreme Court in *Vinson* also provided some guidance on the content of employer policies and complaint procedures. The court stressed the importance that those policies be written to encourage victims of sexual harassment to come forward. In this regard, the Supreme Court made two recommendations: (1) that the sexual harassment policy be particularly enunciated, apart from a general non-discrimination policy, and (2) that the grievance procedure provide a mechanism for employees to take complaints to other than their immediate supervisors.

In developing a written policy prohibiting sexual harassment, the following issues need to be addressed:

1. Scope of application
2. Purpose
3. Zero tolerance statement
4. Define
5. Discipline
6. Reporting procedure
   a. Non-union
   b. Union
7. Investigation
8. Confidentiality
9. Possible use of consent forms
10. Reprisals
11. Dissemination/communications of policy
12. Training

Exhibit 39-1 provides a sample draft of a sexual harassment policy.

Exhibit 39-1

Sample Sexual Harassment Policy Statement

1. ***Purpose:*** The purpose of this policy is to state clearly that (employer) prohibits sexual harassment and to set forth procedures by which allegations of sexual harassment may be filed, investigated, and resolved.

2. ***Policy Statement:*** Sexual harassment of employees or applicants for jobs by employees, supervisors, or agents is unacceptable behavior and will not be tolerated. The company will take appropriate corrective action to remedy any situation which is brought to its attention.

continued

3. ***Definitions:*** Sexual harassment is a type of misconduct that interferes with work productivity and wrongfully deprives employees of the opportunity to work in an environment free from unwelcome sexual overtones. Sexual harassment includes all unwelcome sexual advances, requests for sexual favors, and other verbal or physical conduct of a sexual nature when:

   (a) Submission to such conduct is made either an explicit or implicit term or condition of an individual's employment; or

   (b) Submission to or rejection of the conduct is used as a basis for an employment decision affecting the individual subjecting or submitting to the conduct; or

   (c) Such conduct has the purpose or effect of unreasonably interfering with an individual's work performance or creating an intimidating, hostile, or offensive working environment.

4. No supervisor or any employee shall promise, imply or grant any preferential treatment in connection with another employee or applicant for engaging in sexual conduct.

5. ***Violations:*** Any employee, supervisor, or agent who violates this policy will be subject to discipline up to and including discharge.

6. ***Complaints or Questions:*** Any questions regarding this policy should be addressed to the Personnel Director.

   Any employee who feels that he or she is a victim of sexual harassment, including but not limited to, any of the conduct listed above, by any supervisor, employee, or agent, should immediately bring the matter to the attention of his or her supervisor or designated person or persons in the Personnel or Human Resources Department. An employee who is uncomfortable for any reason in bringing such matter to the attention of his or her supervisor, should report the matter to the designated person or persons in the Personnel or Human Resources Department. Where investigation confirms the offensive behavior, prompt corrective action will be taken.

7. ***Investigation:*** All complaints will be investigated, and information will be treated as confidentially as necessary for the investigation.

8. ***No Reprisals:*** Employees reporting incidents of sexual harassment will be protected from reprisals in any form.

UNDERSTANDING OTHER POTENTIAL PROBLEMS AND LIABILITIES INVOLVING SEXUAL HARASSMENT CLAIMS

In addition to Title VII of the 1964 Civil Rights Act, many states have enacted human rights acts that also prohibit sex discrimination, including sexual harassment. Some state laws may go beyond the typical backpay award and permit punitive damages. Thus, each state law will need to be examined regarding potential liability.

In addition, one matter that arises in some instances in a sexual harassment type claim is a claim under the National Labor Relations Act. The National Labor Relations Act (NLRA), as amended, protects concerted employee activity. 29 U.S.C. Section 151 et seq. Section 8(a)(1) of the NLRA, for example, forbids employers from interfering with, restraining, or coercing employees in the exercise of the right to engage in such concerted activities. Section 7 of the NLRA sets forth the scope of protected activities as follows:

> Employees shall have the right to self-organization, to form, join, or assist labor organizations, to bargain collectively through representatives of their own choosing, and *to engage in other concerted activities for the purpose of* collective bargaining or other *mutual aid or protection* and shall also have the right to refrain from any or all of such activities....

Thus, it is a violation of federal labor law to, for example, discipline or discharge an employee solely because he or she has engaged in any of the activities set forth in Section 7. The typical issue raised is establishing under what circumstances a single employee's activity would be considered "concerted" and therefore protected.

In 1984, the National Labor Relations Board held that for an employee's activity to be "concerted" it would require that the employee be "engaged in with or on the authority of other employees, and not solely by and on behalf of the employee himself." *Myers Industries* I 115 LRRM 1025 (1984); *Myers Industries* II 123 LRRM 1137 (1986).

The NLRB in *Myers* II went on to state that "*Myers* I recognizes that the question of whether an employee has engaged in concerted activities is a factual one based on the totality of the record evidence. When the record evidence demonstrates group activities, whether specifically authorized in a formal agency since, or otherwise, we shall find the conduct to be concerted." *Myers* II 123 LRRM at 1141.

In *Walter Bruker and Company* 118 LRRM 1127 (1984) which was decided subsequent to *Myers* I, the Board found that an individual employee acted on the authority of other employees within the meaning of *Myers* I when that employee discussed with other employees a common wage complaint. The conduct was deemed concerted under the circumstances because a second employee refrained from making his own wage complaint, relying instead on the first employee to resolve the matter. Although there was no specific authorization in the formal agency sense, the record established that the employees acted as a group even though only the first employee further pursued the wage complaint, while the second employee was only generally aware that the first employee would take whatever action he deemed necessary to obtain the information concerning their wage dispute. See also, *NLRB v. City Disposal Systems, Inc.* 465 U.S. 822,115 LRRM 3192 (1984).

An employee who feels that she is being sexually harassed and who has discussed these matters with other employees or more importantly, who has approached management with other employees complaining of the harassment, may file a charge with the National Labor Relations Board. Most often victims file charges with the EEOC.

In addition to potential civil liabilities, there is also potential criminal liabilities that an employee or employer may confront. For example, typically, there are three criminal statutes that may be applicable:

1. Assault
2. Battery
3. Sexual battery

Preventive measures can best protect an employer's interest.

40 Techniques and Tactics in Handling Handicap Discrimination Cases to Comply With the Americans With Disabilities Act

The Americans With Disabilities Act (ADA) was signed by President Bush on July 26, 1990. In determining that such a law was necessary, Congress noted that 43 million Americans have one or more physical or mental disabilities. Further, Congress determined that society has tended to isolate and/or segregate individuals with disabilities. Congress also found that discrimination against the disabled persisted in the areas of employment, housing, public accommodations, education, transportation, communication, recreation, health services, voting, and access to public services. Prior to the ADA's passage, there was only limited protection against discrimination because of handicap. For example, the Rehabilitation Act of 1973 only applied to certain federal contractors and grantees. And, while every state and the District of Columbia has a law that addresses the issue of handicap discrimination, none contain the breadth of protection found in the ADA.

The ADA is divided into five titles:

- Title I covers private sector employment
- Title II addresses programs, activities, and services provided by state and local governments
- Title III regulates public accommodations
- Title IV deals with telecommunications
- Title V contains miscellaneous provisions which, among other things, encourage the use of alternate means of dispute resolution

This chapter will focus on Title I, the employment provisions. These employment provisions become effective for:

- Employers with 25 or more employees—July 26, 1992
- Employers with 15 to 24 employees—July 26, 1994

The law provides that covered entities may not discriminate against any qualified individual with a disability with respect to any term, condition, or privilege of employment.

UNDERSTANDING CRITICAL PROVISIONS OF THE ADA

Defining "Disability" Under the ADA

The ADA has a three-part definition of "disability" that is a mirror image of the definition in the Rehabilitation Act of 1973. Disabilities under the ADA include:

- Physical or mental impairment that substantially limits one or more of an individual's major life activities; or
- Having a record of such impairment; or,
- Being regarded as having such an impairment.

A physical or mental impairment refers to a physiological disorder or condition, cosmetic disfigurement, or anatomical loss such as loss of a limb, sight, hearing, or speech, mental retardation, emotional or mental illness, or specific learning disorder. This term does *not* include left-handedness; obesity (except when caused by some other impairment), or personality traits such as quick temper or poor judgment. Also, environmental disadvantages such as poverty, lack of education, or a prison record are not "physical or mental impairments." Advanced age, alone, is not an impairment, but conditions commonly associated with the aging process, such as hearing loss, osteoporosis, or arthritis, could be. Sexual behavior disorders and certain other conditions are also specifically exempt from the definition of disability.

The definition also speaks in terms of a physical or mental impairment that substantially limits one or more of an individual's "major life activities." Many impairments do not impact an individual's life to the degree that they constitute disabling impairments and only rises to the level of a "disability" if the impairment substantially limits one or more major life activities. The ADA lists caring for oneself, performing manual tasks, walking, seeing, hearing, speaking, breathing, learning, and working as major life activities. This list is certainly not exhaustive and may also include standing, lifting, sitting, and reaching. Some impairments may be disabling for some, but not for others. This determination is not based on the diagnosis, but on the effect the impairment has on the life of the individual.

The term *substantially limits* has been defined in the ADA to mean: (1) unable to perform a major life activity that the average person in the general population can perform; or (2) significantly restricted as to the condition, manner, or duration under which an individual can perform a major life activity as compared to the condition, manner, or duration under which the average person in the general population can perform the same major life activity. There are several factors that will be considered in determining whether an individual is substantially limited in a major life activity which include the following:

- the nature and severity of the impairment
- the duration of the expected impairment
- the permanent or long-term impact or expected permanent or long-term impact of the impairment

With respect to the major life activity of "working," the term *substantially limits* means significantly restricted in the ability to perform either a class of jobs or a broad range of jobs in various classes when compared to the average person having comparable training, skills, and abilities. However, the inability to perform a single, particular job does not constitute a substantial limitation in the major life activity of working.

Other factors that may be considered in determining whether an individual is substantially limited in "working" are:

- the geographical area to which the individual has reasonable access
- the job from which the individual has been disqualified because of the impairment as well as the number and types of jobs using similar training, knowledge, skills or abilities, within that geographical area
- the number and types of *other* jobs from which the individual has been disqualified because of an impairment that do not use similar training, knowledge, skills, and abilities.

One final note on the determination if an individual is substantially limited in the major life activity of working—an individual does *not* have to be totally unable to work in order to be considered substantially limited in the major life activity of working. An individual is substantially limited in working if the individual is significantly restricted in the ability to perform a class or broad range of jobs when compared with the ability of the average person with comparable qualifications to perform those same jobs. The ADA points out that temporary, non-chronic impairments of short duration with little or no long-term or permanent impact are generally not deemed to be disabilities. These include: broken limbs, sprained joints, concussions, influenza, or appendicitis.

Recognizing Limited Protection Under the ADA for Illegal Drug and Alcohol Use

The ADA sets forth what constitutes the illegal use of drugs and alcohol and specifies the actions employers can lawfully take to prohibit substance abuse. It is important to point out that the ADA does not protect individuals who currently use illegal drugs when an employer acts on the basis of that use. However, the ADA includes in the definition of a qualified individual with a disability, one who:

- Has successfully completed a supervised drug rehabilitation program or has otherwise been rehabilitated successfully and is no longer using illegal drugs; or
- Is participating in a supervised rehabilitation program and is no longer using illegal drugs; or
- Is erroneously regarded as using illegal drugs, but is not engaging in such use.

Employer's counsel can help employers protect themselves from hiring current users of illegal drugs by drafting reasonable policies and procedures which may include drug testing which is designed to ensure that a rehabilitated user of illegal drugs is no longer engaged in using those drugs. The ADA exempts testing for illegal drugs from its medical examination limitations, incorporates identical provisions of the Rehabilitation Act of 1973, and authorizes compliance with the Drug Free Workplace Act of 1988.

Qualifying an Individual with a Disability

The employment provisions of ADA in Title I prohibit discrimination against "qualified" individuals with disabilities. A qualified individual with a disability refers to a disabled individual who has the necessary skills, experience, education, and meets the other job-related requirements and who, with or without some form of reasonable accommodation, can perform the *essential functions* of the job. Therefore, to be protected under the ADA's employment title, an individual with a disability must be qualified. Although the ADA doesn't guarantee an individual with a disability the right to a job, an employment decision must be based on reasons unrelated to the presence of a disability.

Employers are obligated to consider applicants and make decisions without regard to an individual's disability or need for accommodation. Importantly, the ADA does *not* require affirmative action—or put another way—employers do not have to prefer a disabled applicant over an applicant without a disability simply because one is disabled.

Determining Essential Job Functions

In order to comply with the requirements of ADA, employers must decide if an individual with a disability can perform the essential job functions of a position, with or without reasonable accommodation. Essential functions refer to the "fundamental" job duties of the position the individual with a disability holds or desires. Essential functions do not refer to non-critical or marginal job functions.

Under the ADA's regulations at 29 C.F.R. Part 1630, to determine whether a job function may be considered essential, the employer should consider a number of factors, including the following:

- Does the position exist simply to perform the function or major task? (i.e., individual is hired to drive a bus, therefore, the ability to drive is an essential function because this is the only reason the position exists)
- How many other employees are able to perform that same job function and can it be distributed among other employees?
- What is the employer's judgment regarding which functions are essential?
- What degree of skill or expertise is required to perform the function?
- Were written job descriptions prepared before advertising or interviewing applicants for the position?
- How much time is spent on a particular function?
- What is the work experience of past incumbents in the job?

There are two areas where the concept of "essential" functions has a practical impact. First, if an individual cannot perform an essential function of the job even *with* reasonable accommodation, this individual is not considered "qualified." Second, an individual who, even with reasonable accommodation, cannot perform the marginal functions, but *can* perform the essential functions will be considered "qualified."

According to the regulations, an "essential job function" is not intended to second guess an employer's business judgment with regard to production standards, either qualitative or quantitative, but if an employer does have a requirement, the reason cannot be for the purpose of excluding individuals with a disability. For example, if an employer requires a typing speed of 75 words per minute accurately, he would not be required to explain why inaccurate work of 65 words per minute would be inadequate, as long as this requirement is the same for all applicants or employees for the position.

Providing Reasonable Accommodation

The ADA provides that employers must make reasonable accommodations for the *known* limitations of a qualified individual with a disability unless the employer can show that the accommodation would impose an undue hardship on its operations.

The ADA defines "reasonable accommodation" as certain actions an employer may take to accommodate a qualified individual with a disability. The regulations implementing ADA indicate that the term "reasonable accommodation" refers to:

- Modifications or adjustments to a job application process to enable a qualified applicant with a disability to be considered for the position he or she desires; or
- Modifications or adjustments to the work environment or the manner or circumstances under which the position held or desired is customarily performed to enable a qualified individual with a disability to perform the essential job functions; or
- Modifications or adjustments that enable an employer's employee with a disability to enjoy equal benefits and privileges of employment as are enjoyed by its other similarly-situated employees without disabilities.

In addition, the regulations state that reasonable accommodations may include:

- Making existing facilities used by employees readily accessible to and usable by individuals with disabilities
- Job restructuring; implementing part-time or modified work schedules; reassigning the individual to a vacant position; acquiring or modifying equipment or devices; making appropriate adjustments or modifications to equipment or devices, as well as to examinations, training materials, or policies; providing qualified readers or interpreters; and making other similar accommodations for individuals with disabilities.

In defining reasonable accommodation, the ADA differs from the Rehabilitation Act of 1973 most notably by requiring employers to consider assigning a disabled employee to a vacant position as a form of reasonable accommodation. Under the Rehabilitation Act the courts had consistently held that reassignment was not required.

Under the ADA, reasonable accommodations should be determined on a case-by-case basis and an employer is free to choose the less expensive accommodation or the one that is easier to implement.

In passing the ADA, Congress was obviously concerned about how people with disabilities are perceived in the workplace. Therefore, employers should not ask if an applicant will require reasonable accommodation *unless* the individual discloses that information. Employers must be careful not to reject an applicant simply because the accommodation request does not appear to be cost efficient.

The courts may consider the balance of the employer's duty to make reasonable accommodation with its right to avoid excessive cost, but will probably err on the side of accommodating the disabled individual.

Determining Undue Hardship

Employers do not have to accommodate an individual with a disability if to do so would constitute an "undue hardship" for the employer. An undue hardship refers to a situation in which an employer incurs significant difficulty or expense in providing a reasonable accommodation. The ADA regulations provide several factors to consider when determining whether an accommodation poses an undue hardship or if an employer has a legal obligation to accommodate an individual with a disability. Some of the factors to be considered are:

- The nature and net cost of the accommodations needed, taking into account the availability of tax credits and deductions and/or outside funding;
- The overall financial resources of the facility or facilities involved in providing the reasonable accommodation, the number of persons employed at the facility, and the accommodation's effect on expenses and resources;
- The employer's overall size and/or financial resources, the overall number of its employees, and the number, type, and location of its facility(s);
- The employer's type of operation(s) (e.g., its workforce composition, structure, and functions), and the geographic separateness and administrative or fiscal relationship of the facility or facilities in question to the employer; and
- The impact of the accommodation upon the operation of the facility, including the impact on the ability of other employees to perform their duties and the impact on the facility's ability to conduct business.

These factors are not exclusive of other factors the courts or administrative agencies may look at to make this determination. For example, one factor to be considered would be the availability of outside funding to pay for accommodations. So, even if a particular accommodation would be an undue hardship because of its high cost, when the funding is made available, the employer may be required to pay the portion of the accommodation that was *not* an undue hardship.

It is important to note that the ADA does not set any financial threshold that would equal an "undue hardship." Instead, this determination is based on whether the expense of accommodation is significant and will be made on a case-by-case basis.

In addition, an employer's good faith efforts to make reasonable accommodation may avoid compensatory and punitive damages now provided for under the Civil Rights Act of 1991. The Civil Rights Act of 1991 provides that "in cases where a discriminatory practice involves the provision of a reasonable accommodation pursuant to [the Act], damages may not be awarded under this section where the covered entity demonstrates good faith efforts in consultation with the person with the disability who has informed the covered entity that accommodation is needed, to identify and make a reasonable accommodation that would provide such individual with an equally effective opportunity and would not cause an undue hardship on the operation of the business."

ENFORCEMENT OF ADA'S EMPLOYMENT PROVISIONS

The ADA incorporates all of the remedies and procedures found in Title VII of the Civil Rights Act of 1964, as amended by the Civil Rights Act of 1991. The Equal Employment Opportunity Commission will be responsible for developing regulations to enforce the provisions of Title I and has indicated that the process will be similar to that of responding to any other charge that may be brought for investigation by that agency. Following administrative processing of the charge, the individual may institute an ADA action upon receiving a right-to-sue letter issued by the EEOC. Therefore, an aggrieved individual would have the right to file a lawsuit only after first filing a charge for violation of the ADA with the Equal Employment Opportunity Commission. Not only will the EEOC have the power to receive and investigate any charges of discrimination, but the Commission may choose to bring civil actions on behalf of the individual discriminated against in certain cases against employers. (See Chapters 34 through 38.)

PRACTICAL PREVENTIVE STEPS TO AVOID VIOLATIONS OF THE ADA

There are a number of steps employers can take in order to comply with the requirements of the Americans With Disabilities Act:

- Establish ADA compliance committee
- Obtain all official publications from EEOC and U.S. Department of Justice
- Review job applications and screening/selection process
- Prepare or modify job descriptions
- Review any employment tests to determine predictable accommodations
- Review status of current employees
- Become familiar with tax incentives and other funding sources for accommodations
- Begin dialogue with disabled persons organizations

- Review current policies, in particular leave of absence, absenteeism/tardies policy, benefits and termination policies and procedures for compliance
- Prepare personnel/medical records systems that will effectuate the level of confidentiality required by the Act
- Determine architectural accessibility
- Identify current situations that will become violations if not addressed
- Comply with all notice posting and recordkeeping requirements
- Educate supervisors and managers regarding compliance with Americans With Disabilities Act

Establish an ADA Compliance Committee

First, employers should identify an individual or a committee to be responsible for compliance with the requirements of the ADA. Preferably a committee should be set up and consist of representatives from various departments such as Human Resources, Communications, Legal, Risk Management, Safety, and so on.

Obtain all Official Publications from EEOC and U.S. Department of Justice

Helpful sources of information include booklets currently available from the Equal Employment Opportunity Commission (one was published by the Civil Rights Division of the U.S. Department of Justice). Those booklets are:

1. "The Americans With Disabilities Act—Your Responsibilities As an Employer"
2. "The Americans With Disabilities Act—Your Employment Rights As an Individual With a Disability"
3. "The Americans With Disabilities Act—Questions and Answers"

These booklets (an EEOC compliance manual should be published in 1992) are available from the Equal Employment Opportunity Commission. For more information, contact: Equal Employment Opportunity Commission, 1801 L Street, N., Washington, D.C. 20507.

Review Job Applications and the Interview/Selection Process

Application Process. The ADA prohibits covered employers from discriminating in the job application process on the basis of a disability. No longer can applications contain a list of potentially disabling impairments and ask an applicant to identify which impairment he or she might have. Employers may, however, ask a question such as: "Are you able to perform the essential functions of the position for which you are applying?" It is important to note, however, that if this question is asked, a job description describing the essential functions of the job or jobs for which the individual is applying should be made available to the applicant.

Screening Process. During the screening process, employers may not ask how the applicant became disabled or the prognosis of the disability. Employers may not ask how often the individual will need leave time as a result of the disability, but employers may state the attendance policy and ask whether the individual can meet the requirements and may inquire as to whether the individual with a disability needs a reasonable accommodation in order to take any pre-employment test. Interviewers may not ask such questions as "Have you ever had a back injury or heart attack?" or, "Are you in good health?" These questions may not be asked in an interview (*or* on the written employment application). Generally, employers should avoid *any* verbal or written inquiry into an applicant's physical status during the pre-offer stage of the employment process. It is important to note that this prohibition against asking these medical questions also includes not asking applicants about their workers' compensation history.

This prohibition also applies to psychological examinations but does *not* apply to tests to determine illegal drug use or physical agility tests. (Note that physical agility tests are subject to the same requirements governing all employment tests.)

Those employers covered by the ADA's employment title may not make inquiries of an employee regarding the existence, nature, or severity of an employee's disability. Employers may ask pre-employment (pre-offer) questions about an applicant's ability to perform job-related functions. Employers may also ask an applicant to describe or demonstrate how, with or without reasonable accommodation, he or she will be able to perform essential job functions. For example, an employer can explain that the job requires reaching books on a high shelf and may lawfully ask the applicant if he or she will be able to perform that task with or without reasonable accommodation. An employer may make such a request of an applicant whose *known* or obvious disability may interfere with or prevent the performance of a job-related function—whether or not the employer makes the same request of *all* applicants for the position.

Hiring Process. During the actual hiring state, an employer may not refuse to hire an applicant with a disability based upon some general fear about safety or an assumption about his or her absenteeism rate.

Pre-Employment/Pre-Offer Medical Examinations. The ADA has a prohibition against discrimination in employment which includes medical examinations. Therefore, a covered employer may not conduct a "pre-employment" medical examination. The purpose of this prohibition is to prevent medical examinations or inquiries that do not serve a legitimate business purpose.

Post-Offer Medical Examination. After an offer of employment has been made to an individual, or before he or she starts to work, however, an employer may lawfully require a medical examination and/or inquiry. Additionally, the employer may condition a job offer on the examination and/or inquiry results as long as the procedures set forth in the ADA regulations are followed which are found at 29 CFR 1630.14(b):

- All entering employees in the same job category are subject to the examination and/or inquiry regardless of disability.
- The information obtained from the examination is collected and maintained on separate forms and treated confidentially. The information may be reviewed by supervisors and managers to identify necessary work restrictions, by safety and first aid personnel if the disability might require emergency treatment, and by government officials investigating compliance with ADA.
- The results of the examination are only used in accordance with the purpose of the ADA and not as a subterfuge for discrimination.

A medical examination conducted according to the above procedures does not have to be job-related and consistent with business necessity. But, if certain criteria are used that screen out employees with disabilities as a result of this medical examination or inquiry, employers must be prepared to demonstrate that the criteria that excluded the person *must* be job related and consistent with business necessity. And, an employer must be able to show that the performance of the essential job functions *cannot* be performed with reasonable accommodation.

Prepare or Modify Job Descriptions

The group can begin the process of determining whether job descriptions are current and whether they actually reflect the "essential functions" and "non-essential functions" of the job in order to determine if an applicant or employee is "otherwise qualified." If they do not accurately characterize the functions as essential versus non-essential, modifications should be made to those written job descriptions.

Although written job descriptions are not required by the law, if written descriptions do not exist, employers would be well-advised to identify the prerequisites for each position and its "essential functions" to determine whether an individual is "qualified" in a written form. Preparing written job descriptions that contain both essential and non-essential functions before advertising or interviewing for a job is critical. Carefully drafted job descriptions may serve as evidence of an employer's nondiscriminatory intent. Similarly, since the terms of a collective bargaining agreement may be relevant to determining whether a particular job function is essential, employers should review them in light of the requirements of the ADA. There may be times when the provisions of a collective bargaining agreement may be in conflict with the ADA. In those cases, the collective bargaining agreement would not protect the employer. For example, physical criteria specified in the collective bargaining agreement that causes a disparate impact on the disabled individual that are not job-related and consistent with business necessity would be illegal under the ADA.

The more difficult question is whether an employer can be required to accommodate a disabled employee if the accommodation would violate the contract. The legislative history to ADA indicates that an employer *would* be required to violate the collective bargaining agreement although the presence of the labor agreement may be considered by a court when determining whether the accommodation would be an undue hardship.

As a result of ADA, new collective bargaining agreements should include a provision allowing the employer to comply with the ADA.

Understanding Requirements for Existing Employees

The ADA prohibits employers from requiring medical examinations or asking medically-related questions of current employees *unless* they are job-related and consistent with business necessity. Employers may lawfully inquire into an employee's ability to perform job-related functions. And, medical exams that may be required by state or federal law may still be conducted.

Additionally, the ADA prohibits discrimination against a qualified individual on the basis of his or her disability with respect to leaves of absence, including sick leave or leaves to pursue training. Leave policies that are uniformly applied to *all* employees will not violate the ADA simply because they do not address the special needs of individuals with disabilities. However, "no leave" policies may be subject to a challenge and an employer may have to consider providing leave as a reasonable accommodation.

Review Any Employment Tests to Determine Predictable Accommodations

For example, contact the publisher of any test used by the company to determine whether those tests are available in alternate formats such as:

- Braille
- Large Print
- Audio Tape
- Electric File on Computer Disk and Electronic Bulletin Board, and so on

Review Status of Current Employees

Employers should establish procedure for evaluating the current workforce in terms of numbers and nature of individuals with disabilities and the existence of possible accommodations for those individuals—but this should be done only after the individuals have disclosed their disabilities to the employer. But once disclosed, an employer should undertake a review of any reasonable accommodation that can be made.

Become Familiar with Tax Incentives and Other Funding Sources for Accommodations

The employer should become familiar with tax incentives and other funding sources for accommodations. Possible sources for assistance in this area would include President's Committee on Employment of People With Disabilities, 1111 20th Street N.W., Washington, D.C. 20036 and Job Accommodations Network of America, Inc., West Virginia University, P.O. Box 6122, Morgantown, West Virginia 26506.

Begin Dialogue with Disabled Persons Organizations

There are a number of organizations established to assist individuals with particular disabilities, such as the National Federation of the Blind. One directory of such organizations is: Directory of National Information Sources on Handicap Conditions and Related Services (1986), GPO Stock Number: 065-000-00254-0, available from U.S. Government Printing Office, Washington, D.C. 20402. In addition, state or local vocational rehabilitation service agencies can also be helpful sources.

Review Current Policies and Procedures for Compliance

Those policies that may be subject to reasonable accommodation are leave of absence policies, absenteeism/tardy policies, benefits, and termination policies and procedures. The company should undertake a review of its entire employment policies, but in particular focus on those policies that may necessitate a reasonable accommodation.

Prepare Personnel/Medical Records Systems for Confidentiality

The Act provides that information collected from a permissible medical examination or inquiry must be collected and maintained on separate forms and separate files and must be treated as confidential. This information should only be shared with:

- supervisors and managers in order to identify restrictions or the employee's work duties or to identify reasonable accommodation
- first aid or safety personnel if the disability might need emergency treatment
- government officials who are investigating compliance with ADA

It is important to note that state workers' compensation laws are not preempted by ADA. Some of these state laws require the collection of certain information for administrative purposes. Therefore, employers may send this required information to state workers' compensation offices or second injury funds and still be within ADA's requirements.

Determine Architectural Accessibility

The employer should begin determining any type of architectural changes that might have to be made to comply with the Act. Helpful information in this regard may be obtained from the American Institute of Architects (AIA). For more information, contact: AIA Public Affairs Department, 1735 New York Avenue, NW Washington, D.C. 20006.

Identify Current Situations That Will Become Violations if Not Addressed

If the employer is aware of a situation that needs to be currently addressed, compliance should be undertaken before a charge is filed with the EEOC.

Comply With All Notice Posting and Recordkeeping Requirements

The ADA requires employers to post a notice that it is covered by ADA *in a format accessible* to applicants and employees describing the applicable provisions of ADA. Obviously, this could include braille notices or other formats for individuals with specific disabilities.

Although the EEOC has not adopted a general requirement that records be made or kept for purposes of enforcing ADA, the EEOC *has* reserved the right to impose recordkeeping requirements whenever they are necessary to accomplish the purposes of ADA.

Employer's counsel should advise the employer to keep employment records such as requests for reasonable accommodation, applications, records regarding hiring, promotion, lay off, termination, rates of pay or selection for training programs for at least one year from the date of the personnel action involved, whichever occurs later. If any charge of discrimination has been filed or an action brought, *all* records must be preserved until final resolution of that action.

Educate Supervisors and Managers Regarding Compliance With Americans With Disabilities Act

All supervisors and managers should be trained in the specifics of the ADA and the do's and don'ts of conducting interviews, and so on. In addition, training programs can be developed to help supervisors and managers address specific needs of workers with disabilities.

41 Defending Veterans Reemployment Rights Cases

The Veterans Reemployment Rights Law protects the jobs of employees entering active military service by requiring employers to restore the employee to his or her former job or a similar job upon the employee's release from military service. The law protects inductees, enlistees, reservists, and National Guardsmen regardless of whether their service was voluntary or involuntary.

The law is administered by the Office of Veterans Reemployment Rights (OVRR) within the Department of Labor. OVRR has the responsibility of investigating cases involving veterans reemployment rights. OVRR does not have, however, any decision-making authority. The OVRR does attempt to settle disputes between employers and returning veterans through voluntary informal conciliation. Employees who have not had their claims resolved through OVRR's conciliation procedures may apply to the United States Attorney's Office to prosecute their claim in federal district court. A federal district court has the authority to require that the employer comply with the Law's provisions and may award damages for loss of wages and benefits.

PRACTICAL POINTS TO CONSIDER REGARDING VETERAN RIGHTS

The primary obligation of an employer is to reinstate the returning employee to his or her previous or similar job, without loss of seniority upon completion of the employee's military service. The employer may require that the returning employee meet the following eligibility conditions for reemployment:

1. ***Previous Job Other Than Temporary.*** The returning employee's previous job must have been more than a temporary position. This eligibility requirement does not mean that probationary employees are considered temporary. Employees who can show that they would have expected to continue indefinitely in the job are not temporary.
2. ***Intent to Perform Military Service.*** The returning employee must have left his or her former job with the intent of performing military service or training. This would include undergoing a pre-induction physical, or other qualifying examination.
3. ***Released Under Honorable Conditions.*** The returning employee must be discharged or released from active duty under honorable conditions.
4. ***Limitation on Duration of Duty.*** Returning employees must not have remained on active duty for more than four years, unless an additional period (no more than one year) is at the request of the federal government.
5. ***Timely Application.*** The returning employee must apply for reemployment within 90 days of separation from military service. If the period of active duty for training is less than twelve consecutive weeks, the returning employee must apply within 31 days after the release.
6. ***Qualified for Job.*** The returning employee must be qualified to perform the duties of the same or similar position. However, employers are required to make reasonable accommodations to the known mental or physical limitations of an otherwise qualified individual with a disability unless the accommodation would impose an undue burden on the employer's business.

CRITICAL RIGHTS THAT AN EMPLOYER MUST RESPECT

If the returning employee meets all of the above listed eligibility requirements, the returning employee is entitled to the following:

1. ***Seniority.*** The returning employee is restored to the seniority he or she would have attained had the employee not left employment for military service.
2. ***Wage Increases.*** The returning employee is restored to the wages, including raises, that he or she would have attained had not the employee left employment for military service. Pay raises that are related to merit or experience are not included.
3. ***Automatic Promotions.*** The returning employees are entitled to the position or rank they would have been promoted had the employee not left employment

for military service, if the promotion was usually granted employees holding same or similar positions.

4. ***Benefits.*** The returning employee is entitled to all the credits that the employee would have attained had the employee not left for military service. The period of military service should be counted as continuous service with the employer when determining benefits such as sick leave, hourly pay, bonuses, vacation, insurance, and retirement benefits.
5. ***Just Cause Employment.*** Returning employees are protected from discharge for one year unless the employer is able to show that the employee was discharged for good cause.

POINTS TO CONSIDER IN DEFENDING A CLAIM UNDER THE VETERANS RIGHTS LAW

If an employer is faced with litigating a case involving an employee returning from military duty, the following checklist of defenses should be considered:

1. The employee's former job was temporary
2. The employee has not received a "satisfactory service" certificate
3. The employee has failed to file a timely application for reemployment (31 or 90 days)
4. The employee left the job originally for a reason other than entering military service
5. The employee is not qualified to perform the duties required of the job
6. The employee would have been laid off had the employee remained employed and not left for military service
7. The employer's circumstances have changed so as to make it impossible to re-employ the returning veteran

(See Chapters 34 through 38.)

VI How to Defend Wage and Hour Cases

42 How to Defend a Wage and Hour Case

The federal wage and hour laws goals have been to provide a minimum standard of living for employees. Two of the most important and comprehensive laws are the Fair Labor Standards Act and the Portal-to-Portal Act. These laws require that an employer pay a minimum wage, pay overtime pay to certain employees, and prohibits the employment of children in certain occupations and limits the number of hours children may work.

FAIR LABOR STANDARDS ACT

The Fair Labor Standards Act (FLSA) was adopted by Congress in 1938 as a means of economic recovery from the Depression by establishing a minimum wage floor and a maximum hour ceiling for employees who were engaged in commerce or the production of goods for commerce, or for employees employed in a business enterprise engaged in commerce or in the production of goods for commerce in any work week. If the maximum ceiling of hours was exceeded for certain employees, employers became required to pay overtime compensation for hours worked in excess of 40 in one work week. In this way, employers were penalized for not spreading their work among a greater number of employees.

The responsibility for the administration and enforcement of the Fair Labor Standards Act lies within the United States Department of Labor. The Wage-Hour Division of that agency issues rules, regulations, and interpretations of the Fair

Labor Standards Act and conducts investigations and compliance reviews. Employees who are entitled to be protected under the Fair Labor Standards Act also have a private right of action to recover minimum wages and overtime compensation. This suit that can be filed by the employee against the employer also would include attorneys' fees and costs and liquidated damages if the violations of the FLSA were found to be willful by the employer.

Employee Coverage Under the Fair Labor Standards Act

In order for an employee to be covered by the Fair Labor Standards Act, there must first exist an employer-employee relationship and the individual employee must personally be engaged in commerce or in the production of goods for commerce ("traditional" or individual basis of coverage) *or* the employee must be employed by an employer in an enterprise engaged in commerce or in the production of goods for commerce ("enterprise" basis of coverage).

The "traditional" or "individual" basis of coverage exists when employees are engaged in interstate or foreign commerce. Activities that constitute "commerce" within the meaning of the phrase "engaged in commerce" are very broadly defined in the FLSA as follows:

> commerce means trade, commerce, transportation, transmission or communication among the several states, or between any state and any place outside thereof.

Courts have also held that employees engaged in activities that merely "affect" commerce are covered by the Act.

Another basis for this "traditional" coverage is if the employee is engaged in the "production of goods for commerce." This coverage extends to manufacturing or packaging goods to be moved in interstate commerce. Also, employees who are involved in the administration, planning, management, supervision, and control of the business that produces the goods for interstate commerce, as well as those employees who perform clerical, accounting, or other business functions for that business are covered. Even if the employee's activities are deemed to be closely related or directly essential to the production process, they are covered.

The concept of "enterprise" coverage extends the wage and hour laws to employees who would not be covered under the "traditional" basis if the employer is an enterprise (usually one or more business unit) that is "engaged in commerce or in the production of goods for commerce." In addition, with exception of certain limited businesses, a dollar volume test that pertains to the gross annual sales of the business must also be met. Whether one or more business units constitutes an enterprise depends on the interrelationship of the activities performed by each unit. Enterprise is defined in Section 3(r) of the FLSA as:

> The related activities performed either through unified operation or common control by any person or persons for a common business purpose, and includes all such activities whether performed in one or more establishments or by one or more corporate

or organizational units including department of an establishment operated through leasing arrangements, but shall not include the related activities performed for such enterprise by an independent contractor.

Therefore, the essential elements of an "enterprise" consist of:

1. The related activities performed;
2. Through unified operation or common control;
3. For a common business purpose.

It does not matter under enterprise coverage that related businesses operate under different trade names.

Once it is determined that a business entity is an "enterprise" engaged in commerce or the production of goods for commerce, an applicable dollar volume test has been set out in the FLSA.

There are, however, certain businesses that only have to satisfy the "commerce" standard in order for enterprise coverage to apply and do not have to satisfy the dollar volume requirements. These enterprises are:

1. Hospitals, nursing homes, and residential institutions that are primarily engaged in the care of the sick, aged, or mentally ill;
2. Pre-schools, elementary or secondary schools, schools for mentally, physically handicapped or gifted children, and institutions of higher education; and,
3. Public agencies.

All other businesses must satisfy an annual dollar volume test to be a covered enterprise under the wage and hour laws.

To determine if an enterprise satisfies this applicable dollar test, annual gross receipts of the enterprise are examined. If the gross receipts are known to be substantially more or less than the cutoff point for the dollar volume test, coverage or exclusion may be obvious. But, if annual gross volume of business fluctuates significantly from year to year or if the business is new, the annual gross volume of sales should be calculated at least until the volume stabilizes.

Determining Compliance with Minimum Wage Requirements. Employees covered by the Fair Labor Standards Act who are not exempt from coverage must receive the stated minimum wage. Currently the minimum wage is $4.25 per hour, effective on April 1, 1991.

Just because the minimum wage specified by the law is stated on an hourly basis, employees may be paid on salary commissions, piecework biweekly, or almost any other basis as long as the wages equal or exceed the minimum wage.

In order to determine if an employee's compensation satisfies the minimum wage requirement of the Act, the work week is the measure used. For example, if an employee works 40 hours in a work week and earns $225.00 dollars, the minimum wage requirement is met, because the employee's hourly rate exceeds the current $4.25 minimum wage ($225.00 / 40 hours = $5.62 hour). However if that same covered employee worked 60 hours in a work week, the minimum wage requirement is not met because the hourly rate is *less* than the applicable minimum wage ($225.00 / 60 hours = $3.75 hour). The FLSA allows employers to include as wages the amount an employee has deducted for the employee's share of Social Security, State Unemployment Insurance, and Federal State and Local taxes. Also, payments the employer makes pursuant to a court order (wage assignments, garnishments) on behalf of or for the benefit of an employee are wages for purposes of minimum wage calculations.

Sub-Minimum and Training Wages. Under some circumstances pursuant to Section 13(a)(7) of the FLSA, covered employees may be paid a wage rate that is less than the statutory minimum wage. Learners, student learners, apprentices, messengers, full-time students, and handicapped workers can be paid at lower rates if they are employed according to special certificates that are issued by the Department of Labor. In addition, teenagers may be paid at a training wage under certain circumstances and as specified in the Act.

State Law on Minimum Wages. Some states have enacted laws that impose a minimum wage greater than or in addition to the FLSA. These state laws are not preempted by the Fair Labor Standards Act. Employers should check for a state law pertaining to the payment of wages.

Definition of Wages. There is no definition in the law for the term "wages", but case law and regulations issued by the Wage & Hour division clearly indicate that wages include more than cash payments for work performed. Other items that may be considered as wages are:

1. Reasonable cost of board, lodging or other facilities furnished to the employee;
2. A portion of tips received by tipped employees; and
3. Taxes collected by the employer that are assessed against the employee.

In contrast, some cash payments made by employers are not considered wages. They include:

1. Benefit plan contributions;
2. Discretionary bonuses;
3. Employee gifts; and
4. Certain premium payments.

Permissible Deductions from Wages. Whether an employer can make deductions from an employee's wages depends on the reason the deduction is being made and whether the deduction would reduce the actual cash payment to the employee *below* the minimum wage rate. Deductions that do not reduce wages below minimum wage are generally allowed. An exception to this rule involves kickbacks. Wages must be paid free and clear and any arrangement that involves the employee paying back a portion of his or her wages strictly for the employer's benefit is not allowed. In addition, there are limitations on deductions in weeks when overtime is worked.

Some of the permissible and most common wage deductions include voluntary wage assignments, loans, advances to the employee, uniforms required by law or by the employer, and employee tax payments (Social Security, Federal tax).

Finally, regardless of the deductions' effect on the net pay, contributions to health or pension plans on behalf of the employee may be taken if the employee voluntarily agreed to the deduction. Also, union dues may be deducted if the deduction is made based on a valid check-off clause in a collective bargaining agreement.

Determining Compliance with Employee Overtime Pay Rates

According to Section 7 of the Fair Labor Standards Act, employees who are not specifically exempt from coverage of the Act are entitled to be paid overtime for each hour worked in excess of 40 in a work week at a rate of not less than one and one-half times their "regular rate of pay." This principle raises three issues for further definition: work week, hours worked, and regular rate of pay.

Work Week. "Work week" is defined in the regulations issued by the wage and hour department as "a fixed and regularly recurring period of 168 hours—seven consecutive 24-hour periods." The work week can start on any day of the week at any hour of the day. Once an employer has established a work week, it is usually intended to be permanent. Any change in the work week cannot be in order to avoid any obligations under the wage and hour laws. Each work week stands on its own.

Hours Worked. "Hours worked" usually includes the time spent by the employee on his or her principal duties and activities as well as any incidental activities. Work performed away from the regular job site or outside an employee's normal shift is usually included as "hours worked." Furthermore, work not requested but "suffered or permitted" will be considered work time if the employer knows or has reason to believe the employee is performing work.

Regular Rate. The employee's regular rate is an employee's hourly rate. So, if the employee is paid in any way other than by the hour, the earnings must be converted to an hourly rate for purposes of computing any overtime that was due. The Fair Labor Standards Act does not require that employees be paid at an hourly rate, but the regular rate must always be re-calculated at an hourly rate in order to determine if the employer has met the obligations of paying the minimum wage and any overtime pay due.

The Fair Labor Standards Act defines the regular rate to include all remuneration for employment paid to or on behalf of, the employee. Therefore, the regular rate includes all cash wages and noncash wages. The Act requires that the following items are to be included in the regular rate of pay calculation, in addition to straight time wage or salary:

1. Non-cash wages in the form of goods, board, lodging, or,
2. Commission payments, and,
3. Nonovertime premium payments and non-discretionary bonus.

Items to be excluded from calculation of the regular rate of pay include such items as:

1. Gifts and payments in the nature of a gift made at Christmas or on other special occasions if the amount is not dependent on the number of hours worked or production.
2. Payment for vacations, holidays, absences, or periods during which no work was performed.
3. Reimbursement for business or travel expenses.
4. Contributions made to employee health and welfare plans.
5. Premium rate paid for overtime work.
6. Extra compensation paid for work done on Saturdays, Sundays, holidays, or the sixth or seventh day of the work week if the premium rate is not less than one and one half times the rate established for the same work performed in non-overtime hours on other days.

The "regular rate" of pay is then determined by adding all remuneration received by the employee, minus any exclusions and dividing that amount by the total number of hours worked during the work week. Overtime would then be calculated by paying the employee one and one-half times the regular rate of pay for all hours worked over 40 in a work week.

SIGNIFICANCE OF RECORDKEEPING REQUIREMENTS UNDER FLSA

Under Section 11(c) of the Fair Labor Standards Act, employers are required to keep records for covered employees. Also, records of exempt employees must also be kept in order to establish the exemption in case of a challenge.

Keeping Records of Information Required

The DOL does not mandate the form of the records to be kept, but sets forth the type of information to be preserved. An employer may not avoid liability in a wage and hour case by arguing that there is insufficient evidence of the claimed hours worked because the employer failed to maintain the required records. In fact, the failure to maintain the required records may even create a presumption in favor of the employees involved in a possible investigation.

With respect to an employee subject to minimum wage and overtime, the following records must be kept:

1. Employee's name in full including any identifying name or symbol used in place of the name on any other records;
2. Home address (with Zip Code);
3. Date of birth if employee is less than nineteen (19) years of age;
4. Employee's sex, and the occupation in which employed;
5. Time of day and day of the week on which the employee's work week begins;
6. Regular hourly rate of pay and the basis on which wages are paid;
7. Hours worked each workday and total hours worked each work week;
8. Total daily or weekly straight-time earnings or wages;
9. Total weekly premium pay for overtime hours worked;
10. Total additions to or deductions from wages paid each pay period;
11. Total wages paid each pay period; and
12. Date of payment and the pay period covered by payment.

For employees who are classified as executive professional, administrative or outside sales persons, and who are therefore exempt from the overtime requirements, only items 1–5 and 11–12 must be maintained. Also, the basis upon which the exempt employees are paid (bi-weekly, monthly, etc.) must be kept with sufficient detail to calculate each exempt employee's total remuneration for each pay period, including fringe benefits.

Preserving Employee Records

Records must be kept either two or three years depending on the type of record. Any document that is a "payroll record" must be kept for three years. "Supplementary records" must only be kept for two years. These records include among others: time cards or earnings cards which contain daily beginning and ending times when those amounts determine the wages of employees; and records that reflect additions or deductions from wages of the employees.

Posting Wage and Hour Law Requirements

A poster showing the requirements of the Wage & Hour Law must be posted in conspicuous places in the workplace. A general notice poster has been designed by the Department of Labor and some State Department of Labor offices have designed special notices pertaining to the requirement of that state.

Verifying Employment Eligibility (Form I–9)

The DOL is also responsible for inspecting an employer's I-9's. Therefore, an I-9 form should be completed for every employee (not for independent contractors).

UNDERSTANDING THE ENFORCEMENT POWERS OF THE DEPARTMENT OF LABOR

The Wage and Hour Division of the Department of Labor (DOL) has been given the authority to enforce compliance with the Fair Labor Standards Act. In doing so, the DOL is authorized to use the services of state and local agencies for the purpose of ensuring compliance with the FLSA. Furthermore, either the Department of Labor or an affected employee(s) may bring suit for alleged violations of the Act. In fact, the Department of Labor is empowered to seek injunctions preventing further violations of the Act, seek criminal penalties, and monetary relief in the amount of unpaid wages as well as an equal amount of liquidated damages in the case of willful violations. To police compliance with the Act, the DOL has the right to enter an employer's workplace, inspect and copy records, and interview employees. If the investigation reveals a violation of the Act the DOL has the authority to demand monetary payment and monitor payment of monies to the affected employee(s).

In addition, a two-year statute of limitations applies to the recovery of backpay, except in cases of willful violation, in which case a three-year statute applies. Thus, in a typical investigation a wage and hour investigator will request to review records for the past two years. If the investigator determines that the violation may be willful, then he or she may request an additional year of records.

PRELIMINARY CONSIDERATIONS REGARDING WAGE AND HOUR INVESTIGATIONS

The Fair Labor Standards Act provides that authorized representatives of the Wage and Hour Division may investigate and gather data regarding the wages, hours, and other conditions of practices of employment. The investigator has the authority to enter the company's premises and inspect records, copy records, transcribe records, and interview employees. An investigation usually has two purposes: the first, to determine whether the company under investigation is covered by the wage and hour laws, and second, whether the company is in compliance with the Act.

An investigation will usually involve:

- Contact with a wage and hour investigator (who may show up at the employer's place of business unannounced or after making an appointment) that the employer is under investigation.
- Opening conference with company representative.
- Inspection of I-9 forms.
- View of required notices to be posted by employer.
- Request for records for two years (possibly three years).
- Request interview with company representative(s).
- Interview of employees (or former employees).
- Investigator's review of all documents.
- Exit interview with company representative.

Typically, wage and hour investigations are initiated by former sour employee(s) or problem employee(s) or employee advocacy groups or even competitors or labor organizations. In addition, the Wage and Hour Division may have targeted the industry or the investigation may be a follow-up to a previous investigation by the Department of Labor. Wage and hour investigators are not required to advise the company of the reasons for the investigation and in most instances the reason will not be disclosed. However, counsel for the employer should inquire about the reason and in some instances the investigator may reveal to the employer the reason or inadvertently mention that it was a disgruntled former employee who filed a complaint. (As a result, the employer can provide to the investigator information pertaining to the employee. For example, if employee was discharged for drug use, this may undercut the former employee's credibility with the investigator.)

Question the Reason for the Investigation

When contacted by a wage and hour investigator an employer should request review of the investigator's credentials and ask why the employer's place of business was chosen for an investigation. Typically, an employer may request that the wage and hour investigator return at a more convenient time or after the employer has consulted with counsel. The company should consider not automatically turning over records without prior consultation with counsel. (At times, government agents have been impersonated by unscrupulous individuals seeking confidential information about the company.) Counsel can then perform an internal audit and supervise and coordinate with the investigators matters such as the production of records, interviewing of employees, and taking of employer affidavits, if deemed necessary by the investigator. In addition, in this interval the employer can complete I-9 forms and post notices if not already done.

Confer with the Investigator

Once entry is allowed (and usually the marginal benefits that may accrue from the absolute refusal of allowing entry are outweighed by the risk of an investigator undertaking a much more rigorous inspection if a subpoena is necessary), counsel for the employer should engage in an opening conference with the investigator. Typically, a wage and hour investigator will:

1. Advise the employer that the purpose of the visit is to make an investigation to determine compliance with federal wage and hour laws
2. Request to inspect I-9 forms on all employees
3. Advise the company of the scope of the investigation
4. Detail the records and documents to be reviewed
5. Request the employer's permission to conduct interviews with certain management representatives
6. Request of the employer to make office space available for the investigator's use
7. Advise the employer that at the conclusion of the investigation a final conference will be held to discuss the investigator's findings

Although the wage and hour laws may appear to be rather mechanically applied, there is in fact room for interpretation and application of the facts to an investigator's interpretations. Thus, an employer who can marshall the facts as well as legal arguments will be in a stronger position to respond successfully to an investigator's claim of non-compliance.

STRATEGIC STEPS IN DEALING WITH WAGE AND HOUR INVESTIGATIONS

In responding to a request for an investigation by a wage and hour agent, counsel for the employer should consider the following action:

- Conduct a telephone conference with the wage and hour investigator to elicit information about the investigation including any problem areas that the investigator may already be aware of;

- Advise the employer to, if not already done so, complete all I-9 forms and copy all employees' I-9's for presentation to the investigator when requested;
- Advise the company to post all required federal and state posters;
- Conduct an internal audit of the company's wage and hour practices prior to the time for the date set for the opening conference (usually counsel will be able to delay the investigation by several days, if not several weeks). The internal audit should focus on any issue discussed with the wage and hour investigator by phone or on any issue that counsel may discover during his or her discussion with company representatives or review of any documents. Counsel should generally focus on the following issues:

    1. Is the employer and/or employee covered by the wage and hour laws?
    2. Is there an employer-employee relationship (as opposed to independent contractor)?
    3. Determine which, if any, employees may be exempt from the minimum wage or overtime requirements.
    4. On non-exempt employees determine whether the company has complied with wage and hour requirements.

This early internal audit is very useful to a company in order to present the best possible case to an investigator. Without this initial audit, sometimes investigators will "grab" documents and, without necessarily getting all the facts (due to the fault of the employer), make an early determination of liability. Now the employer has to dig out of a hole which is much more difficult than convincing the investigator on the front end that there is no liability. Furthermore, this also gives the employer an opportunity to assess liability; and if it is clear that there will be liability, attempt to reduce that liability. In those instances where an employer may know that they are in violation of the wage and hour laws, counsel for the employer should advise and assist the company in getting into immediate compliance with the law. Then, of course, if the investigation takes several weeks or several months, the amount of backpay liability may be reduced because the relevant statute of limitations for non-compliance has been reduced.

Meeting with the Investigator

Counsel, after an audit, is prepared to meet with the investigator. During this opening conference, counsel for the employer should take notes. In particular, counsel for the employer should determine exactly what the investigator is requesting to review and the scope of the investigation. More specifically, if at this point the investigator is aware of the specific issue, elicit all information from the investigator as to why there may be a problem for the employer. At this initial meeting counsel should also have available (if requested) copies of all I-9's for company employees. In addition, in the event that the wage and hour investigator wants to "view" for notices, counsel should make sure that all notices have been properly posted; particularly those that deal with wage and hour laws. During this meeting the investigator will request records going back two years (possibly three if the investigator believes the violation is willful). In summary, during this initial meeting counsel should elicit as much information from the wage and hour investigator as possible, including specifically what records the investigator wants to review. Typically, counsel will advise the investigator that the records will be gathered and that they will be made available at a later date to the investigator either at the company or at counsel's office.

At the next meeting, in which records are produced, counsel should again have an opening conference with the wage and hour investigator and provide copies of requested information (although counsel will want to have available the original in the event that the wage and hour investigator requests to review the original of any document). In the event that the wage and hour investigator desires to copy certain documents, counsel should supply the wage and hour investigator with some method to mark (such as paper clips to show what documents the investigator desires to have in his or her file) the documents to be copied. In this way, counsel can know exactly what documents will be contained in the wage and hour investigator's file.

The wage and hour investigator may also request to interview or take the affidavit of a management representative. Counsel for the company has the right to be present during this investigation and should interview the management person prior to his or her interview with the wage and hour investigator. Of course, the individual needs to be told to tell the truth to the wage and hour investigator. However, an initial interview is helpful in reviewing job responsibilities and duties with a management representative. Furthermore, the wage and hour investigator may already be interviewing former employees or have requested names, addresses, and telephone numbers of employees. Counsel for the employer may want the company to advise its employees that a wage and hour investigator is present and he or she may be interviewed by the wage and hour investigator. It must be emphasized that at no time should the company in any way intimidate or coerce employees or retaliate against any employee who has cooperated in any investigation.

Counsel should also request that the investigator notify counsel of any compliance problems even prior to the exit interview. As a result, counsel can be marshalling any additional facts to argue that the company is in compliance before the investigator has completed the investigation.

Conducting the Exit Conference with the Investigator

Once the wage and hour agent has completed the investigation, there will be an exit conference with the employer or counsel for the employer. At this meeting the investigator will advise the company of his or her findings and, if non-compliance is determined, the amount of backpay liability. Counsel should make detailed notes and also request a copy of any notes or wage transcriptions sheets that the investigator is willing to provide. In most instances wage and hour investigators will provide counsel with their transcription sheets showing the period of time under investigation and the amount of backpay allegedly owed. Counsel should review with the investigator the following:

- Each person allegedly owed backpay
- Amount of backpay for each person
- The reason for backpay liability (e.g., non-compliance because the person is not exempt as an administrator)
- The legal criteria employed by the investigator to reach his or her conclusion
- The specific facts relied upon by the investigator in determining non-compliance
- The method of calculation used by the investigator in arriving at backpay liability
- Specific information relied upon in making the calculations (e.g., company had no records and employees say they worked 50 hours a week)
- The total amount of backpay

Once reviewed with the investigator, counsel should take this opportunity to either convince or create doubt in the investigator's mind regarding whether there is any violation or non-compliance on the part of the company. In addition, this may be the time to begin discussing steps for compliance as well as how the matter will be resolved. Set forth in the next section are those defenses that will be typically asserted by an employer either during investigation or in a lawsuit.

SIGNIFICANT DEFENSES AN EMPLOYER MAY ASSERT IN A WAGE AND HOUR CASE

In the typical wage and hour case the Department of Labor (or an aggrieved employee) will assess:

1. Coverage under the act
2. An employer-employee relationship
3. Violation of the Fair Labor Standards Act

4. Actions commenced within the applicable statute of limitations
5. Good faith defense

Thus, counsel for the employer will want to determine whether each of the above requirements can be met by the Wage and Hour Division or the plaintiff in a wage and hour case.

The Defense of No Coverage

As previously mentioned, the Fair Labor Standards Act has three bases for coverage. Employees are covered if they are:

- engaged in interstate commerce
- engaged in the production of goods for commerce
- employed in an enterprise engaged in commerce or the production of goods for commerce

Each of these bases for coverage is discussed in the following paragraphs.

Employees Engaged in Interstate Commerce. Although the Wage and Hour Division takes a rather expansive view of "engaged in commerce," counsel for the employer should carefully review the employee or employees' work. Although in most instances the employee will be covered, a careful review may indicate non-coverage or at least create a question regarding coverage that may assist counsel in a more favorable resolution of the case.

Employees Engaged in the Production of Goods for Commerce. A second basis for coverage includes those employees who are engaged in the "production of goods for commerce." Again, the Wage and Hour Division gives a very expansive definition to these words and even though an employee is not directly engaged in "production," the employee will still be covered if those activities are closely related or essential to the production process. Thus, in those instances in which an employee's job duties are remote to "the production of goods," counsel may assert lack of coverage. And even if the investigator is not convinced, it may assist in selling the Wage and Hour Division enough uncertainty to obtain for the company a more favorable resolution of the matter.

Employees Employed in "an Enterprise Engaged in Commerce or the Production of Goods for Commerce." Employees who are not otherwise covered, will be covered if they work for an employer who meets the enterprise requirement. Under this basis of coverage all of the employees of a company may be covered regardless of whether they meet the other two bases for coverage. In addition to meeting the requirement of being a "enterprise," there are dollar volume tests that must be met. Thus, counsel for the employer will want to determine whether there is "enterprise" coverage and again, if any doubt whatsoever, this should be asserted as a defense if for no other reason then to sell uncertainty to obtain a more favorable settlement.

Defense of No Violation

There are numerous exemptions available under the wage and hour laws and counsel for the employer must undertake a careful review of each exemption to ascertain whether a specific exemption can be raised as a defense in a wage and hour investigation. Again, an internal audit and review by counsel for the employer will determine whether an exemption is available or, in any event, whether counsel can in good faith assert an exemption, thereby creating doubt in the investigator's mind, either resulting in no liability, or if enough doubt is raised to result in a more favorable settlement. A form such as the one depicted in Exhibit 42–1 (pages 404–408) will assist counsel in making this type of determination.

Statute of Limitations Defense

Actions for wages under the Fair Labor Standards Act must be brought within two years of their accrual except in those instances where there is a "willful" violation, then the statute of limitations is three years. Thus, it is important to review with the Department of Labor investigator the period of time under investigation. Depending upon the circumstances, in some instances where counsel finds that an employer has undoubtedly violated the wage and hour laws, the employer should be urged to get in immediate compliance and then, if significant sums of money are involved, may wish to defer as long as possible the resolution of the matter.

Defense of No Employer-Employee Relationship

Independent contractors who are not employees under the Fair Labor Standards Act are not subject to the Act's provisions. This distinction is extremely important since misclassification of an employee as an independent contractor may not only subject an employer to violations of the Fair Labor Standards Act, but will also subject the employer to liability under the Internal Revenue Act as well as other state and federal unemployment and workers' compensation laws. Thus, counsel for the employer must understand the distinction between an employee and independent contractor. A misclassification by the employer, either intentionally or unintentionally, can result in enormous unexpected legal liability in both the employment and tax law areas. Merely labelling someone an "independent contractor" does not make it so. In making the distinction, the ultimate concern is whether, as a matter of "economic reality," the individual depends upon

EXHIBIT 42-1

Sample Form for Determining Whether an Employee Is Exempt from Wage and Hour Laws

NAME: ____

JOB DESCRIPTION

POSITION TITLE: ____________________________________

POSITION SUMMARY

____

____

____

____

____

____

QUALIFICATIONS

EDUCATION REQUIRED ____

____

____

____

TRAINING AND EXPERIENCE REQUIRED ___________________________

____

____

KNOWLEDGE REQUIRED _______________________________________

____

____

____

MAJOR DUTIES AND RESPONSIBILITIES

(Include percentage of time spent on each major duty)

POSITION RELATIONSHIPS

SUPERVISED BY ______________________________

NUMBER AND JOB TITLES OF OTHER POSITIONS SUPERVISED (Include percentage of time spent in supervising others): ______________________________

MATERIALS AND EQUIPMENT UTILIZED

____

____

____

PHYSICAL DEMANDS

____

____

____

Salary $ ______________ per ____________________

Is employee "docked" for missing work? ____________________

Does employee ever work over 40 hours per week? ________________

Executive Exemption

a) Does employee's primary duty consist of management of the enterprise or a customarily recognized department or subdivision? ______ Which department or subdivision? ______________________________

b) Does employee customarily and regularly direct the work of two or more other employees? ______

c) Does employee have the authority to hire or fire? ______ If not, are employee's suggestions on hiring, firing, advancement, and promotion given particular weight? ______

d) Does employee regularly and customarily exercise discretionary powers? ______ In what areas? ____________________ ________________

____

e) Does employee devote more than 20% of his/her hours worked to activities which are *not* directly and closely related to work described in paragraphs a–d above? ______ If so, does he/she devote as much as 40% of hours worked to activities *not* directly and closely related to work described in paragraphs a–d above? ______

f) Is employee in sole charge of an independent establishment or physically separated branch establishment? ______ Does employee own at least 20% of the Company? ______

Administrative Exemption

a) Does employee's primary duty consist of office or non-manual work directly related to management policies or general business operations of the Company or its customers? _______

b) Does employee customarily and regularly exercise discretion and independent judgment? _______ In what areas? ______________________________

____

____

c) Does employee regularly and directly assist a proprietor or bona fide executive or administrative employee? _______ If so, give that person's name and job title ______________________. Does employee perform under only general supervision work along specialized lines requiring special training, experience, or knowledge? _______ If so, describe the required training, experience, or knowledge. ______________________________

____

____

Does employee execute under only general supervision special assignments and tasks? ______________

d) Does employee devote more than 20% of his/her hours worked to activities *not* directly and closely related to work described in paragraphs a–c above? _______ If so, does he/she devote as much as 40% of hours worked to activities *not* directly and closely related to work described in paragraphs a–c.

Professional Exemption

a) Does employee's primary duty consist of:

1) Work requiring knowledge of an advanced type in a field of science or learning customarily acquired by a prolonged course of intellectual instruction and study (as opposed to general academic instruction or apprenticeship or training in routine mental, manual, or physical processes)? _______ If so, what is the field of science or learning? ____ ______________________ What course of intellectual instruction and study is required? ______________________

2) Work that is original and creative in character in a recognized field of artistic endeavor (as opposed to work which can be produced by a person with general manual or intellectual ability and training)? ____ If so, does the result of the work depend primarily on the invention, imagination, or talent of employee? _______ What is the recognized field of artistic endeavor that is involved? ______________________

b) Does employee's work require consistent exercise of discretion and judgment? _______ In what areas? ____

____

____

c) Is employee's work predominantly intellectual and varied (as opposed to routine mental, manual, or physical work)? _______ Is employee's work of the character that the output or result cannot be standardized in relation to a given period of time? _______

d) Does employee devote more than 20% of his/her hours worked to activities which are *not* an essential part of and necessarily incident to the work described in paragraphs a–c above? _______

Outside Sales Exemption

a) Is employee employed for the purpose of and customarily and regularly working *away from* your premises either making sales or obtaining orders? _______

b) Does employee spend more than 20% of his/her work time in performing work that is *not* incidental to or in conjunction with his/her own outside sales or solicitations? _______

---

someone else's business for the opportunity to perform his services, or if he is in business for himself. Typically, "employees" work for wages and salaries under direct supervision while "independent contractors" undertake to do a job for a price, decide how the work will be done, may hire others to actually do the work, and depend for their income, not upon wages, but upon the difference between what they pay for goods, materials and labor, and what they receive for the end result. See *Brock v. Superior Care, Inc.*, 28 WH Cases 940 (2nd Cir. 1988).

There are many different factors or tests used by the courts in order to make this determination, but generally, they have looked at the six criteria described in the following paragraphs. Neither the presence nor absence of any *one* of these particular factors is dispositive on the determination of the issue.

1. Whether the work is an integral or essential part of the employer's business. This relates to the type of work performed by the individual. If the individual is doing exactly the same type work that the employer is engaged in, this would suggest an employer-employee relationship.
2. The worker's opportunity for profit or risk of loss and his or her investment in the business. Where the individual provides the necessary tools and

materials to do the job (i.e., his or her investment in the business), he or she will more likely be viewed as an independent contractor. If the individual has the authority to set the rates he or she will charge for his or her services and risks a financial loss or has an opportunity to profit after all expenses are paid, these facts will also tend to support the conclusion that the individual is an independent contractor.

3. The permanence of the working relationship, which may be indicative of "employee" status. If the relationship is transitory and the individual transfers his or her services to other organizations following the completion of work for the particular business, then this suggests the relationship is one of an independent contractor.
4. The intention of the parties or the relationship which the parties believe they have created. This is another factor to be considered in determining whether the status is that of employee or independent contractor. An employer-employee relationship may be found, however, even where the parties agreed in writing to an independent contractor relationship.
5. The degree of skill, initiative, and judgment required in the particular occupation. Services provided by an individual engaged in work requiring specialized knowledge or skills that may be attained through either recognized courses of instruction or experience may lead to the result that the individual is an independent contractor.
6. The extent to which the employer has the right to control and direct the work of the individual. In general terms, this means that if the employer can dictate only the result of the work, the individual is more likely an independent contractor. In contrast, if the employer can dictate both the means by which the worker will perform as well as the result of the work, then the individual will probably be viewed as an employee. It is important to note that it is the *right* to control the individual and not the actual *exercise* of that right that is the key element in determining an individual's status. Thus, an individual will be deemed an employee if the employer has the right to control the work—even if he or she does not actually exercise that right. The IRS lists a number of factors that may help determine if the right of control by the employer exists which would be indicative of employee status. A summary of those factors includes:
   - whether the worker is required to comply with an employer's instructions regarding when, where, and how to work
   - whether the employer trains the worker
   - whether the employer requires that the worker render the services personally
   - who hires, pays, and supervises assistants for the worker
   - whether the employer establishes set hours of work
   - whether the worker does the work on the employer's premises

- whether the employer requires the worker to regularly submit written or oral reports
- whether payment to the worker is by the hour, week, or month rather than by the job or on commission
- whether the employer pays business and/or travel expenses of the worker
- whether the employer furnishes tools and materials for the worker

In general, the Wage and Hour Division (or a court) will look closely at the employer's right of control in order to make a determination on this issue. However, the other factors listed above will also be considered in making the ultimate decision. The sheer number of factors to be considered makes it almost impossible for a routine formula to be applied. The dilemma with the number of factors involved becomes compounded by the fact that the various factors must be weighed differently and the fact that different factors are considered more important under different laws. Sadly, an individual can be considered an independent contract under some laws and an employee under others. It is clear, however, that the courts will look at the circumstances of the whole activity and of the total relationship between the employer and the individual when making this crucial distinction. See *Donovan v. Dial America Marketing, Inc.*, 757 F.2d 1376 (3d Cir. 1985); *McLaughlin v. Seafood, Inc.*, 861 F.2d 450 (5th Cir. 1988).

The IRS has available a form that provides help in making the distinction. This form SS8 is useful in helping counsel to determine (even in a wage and hour case) whether a worker is an employee or independent contractor.

Good Faith as a Defense

It is important to note that an employer, except in very limited circumstances, cannot defend on the grounds that it did not intend to violate the law. Wage and hour cases are typically viewed like strict liability cases and intent or state of mind of the employer is not relevant except if the employer can assert that the action taken in good faith was in reliance upon a written ruling of the wage and hour administrator. In these instances the employer must also show that his or her reliance was "in conformity" with the wage and hour ruling. Thus, if there are any distinctions between the specific facts of the company's case and the factual circumstances set forth in the ruling, the defense will be meritless. Second, good faith is a defense available in actions in which liquidated damages are pursued. In these instances a court may deny or reduce liquidated damages and this defense is not tied to reliance on an administrative ruling.

43 Defending Claims Under the Equal Pay Act

The Equal Pay Act (EPA) was an amendment to the Fair Labor Standards Act in 1963. This statute provides that it is unlawful for an employer to discriminate on the basis of sex in the wage rates of male and female employees performing jobs which require equal skill, effort and responsibility and which are performed under similar working conditions. Employees may be paid different wages, however, if the differential is based on one of the exceptions provided in the statute.

Since July 1, 1979, the responsibility and authority for the administration and enforcement of the Equal Pay Act has been with the Equal Employment Opportunity Commission (EEOC). This authority previously was reposed with the Department of Labor, but was transferred pursuant to the Reorganization Plan No. 1 of 1978 by President Jimmy Carter.

Generally, the Equal Pay Act applies to employees who are subject to the Fair Labor Standards Act. However, employees who are bona fide executives, administrative professionals or outside sales persons who are exempt from the minimum wage and overtime requirements of the wage and hour laws are still protected under the Equal Pay Act.

HOW TO DETERMINE EQUALITY OF WORK STANDARDS

Although it is a violation of the Equal Pay Act for an employer to provide disparate pay *or* benefits to male and female employees for "equal work" performed, "equal" has been interpreted by the courts to mean only substantially equal and not "identical." In order to determine compliance with the Equal Pay Act, certain general principles apply when comparing jobs to determine if they are "equal." Job requirements and the duties actually performed determine, in part, whether jobs are equal while job titles or classifications will not be controlling. Four work standards are considered in making the actual determination: skill, effort, responsibility, and working conditions.

Determining Equal Skill

The equal pay work standard does not apply if the amount or degree of skill required to perform one job differs significantly from the degree of skill required to perform another job. The Equal Pay Act's administrative interpretations, as well as the courts, have looked at whether various jobs require equal skill by looking at factors such as experience, training, education, and ability. The skills that are not essential to the performance of the job are irrelevant in determining the equality of jobs. The key is whether the job requires or utilizes the skill and not whether the employee possesses the skill.

Determining Equal Effort

In determining whether equal effort is similar for different jobs, both mental and physical exertion that is needed to perform the job will be measured. The occasional performance of work requiring additional mental or physical exertion will not make jobs unequal that were otherwise substantially equal. Also, different kinds of effort required in the performance of jobs will not make those jobs unequal if the amount or degree of effort exerted is substantially equal.

Determining Equal Responsibility

The term "responsibility" refers to the degree of accountability in performing the job for equal pay purposes. A minor or inconsequential additional responsibility will not make one job unequal from another. Generally, if an employee is required to make decisions that may materially affect the business operations of the employer, that additional responsibility may justify a higher rate of pay. Even an occasional added responsibility may justify a wage increase during the period of actual increased responsibility as long as the higher rate is paid to either sex performing the increased responsibilities.

Determining Similar Working Conditions

A wage differential paid between males and females will not violate the Equal Pay Act if the jobs are performed under substantially different working conditions.

Slight differences will not make otherwise equal jobs unequal. In determining whether the performance of certain jobs involves similar working conditions, the factors considered include both physical surroundings as well as the job's hazards. Some examples for comparison are: inside versus outside work, exposure to outside elements of heat, cold, noise, wetness and hazards from toxic fumes, odors and dust. Working conditions are not similar if the risks of one are greater than the risks of the other.

PERMISSIBLE EXCEPTIONS FOR WAGE DIFFERENTIALS

The Equal Pay Act *only* prohibits wage differentials that are based solely on sex. However, the Act does not extend to differences in wages paid if those differences are based on factors *other than sex*, such as those described in the following paragraphs.

Seniority Systems

An employer will not violate the Equal Pay Act when wage differentials are based on seniority if the system is applied equally to employees of both sexes. While the term seniority "system" seems to contemplate a formal or existing plan, the plan need not be—it just must be an established plan and one where the terms and conditions have been communicated to the affected employees.

Merit and Incentive Programs

Again, these programs need not be formal or written, just clearly communicated to the affected employees. Incentive payments, performance raises, and production bonuses paid will not violate the Equal Pay Act as long as they are applied equally without regard to the sex of the employee. A merit system will not violate the Act as long as the system measures earnings based on a predetermined set of criteria such as quality or quantity of production. A merit system that is based solely on the subjective opinion of a manager or supervisor, for example, fails to qualify as a bona fide system for equal pay purposes.

Training Programs

A bona fide training program may qualify as an exception to the equal pay work standards and be used as a basis to pay a wage differential as long as it is applied without distinction between the sexes. To be a bona fide training program, the Equal Employment Opportunity Commission has indicated that the program must:

- Be open to both sexes;
- Have an ascertainable beginning and ending point with ultimate advancement to a higher position depending on completion of the program;
- Have definite form and content; and,
- Reflect a reasonable progression from simple tasks to more difficult or complicated ones.

Shift Differentials

Generally, shift differentials do not constitute dissimilar working conditions for equal pay purposes. Night-shift employees are frequently paid higher wages than day-shift employees, since night shifts are usually considered less desirable and higher wages must be paid to attract employees to this shift. This difference will not violate the Equal Pay Act as long as the shift differential is not paid based on gender.

Red Circle Rates

This term has been used to describe certain higher-than-normal wage rates which are paid for reasons unrelated to sex. Typically, "red-circling" is used in connection with a temporary reassignment or situations involving permanent part-time or temporary employees. As long as the reassignment is temporary, the "red-circling" of the wage will account for any wage differentials that occur between members of the opposite sex.

Miscellaneous Factors

There are other miscellaneous factors which may justify a wage differential based upon a factor other than sex. Some of these include:

- Status as a probationary employee; and
- Status as a part-time employee.

PRACTICAL STEPS TO COMPLY WITH RECORDKEEPING REQUIREMENTS OF THE EQUAL PAY ACT

Employers subject to the Equal Pay Act are required to preserve and maintain records and documents that relate to the payment of wages, wage rates, job evaluations, incentive systems, merit systems, seniority systems, and any records or documents that would explain the basis for paying differentials in wages. A violation of the recordkeeping requirements of the law involves consequences that vary according to the nature of the violation. Some violations are classified as willful falsification. This is an offense for which a criminal action may be brought. The non-willful failure to keep records is a civil action and will deprive an employer of any defenses he or she might have. Difficulty in keeping records is no excuse for the failure to keep records as required by the law. Records maintained must be kept for a period of at least two years.

PRACTICAL POINTS TO CONSIDER IN DEFENDING AN EQUAL PAY ACT CLAIM

Once a charge is filed, the EEOC will conduct an investigation. (See Chapters 34–38.) The employer who must defend an equal pay lawsuit may show that the wage differential paid was based on one of the permissible exceptions provided in the statute. Differentials that can be justified based on a seniority system, merit-pay system, productivity system, or training programs are fairly specific and are easier to show. However, the catch-all exception, where differentials are based "on factors other than sex," is much broader and generates considerable interpretation. If an employer can establish any one of these affirmative defenses, however, he or she may not be found in violation of the Equal Pay Act.

Another affirmative defense the employer may choose to use is that the action was not timely filed with the EEOC. Currently, an action under the Equal Pay Act must be brought within two years from the time of the alleged violation and within three years if the violations of the Act were willful. However, some courts have held that violations of the Equal Pay Act where wage differentials are based on sex constitute "continuing violations." Therefore, the two- and three-year statute of limitations periods do not necessarily run from the date the employer allegedly failed to pay the proper wage amounts.

Other possible defenses that an employer may raise are:

- The employer is exempt from the Act
- Proper wages were paid
- The employer relied in good faith on applicable or administrative rulings and regulations

It is important to note that an employer found to have willfully violated the Equal Pay Act may be subject to criminal prosecution with significant fines and possible imprisonment as potential consequences.

44 How to Defend Against a Child Labor Law Violation

The Fair Labor Standards Act contains essentially two prohibitions in the use of child labor. First, the Fair Labor Standards Act prohibits the employment of any "oppressive child labor" in commerce, in the production of goods for commerce, or in any enterprise covered under the Act by virtue of being engaged in commerce or in production of goods for commerce. This prohibition encompasses both the traditional and enterprise bases for coverage.

Child labor is considered "oppressive" if a minor is employed below the minimum age specified for a particular occupation. Generally, the minimum age in order to be employed is sixteen years of age although in some dangerous or hazardous occupations the minimum age may be eighteen years of age.

The second prohibition is more indirect in nature. The Act contains a section called the "hot goods provision" where producers, manufacturers, and dealers are *prohibited* from shipping or delivering for shipment any goods produced where, within 30 days prior to the removal of the goods any oppressive child labor was used. This provision applies no matter in what capacity the child was employed.

Unless there is an order or regulation issued by the Secretary of Labor, children below the age of sixteen may not be employed in a business establishment. There are some exceptions, however, for children who deliver newspapers, work in the theater or theatrical fields, agriculture, and some minors who work at home or for parents or guardians.

Certain occupations are deemed as "hazardous occupations" and only those eighteen years or older may work in these occupations. The determination of whether an occupation is hazardous is made by the Secretary of Labor. Seventeen occupations have been deemed hazardous which include construction, demolition, repair, mining, wood-working with power-driven machines, plants that manufacture explosives, radioactive substances, power-driven machines, among others.

Even though age sixteen is the minimum age generally applicable to non-hazardous occupations, there are regulations issued that authorize minors aged fourteen and fifteen to work *if* the working conditions don't interfere with their schooling, health and well-being. Children in this age group may be employed in occupations that do not require a minimum age of sixteen or eighteen as long as the employment is:

1. Performed outside of school hours;
2. Performed between the hours of 7:00 a.m. and 7:00 p.m., except during the summer when children may work until 9:00 p.m.;
3. During the school year, children may work only three hours per day on school days and eight on non-school days; and
4. May not work more than eighteen hours per week when school is in session and no more than forty when school is not in session.

STRATEGIES EMPLOYERS MAY USE TO AVOID CHILD LABOR LAW CHARGES

Employers of minors should:

1. Post in a conspicuous place on the business premises a notice of the Child Labor Act that is furnished by the Department of Labor;
2. Maintain a separate file for each minor employed which includes (a) an employment application, (b) a copy of the minor's birth certificate or other proof of age, (c) accurate daily time records for all fourteen- and fifteen-year-old minors subject to the Act and (d) any records that could exempt a minor from coverage such as house work in the minor's own home, employment by a parent or guardian in a non-hazardous occupation, newspaper sales or delivery, is a musician or entertainer, or as provided by individual state statutes.

Employers can also protect themselves from child labor law violations by requiring that the minor provide an age certificate. This is an official statement of the minor's age based upon the best available evidence of that age. It is signed both by the minor and the issuing official and is designed to provide reliable proof to an employer of a minor's age. An employer will be protected against unintentional violations of the child labor laws if he or she relies on an unexpired age certificate which meets all wage and hour standards.

DEFENSES TO ASSERT IN CHILD LABOR LAW CASES

Obviously, one of the best defenses an employer's counsel can use against a charge of a violation of the child labor laws is to be able to produce a legitimate copy of a birth certificate or age certificate as proof of the age of the minor involved. With accurate time records kept, an employer's counsel can argue that minors aged fourteen and fifteen did not work during any of the prohibited hours or more than the maximum allowed during school weeks. Another defense is to show that the occupation the minor is employed in is not one of the prohibited occupations that is considered "hazardous." If the occupation is one defined as hazardous, then proof that the minor is at least eighteen years of age would be the best defense for the employer.

SUCCESSFUL COMPLIANCE WITH CHILD LABOR LAWS

If an employer becomes aware there has been a child labor violation, one solution would be to immediately remove the minor from the prohibited occupation or change the hours of work in order that the minor might continue to be employed. Or, if the minor works in an establishment and takes orders for intoxicating beverages sold, the minor could be moved to another position where taking orders for drinks is not required. If the number of hours worked or the time period of the hours is a problem, then the minor's shift could be adjusted to comply if he or she is in the fourteen- to fifteen-year-age bracket.

Again, compliance is the key to avoid trouble with child labor laws.

45 How to Handle Wage and Hour Disputes Regarding Federal Construction Projects

Laws covering employees performing work on federal construction projects are primarily regulated by the following laws:

- Davis-Bacon Act and related laws making the Act applicable to federally assisted construction
- Copeland Act, "Anti Kickback Act"
- Contract Hours and Safety Standards Act

These laws in conjunction with the Fair Labor Standards Act are not mutually exclusive, but rather supplement each other. In addition, there are other similar laws such as Walsh Healy (Federal Supply Contracts) and Service Contract Act (Federal Service Contract) that may be applicable to services or supplies provided for government jobs. The focus here is on work performed on federal construction projects.

The centrally implicated law with federal construction projects is the Davis-Bacon Act, which requires the payment of prevailing wages and fringe benefits to laborers and mechanics employed on public works projects.

There are four requirements that must be met for the contractor to be covered under the Davis-Bacon Act:

1. The contract amount must be in excess of $2,000.00.
2. The contract must be for "construction, alteration, and/or repair" as those terms are defined in the Act.
3. The contract work must be performed on "public buildings or public works of the United States or the District of Columbia."
4. Last, the work must "require or involve employment of mechanics and/or laborers" directly upon the site of the contract work. And, at least one court has held that the mechanics and laborers must actually be working on the project site to be covered. In that case, the court held that a material delivery truck driver who came onto the work site merely to drop off the truck's materials was *not* covered by the Davis-Bacon Act. Generally excluded are executive, administrative professional, and clerical employees. The laborers and mechanics must be employed by a federal contractor or subcontractor in construction-type activity for the Davis-Bacon Act to apply.

Thus, it is of critical importance that a contractor determine whether a construction contract falls under the Act before any bid is prepared. Typically, the contractor can determine this by:

1. Reviewing the prime contract or any subcontracts;
2. Wage determinations included with any contract or subcontract; or
3. If still not certain, the contractor should discuss the matter with the owner or contracting officer directly as to whether the project is a Davis-Bacon project (or possibly a state prevailing-wage job).

If the project is covered, the Davis-Bacon Act requires compliance with its wage determination, overtime requirements of the contract Work Hours and Safety Standards Act, compliance with the Copeland Act's recordkeeping and payroll requirements, and certification that neither the contractor nor subcontractor are currently debarred from performing government contract work. Most significantly, the Davis-Bacon Act requires that an employer pay the minimum wages and any specified fringe benefits for covered laborers and mechanics. Thus, if it is determined that the project is covered by the Davis-Bacon Act, the contractor or subcontractor should carefully review all wage determinations and their required wage rates and fringe benefit requirements, if any.

Contractors and subcontractors should be aware that the area wage determination sets the *minimum* standards for employee wages and fringe benefits. If higher wages are required by, for example, a collective bargaining agreement, the extra compensation will *not* be reimbursed by the federal government.

STRATEGIC STEPS FOR AVOIDING PROBLEMS UNDER THE DAVIS-BACON ACT

It would seem that the requirements of the Davis-Bacon Act are straightforward and would not create any compliance problems for a contractor. However, many contractors, either inadvertently or intentionally, have run afoul of provisions of the Davis-Bacon Act. The following sections describe some of the problems that a contractor may confront.

Problem 1: Failure to Pay the Wage Rates or Fringe Benefits Specified by the Wage Determination

Obviously, the failure of the contractor to pay the wages or fringe benefits and to certify the payroll is sure to draw an immediate complaint by an employee to the Department of Labor. The Department of Labor has a wide range of sanctions including debarment, cancellation of the contract, and, for willful violations, criminal sanctions may be imposed through the United States Attorney General. If there is a delay with payment, it is better practice to discuss the delay, and reasons for the delay, with the contracting officer.

Problem 2: Misclassification of an Employee Resulting in Contractor Paying a Lesser Wage Than That Required by the Wage Determination

A wage determination will contain a number of job classifications and the required pay for each classification. Thus, carpentry work will be paid at the carpenter's rate. Therefore, if a contractor's employee is performing carpentry work, but has been classified as a laborer by the contractor and paid at a lower rate, this will result in liability. If there is any question as to how, for example, carpentry or any other classification is defined, the contractor should discuss the matter with the contracting agency or request definitions through the Department of Labor. This is a common problem for contractors and, as a result, contractors need to monitor this very carefully.

Problem 3: Utilizing an Employee to Perform Work in More Than One Davis-Bacon Classification (Split Work)

A contractor runs a real danger by working one employee in two separate wage determination classifications. Typically, the contractor fails to keep specific and accurate records regarding the amount of time spent doing work in each classification, resulting in the Department of Labor classifying the employee at the higher classification rate, resulting in backpay liability. Therefore, unless the contractor is prepared to keep daily precise records regarding allocation of work of one employee, the contractor should pay the employee at the higher classification rate.

Problem 4: Utilizing the Wrong Wage Schedule

In some instances, it's possible that because of the different types of construction (e.g., building and heavy), more than one wage schedule may be applicable. Contractors must avoid utilizing the wrong schedule for the particular type of work being performed by the contractor. Careful review and, if necessary, discussions with the contracting officer will avoid this problem.

Problem 5: Use of Apprentices, Trainees, or Helpers

It is important to note that apprentices and trainees who are employed under a registered, bona fide apprenticeship or trainee program may be paid at a lower rate if certain requirements are met.

The contractor must certify in writing to the contracting agency that an employee is enrolled in an apprenticeship or training program registered with either the Bureau of Apprenticeship Training or a state apprenticeship agency recognized by the Bureau of Apprenticeship Training. In addition, the ratio of apprentices and trainees to journeymen cannot exceed that as designated by the program's requirements. If a contractor works an apprentice or trainee who is registered or who is in a registered program, the wage rate provided for in the program may be used. Employees who are enrolled in uncertified programs must be paid the journeyman rate in the wage determination for the job for which they are performing.

Another area where contractors run into trouble on Davis-Bacon jobs is by using "helpers" when this classification does not appear in the wage determination. Although the Department of Labor has attempted to revise the Davis-Bacon regulations defining helpers as semi-skilled employees who work under the direction of and assisting a journeyman, the efforts to achieve finality on these new regulations have been blocked. Unless and until these new regulations are finally approved, it is imperative that contractors understand the *existing* procedures. That procedure is that "helpers" can be used only if there is a "helper" classification found in the wage determination. The Department of Labor will not include a "helper" classification in a wage determination unless helpers prevail in the area. Helpers do not usually do work commonly done by journeymen and they do not use the tools of the trade, so this classification is rarely found in a wage determination.

Problem 6: Making Improper Deductions from an Employee's Paycheck

Those covered by the Davis-Bacon Act are also covered by the Copeland Act which permits some authorized deductions to be made from an employee's wages. "Authorized deductions" are defined in the Copeland Act as those required by law (i.e., federal and state taxes, Social Security taxes, deductions required by court process to be paid to another, employee contributions made to fund medical hospital care, pensions, deductions for union dues and fees, deductions for cost of safety equipment for employees' personal use, etc.).

Problem 7: Miscalculation of Required Fringe Benefits

Most wage determinations contain provisions for the payment of fringe benefits to laborers and mechanics. Some of the benefits include: medical or hospital care, pensions, retirement life insurance, disability insurance, holiday pay, costs of apprenticeship training programs, etc.

The fringe benefit obligation may be met by allowing the contractor or subcontractor to pay the amount in cash (but, taxes have to be paid), or it can pay a combination of cash to the employee and contribute directly to a bona fide fringe benefit fund on behalf of the employee. It is important to note that although there is some flexibility regarding contribution for fringe benefits, the amount that may be considered as payment toward the fringe benefits under the wage determination must actually represent the cost or contribution rate required to provide benefits for the employees. A contractor may not include amounts paid in for workers' compensation insurance premiums or unemployment insurance premiums as part of the fringe benefits package. Bona fide fringe benefits are items such as hospitalization, medical or life insurance, pension plans, disability insurance plans, etc. A contractor may, with authorization from the DOL, take credit for a bona fide unfunded benefit plan. This credit will probably be approved if the contractor cannot direct or recoup the funds for personal benefit.

Most important, a contractor must make sure that the total paid for wages and bona fide fringes must equal or exceed the wage determination total rate. Furthermore, in determining the employee's base rate of pay for overtime calculation purposes, the Davis-Bacon Act permits the exclusion of fringe benefits. So, if the applicable wage determination requires a base cash wage of $14 an hour plus $2 an hour as a continuation to a health and welfare and a pension plan, for purposes of determining overtime pay for all hours worked over 40 in a work week, the $2 contribution for the benefits is excluded and the employee's overtime pay is calculated on the employee's rate of $14 an hour.

Problem 8: Failure of the Contractor to Obtain a Conforming Rate for a Missing Classification

Occasionally a classification (used by the contractor) is not set forth in the wage determination. Thus, bid documents must be reviewed to determine whether all of the necessary craft classifications are listed for the project. If they are not, the contractor must ask the contracting officer to promptly submit a request to the Department of Labor for the missing classifications. One way to avoid this problem is by not using classifications (if possible) that are not listed in the project's wage determinations. If missing classifications must be used, ask the contracting officer to reach an agreement *in writing* for the missing craft. In making this request it is important for the contractor to show that the work to be performed by the classification is not already in the wage determination and that the classification proposed to be used is utilized in the area by the construction industry. The contractor should supply supporting documentation because this will influence the Department's decision. Failure to supply the information may result in a wage rate that the contractor believes is inaccurate; remember, trying to change a decision already made is more difficult than influencing a decision prior to its making. So, supply the documentation.

HOW TO CHALLENGE A WAGE DETERMINATION

Contractors should have an interest in assuring that wage rates issued are accurate. Therefore, a close review of the wage determinations should be one of the first items on a contractor's checklist.

Any contractor, subcontractor, or other interested person who wants a modification or other change in a wage determination and who has requested the administrative officer authorized to make this modification and the request has been denied, may petition for review of the action taken by that officer.

This petition for review (an original and four copies), accompanied by a statement of service, must be filed with the Wage Appeals Board at the Department of Labor. Also, copies of the petition must be served upon the federal, state or local agency involved; the officer issuing the wage determination; and, any other person or persons reasonably expected to be interested in the position.

The request for review of a wage determination must be "timely" made and whether the request is timely or not depends on the particular facts and circumstances involved. Some of the considerations include the contract schedule of the administering agency, the kind of work involved, and its location. The Wage Appeals Board will not postpone any contract action because a petition for review has been filed.

The petition for review of a wage determination must be in writing signed by the individual requesting review (petitioner) or his or her counsel; identify the wage determination, location of the project and the agency involved; state that the petitioner has requested reconsideration of the wage determination and the grounds for review; include supporting data; and, whether the petitioner consents to the disposition of the questions involved by a single member of the Wage Appeals Board.

The Wage Appeals Board may decline to review any case whenever, in its judgment, review would be inappropriate or is untimely or for other reasons. The Board must decide the case based on the matter contained in the record before it and notify the interested persons of its decision.

HELPFUL HINTS FOR COMPLIANCE WITH DAVIS-BACON REQUIREMENTS

There are specific recordkeeping requirements under the Davis-Bacon Act. Payrolls and basic records relating to a contract covered by the Davis-Bacon Act must be maintained during the course of the work and preserved for a period of three years for all laborers and mechanics working at the site of the project. These records must contain:

- The name, address, and social security number of each employee
- Each employee's correct classification
- Rates of pay (including rates of fringe benefit contributions or costs anticipated
- Daily and weekly number of hours worked
- Deductions made
- Amount of actual wages paid

The contractor must also submit a weekly copy of all payrolls to the contracting agency. This copy must be sent along with a statement signed by the employer or his or her agent indicating that the payrolls are correct and complete, that the wage rates paid are not less than those determined by the wage determination issued, and that the classifications set forth for each laborer or mechanic conform with the work performed. Also, the prime contractor is responsible for submission of copies of the payrolls of all subcontractors. The contractor must make the required records available for inspection by the authorized representatives of the contracting agency and the Department of Labor and permit representatives from those agencies to interview employees during working hours on the job.

In addition, every contract covered by the Davis-Bacon Act must contain a stipulation that the scale of wages to be paid must be posted by the contractor in a prominent and accessible place at the site of the work.

PRACTICAL POINTS TO PONDER FOR FAILURE TO COMPLY—SANCTIONS

A number of sanctions may be imposed for non-compliance with the requirements of the Davis-Bacon Act. Every contract must contain a stipulation that enough of the accrued payments as considered necessary by the contracting officer to pay laborers and mechanics the difference between the required wage rates under the contract and the rates they may actually have received may be withheld from the contractor or subcontractor. According to Department of Labor regulations, in the event a contractor or subcontractor fails or refuses to comply with the labor standards required by Davis-Bacon, the agency may cause the suspension of payment until such time as the violations are discontinued or until sufficient funds are withheld to pay the employees the wages to which they are entitled.

There may be criminal sanctions if the Department of Labor finds substantial evidence that any violations of the labor standards classes are willful and in violation of a criminal statute. In those cases, the matter must be forwarded to the United States Attorney General for prosecution.

Another sanction may be the cancellation of the contract. Every contract within the scope of the Davis-Bacon Act must contain the provision that in the event it is found that any laborer or mechanic employed by the contractor or subcontractor has been or is being paid a wage rate less than the rate required by the contractor, the government may, by written notice to the contractor, terminate his or her right to proceed with the work and then proceed with the work, in part, at the contractor's expense.

A final sanction available for non-compliance is debarment. Either the contracting agency or the Department of Labor may recommend debarment to the United States Comptroller General. If debarment is imposed, the contractor and any firm, corporation, partnership, or association in which he or she has an interest, is excluded from government contracting or subcontracting for a period of three years. This procedure is effected by the Comptroller General circulating a list of all the names of persons or firms who have been found to have disregarded their obligations to employees and subcontractors.

VII How to Defend Employment Safety and Welfare Cases

46 Strategic Steps to Avoid Violation of Plant Closure Laws

The Workers Adjustment and Retraining Notification Act (WARN) requires employers to give 60 days' notice before closing a facility or implementing a mass layoff. The Act applies to employers who employ either:

1. 100 or more employees excluding part-time; or
2. 100 or more employees, including part-time, who in the aggregate work at least 40,000 hours per week not including overtime.

Part-time employment is defined under the Act as an employee who averages less than twenty hours per week or has been employed for fewer than six of the twelve months preceding the date notice would be required.

What Triggers the Notice Requirement. Covered employers must provide sixty days' notice of a plant closing or mass layoff. A plant closing is any permanent or temporary closing of a single site of employment or one or more facilities within a single site if an employment loss results for fifty or more employees, excluding part-time employees.

An employment loss means an employment termination other than a voluntary quit, retirement, or discharge for cause. An employment loss means a layoff which exceeds six months and a reduction of work hours by more than 50% during each month of any six-month period.

A mass layoff is a reduction in force that results in an employment loss for at least 33% of the employees at the single site excluding part-time employees, that affects at least fifty employees excluding part-time. By way of example, if 33% plus of the employees were laid off, but the number of employees totaled less than fifty, the notice provisions would not be triggered. If, for example, 200 employees were laid off, but the percentage was less than 33% of the overall workforce, the notice requirements would not be triggered. The Act provides further, however, that if 500 or more employees are laid off, excluding part-time, the notice requirement is triggered regardless of the percentage affected.

The notification requirement for plant closing and mass layoff apply where the employment loss occurs within a thirty-day period. For example, if 250 employees are laid off the first of the month and three weeks later 250 more employees are laid off, all 500 employees would be entitled to 60 days' advance notice under the Act. In addition, if the employer laid off two or more groups at a single site that were each less than the specified number or percentage, but which in the aggregate trigger the notice requirement, and which occur within any ninety-day period, shall constitute a mass layoff or plant closing unless the employer can show that the layoffs were the result of a separate and distinct cause and were not an attempt to evade the Act. In other words, an employer cannot attempt to evade the notice requirements by laying off employees a few at a time over a 90-day period.

Exclusions and Exemptions. The notice requirements are not applicable to situations where the closing or layoff results from a relocation or consolidation if prior to the closing or layoff:

1. The employer offers to transfer the employee to a different location within a reasonable commuting distance with no more than a six-month break in employment; or
2. The employer offers to transfer the employee to another location, regardless of distance, with no more than a six-month break in employment and the employee accepts within thirty days of the offer or within thirty days of the closing or layoff.

The Act shall not apply to a closing or mass layoff if either constitute a strike or lockout not intended to evade the Act. Notice is not required when permanently replacing an employee deemed to be an economic striker under the National Labor Relations Act.

The notice provisions do not apply if the closing or layoff is the result of the completion of a particular project, where the employees were hired with the understanding that their employment duration was limited to only as long as it took to complete the particular project or undertaking. Employers seeking to rely upon this exclusion should be sure to have the employee sign a written statement of understanding.

Notice may be given less than 60 days in advance under the following circumstances:

1. If at the time notice was required for a closing the employer is actively seeking capital or business which if obtained would enable the employer to avoid or postpone the closing. In order for this exception to apply, the employer must be also able to show that it had a reasonable good faith belief that giving the notice would prevent the employer from obtaining the needed capital or business.
2. If at the time notice should be given the plant closing or mass layoff is caused by business reasons not reasonably foreseeable at the time the notice was required.
3. If the plant closing or mass layoff was caused by a natural disaster.

PRACTICAL STEPS TO ACHIEVE COMPLIANCE WITH WARNING NOTICE REQUIREMENTS

The 60-day notice should be specific as to the date the layoff or closure will take place. Advance notice must be given to the following:

1. If the affected employees are represented by a labor organization, notice must be given to the representative; or if the affected employees are not represented by a labor organization, then notice must be given directly to all affected employees.
2. Notice must be given to the state dislocated worker unit.
3. Notice must be given to the chief elected official of the local government.

If the employer chooses to mail the notice it should be mailed well enough in advance so that the notice is received 60 days in advance of the closing or layoff. Mailing notice to the employee's last-known address or inserting the notice in the employee's paycheck are acceptable methods of serving notice under the Act's regulations.

UNDERSTANDING SIGNIFICANT PENALTIES UNDER WARN AND OTHER LAWS INVOLVING PLANT CLOSURE

Under WARN

Employees who suffer an employment loss and do not receive 60 days' advance notice as required by the Act have a private right of action and may bring a lawsuit against the employer to recover backpay and benefits he or she would have been entitled had the employment loss not occurred. Of course, this liability to the employee or each employee is limited to 60 days. By way of example, if the employer provided the employees five days' notice of a mass layoff, where the Act required 60 days' notice, the employer may be held liable for 55 days of backpay and benefits for each employee affected under the Act. The Act also limits liability to no more than one-half the number of days the employee was employed by the employer.

Employers may also face liability with respect to the required notice to a unit of local government at a rate of $500 for each day of the violation. This penalty does not apply if the employer pays the employees suffering the employment loss the amount to which they are entitled within three weeks from the date the employer orders the closing or mass layoff. An employer may have its liability reduced in the discretion of the court upon a showing that the employer had reasonable grounds to believe that its acts or omissions did not violate the Act.

In addition, the court in its discretion may allow the prevailing party to recover attorney's fees as part of its costs.

Liability Other than WARN

Employers should be aware that their exposure to liability when confronting a plant closing or mass layoff is not limited to that found under WARN. Employers may also face potential breach of contract claims either based on a written agreement such as a collective bargaining agreement or based upon an employee handbook. There could also be ramifications under the National Labor Relations Act or even Title VII or the Age Discrimination in Employment Act.

In addition, many states have passed their own notice of closure laws that apply to employers that are not covered by the federal WARN statute. Employers should check their own state laws before concluding that they are not covered by WARN and not required to provide advance notice. The number and percentage of employees with an employment loss triggering advance notice are often much less under the state laws than is found under WARN. Some states even require more than 60 days' advance notice.

STRATEGIC STEPS FOR PREVAILING UNDER WARN

In order to prevail on claims brought under the Act, employers should consider the following checklist when faced with a situation involving a plant closure or layoff:

1. Determine whether you are an employer covered either by WARN or the law of your state concerning notice of plant closure or layoff.

2. Determine whether the number of employees affected triggers the advance notice requirement.
3. If advance notice is required, provide the notice in writing. If the notices are mailed, make sure that they are mailed well in advance so that they will be received at least 60 days in advance of the identified date of closure or layoff. Notice letters mailed to union representatives or employees, the dislocated workers unit, and the chief elected official of local government should be sent registered mail/certified receipt requested, so that the employer has proof of when the notice was received. Because some employees may not have someone at their address to sign for the registered letter and may not promptly pick up their registered mail, it is suggested that employers in addition to sending out the registered letter also provide the employees with a letter sent through the regular mail or provide the employee with written notice at the workplace. This could be done through a supervisor or could be included in the employee's payroll check.
4. If the employer seeks to avail itself of one of the Act's exemptions, the employer should still provide as much advance notice as practicable. The employer should have its basis for the exemption well documented as the employer will most likely face the burden of proving the exemption.

47 Strategic Steps to Follow in Defending Against Unemployment Compensation Claims

In 1935, President Roosevelt signed as part of the Social Security Act a federal-state unemployment insurance system that was designed to provide weekly cash benefits to workers who become unemployed because of cyclical or structural changes in the economy. Therefore, an insurance-type fund was established to pay people who became unemployed through no fault of their own. The purpose of this fund was to provide a type of insurance to workers as a budgeting aid, to provide unemployed workers with income while they searched for a new job and to stabilize the overall economy.

Unlike social welfare programs which are based on the need of the recipient, unemployment compensation is provided without regard to the economic condition of the claimant. Each state is responsible for funding its own unemployment benefit costs no matter how severe unemployment may become. State unemployment tax contributions which are not paid out immediately are used to build up the state's reserves.

Each individual state administers its unemployment compensation program, within certain federal guidelines. These benefits are financed by a payroll tax assessed against an employer's defined payroll. The level of the benefit and tax contribution rates vary from state to state and are usually influenced by the number of claims filed.

The eligibility requirements also vary from state to state, but generally, to be eligible a claimant must have worked a specified amount of time in a base period that precedes the claim. The amount of this base period and the level of earnings is established by state law. The work does not have to be with one employer and can include several employers combined.

POINTS TO CONSIDER IN ANALYZING ADMINISTRATIVE REQUIREMENTS

There are several obligations imposed on employers by the unemployment compensation laws. Not only are employers required to pay the payroll tax but also notice posters and several reports are required.

Each state's Unemployment Compensation Division or Department of Employment Security will furnish the employer with the poster which notifies workers that they may become eligible for unemployment compensation if they should lose their job. These posters should be placed where they are likely to be seen by all employees. By posting this information, the employer, under most state laws, is no longer obligated to notify each worker individually of their possible eligibility for benefits if the worker is ever laid off or terminated.

Another preliminary detail is that when any employee is terminated from employment, some states require that each separated employee be provided with a Separation Notice within 24 hours of the separation from employment. These separation notices reduce the administrative costs of processing the claim and enable the Department of Employment Security or other state agency to make a more accurate determination of a claimant's eligibility for benefits.

Another administrative obligation usually imposed on employers is to complete and return to the Unemployment Compensation Division any required benefit-related reports. When an employee files for unemployment, a report form is usually sent to the employer. The employer should complete the form which will ask how many weeks the employee worked, and what the earnings were for those weeks. These facts are then used to determine if the claimant is eligible for benefits. It is at this point that the employer can begin to contest benefits since this form will usually request the employer to indicate any legal reason why the employee is ineligible for benefits. If this report is filed *without* the employer contesting benefit payments, usually the claimant will begin receiving unemployment compensation benefits. The importance of completing and returning this form is obvious—unless the payment of these benefits is contested by the employer, any and all claims will be treated as if the employer has conceded that the employee is eligible for the benefits.

PRACTICAL STEPS IN MINIMIZING UNEMPLOYMENT CLAIMS

Eligibility for unemployment compensation benefits is usually based upon two factors: (1) the employee must have earned enough money in a "base period" to be monetarily eligible, and (2) the employee must have been separated from his or her employment through no fault of the employee.

If an employee can meet the state's monetary eligibility requirements, then a determination of eligibility will depend on the reasons for the separation. Separations reasons include:

Reason 1: Lack of Work

Obviously, an employee who is laid off will undoubtedly be entitled to unemployment compensation benefits, if all other eligibility requirements have been met. A bad practice for the employer is to allow the employee to induce the employer to lay the employee off when in fact the employee had been discharged or the employee was going to quit for personal reasons. Sometimes employers lead with their hearts and as a result issue a layoff notice in order to help out the employee (and also hope that this will somehow minimize the risk of other charges or lawsuits). Aside from the misrepresentation committed on the Unemployment Compensation Office, an employer is also setting itself up for other charges, e.g., discrimination. For example, an employer who hires a replacement for the "laid off" employee may be confronted with a charge of race, sex or age discrimination by the "laid off" employee. The real kicker is when the "laid off" employee has also cajoled the employer into writing a satisfactory letter of reference. Issuing a layoff notice for an employee who is about to be discharged has always been a bad practice; now, however, the practice carries with it even greater dangers in view of the 1991 Civil Rights Act that allows compensatory and punitive damages.

Reason 2: Voluntary Quit

A quit results in disqualification of the employee. A voluntarily quitting may not be a disqualification where the employee can show that he or she has left the job for "good cause connected with his or her work." In other words, if an employee quits his or her job because the employee's spouse is relocating, the employee will be denied unemployment compensation because the quit was not a "work-related good cause." However, in some instances employees will allege that they quit, for example, because they were sexually harassed on the job or the employer's work environment was dangerous. As a result, even though an employee may quit, if the quit is work related and for good cause the employee under many states' statutes may still be entitled to unemployment compensation. In addition, many times employees "quit" when threatened with discharge. In these circumstances an employee may still assert that he or she was discharged by the employer and the issue will then shift from whether the employee quit for good cause connected with his or her work to the issue of whether the discharge was for misconduct related to his or her work. In either instance the issue has a causal connection to whether the separation was work related.

In a typical situation an employer should request that the employee sign a resignation letter or at least confirm the employee's quit in writing. In this way it will make it more difficult for the employee to allege that he or she was "constructively discharged." In addition, there are other circumstances where an employer alleges that an employee quit that may be analyzed under either the quit or discharge criteria. For example, many companies have policies that provide that if an employee is absent a certain number of days without reporting or without notice to the company, the employee will be considered to have quit the job. Under either analysis it is important for the company to have established such a policy and be prepared to submit it to the Unemployment Compensation Office.

Reason 3: Work-related Misconduct.

The next most significant issue regarding eligibility is whether the employee was discharged for misconduct connected with his or her work. Misconduct such as dishonesty, theft, insubordination, etc., are reasons for denying unemployment compensation. If the employee is discharged due to his or her negligence, typically, an employer will need to establish that the negligence was either gross or that the conduct was part of a continuing pattern of negligent behavior. However, in most instances, state agencies and courts will look for the following factors in making a decision as to whether the misconduct was work related:

1. Did the employee violate a written rule or regulation of the employer?
2. Was the employee given warnings prior to his or her discharge?
3. Documentation by the employer (for example, statement of receipts that the employee was aware of the work rules; warning letters; write-ups; etc.).
4. Whether the work-related misconduct was the fault of the employee; for example, this usually is evaluated in "fighting on the job" cases. If the employee was not the aggressor but was deemed defending himself or herself, even though the offense was a dischargeable one under the company's work rules, the employee may still be entitled to unemployment compensation because the employee is "not at fault."

WHY AN EMPLOYER SHOULD PROTEST AND ATTEND A CLAIMANT'S UNEMPLOYMENT COMPENSATION HEARING

Employers, depending upon the circumstances, may take a different attitude toward an employee's unemployment compensation case. Many employers simply do not fight unemployment compensation claims. And, of course, should not do so if it cannot in good faith make an assertion that the employee is not entitled to unemployment compensation. However, in those cases where the employer determines that the employee is not entitled to unemployment, the company should defend. Employees, in addition to filing discrimination claims before agencies or courts, are also suing more frequently for wrongful discharge. Thus, employers may decide to fight an unemployment compensation claim where it anticipates that some other type of charge or lawsuit will be filed as a result of the employer's action against the employee. Obviously, an employer can use the unemployment compensation proceeding to determine the employee's contentions as well as obtain evidence that may result in the impeachment of the employee who changes his or her story in a different forum.

In addition, there is another significant reason why employers should consider responding to and fighting claims that the employer believes are not valid. Plaintiffs' attorneys are now alleging that the issue of whether the employee was discharged for "work-related misconduct" should be binding in subsequent proceedings. The argument is that if the unemployment compensation agency determines no misconduct, that finding should be binding upon any state court or state agency. Plaintiffs' attorneys state that the employer is "collaterally estopped" to argue differently. Although the findings typically are not held to be final and binding in most states, this assertion will be raised and, as a result, employers can no longer disregard unemployment compensation claims or run the risk of going unprepared to such a hearing.

PRACTICAL POINTS TO CONSIDER IN OPPOSING AN UNEMPLOYMENT CLAIM

Generally, when a claim for benefits is filed, a statement is taken from the claimant by the particular state's Department of Employment Security or similar agency. Then, a form that indicates a claim has been filed and that there is a request for separation information is mailed to the employer asking for the reason for the separation. It is very important for an employer to complete and return this information promptly; otherwise, the determination of whether the claimant will receive benefits will be based on the claimant's statement or any other available information. At this point an agency decision is issued after all the information has been received either approving or rejecting the claim. Then, there is a set number of days within which to appeal the decision if either party disagrees with the findings.

An appeal will not interrupt benefit payments if the appeal is from an approved agency decision. However, any benefit payments are, usually, subject to repayment by the claimant if an appeal results in the employer's favor.

If an employer wishes to appeal a decision, he or she should do so at the earliest possible date. An employer should be prepared to present his or her case on the designated date for the hearing. Hearings are typically scheduled as quickly as possible since any delay could increase the amounts of overpayment on an approved claim. It is possible, in most states, to be granted a continuance for the hearing, but these are reserved only for the most compelling circumstances.

At this hearing, which is usually presided over by a referee or judge (or whatever title is bestowed by the state) an actual record of the case is made either by tape or typed transcript. If counsel believes the former employee will also file other charges with other agencies, consideration should be given to having a court reporter present. This record usually forms the basis of review for any further appeals (and possible use for impeachment in other hearings, e.g., NLRB, EEOC).

In order to prevail in an unemployment hearing, the best results are obtained when:

1. The employer has responded to all inquiries and met all deadlines
2. The employer has *prior* to the hearing (if the agency will make it available), reviewed the unemployment compensation file which typically includes statements by the claimants and any notes regarding the initial determination
3. The company prepares its case and attends the hearing as opposed to merely writing a responsive letter
4. Those individuals with first-hand knowledge of the facts are in attendance at the hearing (particularly if the claimant may be testifying to certain facts that are adverse to the employer—the employer will need to determine who can counter such allegations)
5. Prepare exhibits including originals and copies of work rules, warnings, statements
6. If necessary have the custodian of records present in order to introduce the documents in an employee's personnel file

UNDERSTANDING APPEAL RIGHTS OF EMPLOYERS AND EMPLOYEES

In most states, there will exist one last level of appeal available to the employer or claimant from an adverse decision at the agency level. In some states, this body is called the Board of Review. The agency decision usually becomes final within a set number of days, unless a letter indicating the desire for a notice of appeal or an actual notice of appeal form is filed with the review board.

Usually, appeals to this final review board are decided based on the evidence already in the record from the agency hearing previously described, or this board may choose to accept additional evidence in order to enable it to reach a decision. If an additional hearing is scheduled, it is vital that the employer or employer's counsel appear. If a hearing or oral argument is not granted, the parties may be able to submit written arguments. This reviewing board may reserve the right to affirm, modify, or set aside the lower agency's decision.

Finally, in some states, after this review board's decision has become final, an action may be brought in the appropriate state court to seek a judicial review of the decision.

48 Strategies and Techniques in Defending Against OSHA Inspections and Lawsuits

The Occupational Safety & Health Act of 1970 (OSHA) applies to private employers "engaged in business affecting commerce; and requires employers to provide a place of employment free of recognized hazards that are causing or are likely to cause death or serious physical harm to its employees." In addition, employers must comply with promulgated health and safety standards. The Act defines "occupational safety and health standards" as follows:

> "[a] standard which requires condition, or the adoption or use of one or more practices, means, methods, operations or processes reasonably necessary or appropriate to provide safe or healthful employment or places of employment."

OSHA's promulgated safety and health standards are broken down into those applicable to specific types of industries and those applicable to industry generally. Some areas in industry generally include: wiring and electrical, machine guarding, hazardous fumes, storage of flammable materials, fire protection equipment, personal protective equipment, and general housekeeping. These are just examples; there are thousands of standards that may apply. Employers are encouraged to obtain a current copy of the General Industry Standards in order to comply with the requirements applicable to their specific industry by writing to:

United States Department of Labor
Office of Information
200 Connecticut Avenue, N.W.
Washington, D.C. 20210

In addition, the Act prohibits discharging or otherwise discriminating against any employee who files a complaint, instituted, testified or participated in any proceeding, or otherwise exercised any right under the Act. Employees who file complaints alleging discrimination must do so within thirty days of the alleged violations.

Employees have no private right of action to bring a lawsuit under the Act. The Secretary of Labor has the responsibility and authority to enforce the Act's provisions. This applies not only to alleged discrimination claims but also any claim of injury due to unsafe conditions an employee might allege under the Act.

PRACTICAL POINTS TO CONSIDER IN RESPONDING AND DEALING WITH AN OSHA INSPECTION

OSHA gives the Secretary of Labor the authority to conduct investigations and on-site inspections to enforce the employer's obligations under the Act. OSHA expressly provides that employees and their authorized representatives (union) have the right to request an inspection. OSHA may conduct an inspection in response to employee complaints. Inspections may also be conducted as a follow-up to check whether previous violations have been abated. "Programmed" inspections for high-hazard industries are undertaken pursuant to an inspection schedule.

In most cases OSHA does not provide employers with advance notice of an inspection. If the employer refuses entry for the inspection, OSHA may obtain a search warrant and obtain access to the employer's facility. Although employers cannot be penalized for demanding that OSHA representatives obtain a search warrant, there are some practical considerations that militate in favor of consenting to the inspection and not demanding OSHA obtain a search warrant. For example, if an inspector is required to get a warrant, the inspector may suspect a violation and subject the employer to a more thorough inspection than otherwise. Although all inspections must be conducted in a reasonable manner, employers should not underestimate the importance of a good relationship with the investigator.

If the employer for good reason refuses to consent to an OSHA inspection and OSHA obtains a search warrant, an employer may challenge the validity of the search warrant. Very few employers will find it advisable to pursue such a challenge since successful challenges to OSHA warrants have been few. There are essentially two ways to contest the validity of a warrant:

1. Enjoin the issuance of the warrant in federal district court
2. After the warrant is issued, refuse inspection and present your defenses in a civil contempt proceeding brought by OSHA

Before challenging the search warrant an employer should consider the alternatives. Employers with legitimate concerns about an inspection such as the disruption of work, possible revealing of trade secrets, or undue influence on labor disputes should consider seeking a protective order modifying the terms of the inspection. This alternative is less confrontational, yet allows the employer to demonstrate the specific harm that a modification would prevent.

How to Handle an OSHA Inspection

There are a number of things an employer should be prepared to do in the event an OSHA inspector arrives without advance notice. If the employer consents to the inspection, the following checklist should be considered:

1. Request to see the inspector's official credentials. An OSHA inspector should have a U.S. Department of Labor identification with his or her photograph and a serial number.
2. Make a determination as to whether the company will require the investigator to obtain a warrant. Obviously, the company will need to determine whether the potential benefits will outweigh the risk of the possibility of a more rigorous inspection if a warrant is obtained for a search of the premises. For example, if the company knows that there are obvious hazards in the plant, company officials may want to request that the investigator return after first talking with the company attorney, or tell the investigator that they will talk with their attorney and evaluate whether a warrant will be needed. Thus, an employer may be able to buy additional time in order to prepare its facility for the inspection (which includes posting notices required by OSHA).
3. During the initial meeting with the investigator, one member of management familiar with the plant operation, its safety standards, and OSHA standards should be selected as the representative to deal with the OSHA investigator. During this initial meeting the employer representative should appear reasonable and leave the OSHA investigator with as good an impression as possible.
4. Ask what type of inspection will be conducted. It should be either a (1) fatality or catastrophe; (2) a general compliance inspection; or (3) an employee complaint. If the inspection is due to an employee complaint, request a copy of the complaint. In addition to the employer representative talking with the OSHA investigator, there should be another representative present taking notes. These notes are company notes and should not be given to the OSHA officer.
5. Before beginning the investigation, ask which areas will be inspected and which records they need. (OSHA inspectors usually want to see OSHA Forms 101 and 200.) In addition, prior to commencement of the investigation, counsel may want to negotiate limitations on the search. Such limitations

might include confidentiality regarding photographs or samples, and so forth.

6. Designate a management official to accompany the inspector during the investigation. The management official should be warned that anything he or she says can be used against the employer. Without appearing uncooperative, the designated management official should avoid talking anymore than necessary about facility equipment and operations. Management officials should also be careful not to admit to any violations that the inspector may allege during the course of the investigation.
7. During the walk around, make sure that the OSHA inspector complies with all safety procedures for walking through the plant. In addition, in the event that the inspector points out something that can be fixed immediately, try to have a maintenance person available to do the repair and possibly advise the inspector that the problem has been corrected even prior to his or her departure.
8. If the inspector takes photographs during the inspection, the designated management official should request that the inspector explain the purpose of the photographs. After the inspector leaves, the designated management official should document the reasons given for the photographs, and the time and area the photographs were taken. In addition, the company should take its own photographs from the same view as those taken by OSHA. Furthermore, additional photographs from different angles should be taken by the company.
9. Inspectors have the right to interview employees, but only when it will not disrupt work. After the inspector leaves, make notes of what was said by whom during the interview. Be cautioned, however, that it is unlawful to discriminate against an employee for participating in an OSHA investigation.
10. At the conclusion of the investigation, the employer should have an exit conference with the inspector. Counsel should keep complete and thorough notes regarding this meeting. In particular, the inspector should be questioned as to all areas of possible and probable violations. During the questioning, counsel or management representatives must never admit that something is wrong. This is the time to listen to the inspector. At the conclusion ask the inspector what will be required for compliance and make careful notes of the inspector's statement.

PRACTICAL POINTS TO CONSIDER IN CONTESTING CITATIONS AND PENALTIES

If the inspector's report indicates that an OSHA violation has occurred, the area director is required to issue a citation. Citations must be issued within six months of the inspection. The citation and notice of penalty must be written, describe the violation, and identify the rule, standard, or regulation that was violated. The citation must also submit a deadline date for the employer to correct any alleged violation. This is referred to as the abatement period.

The Act provides for various degrees of violations as follows:

1. De minimis violations may be claimed by OSHA where the cited conditions have no direct relationship to safety and health. There is no fine for de minimis violations.
2. Intermediate or non-serious violations are cited where the conditions have a direct relationship to safety and health, but do not raise a substantial probability that death or serious physical harm could result from a violation. The maximum fine for an intermediate or non-serious violation is $7,000.
3. Serious violations are cited if there is a substantial probability that death or serious physical harm could result from the conditions. The maximum fine for a serious violation is $7,000.
4. Repeat violations occur where there has been a final OSHA order issued previously for the same or substantially similar violations. The maximum fine for a repeat violation is $70,000.
5. Willful violations are cited where the employer has knowledge of the regulations being violated and shows a willful or intentional disregard for the Act's requirements. The maximum fine for a willful violation is $70,000.
6. Criminal violations result where a willful violation causes the death of an employee. The penalty provides for a fine of not more than $10,000 or imprisonment up to six months.
7. Posting requirement violations result when an employer fails to post in a conspicuous place the "Safety & Health Protection on the Job" poster and the "Hazardous Chemical Right-to-Know" poster. The maximum penalty is $7,000 for each violation.
8. Failure-to-abate violations result when the employer fails to correct the violations during the abatement period. The maximum fine for failure to abate is $7,000 per day. (Employers who find it impossible to comply with the citation's deadline should file a petition to modify abatement and seek, for good cause shown, an extension of the deadline.)

Employers have fifteen working days after receiving a citation and notification of proposed penalty to file a notice of contest. If the employer fails to timely file a notice of contest the penalty becomes a final order, and the penalty must be paid within thirty days. After the employer has filed a notice of contest the Secretary of Labor must file a complaint within twenty days. The employer has fifteen days to file its answer to the complaint.

In addition to filing a notice of contest, employers may request an informal conference with the assistant regional director. These conferences most often take place with the area director. The informal conference provides the opportunity to (1) clarify what specific standards were violated; (2) seek to modify abatement dates; (3) attempt to have citations withdrawn or penalties reduced; or (4) attempt to resolve any or all disputed issues. Employers should note, however, that the informal conference does not affect or delay the requirement that the notice of contest must be filed within fifteen working days.

The notice of contest should address each citation. If the employer contests some, but not all of the citations, the employer risks that those uncontested citations will become final. Therefore, where the employer has a legitimate defense to each particular citation, it should be raised.

SIGNIFICANT PROCEDURAL AND SUBSTANTIVE DEFENSES AVAILABLE TO AN EMPLOYER

Employer defenses generally fall into either of two categories, procedural or substantive. The following sections describe the more common procedural defenses.

Statute of Limitations Defense

If the citation is not issued within six months of the date of the alleged violation, it is barred by the six-month statute of limitations.

Lack of Reasonable Promptness Defense

Unlike the statute of limitations defense, this defense is not an absolute defense to a citation. The Act provides that citations shall be issued with reasonable promptness after the inspection has found violations. This defense depends on a number of factors in determining "reasonable promptness" such as the reason for the delay, and whether the delay prejudiced the employer. This defense should be raised by the employer at its first opportunity.

Lack of Particularity Defense

The Act requires that violations be cited with particularity. This defense should be raised in circumstances where the citation is not specific enough to give the employer notice of the violation, or the cited standard was not specific enough to let the employer know what corrective steps should have been taken.

Vagueness Defense

This defense applies where the OSHA standard cited is vague and does not provide employers with adequate notice of the measures that are necessary in order to comply.

SUBSTANTIVE DEFENSES

Some of the more common substantive or factual defenses are described in the following sections.

Isolated Incident Defense

This defense applies where the alleged violation resulted solely from an employee's misconduct. In order to prevail on this defense the employer must show the following:

- the violation resulted exclusively from an employee and not a supervisor or manager
- the violation was not observed or performed with the knowledge of a manager
- the employee's conduct violated the employer's well-established, well-publicized, and actively enforced policy or work rules
- the employer must have a safety program that instructs employees in safe and healthful work practices

Compliance Is Greater Hazard Defense

This defense applies when compliance with the OSHA standard would create a more dangerous hazard than the employer's current practices for which it was cited. The employer must be able to show that complying with the standard results in a greater hazard that cannot be eliminated, and for which no alternative means of protection are available.

Impossibility of Compliance Defense

Here the employer must show that compliance is impossible due to the nature of work being performed. The employer faces a very heavy burden in prevailing on this defense.

Lack of Knowledge Defense

In proving serious violations of the Act, OSHA must show that the employer knew or should have known of the presence of the violation. This defense would be applicable where the employer did not and could not with the exercise of reasonable diligence know of the conditions in violation of the Act.

Equipment Not-In-Use Defense

This defense may apply where the equipment or materials involved in an alleged violation are not in use and because of their non-use do not present any safety or health hazard.

TACTICAL CONSIDERATIONS REGARDING OSHA VARIANCES, HEARINGS AND APPEALS

Variances

The Act provides that OSHA may grant variances in limited circumstances in order to permit employers to use alternative means to ensure a safe and healthy work environment. Variances may be obtained for national defense needs or on a temporary or permanent basis. For a permanent variance the employer must show that the alternatives being used protect employees from hazards to the same degree as if the employer complied with the OHSA standard. An employer may apply for a temporary variance from the requirements of a specific standard in the following circumstances:

1. inability to comply because of a lack of technical personnel
2. unavailability of materials or equipment
3. necessary construction or alteration cannot be completed by the standard's effective date

The employer must show that it is taking all the steps necessary for compliance as quickly as possible and that in the meantime all available measures are being taken to provide a safe and healthy work environment.

OSHA Hearings and Appeals.

Hearings under OSHA are subject to the Administrative Procedure Act and are presided over by an administrative law judge (ALJ). The Federal Rules of Civil Procedure and the Federal Rules of Evidence generally govern the proceedings. The ALJ hears the evidence and makes finding of fact and issues his or her recommendation. The ALJ does not render an enforceable decision. The decision only becomes enforceable when adopted by the Commission. The decision then only becomes final thirty days after the Executive Secretary receives it.

An employer's appeal arises only from a final order and lies in the Court of Appeals. A request for review must be filed within sixty days of service of the final order. Employers should be warned that the filing of a request for review does not operate as an automatic stay. Employers should seek such a stay in whole or in part pending court review by applying directly to OSHA.

The reviewing court applies a "substantial evidence" test. If the court determines that the findings of fact are supported by substantial evidence, the court will defer to OSHA and uphold its final order.

49 Successful Safeguards in Handling Violations of the Employee Polygraph Protection Act

The Employee Polygraph Protection Act of 1988 sharply restricts the use of lie detectors by private sector employers. The term "lie detector" is broadly defined to include a polygraph, deceptograph, voice stress analyzer, psychological stress evaluator, or any other device that is used for the purpose of determining the honesty or dishonesty of an individual. Employers are prohibited (except in limited circumstances) from directly or indirectly requiring, requesting, or causing any employee or applicant to take a lie detector test. The Act also prohibits employers from using, accepting, referring to, or inquiring about the results of any lie detector test taken by an employee or applicant. Employers are prohibited from taking adverse action against an employee or applicant who refuses, declines, or fails to submit to a lie detector test. Furthermore, employers must post in a conspicuous place a notice prepared by the U.S. Department of Labor informing employees and applicants of their rights under the Act.

ENFORCEMENT AND PENALTIES

The act authorizes enforcement by the Secretary of Labor to seek injunctions for violation of the Act, and civil penalties up to $10,000. In addition, employees or applicants may file private lawsuits in federal or state court. Employees or applicants bringing private actions may sue to recover lost wages and benefits, reinstatement, promotion, and general damages. Attorney's fees are recoverable by the prevailing party in the court's discretion. The Act's provision allowing for "legal" as well as equitable relief means that either party has the right to trial by jury. Both private actions and actions brought by the Secretary of State are subject to a three-year statute of limitations.

HELPFUL HINTS FOR UNDERSTANDING EXEMPTIONS UNDER THE ACT

All governmental employers (local, state, or federal) are exempt from coverage under the Act. This exemption extends to experts or consultants with the Department of Defense and to the employees of such contractors. The exemption also extends to consultants or experts and their employees under contract with the Department of Energy if they work in connection with that Department's atomic energy defense activities. In addition, individuals or any employee thereof under contract to any federal agency with access to top secret information and to employees of those who contract with the FBI are exempt.

The Act provides a limited exemption for certain private security employers (armored car and those engaged in design, installation, and maintenance of security alarm systems), which allows for the use of polygraphs in pre-employment screening of prospective employees. This exemption also applies to employers who employ security personnel, so long as their function includes protection of nuclear power plants, public water supply facilities, or other facilities that have a significant impact on public safety.

The Act contains a limited exemption for drug companies who are authorized to manufacture, distribute, or dispense controlled substances. Such employers may administer polygraph tests to prospective employees who would have direct access to the manufacture, storage, distribution, or sale of any controlled substance. Such employers may administer a polygraph test to current employees in the connection with an ongoing investigation of criminal or other misconduct involving loss or injury to the manufacture, distribution, or dispensing of any controlled substance if the employee had access to the person or property that is the subject of the investigation.

UNDERSTANDING THE RESTRICTIONS ON USE OF THE POLYGRAPH

Private employers who do not come within any of the Act's exemptions mentioned above may, under very limited circumstances, use the polygraph. Private employers may request that an employee submit to a polygraph test in connection with an ongoing investigation of economic loss or injury to the employer's business such as theft, embezzlement, misappropriation, or an act of industrial espionage or sabotage. The polygraph test may only be requested if the employee had access to the property in question, and the employer must have a reasonable suspicion that the employee was involved in the activity under investigation.

Before the test is administered, the employer must provide the employee a statement that sets forth the specific incident or activity being investigated, and describes the basis of the employer's reasonable suspicion.

Employers that come within the security or drug company exemption, or the "ongoing" investigation exemption, who use the polygraph must meet a number of requirements when administering the test. During all phases of the polygraph testing, the person being examined must be given the following rights:

1. That he or she may terminate the test at any time
2. The question may not be asked in a degrading or unnecessarily intrusive manner
3. The question asked may not deal with religious beliefs or affiliations; beliefs regarding racial matters; political beliefs or affiliations; sexual preferences or behavior; or beliefs, affiliations, or lawful activities concerning unions

Before the test is administered, the examinee must be provided within 48 hours of the examination written notice in understandable language as to when and where the examination will occur and that the examinee has the right to consult with legal counsel or an employee representative before each phase of the test. It should be noted, however, that the right to consult with legal counsel or a representative before each phase of the test does not mean that they have the right to be present during the actual test. The written notice must also include all of the examinee's rights mentioned above as well as the following:

1. Whether or not the examination area contains a two-way mirror, camera or other recording device by which he or she could be heard or observed;
2. That both parties have the right to electronically record the entire examination;
3. That the examinee has the right to review all questions to be asked during the examination;
4. That the test may not be conducted if there is sufficient written evidence by a physician that the examinee is suffering from a medical or psychological condition that might cause abnormal responses;
5. That the test is not and cannot be required as a condition of employment;
6. That the employer may not discharge, discipline, deny employment or promotion, or otherwise discriminate against the examinee based on the test or the examinee's refusal to take such a test without additional evidence which would support such action;
7. That any statement made by the examinee before or during the test may serve as additional supporting evidence for taking an adverse employment

action, and that an admission of criminal conduct may be given to the appropriate law enforcement agency;

8. That information received from a polygraph test may be disclosed only to the examinee, the employer that requested the test, a U.S. Department of Labor official, or to a court, arbitrator or agency by court order;
9. That if any of examinee's rights are violated, the examinee has the right to file a complaint with the Department of Labor or file a court action against the employer; and
10. That the examinee's rights under the Act may not be waived.

The test itself shall not be less than ninety minutes, unless the examinee terminates the test.

During the actual testing, the examiner is prohibited from asking any question that was not presented in writing for review prior to the test. After the test and before the employer takes any adverse action against the employee, the employer must give the examinee a written copy of any opinions or conclusions rendered in response to the test as well as the charted responses to the questions.

Of course, not just anyone can administer a polygraph examination. Under the Act, an examiner must have a current state license and carry a minimum bond of $50,000. The examiner must observe all the rights of the examinee under the Act. Both the employer and the examiner are prohibited from unauthorized disclosure of any information obtained during a polygraph test.

SUCCESSFUL STEPS TO PREVAIL IN LAWSUITS BROUGHT UNDER THE POLYGRAPH PROTECTION ACT

Employers that are covered by the Act's prohibitions will most commonly face lawsuits only when they have taken some sort of adverse action based on either the results of a test or on an employee's refusal to take the test. An employer should be able to successfully defend such lawsuits by having enough documented evidence of whatever misconduct is involved that would justify the adverse action taken regardless of the outcome of the polygraph examination. In this way the polygraph is only used to potentially exonerate the employee, but not convict the employee. Of course, a polygraph can only be administered when the specific misconduct involves economic loss or injury to the employer's business. The nature and extent of the economic loss or injury should also be well documented.

The crucial issue in most cases will most likely be whether the employer had sufficient additional evidence to support the adverse action taken. Again, like so many of the laws that protect employees, a critical inquiry will be consistency with rules and past precedent. In other words, were other similarly situated employees who found themselves under similar suspicion treated the same as the employee who took or refused to take the polygraph test.

In order to avoid liability, employers should consider the following checklist when having an applicant or employee undergo a polygraph test:

1. Have the examinee sign a statement that he or she has been provided 48-hour advance written notice of examinee rights. The statement should be attached to the complete list of examinee rights.
2. Have the examinee sign a statement that all the listed preliminary requirements were followed.
3. During the test, ensure that the examiner follows all the requirements in administering the test.

If the employer is relying upon the reasonable suspicion of ongoing investigation of economic loss exemption, the employer, in testing the reasonableness of the suspicion, should consider the following:

1. Did the employee have access to the property at issue?
2. Does the finger of suspicion point to the employee?
3. Does the finger of suspicion point to other employees as well and are they being tested?
4. Is there enough suspicion to take some adverse action consistent with your rules or past practice?

Index

A

D

E

F

G

H

I

P

Q

R

T

U

V

W